German A. Duarte
Fractal Narrative

Media Studies

German A. Duarte holds a Ph.D. (2013) in Media Studies, Ruhr-Universität Bochum. His research interests include history of media, film history, new technologies in audiovisual narratives, cognitive-cultural economy and philosophy.

German A. Duarte

Fractal Narrative

**About the Relationship Between Geometries and Technology
and Its Impact on Narrative Spaces**

[transcript]

Bibliographic Information published by the Deutsche Nationalbibliothek
The Deutsche Nationalbibliothek lists this publication in the Deutsche Nationalbibliografie; detailed bibliographic data are available in the Internet at http://dnb.d-nb.de

Cover layout: Kordula Röckenhaus, Bielefeld
Cover illustration: himberry / photocase.de
Typeset by German A. Duarte
Printed by Majuskel Medienproduktion GmbH, Wetzlar
Print-ISBN 978-3-8376-2829-6
PDF-ISBN 978-3-8394-2829-0

In memory of Adela Vélez Rezk and Antonio Caronia

Quis desiderio sit pudor aut modus
tam cari capitis? praecipe lugubris
cantus, Melpomene, cui liquidam pater vocem cum cithara dedit.
(Horace, Odes, I 24)

Table of Contents

Acknowledgements

This volume continues and elaborates my Ph.D. dissertation 'Fractal Narrative' submitted to RUHR-Universität Bochum, July 2013.

I would like to take this opportunity to gratefully acknowledge the guidance of some professors, scholars and friends who believed in this work and supported me from the very beginning of my research.

My deepest appreciation and gratitude go to my mentor and friend Antonio Caronia, who kindly followed the development of this book until he passed away in January 2013. Without his friendship, his advice and his encouragement I would never have started this research. I will always be grateful for his friendship and for all the conversations we had, which were always a source of inspiration for me.

Special thanks are offered to my doctoral adviser Oliver Fahle for following this work in all its stages and for his comments and suggestions. It is also my duty and pleasure to thank Erich Hörl for his guidance during the drafting of this text.

My gratitude also goes to many friends and colleagues who, during the years devoted to the research, offered me their assistance and advice. I mention them in alphabetic order: Justin Battin, Unai Begiristain, Wil Chang, Lázaro Echegaray, Alessandra Luciano, Eva Oer, Rebekka Reichold, Alfredo Rizza, Sven Speek and Mike Yung.

To Maria Elena and to my parents go my thanks for their unlimited support, and their inexhaustible patience all through my research work.

Berlin
May 2014

Preface

Fractals suggest recursivity, infinity and the repetition of a principle of order. But they are not just infinite images, wonderful infinite images in a space. They are processes. Fractals are digital pictures of the universe's continuous movement. Attempting to explain the state of fractals, one can only posit that their state is pure becoming. For this reason fractal geometry was understood as a geometry that can recognize nature, its irregular shapes, its perpetual mutation and its chaotic characteristics.

The present work attempts to demonstrate that fractals are more than an instrument of scientists, more than just one of the features of our scientific context. Indeed, these forms have accompanied mankind over millennia. Consider, for instance, not only the fractal shape of mountains, trees and human lungs, but also Islamic art, African architecture, Hokusai's works and many other artistic expressions that are able to display these infinite forms and show us that they are also part of mankind's deepest unconscious.

Notwithstanding the irregularity and infiniteness of nature, starting from the 4th century B.C. onwards, philosophy developed a linear thought called logic and opposed the *alogon* to it. According to this framework, what is not linear is inexplicable and therefore a paradox. At the same time, geometry and mathematics developed a science able to explain nature and natural phenomena through abstract and simple forms that do not exist in nature, that is, through lines that only exist in the human mind. As a result, the *logos* became the only rule and was considered the only truth. Geometry, which was an indispensable instrument for analyzing nature, was also governed by logic, mostly embodied in the axioms of Euclid.

Through geometry, 'real things,' fruits of the observation of nature, were identified with the fruits of the intellect, that is, with geometrical figures that, in turn, were perceived as 'real.' As a consequence, geometry could create 'reality' through abstractions, through figures created by the intellect. At that point, the rational translation of natural objects through the science of geometry started to be seen as an objective translation of nature. This impression of objectivity, derived from a kind of Pythagorean thought in which nature can be translated into numbers, started to impose a new relationship between man and nature. On the one hand, one started to see nature as a regular entity that could be embraced by *logos*. On the other hand, one assumed that the human senses where insufficient to understand some phenomena. Therefore, geometry was employed to translate objects and phenomena onto another plane where human perception could analyze them.

The idea that nature could be translated into the language of numbers generated the erroneous conception that natural processes are regular, that is to say, that they can be predicted and imitated by finding their correspondence with numbers or Euclidean geometrical figures. This idea is exemplified by the Greek concept of truth (*aletheia*), the literal meaning of which is 'the state of not being hidden, of being evident,' or in Heidegger's translation, the state of '*Unverborgenheit*.'

This concept of truth governed mankind's relationship with nature from the classical period up to the Modern Age. During this period, truth and nature were seen as eternal and immutable entities that could only be understood by decoding them using numbers. Thus, nature could only be contemplated, because only through contemplation could mankind decipher it and disclose its secrets. Consequently, the scientific knowledge, namely the *theoria* of the Greeks and the *contemplatio* of the Romans, subdued the *praxis*.

However, through the mediation of Christian thought, in the Modern Age, scientific knowledge was no longer understood as the *fine ultimo* to which *praxis* should be subordinated. *Theoria* and *contemplatio* became operative instruments. From that moment on, man began seeing his presence in the world as a chance – almost as a mission – to become the 'dominator' of nature. And man's supremacy over nature is expressed in his act of making truth. This truth is no longer the Greek *aletheia*, but the Hebrew '*emet*' whose root is strongly related to the verb 'to do.' More specifically, the difference between the Greek and Hebraic truths lies in that the first one is something that man 'knows,' whereas the second is something in the sphere of what man 'practices.' In the Hebrew conception of truth, there is something formed in time, something created in time and by time, which implies that every historical period generates its own truth. The old idea of an untouchable and everlasting truth was replaced by a completely different concept. The human being acquired the capacity to 'act' upon nature thus establishing a continuous creation of truth. Therefore, scientific knowledge also started to be understood as a means to improve technology with the aim of creating truth by transforming nature. But if technology represented the only means to transform nature and supply human sensorial weakness, then geometry represented the instrument to translate nature 'objectively.' In addition, geometry was a means to improve – and also to prove – the efficacy of technology, which, in turn, offered the possibility to study, represent and simulate the human body and its functions. Consider, for instance, the technique of perspective developed during the Renaissance, which, by applying the geometrical rules developed by Euclid, allowed not only the analysis of the human sense of sight, but also its representation and simulation.

During the Renaissance, the desire to represent natural objects with a high degree of objectivity created a different relationship with nature. The Renaissance took on as a goal the construction of an image on a two-dimensional surface able to produce for the beholder an illusion of a three-dimensional object, a simulation of our perception of natural objects. The principal aim of perspective was to achieve a perfect translation of nature in order to produce in the beholder, in Gombrich's words, an effect 'akin to visual hallucination.' Perspective aims to attain the correct equation such that the image appears like the object and the object like the image. In addition, this technique generates a kind of mechanization of the representation of natural objects. It was a mechanization of the natural function of sight that was simulated through the device of the camera obscura. As a prosthesis able to realize translations of nature, which are seen as objective due to its scientific component, the camera obscura started a phenomenon of alienation of mankind from the representation of the world. The camera obscura represents the first of a series of visual media that translated nature under a Euclidean *ordino*.

In the field of cinematographic studies, when the formalist influence on the study of cinematography came to an end, some narrative constructions started to be seen as narrative constructions that do not represent Euclidean spaces. In other words, it became quite clear that even though the cinematographic camera was a direct heir of the camera obscura and, for this reason, a geometrical machine governed by Euclidean rules, it was able to develop non-Euclidean narrative spaces that share some features with fractal forms.

The primary aim of the present work is to analyze the influence of fractal geometry on the organization of contemporary narrative spaces. As noted by Simmel (see Simmel G. 1908, esp. pp. 614-708), society is not only developed into the space – that is, the social space is not only a spatial manifestation or development – but it also constructs a spatial organization that is perceptible. Certainly, technology and geometry play a fundamental role in the construction of the social space. Our society, strongly influenced by contemporary mass media, has started to see a new way to articulate narrative spaces, displaying a type of organization that I call in this text fractal. In my view, society is moving towards the construction of fractal social spaces that will, in the near future, completely modify social dynamics and structures, class struggles, and so on. At the moment, we see only one aspect of the impact that fractal geometry has on the organization of narrative spaces: on the aesthetics of some narrative constructions and on the creation of open spaces for discussion and sharing information. My research, by analyzing the symbiosis between man and technology and between man and geometry, aims at developing an instrument of analysis that could represent a new way to understand the contemporary narrative act, which is no longer the creation of a linear succession of information governed by fixed Euclidean rules, but the construction of infinite fractal spaces in which man and technology establish a new relationship.

In the first part, I first outline the development of geometry, Euclid's contribution, as well as the scientific research that allowed the theorization of non-Euclidean geometries. After that, I deal with the fundamental concepts of topology and proto-fractal objects that in the 1970s allowed Benoit Mandelbrot to create fractal geometry.

The second part is focused on the development of the technological devices that influenced the analysis of space and allowed the theorization of new kinds of structures, new ways of organizing the universe. Each visual medium considered in this second part is analyzed from a historical point of view that enables us to highlight a common process shared by all the devices discussed. Indeed, every visual medium was developed within the scientific field with the purpose of improving mankind's analysis of nature. As prostheses that supplies human sensorial weakness, these apparatuses represented extensions of the human senses and allowed a better understanding of nature and natural phenomena. However, when these apparatuses are introduced to the large public, they become narrative instruments that not only modify the social understanding of 'objective representation' but also influence the way mankind constructs narrative spaces, the way mankind communicates. Particular attention is drawn to the microscope, which influenced Leibniz's theories of *Analysis Situs* and Monadology, through which I analyze important characteristics of fractal objects that are present in the organization of some narrative spaces. But I also deal with the invention of the cinematographic camera, which allowed Bergson to theorize a new universal structure, and the Panorama, the aim of which was to concentrate in a single place huge quantities of information, always attempting to create an infinite space where information could be preserved.

The third part of this work focuses on the introduction of non-Euclidean geometries into art, on the way fractal spaces can be illustrated through pictorial representations, and on how these spaces, particularly as displayed in African art, were introduced into and interpreted by Western artistic expression. I also examine some scientific theories, like Poincaré's *Analysis Situs,* and how these theories were incorporated into artistic expression. From there I am able to start an analysis on the influences of both Euclidean geometry and linguistics on the organization of narrative spaces, and on how Deleuze, by analyzing the cinematographic camera as an instrument able to construct non-Euclidean spaces, made possible the understanding of audiovisual narrative as a pure spatial organization, which, after the Second World War, started to be organized following some non-Euclidean laws. Following in the footsteps of Deleuze, I attempt to create a parallel between the development of non-Euclidean geometries and the audiovisual narrative spaces constructed after the Second World War. The comparison between the development of non-Euclidean geometries and the construction of non-Euclidean narrative spaces takes into account the role played by technology. I theorize that every technological improvement generated a new way of organizing narrative spaces. Thus, I argue that video technology enabled the development of a kind of image that shares some characteristics with Proto-Fractal objects. I analyze the digital image and the organization of audiovisual narrative spaces through a comparison with the characteristics of fractal forms. In this part, I used as a framework the theory developed in the text to analyze some mainstream films. While analyzing these films, I also attempt to highlight the existence of fractal narratives and how they function. Indeed, even though the narrative spaces developed in the films under analysis have already been studied, I decode them in a completely new way, that is, through the innovative instrument of analysis offered by fractal geometry.

The fourth and last part is focused on the current status of audiovisual narrative. I deal in particular with the narratives developed in recent times on the World Wide Web, and I inquiry into the social role that these narratives play and can play in the future. I also propose a geometrical demonstration of the fractal narrative in order to better define its essence and potentialities.

1 Some Notions of an Infinite Space

Est-ce simplement que les choses qui nous semblent belles sont celles qui s'adaptent le mieux à notre intelligence, et que par suite elles sont en même temps l'outil que cette intelligence sait le mieux manier ?[1]

1.1 GEODESY, OR THE FIRST TRANSLATIONS OF NATURE

The Greeks developed Geometry as an abstraction of familiar things, the abstraction of the reality around them.[2] Thales of Miletus (ca. 625-547 B.C.) is commonly considered the first philosopher to realize a system in which all things derive from a

---

1 | Poincaré H. 1908, p. 17.

2 | With this I do not want to state that geometry is a Greek invention. Geometry has an universal character that all cultures have faced. The interest here is in the process that Greeks developed over centuries and which developed a strong influence on the human perception of space and therefore its representation. When one talks about geometry it is necessary to talk about geometries. This is due to the fact that every culture and every era has constructed its own view of space. As Serres posited questioning the history of this noble science: "Commençons par l'histoire de la géométrie: peut-on décider ce que désigne cette science? La mesure, ancienne et moderne, de la terre, arable ou constructible, celle des cultivateurs ou des maçons? Les figures archaïques de l'arithmétique pythagoricienne? Celles de l'école de Chio? Les formes ou les idées platoniciennes? Les livres des Éléments d'Euclide? Ce qui nous reste d'Archimède ou d'Apollonius? La représentation Cartésienne? Les épures descriptives du siècle passé? Les reconstructions non euclidiennes? L'analysis situs de Leibniz, la topologie d'Euler, Riemann et Poincaré? Les démonstrations formelles de Hilbert? La géométrie algébrique contemporaine? Les plans des programmateurs de mouvements robotiques...? L'universel, vu de loin, se transforme, de près, en une jungle de sciences si différentes que surabonderait le nombre des histoires à relater, toutes divergentes et enracinées dans des passés oubliés." (Serres M. 1993, p. 16.)

principle formulated through geometric analysis and through geometric theorems. In fact, he developed both the concept of model and of scale.

The first geometrical theorems were diagrams that showed a strong relationship with the visible and were also used to prove natural phenomena. By using the spatial character offered by geometry, the proven phenomena acquired additional veracity because they displayed a direct relationship with the 'things' themselves. Aiming at measuring proportions that surpassed the human scale, Thales created a spatial *re*-organization through observations and worked on optical representations of objects at a lower scale. Indeed, he translated the visible into a tangible form through abstractions. He measured and measuring means to compare, and to compare is an act of transport, of translation, of the rule, the point of view or the things covered by an alignment.[3]

At that time geometry benefited from a field of study that, while still belonging to geometry, was also seen as an isolated subject. This was geodesy (γεωδαισια), a science that dealt with sensitive and corruptible objects. Conversely, geometry was applied to the treatment of non-sensitive entities.

How do we approach astronomy that would have as a matter of study the sensitive sizes? How do we see the sky that is above our heads?

"Nor would astronomy be concerned with sensible magnitudes or with this heaven. For neither are sensible lines such as the geometrician speaks of (for no sensible thing is straight or round in the sense in which he uses the terms 'straight' and 'round'; for the circle touches the ruler not at that point, but in the way in which Protagoras used to say in refuting the geometricians), nor are the motions and the orbits of the heavenly bodies similar to those discussed by astronomy, nor do points have the same nature as the stars."[4]

Traditionally, Egypt is considered the birthplace of geometry. As narrated by Herodotus, Ramses II (ca. mid 13th century B.C.) developed a system of equal distribution of lands. Agricultural lands were divided into equal rectangles and when the Nile rose and the water carried off a portion of land, the system used by Ramses II acted to affix the corresponding reduction of taxes related to the portion of land lost as caused by the effluent.[5]

Also in Plato's Phaedrus, the origins of geometry are placed in Egypt.

Socrates: "Very well. The story is that in the region of Naucratis in Egypt there dwelt one of the old gods of the country, the god to whom the bird called Ibis is sacred, his own

---

3 | Serres M. 1993, p. 198.

4 | Aristotle, *Metaphysics*, B.2, 998 a 2, 5. (Translation: Apostle H.G. 1966.)

5 | Consider, for instance, what had been observed by the Greek historian Herodotus (5th century BC) in his Histories (Histories ii. 109).

name being Theuth. He it was that invented number and calculation, geometry and astronomy, not to speak of draughts and dice, and above all writing."[6]

In Aristotle's Metaphysics, geometry developed in Egypt as a wise need for priests, rather than an instrument to measure and divide land.

"As more arts were arrived at, some for the necessities of life and others as the only ends of *activity*, those who arrived at the arts for the latter purpose were always believed to be the wiser than those who did so for the former because their sciences were not instrumental to something else. Now when all such arts were already developed, the sciences concerned neither with giving pleasures to others nor with the necessities of life were discovered, and first in such places where men had leisure. Accordingly, it was in Egypt that the mathematical arts were first formed, for there the priestly class was allowed leisure."[7]

Let us go back to Thales. Thales went first to Egypt, and then, upon his return to Greece, he introduced the study of geometry.[8] Geometry with Thales became a deductive science ruled by general propositions. In Laertius's writings, Hieronymus, a pupil of Aristotle, tells how Thales, using the shadow projected by the pyramids, could carry such colossal structures on paper.

|*Fig. 1.1*|

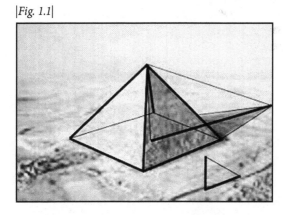

"Hieronymus says that he even succeeded in measuring the pyramids by observation of the length of their shadow at the moment when our shadows are equal to our own height."[9]

---

6 | Plato, *Phaedrus*, 274 c-d (Translation: Hackforth R. 1952.)
7 | Aristotle, *Metaphysics*, A.1, 981 b 17-24 (Translation: Apostle H.G. 1966.)
8 | See Heath T. 1981.
9 | Diógenes Laertius i. 27.

Thanks to the possibility to 'translate' objects through geometry, it was also possible to reach general conclusions from specific diagrams.[10] However, the presence of fixed laws in this spatial organization became essential. Michel Serres described the phenomenon as follows:

"Le réalisme des idéalités s'alourdit et reprend une compacité qu'avait dissoute le soleil platonicien. Pleines d'ombre, les idéalités pures ou abstraites redeviennent noires comme les Pyramides, et comme elles, font de l'ombre."[11]

The interpretation of nature through points and lines started to be ordered through the fixed laws guided by logic, which give to the geometrical representation its final signification. In fact, these figures had to meet specific laws, axioms that would govern this creative process and guide the projection of these analyses.

The axioms formulated by Euclid in the thirteen books of his work *Elements* guided the human perception of space through centuries. In this work, he established the properties of figures placed in the plane. These figures, in turn, structured the analysis of space. Through Euclid's axioms, the abstractions of nature acquired truth-value, since they responded to a logical system of rules; Euclid's axioms.

Let's see how Euclid constructed his work *Elements*. The first book begins with a list of assumptions ordered as follows:

- Definitions
- Postulates
- Common Notions

By using the term 'common notions', Euclid follows Aristotle. The latter used the term 'common (things)' and 'common opinions' as an alternative to the word 'axiom'. In the books II, IV, V, VI, VII and XI, one finds some additional definitions. The remaining books present proposals and problems that can be solved by means of hypotheses.[12] In the first book there are twenty-three definitions. They deal with the notions of point, line, angle, etc. The arrangement of the first book and especially the section dedicated to definitions can be understood, following Serres, as a typical grammar in which first the morphology and then the syntax is analyzed.[13] The definitions and assumptions (syntax) give sense to lines or elements constructed by means of the ruler and the compass (morphology). The definitions and assumptions also make possible the development of a system – Euclidean geometry – which can be defined as a lan-

---

10 | In this regard see Plato, *Meno* 80d-86c, where one can see how Socrates, in order to prove the existence of reminiscence during his discussion with Meno, draws from the slave's soul his knowledge of geometric abstraction.

11 | Serres M. 1993, p. 214.

12 | See Torretti R. 1978.

13 | Serres M. 1993, p. 251.

guage of infinite possibilities and performances.[14] These definitions and assumptions represent proper principles; they are "truths whose existence is impossible to prove."[15]

However, what is the difference between postulate and hypothesis? Indeed, between these two words, there is a huge semantic difference.

"Thus any probable proposition that the teacher assumes without proving it, if the student accepts it, is a hypothesis – a hypothesis not absolutely but relatively to the student; but the same assumption, if it is made when the student has no opinion or a contrary opinion about it, is a postulate."[16]

That is to say, a postulate is an improbable proposition that the master asks the disciple to grant him.

"This is the difference between a hypothesis and a postulate; the latter is the contrary of the student's opinion, or any provable proposition that is assumed and used without being proved."[17]

Following this short passage from Aristotle, Euclid's postulates became the instruments through which mankind constructs its 'reality'.[18] As mentioned above, the use of lines, circles and areas simplify the analysis, since all these elements deal with 'existing' things. Geometry made the world of mathematics fully intelligible. Thanks to the abstractions offered by the geometric knowledge, nature became more deductible. Geometric knowledge, which allowed man to explain phenomena by describing the reality, became a 'mediator' between human cognition and the nature of existing things.[19] Thus, geometry became essential to make direct confrontations with the result of mathematical analysis, i.e. with numbers. Thanks to geometry, the 'real things', fruits of the observation of nature, could be identified with the fruits of intellect, that

---

14 | Heath T. 1981, p. 373.

15 | Aristotle, *Posterior Analytics*, 76a, 31. (Translation: Tredennick H. 1960.)

16 | Aristotle, *Posterior Analytics*, 76b, 30. (Translation: Tredennick H. 1960.)

17 | Aristotle, *Posterior Analytics*, 76b 32-34. (Translation: Tredenneck H. 1960.)

18 | In this regard, it is important to remember the strong bond between the meaning of Truth and *ideîn* (to see) in the ancient Greek world. For the Greeks, mathematics represented the order of nature, which was manifested to man: $\alpha\lambda\eta\theta\epsilon\iota\alpha$ (*alétheia*) "truth" in the meaning of revelation, but also in the meaning of reality. *Aletheia* is the truth-reality that is manifested to humans through mathematics, and it can be seen (*ideîn*) through numbers. Conversely, for the scientist of the modern era, truth does not imply the Greek 'passivity' imposed by the action of "to see". It is strongly associated with the Hebrew meaning of *'emet* (אמת) or "doing truth". The latter implies an action upon nature. Thus, truth in the modern era is the order that mankind assigns to nature. See, Galimberti U. 2005[4], p. 312. This point will be discussed in more detail in the following chapters.

19 | See Gray J. 1989[2].

is, geometrical figures that were also 'real'. In fact, geometry creates 'reality' through abstractions, that is, through figures created by the intellect.

Contemporary to the process of abstraction initiated by geometry, Pythagorean mathematics developed. Pythagoras advocated that mathematical principles could be applied to any existing thing. The idea of the 'superiority' of the science of numbers was born when Pythagoras (or perhaps one of his students) found a mathematical relationship in the consonance of sounds of musical instruments. This fact encouraged the Pythagoreans to establish further connections between numbers and natural phenomena. According to Pythagoreans, the analysis of nature should pass through the science of numbers, i.e. nature could be translated into the language of numbers.

"Contemporaneously with these thinkers, and even before them, the so-called Pythagoreans, who were engaged in the study of mathematical objects, were the first to advance this study, and having been brought up in it, they regarded the principles of mathematical objects as the principles of all things. Since of mathematical objects numbers are by nature first, and (a) they seemed to observe in numbers, rather than fire or earth or water, many likenesses to things, both existing and in generation (and so they regarded such an attribute of numbers as justice, such other as soul or intellect, another as opportunity, and similarly with almost all of the others), and (b) they also observed numerical *attributes* and ratios in the objects of harmonics; since, then, all other things appeared in their nature to be likenesses of numbers, and numbers to be first in the whole of nature, they came to the belief that the elements of numbers are the elements of all things and that the whole heaven is a harmony and a number."[20]

The analysis of the real by means of numbers encountered a crisis due to the discovery of the diagonal of the square, in other words, the discovery of the irrational numbers: $\sqrt{2}$. History attributed their discovery to Pythagoras despite the fact that some authors attested that he did not discover the irrationals.[21] One supposes that their discovery remained a secret for years – almost a century – and this long silence cre-

---

20 | Aristotle, *Metaphysics*, 985b 23 - 986a 4. (Translation: Apostle H.G. 1966.)

21 | One of these texts, which questions the discovery of irrationals by Pytagoras, is Plato's Theaetetus. In this discussion between Socrates and Theaetetus one can see how the irrationals were found.

"**Theaet.** We divided all numbers into two classes. The one, the numbers which can be formed by multiplying equal factors, we represented by the shape of the square and called square or equilateral numbers.

Soc. Well done!

Theaet. The numbers between these, such as three and five and all numbers which cannot be formed by multiplying equal factors, but only by multiplying a greater by a less or a less by a greater, and are therefore always contained in unequal sides, we represented by the shape of the oblong rectangle and called oblong numbers.

Soc. Very good; and what next?

ated the doubt over the attribution of this discovery to Pythagoras. In addition, it is also impossible to date with precision the discovery of irrationals.[22] However, thanks to the testimony given by several texts about the crisis generated by the discovery of irrationals, it is possible to understand how geometry was developed on the basis of the theory of numbers.[23]

The primitive Pythagorean arithmetic only admitted integers. Therefore, the diagonal of the square shows, in the geometric space, existing and reproducible lengths that are unrecognizable by calculation. Thus, the measurement of the diagonal requires a non-Pythagorean notion, which demonstrates the existence of an irrational, a non-being, an afterlife. Going beyond the concepts of known ratios, the diagonal became a measure, "**irrational and inexpressible in its essence.**"[24]

What happens if something can be represented by geometry but not by the science of numbers? How do we represent the complexity of this non-being and most importantly, how to accept the existence of a non-being, of an afterlife?[25]

The ratio of the diagonal of the square, inexplicable through natural numbers, was historically seen as the drama of irrationality and (in some ways) as the death of pure thought.[26] If the *logos* means proportion, ratio or the action, *alogon* means irrational, it prohibits measuring. If *logos* means speech, *alogon* is opposed to any word. Thus, accuracy is condemned to collapse and reason to keep silent.[27]

In order to accept the existence of the diagonal and to assign a measurement to it, one must take into account another dimension, a space that accepts the existence of such a segment. First, we must overcome the one-dimensional world of the straight line, and then it is necessary to go out into an 'ultra-dimensional' world where the line is submerged.[28] The measurement of such a segment (the diagonal) means the

---

Theaet. All the lines which form the four sides of the equilateral or square numbers we called lengths, and those which form oblong numbers we called surds, because they are not commensurable with the others in length, but only in the areas of the planes which they have the power to form. And similarly in the case of solids." (Plato, *Theaetetus*, 147e – 148 b. - Translation: Fowler H.N. 1921.)

22 | It is interesting to see how irrationals started to be accepted. Thomas Heath analyzes this assimilation through Plato, (*Republic* vii. 546 D.) where irrationals seem to be totally assimilated. See Heath T. 1981, p. 157.

23 | See Heath T. *A history of Greek Mathematics*. Volume I. *The Irracional*, p. 154.

24 | Toth I. 1991, p. 65.

25 | That is why one needed to accept the realistic theory that states that things in our intellect are more real than reality. From this premise, mathematics could be assimilated as an abstract form of real objects. See Dicks D.R. 1970 and Körner S. 1960.

26 | Serres M. 1993, p. 20.

27 | Serres M. 1993, p. 146.

28 | Toth I. 1991, p. 95.

recognition of the incommensurability, of the non-Pythagorean.[29] What allowed the recognition of the diagonal on a flat universe was that it had been recognized independently, it was recognized as *the measurement of the diagonal*. Even if it was not representable with Pythagorean numbers, it became an existing measurement because it acquired its own existence as *the diagonal of the square*; it belonged to the field of irrational numbers.[30]

---

29 | The diagonal needs to be broken down in this way and its analysis requires a recursive operation. See Toth I. 1991, p. 65.

30 | One can observe the same phenomenon in the Greek π. This ratio, which is documented in 1650 B.C. in the Rhind papyrus, is the constant ratio between the length of a circumference to the diameter of the same. In the Rhind papyrus, this ratio was calculated as 3.16049... Thanks to Archimedes π was calculated with more precision. Archimedes found that the length of the circumference could be approximated with the perimeter of regular polygons inscribed and circumscribed to the circumference. This measurement became even more precise by increasing the number of sides of the polygons, which tend to multiply endlessly. By multiplying its sides to 96, Archimedes found that the result was 3.14271... The definition of this irrational was corrected by Lambert in the seventeenth century.

1.2 Recursion as Creator of Infinity

The number theory, our sense of measurement, and even deeper thoughts on the irrational and rational are fruits of the diagonal of the square and of the abstract figures developed by Greek thought and its relationship with space. From these concepts, other languages started to be developed, which use even more complex abstractions in order to reproduce and explain natural phenomena. These languages became even better instruments for mediating the relationship between man and nature. By means of some of these languages and their relationship with other sciences and concepts, mankind was able to approach natural phenomena and concepts from another point of view. This was the case of the relationship between the algorithms and paradoxes of Zeno. Zeno's paradoxes enable us to understand how using the abstractions offered by numbers, the divisibility of space was postulated by applying a recursive operation. In turn, this allowed us to question the existence of movement.

|Prop. XVI| Zeno showed how the idealization of infinity is based on the concept of recursion. It is important to remember that Zeno's paradoxes were created to support Parmenides of Elea's thoughts on motionlessness (ἀτρεμής), a concept developed in his unique surviving (in a fragmentary form) work, *On Nature*. In this important work, which influenced many aspects of western philosophy, Parmenides deals with the concept of **reality** (in his words, "what-is"). Reality was described as one, change was considered impossible and entities were thought to be unchanging. He also developed an interesting way of inquiry grounded in the opposition, that it is (ὅπως ἐστίν) – that is not (ὡς οὐκ ἐστίν). In his work, Parmenides asserts that an entity always stays in its place. His aim was to place reality exclusively in the *logos* and not in perception because, according to him, perception (doxa – δόξα: a Greek word that describes common beliefs or popular opinions) is misled. Thus, he theorized an eternal reality (*aletheia*), which is static and immutable.

Zeno was a member of the Eleatic School founded by Parmenides. His most famous paradoxes are known as "Arguments Against Motion."[1] Zeno created the paradoxes in order to support Parmenides' doctrine that "all is one." Zeno, following the logic that states that the analysis of reality must be effectuated through the *logos*, and arguing that no change is possible, concluded that motion is just an illusion.

Let us focus more closely on these Arguments. In the case of the dichotomy paradox, Zeno states that a moving body that must arrive at point B from point A will never get there. The body must first cover the first half of the course, but before doing that, it must reach half of the half, and half of that half, and so on to infinity. This recursive operation divides the space to cover an infinite number of times; consequently, the body will never arrive at point B.

---

1 | According to Plato, the creation of these paradoxes was a response to some philosophers who had created some paradoxes to contradict Parmenides' philosophy.

|*Fig. 1.2*|

Zeno's arguments accomplished his goal of defending Parmenides' thesis. However, as we will see in the following chapters, Zeno's approach to the analysis of movement – which is an action and consequently, is indivisible, like time – leads us to apply the same approach to the analysis of time, thus giving rise to the erroneous analysis of time by means of spatial notions. Let us delve into this last point.

|**Prop. VIII, IX**| The spatial representation provided by Zeno is inexhaustible. In mathematical terms, it means the impossibility of representing the calculation of this movement, i.e. $\frac{1}{2} + \frac{1}{4} + \frac{1}{8}$ ... Through this paradox, Zeno also argued that due to being on a infinitely divisible space, the body also needs an infinite time to cover it. Consequently, in this paradox, time is represented by spatial notions, by a geometric line of infinite length.[2] The imaginary straight line, covered by the body in the paradox, represents the domain of natural numbers, which are infinite. In fact, if each point of the line represents a natural number, consequently they are also immeasurables. However, let us look closely at what the line represents. As it is composed of an infinite number of points, it could help us to understand the particular geometrical structures that we will analyze in this text. The first question we should deal with is: what is a point in the line? It is clear that the point is a semantic value given to a unitary and indivisible element. However, our interest now is focused on how this element is defined by mathematics. The point has been understood in three different ways. According to the first way, the point is a kind of generator element whose movement builds the line. Alternatively, the point has been seen as an intersection between two lines. Thirdly, it has also been seen as a "limiting position in a infinite process applied to a segment of a line."[3] These three ways of defining the point allow us to understand not only the nature of the line but also the nature of infinite sets.[4] An infinite structure, like the line, is something that requires a successor, thus it needs a recursive operation. In the case of the straight line, the required element is a point, in the case of natural integers it is another natural integer. Consequently, any number – or object – in such systems allows the operation $x + n$, where the addition of another number or figure is always possible. As in Zeno's paradoxes, repetition generates repetition.[5] It is possible to deduce that the fundamental condition of an infinite space, and thus the essence

---

2 | In this regard, Danzig states that this is the fundamental principle of our world of relativity. See Dantzig T. 1954⁴, p. 124.

3 | Dantzig T. 1954⁴, p. 142.

4 | Engell defines the point as a metaphor for something that is not possible to represent, a metaphor for space through time and time through space. See Engell L. 1999.

5 | Serres M. 1993, p. 288.

of infinite sets, is the generating element, which, due to its nature, requires or allows a successor.

Through the definition of the inner nature of the straight line, one can define recursion as a means of creation of immeasurable spaces. The capacity to accept a recursive operation is what gives infiniteness to the straight line and represents the essence of this structure. The straight line, being an infinite succession of points, was evidence of the existence of infinite spaces. Not accepting the existence of infinity means the non-existence of natural numbers. The absence of infinity also means the beginning and end of time, the impossibility of dividing magnitudes into magnitudes.[6]

"If there were no infinity, all magnitudes would be commensurable and there would be nothing inexpressible or irrational, features that are thought to distinguish geometry from arithmetic; nor could numbers exhibit the generative power of the monad, nor would they have in them all the ratios -such as multiple and super particular- that are in things."[7]

|Prop. XV| If we return to Zeno's paradox, the existence of two kinds of infinities seems to emerge from it. Aristotle argued that, when one talks about infinity, it is essential to distinguish between *potential infinity* and *actual infinity*. The first one is accessible through human cognition, the second one represents a vague idea and is inaccessible to the human being.

We have outlined above the essence of infinity. In particular, it is the result of an endless succession (as in the case of natural numbers and straight line) and it derives from a recursive operation. This infinity can be denoted as potential infinity. The limit of human perception appears when one tries to identify a single entity of infinite size as a uniqueness. This represents the actual infinity and exceeds the limits of our intellect.

The duality depicted above has been described by Leibniz as "*infinitum actu non datur*":

"Prennons une ligne droite et prolongeons la, ensorte qu'elle soit double de la première. Or il est claire, que la seconde, estant parfaitement semblable à la première, peutestre doublée de même, pour avoir la troisième qui est encor semblable aux precedentes; et la même raison ayant tousjours lieu, il n'est jamais possible qu'on soit arresté; ainsi la ligne peut estre prolongée à l'infini, de sorte que la consideration de l'infini vient de celle de la similitude ou de la même raison, et son origine est la même avec celle des verités universelles et necessaires. Cela fait voir comment ce qui donne de l'accomplissement à la conception de cette idée, se trouve en nous mêmes, et ne sauriot venir des expe-

6 | Fauvel J. - Gray J. 1987, p. 96.

7 | Proclus, A Commentary on the first Book of Euclid's Elements (ed. and tranlated by Morrow G.R. 1970, p. 5.)

riences des sens, tout comme les verités necessaires ne sauroient estre prouvées par l'induction ny par les sens."[8]

Leibniz also states that :

"Mais on se trompe en voulant s'imaginer un espace absolu qui soit tout infini composé de parties, il n'y a rien de tel, c'est une notion qui implique contradiction, et ces touts infinis et leur opposés infiniment petits, ne sont de mise que dans le calcul des Geometres, tout comme les racines imaginaires de l'Algèbre."[9]

In Zeno's paradoxes the succession $\frac{1}{2} + \frac{1}{4} + \frac{1}{8}$... shows that the recursive operation is the source of the existence of the potential infinity. However, the vision of an immeasurable entity was unacceptable by the human intellect, as attested by Leibniz.

8 | Leibniz G.W. 1996a (1765), p. 212.

9 | Leibniz G.W. 1996a (1765), p. 214.

1.3 THE DESTRUCTION OF SPACE

In the previous chapters I have tried to highlight, through the example of the diagonal, the notions of ratio and scale. Thanks to these notions, an immeasurable object, being recognized as an entity itself, becomes recognizable and therefore measurable. In particular, the notion of relation, of ratio, is essential in a hierarchical system. In Serres words:

"Qu'il s'agisse de monde ou de religion, de politique, de la maison... de langue, savoir, vue, théorie... l'essentiel gît dans le rapport. Prenez un ensemble quelconque d'astre, de dieux, d'individus, de rues, de pierres, de mots, de sites, d'abstractions, il ne peut devenir système rationnel que s'il est lié par une référence. Le rationnel est prisonnier du référé. La raison est gelée dans la hiérarchie."[1]

The impossibility of comparing means the impossibility of measuring. In the case of the diagonal, to overcome this obstacle, the 'diagonal' itself became a concept. This phenomenon of recognition, as we will see in this text, repeats itself throughout the history of geometry. However, our interest now is focused on the crisis produced by the need to represent phenomena in spaces that do not correspond to those constructed by Euclid.

At the beginning of the 19th century, the 'destruction' of the Euclidean space was possible because of the nature of the fifth postulate, the so-called Parallel Postulate, which was considered Euclid's major innovation, but which was also the most criticized.

|Fig. 1.3|

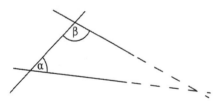

"if a straight line falling on two straight lines make the interior angles on the same side less than two right angles, the straight lines, if produced indefinitely, meet on that side on which are the angles less than two right angles."[2]

Some commentators of Euclid, like Ptolemy, Proclus or Posidonius, doubted the demonstrability of this postulate. It is also possible to find severe criticisms of the fifth postulate of Euclid's *Elements,* dated to the twelfth and thirteenth century in some Arabic, as well as in some Greek texts of the fifteenth and the early sixteenth century.

---

1 | Serres M. 1993, p. 137.

2 | Euclid's *Elements* (Translation: Heath T.L. 1926 I, p. 155.)

Before we deal with the process that initiated the recognition of a geometry that does not meet the Euclidean notions, it would be interesting to make a short digression on the revolution started by Descartes in 1637.

With his work *La géométrie,* Descartes provided a revolutionary concept: the Cartesian coordinated system. Thanks to René Descartes, geometry could be 'conjugate' with algebra. Inventing algebraic geometry, he created a language able to express visible variation with formulas.[3] In *La géométrie,* known as the first book of modern mathematics, Descartes claims that:

"Tous les problemes de Geometrie se peuuent facilement reduire a tels termes, qu'il n'est besoin pas aprés que de connoistre la longeur de quelques lignes droites, pour les construire."[4]

Descartes encouraged the study of geometry through the methods of algebra, and from this combination derived the idea of coordinates. The Cartesian Coordinate System allows specifying points with coordinates, which correspond to equations that in turn can be identified with geometric groups. In other words, it is a translation of geometry into algebra. The method used by Descartes shows that numbers are able to represent geometrical objects. It also demonstrates that it is possible to solve some problems belonging to the field of geometry through arithmetic operations. Descartes developed a system that grants a letter to each line in order to perform the geometric operation in the field of algebra.[5] This method allowed the scientist to have parametric representations of geometric objects.[6] Thanks to the notion of coordinates and the approach to equations, science was able to **create forms through equations.** Descartes' idea was the possibility to draw with equations as with the ruler and the compass. His aim was to translate a geometrical problem into algebraic language, solve the problem, and then translate it back into geometric figures. This process was useful for solving some mechanical problems, calculations that could be represented by curves. However, Descartes' *La Géométrie* offered more than one method of analysis. Thanks to Descartes, geometry acquires a still greater range in that it started to concern the field of specificity, demonstrability and constructiveness.[7] The possibility of translating images – geometric objects – into the field of numbers granted a higher dimension of 'truth' and accuracy to calculations. This phenomenon was emphasized because, in a successive stage, it was applied to machinery and mechanisms in order to prove their functionality.

---

3 | Serres M. 1993, p. 168.

4 | "Any problem in geometry can easily be reduced to such terms that a knowledge of the lengths of certain straight lines is sufficient for its construction" (Descartes R. *La Géométrie.* – Tranlation: Smith D.E. - Latham M.L. 1925, p. 2.)

5 | See Reed D. 1995.

6 | See Smith D.E. - Latham M.L. 1925.

7 | Reed D. 1995, p. 30.

The foundations for the creation of a new geometry, and an alternative to the Euclidean one, were laid in the eighteenth century. After the contribution of John Wallis (1616-1703), the mathematician and Jesuit Gerolamo Saccheri (1667-1733) devoted a work to the demonstration of Euclid's fifth postulate.[8] In his work *Euclides ab omni naevo vindicatus : sive conatus geometricus quo stabiliuntur prima ipsa universae Geometriae principia*, of 1733, he developed a very special reasoning. Saccheri adopted as premises the first twenty-six of Euclid's propositions and assumed as hypothesis that the fifth postulate was false in order to prove, through this hypothesis, that it was true.[9] Saccheri's conclusion was that the fifth postulate cannot be demonstrated. In turn, Johann Heinrich Lambert (1728-1777) attempted to develop contradictions that could create alternative postulates. Consequently, Lambert left several geometric theorems developed in non-Euclidean parallels systems.[10]

At that time, the proposal of a new geometry was considered a heresy. However, after Saccheri's and Lambert's works, many criticisms of Euclidean geometry and several new geometries emerged. It was during the early nineteenth century that a real breaking away from Euclidean space occurred. This revolution started becoming more concrete thanks to Johann Carl Friedrich Gauss (1777-1855) and Georg Friedrich Bernhard Riemann (1826-1866). Gauss did not seek to contradict the existing geometry, he sought to create a **new geometry**, a non-Euclidean geometry. This revolutionary topic was certainly a problem at the time. To theorize a new geometry meant not only to go against the scientific world, but also to attack both science and Western Culture. As a consequence, Gauss's work remained unpublished.[11]

The first publications theorizing a non-Euclidean geometry are the result of the research of two Russian authors: Nikolai I. Lobachevsky (1792-1856) and Janos Bolyai (1802-1860) published in 1830.[12] They both concluded that there is not a 'universal geometry', rather each field requires a special geometry. They assumed that Euclidean geometry is more adapted to human senses, to our perception of the world, whereas other perspectives, for example atomic or planetary ones, require a different kind of geometry.[13] For example, a planetary perspective, being planets spheres and their or-

---

8 | See Gray J. 1989[2].

9 | See Bonola R. 1955. Chapter II. *The Foreruners of Non-Euclidean Geometry. Gerolamo Saccheri.*

10 | It is very interesting to note the spherical geometry invented by Thomas Reid in the eighteenth century. This geometry was based on the idea of the perceptual space, i.e. the world is presented as a hemisphere centered in the human eye.

11 | See Henderson D.L. 1983.

12 | For a more detailed analysis of this process see Leonesi S. – Toffalori C. 2007.

13 | Note that Lobachevsky and Gauss tried to demonstrate that their new geometry could exist in natural space. In fact, they investigated if there were elements of non-Euclidean geometry in natural space. For instance, Gauss attempted to measure the angle sum of an immense triangle formed by three mountain peaks. See Henderson D.L. 1983.

bits circumferences or ellipses, justifies the elliptic geometry theorized by Riemann, in which the plane manifests some spherical surfaces. From this new perspective, a straight line must be understood as a circle of maximum radius.[14] In addition, through his elliptic geometry, Riemann realized for the first time the important distinction between unbounded space and infinite space.[15] The sphere represented both a finite surface and an unbounded space in which the line cannot be extended infinitely, contrary to Euclid's postulates. Thus, in this space a parallel line cannot be drawn to a given line.[16] Thanks to Riemann, there arose the will to develop new geometrical spaces, such as the topological space. In fact, Riemann also proposed some surfaces that curvature might vary. In such spaces, composed by irregular shapes, the movement of objects implies changes in their shape as well as in their properties.[17] Through this theory, the principle of indeformability established by Euclid was completely negated. Additionally, some important research developed during the nineteenth century also

---

14 | See Leonesi S. – Toffalori C. 2007.

15 | It is interesting to quote Riemann's words about the development of a multidimensional space. "Diese Dunkelheit wurde auch von Euklid bis auf Legendre, um den berühmtesten neueren Bearbeiter der Geometrie zu nennen, weder von dem Mathematikern noch von den Philosophen, welche sich damit beschäftigten, gehoben. Es hatte dies seinen Grund wohl darin, daß der allgemeine Begriff mehrfach ausgedehnter Größen, unter welchem die Raumgrößen enthalten sind, ganz unbearbeitet blieb. Ich habe mir daher zunächst die Aufgabe gestellt, den Begriff einer mehrfach ausgedehnten Größe aus allgemeinen Größenbegriffen zu konstruieren. Es wird daraus hervorgehen, daß eine mehrfach ausgedehnte Größe verschiedener Maßverhältnisse fähig ist und der Raum also nur einen besonderen Fall einer dreifach ausgedehnten Größe bildet. Hiervon aber ist eine notwendige Folge, daß die Sätze der Geometrie sich nicht aus allgemeinen Größenbegriffen ableiten lassen, sondern daß diejenigen Eingenschaften, durch welche sich der Raum von anderen denkbaren dreifach ausgedehnten Größen unterscheidet, nur aus der Erfahrung entnommen werden können. Hieraus entsteht die Aufgabe, die einfachsten Tatsachen aufzusuchen, aus denen sich die Maßverhältnisse des Raumes bestimmen lassen – einige Aufgabe, die der Natur der Sache nach nicht völlig bestimmt ist; denn es lassen sich mehrere Systeme einfacher Tatsachen angeben, welcher zur Bestimmung der Maßverhältnisse des Raumes hinreichen; am wichtigsten ist für den gegenwärtigen Zweck das von Euklid zugrunde gelegte. Diese Tatsachen sind wie alle Tatsachen nicht notwendig, sondern nur von empirischer Gewißheit, sie sind Hypothesen; man kann also ihre Wahrscheinlichkeit, welche innerhalb der Grenzen der Beobachtung allerdings sehr groß ist, untersuchen und hiernach über die Zulässigkeit ihrer Ausdehnung jenseits der Grenzen der Beobachtung sowohl nach der Seite des Unmeßbargroßen, als nach der Seite des Unmeßbarkleinen urteilen." (Riemann B. 1919, pp. 1-2.)

16 | See Wolfe H.E. 1945.

17 | See Bonola R. 1955.

created the need to develop new mathematical spaces, as Jean-Victor Poncelet did through pure imaginary numbers.

During the early nineteenth century, pure imaginary numbers were a scandalous topic but at the same time, very useful. In this regard, Poncelet, trying to explain the usefulness of imaginary numbers, used the method of postulation. He claimed that mathematical reasoning can be thought of as a mechanical operation using abstract signs. From the moment that the new sort of numbers was accepted in mathematical analysis, Poncelet argued that geometry is equally able to use abstract signs.[18] Therefore, Poncelet made a great contribution to science by working on the combination of mathematics and geometry. He opened a path of analysis based on the method of postulation, a kind of analysis that helped to theorize non-Euclidean geometries.[19]

In 1899 David Hilbert (1862-1943) published *Grundlage der Geometrie*, where he wrote an important analysis of the method of postulation. Hilbert's work represents a break with the semantic space constructed by Euclid nearly two millennia earlier. To understand Hilbert's contribution one must remember Descartes' *La géométrie*. As noted above, Descartes provided a method of operation. For Descartes, axioms do not really matter: the problems' resolution passes through the construction and its demonstration. Instead, Hilbert deals with a different kind of problem. In his work, there is no longer a Cartesian construction and the method of postulation becomes fundamental.

"Die Geometrie bedarf – ebenso wie die Arithmetik – zu ihrem folgerichtigen Aufbau nur weniger und einfacher Grundsätze. Diese Grundsätze heißen Axiome der Geometrie. Die Aufstellung der Axiome der Geometrie und die Erforschung ihres Zusammenhanges ist eine Aufgabe, die seit Euklid in zahlreichen vortrefflichen Abhandlungen der mathematischen Literatur sich erörtert findet. Die bezeichnete Aufgabe läuft auf die logische Analyse unserer räumlichen Anschauung hinaus."[20]

This excerpt shows that from the interest in axioms derived a logical analysis instead of the former constructive examination proposed by Descartes. This meant a radical change in the method used to study spaces and also to represent them.

Hilbert proposed three kinds of objects: points, lines and planes, whose properties are described by words like "between" and "congruent." These families of objects are defined by five axioms: incidence, order, parallelism, continuity and congruence. In this way, Hilbert conceptualized the point, the line and the plane. He considered these concepts in a purely formal way. That is to say, these concepts – line, point and plane – do not represent a physical or intuitive idea; rather, their existence is only justified because they obey the 21 laws set by Hilbert himself.[21] Any object that meets

---

18 | Shapiro S. 1997, p. 146.
19 | See Poncelet J.V. 1822.
20 | Hilbert D. 1962, p. 2.
21 | In this regard see Toepell M. 1986.

these conditions will be or will have the right to be interpreted, and therefore, called point, line or plane.[22]

Thanks to Hilbert, the science of geometry underwent a big change. On the one hand, Descartes developed methods to solve problems; on the other hand, Hilbert developed an analysis of logical relations between propositions. Hilbert determined kinds of geometries; conversely, Descartes constructed types of curves.[23] Following Hilbert's contribution, the scientific world started a discussion about the nature of space as well as a debate about the objects that humanity had placed in this space since antiquity.

22 | Leonesi S. - Toffalori C. 2007, Chapter 3, *Dondamenti e turbamenti.*
23 | Reed D. 1995, p. 38.

1.4 TOWARD FRACTALITY

The apparent weakness of the fifth postulate allowed the development of a new theory of space. Scientists started to create new postulates for new geometries that responded to new mathematical objects. Hilbert made this possible through new axioms that rendered geometry a logical analysis of spaces and structures. In fact, a new logic, governed by axioms different from those of Euclid, allowed the representation of new spaces.

Fig. 1.4

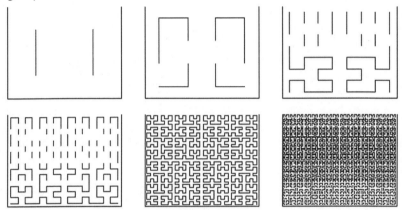

Towards the end of the nineteenth century, Giuseppe Peano, achieving Hilbert's theories, showed that the traditional notion of the curve was naïve and tried to develop a very particular space.[1] He built a curve, which was supposed to cover all the points in a square.[2] Peano's curves obliged the scientific world to think on the nature of this geometric figure and, therefore, to propose alternative definitions of curve.

Traditionally, the curve was considered as a one-dimensional object placed in a two-dimensional plane. Peano's curve, as one can observe in the figure above (fig. 1.4), represents a one-dimensional object that fills the two-dimensional plane. Hence the curve is considered a two-dimensional object.[3]

---

1 | See Hilbert D. 1891.

2 | See Peano G. 1890.

3 | In this regard it is important to quote Peitgen, Jürgens and Saupe. This phenomenon, which occurs in nature, was highlighted by fractal geometry. Thanks to fractal geometry, mankind could understand and, therefore, apply this "space-filling structure" to complex systems. "In Nature the organization of space filling structures is one of the fundamental building blocks of living beings. An organ must be supplied with the necessary supporting substances such as water and oxygen. In many cases these substances will be transported through vessel systems that must reach every point in the volume of the organ.

Through the nineteenth century, there were several attempts to 'conjugate' mathematical analysis with forms. Geometry was proposed as a **field of analysis of structures and phenomena**. It led to the introduction of particular figures into space, of **ideal elements**.

Justus Grassmann, with his work on crystallography, demonstrated that the development of a new geometry was of primary importance for the industry. According to Grassmann, in this particular domain, geometrical analysis was more appropriate than the application of concepts of pure mathematics. But why was it necessary to theorize a new geometry? In other words, what is the point of the change from geometry as a physical or spatial study to a geometry that deals with independent structures and complex sets? Most likely, the idea lying at the bottom of new geometries was that by means of another kind of perspective, the spatial relations, which do not provide fixed distances or specific magnitudes, could be better analyzed. This kind of perspective was highly useful for the study of surfaces such as those of crystals carried out by Grassmann.[4]

Grassmann developed a stronger connection between arithmetic, which has as its subject of study quantity, and geometry, which deals with physical bodies and spaces. J. Grassmann worked under the influence of his father, Hermann Grassmann (1809-1877), who, with his work *Die Ausdehnungslehre von 1844*, developed geometry as a science of forms.[5] Under H. Grassmann geometry acquired the ability to accept either abstractions or interpretations from any language. According to H. Grassmann, geometry assigns meaning to objects. Therefore, the object itself is totally irrelevant;

For example, the kidney houses three interwoven tree-like vessel systems, the arterial, the venous, and the urinary system. Each one of them has access to every part of the kidney. Fractals solve the problem of how to organize such a complicated structure in an efficient way. Of course, this was not what Peano and Hilbert were interested in almost 100 years ago. It is only now, after Mandelbrot's work, that the omnipresence of fractal becomes apparent." (Petingen H.O. - Jürgens H. - Saupe D. 1992, p. 94.) Note that these curves are now used in printing and in the creation of digital images.

4 | See Lewis C.A. 1975.

5 | As we might suppose, after Leibniz's *Analysis Situs* the idea of the conjugation of algebra with geometry became a necessity in the scientific field. Grassmann developed an important example of a topologic space. Further, he developed an interesting continuous form. However, I would like to quote Listing's words about topology. In fact, he coined the term. "Unter der Topologie soll also die Lehre von den modalen Verhältnissen räumlicher Gebilde verstanden werden, oder von Gesetzen des Zusammenhangs, der gegenseitigen Lage und der Aufeinanderfolge von Punkten, Linien, Flächen, Körpern und ihren Teilen oder ihren Aggregaten im Raume, abgesehen von den Maß- und Großenverhältnissen." (Listing J.B. 1848, p. 6.) It is interesting to note that contrary to Leibniz, who was primarily interested in the possibilities of the movement of variable points in space, Listing focused on the complexity of the set. Indeed, he was interested in the development of a *complexus*. See Heuser M.-L. 2007.

what is important is the meaning granted to the object.[6] Thus, geometry became a language able to express any concept through forms. This desire was driven by an interesting remark on mathematical science:

"Die reine Mathematik ist daher die Wissenschaft der **besonderen** Seins als eines durch das Denken **gewordenen**."[7]

|Prop. X| The main problem was that mathematics had no spatial concepts. In order to solve this problem, H. Grassmann proposed a new relationship between mathematics and many other scientific fields. With this aim, he attempted to develop a basic concept of 'continuous', in which the notion of 'becoming' derives from a spatial continuous form.[8] This continuous form is characterized by three major phenomena: *Erzeugen* (generation), *Setzen* (positioning) and *Verknüpfen* (bonding). The becoming, being the essence of infinity, is represented by H. Grassmann as a continuous form that presents a generating phenomenon. But his analysis is not limited to the generating element. Through the concepts of *Setzen* and *Verknüpfen*, H. Grassmann assigns a spatial nature to the becoming. As pointed out above, the first condition to create an infinite space is the generation (*Erzeugen*). The generating element represents the possibility to apply a recursive operation. As long as we accept an infinite space created by means of Grassmann's continuous form, we are obliged to recognize the position (*Setzen*) of its elements and its direct relationship (*Verknüpfen*) with the whole set. Such recognition not only allows the creation of a topology or map of an infinite space (because it is in constant self-reproduction) but it also allows the analysis of the character of a given object in its relationship with the others in the set. In this new kind of space, the objects are analyzed as sets without losing their unitary nature. Each object has a relationship with each other and with the whole. According to Grassmann, the process of continuous form characterizes the essence of all things that are created by the human thought.[9] It is important to remember that Grassmann's work represents the first fundamental investigation into a multidimensional geometry.[10]

It was only with the work of Karl Georg Christian von Staudt (1798-1867) that it became possible to realize Grassmann's theories on space. In fact, before reaching that stage it was necessary to build new elements and to develop a new interpretation of accepted geometrical elements. For example, points, contrary to Euclid's definition

---

6 | See Grassmann H. 1878.

7 | Grassmann H. 1878, *Einleitung XXII*.

8 | Lewis C.A. 1975, p. 98.

9 | As we will see in the last part of this text, Vannevar Bush, in his attempt to develop the first hypertext, highlighted the same phenomenon.

10 | For a further analysis of these works, see Grassmann H. 1878, Lewis C.A. 1975, Kolmogorov A.N and Yushkevich A.P. 1996, which treats the subject from a scientific perspective.

stating that a point has no parts (= is indivisible), were defined as elements having an internal structure.

"We are accustomed, even today, to think of a line as a locus of points. However, one can just as well think of a point as a locus of lines."[11]

Thanks to these innovative theories, the objects of classic geometry acquired another identity. Thus, the search for a new axiomatic changed the focus of geometry. Geometry was no longer interested in the classic geometrical objects, like triangles, squares and circles, but started to develop the study of geometric forms as a unity, a flexible unity that allows transformations.[12] The acknowledgement of new axioms offered the possibility to build a space where the existence of points presenting an internal structure was accepted. In adition, this new vision of geometry allowed the representation, through forms, of complex operations belonging to mathematics.

After the research of Grassmann and Staudt, several objects of great rarity emerged in the scientific world. For example, scientists had always believed that every curve has a tangent at every point, except in obvious cases of curves that showed a sharp reversal of direction. Thanks to the research improvements in the field of mathematics in the nineteenth century, scientists discovered some special properties of curves. They realized that it is possible to construct a curve that manifests no tangent at any point. It was Bernhard Riemann (1826-1866) who revealed for the first time this geometrical object, which was demonstrated through the examples of Weierstraß (1815-1897) in 1860. Thanks to Weierstraß's contributions on this subject, the basic concepts of topology were established: proximity, open sets, and accumulations of points of the infinite set. The multiplication of dimensions created a new space where the traditional objects could manifest drastic changes. Riemann also carried out an expansion of classic metric notions: length, area and volume. He also worked on the notion of surfaces and created several new ones. Some of them are designed as completely break up entities, as a reunion of pieces connected by 'laces' coming from the same point. Among the surfaces theorized by Riemann there is a surface made up several 'layers' that can also be interconnected along the lines of passage.[13] He also created families of curves or surfaces that are considered "multiplicities" of infinite dimension. The scientific community rejected these curves, and some of them could even properly be described as 'monsters'.[14]

|Prop. III| One of the most important contributions to this revolution in geometry was given by Georg Cantor. However, before analyzing Cantor's work, it is necessary to know what his aims were. Cantor began his research with the analysis of the paradoxes of both Albert of Saxony (Albertus de Saxonia 1316-1390) and Galileo Gali-

---

11 | Shapiro S. 1997, p. 148.

12 | See Heuser M.-L. 2007, pp. 197-198.

13 | Dieudonné J. 1994, p. 37.

14 | See Gray J. 1994.

lei (1564-1642). In his paradox, Albert of Saxony states that by cutting up a beam of infinite length into cubes of the same size and then placing the cubes in such a way as to make another cube, it is possible to fill an infinite three-dimensional space.[15] By means of this paradox, he compared two infinite spaces and attempted to establish relationships of magnitude between them. Galileo undertook the same operation but with numbers. He took the positive numbers, 1,2,3,4,5,6,7... to infinity. Then he squared all the numbers as follows: 1x1=1, 2x2=4, 3x3=9, 4x4=16 5x5=25, etc. The series of numbers obtained by means of this operation (1, 4, 9, 16, 25...) is also infinite because it is in one-to-one correspondence with positives numbers. At that point, Galileo wondered which group has the largest number of elements, being both infinite sets. Each item in the list of squares corresponds to an item of the list of positive numbers. The paradox lies in the fact that the set of numbers obtained by squaring the integers is also in the set of integers. Thus, it suggests that the list of positive numbers is bigger than the list of numbers obtained from this group, i.e. the powers. Galileo's conclusion is that one should not try to measure or compare infinite sets because it is impossible to know which 'infinite' is bigger.

Cantor's revolution consists in considering the infinite not as a succession (= the Aristotelian potential infinite), but as a totality, as an object which must be perceived by the intellect as an entire entity, even if it is infinite.[16] Thanks to Cantor, the existence of the actual infinity started to be accepted.

"By arranging the integers not in their natural order but according to the sequence 0, 1, -1, 2 -2, 3, -3, ..., we see at once that the distinction becomes meaningless. (According to the definition of set, the order in which we place the individual elements in a set is immaterial. Thus the set consisting of the letters a, b, c is the same as that consisting of b, a, c.) Moreover, Cantor argued that to deny the actual infinite means to deny the existence of irrational numbers, for such numbers have an infinite decimal expansion, whereas any finite decimal would only be a rational approximation."[17]

Cantor's theories lead to the acceptance of a hierarchy of infinities. He demonstrated to the scientific world that from an infinite set it can derive a new set that has more elements than the original set:

"If from any given set – finite or infinite – one can create ('more' in the ordinary sense of the word for finite sets, and in the sense of power for infinite ones), then this process can be repeated; that is, from the new set we can create a set with still more elements, and so on *ad infinitum!*"[18]

---

15 | See Barrow J.D. 2005.
16 | Maor E. 1987, p. 54.
17 | Maor E. 1987, p. 54.
18 | Maor E. 1987, p. 62.

Thanks to Cantor, who compared infinite sets, it was possible to recognize infinites bigger than others and therefore also measurable infinities and non-measurable ones. Cantor reached this conclusion by making one-to-one correspondences between sets. For example, if one has a set composed of the letters *a*, *b*, *c* and another composed by the numbers 1, 2, 3, it is possible to create a 1:1 correspondence, as follows: 1 with *a*, 2 with *b* and 3 with *c*. There can also be a correspondence 1 with *b*, 2 with *a* and 3 with *c*. These correspondences are possible because the number of objects of each set is the same. If the 1:1 correspondence is possible between finite sets it is because they have the same quantity of elements. Cantor followed the same process but with infinite sets. He stated that when a 1:1 correspondence can be made between two infinite sets it means that they have the same amount of items. Thus, he demonstrated that there is the same quantity of points in the straight line as in a part of it. It is important to note that this conclusion contradicts the postulate of Euclid asserting that the whole is greater than the part.

"Un ensemble infini se reconnaît à ceci, qu'il peut être mis en correspondance terme à terme avec une vraie partie de lui-même, c'est-à-dire appliqué et comme remplié sur cette partie. Ainsi l'ensemble des nombres entiers peut être appliqué sur l'ensemble des nombres pairs, ou sur celui des carrés parfaits qui sont pourtant contenus en lui: il suffit d'écrire en face de tout nombre son double, ou son carré; on se trouve alors avoir passé en revue tous les termes possibles, dans chacune des deux séries."[19]

By demonstrating that there is a one-to-one correspondence between the points of the curve and the points of the plane, Cantor opened many useful possibilities to understanding the relationship between curves and planes. These relationships were very useful in the topological dimension that, at that period, was in its first phase of development.

In 1892, Henri Poincaré (1854 -1912) laid the foundations for a critical theory known as topology.

To understand complexity, which became a topic of study to the scientific world, it was extremely important to develop a space where it would be possible to make abstractions of complex phenomena. The *Analysis Situs*[20] of Poincaré was the creation of a space that allowed scientists to explain phenomena through abstractions that enable a new character of spatial structures that are highly transformative.[21] Let us see how Poincaré expressed the need for such a space:

---

19 | Bolzano-Weierstraß, in Dällenbach L. 1977, p. 33.

20 | Through the *analysis situs*, Leibniz attempted to describe a new way of representing space based on the relationships between objects. It is important to remember that Leibniz's ideas about the *analysis situs* are formed within the algebra, and its primary aim was to prove mechanical systems.

21 | On the development of the *Analysis Situs*, see Dieudonné J. 1989, especially *The Work of Poincaré*.

"Il faut qu'on arrive à le construire [l'Analysis Situs] complètement dans des espaces supérieurs ; on aura alors un instrument qui permettra réellement de voir dans l'hyperespace et de suppléer à nos sens."[22]

Topology represents a violent departure from the space built by the Greeks:

"La topologie impose l'oubli de la tradition et le souvenir d'une constitution spatiale recouverte par l'équivoque du miracle grec, suspend le langage traditionnel comme ambigu et pratique la dissociation liminaire de la pureté non métrique et de la mesure."[23]

But how does one imagine this space?

A factor that helped in designing the topological dimension was the relativity of space theorized by Poincaré. He stated in the early twentieth century that space was amorphous and that the objects placed into space gave it shape.[24] In Günzel's words:

"Für die topologische Raumbescreibung hilfreich sind dabei Relativierungen, welche von Seiten der Mathematik und Physik nach Newton hinsichtlich der Raumauffassung vorgenommen wurden: Raum wird im Zuge dessen nicht mehr als eine dreifach dimensionierte Entität oder formale Einheit gefasst, sondern anhand von Elementen beschreiben, die relational zueinander bestimmt werden. –Mit anderen Worten: An die Stelle des Ausdehnungsaprioris tritt eine Strukturdarstellung von Raum."[25]

|Prop. XI| This new character of the space, clearly influenced by Leibniz's ideas, represents the peak of the revolutionary ideas of topology in the new way of conceiving space.[26] These shapes are placed into a space composed of a number of dimensions that are assigned by our intellect.[27] The space, at that point, could be understood as a composition of dimensions necessary to respond to movements and forms derived from a complex thought.[28] Further, directly influenced by Leibniz's theory of *Analysis*

---

22 | Poincaré H. 1908, p. 40.

23 | Serres M. 1993, p. 21.

24 | Poincaré H. 1908, p. 103.

25 | Günzel S. 2007, p. 17.

26 | See Günzel S. 2007.

27 | See Lefèbvre H. 2000[4], especially *Dessin de l'ouvrage.*

28 | Note that thanks to Poincaré and Helmholtz the scientific world and the larger public recognized that sense perceptions were relative. One can find, after Poincaré's studies, many articles and scientific researches focused on the relativity of the space theorized by Poincaré, theories that imply a non-Euclidean geometry as well as the existence of more than three dimensions in space. Examples include Sir William Crookes *De la relativité des connaissances humaines*, published in 1897 and Gaston Moch's analysis of it published in the *Revue Scientifique* the same year. Another interesting example is *La relativité de l'espace euclidien* (1903) by Maurice Boucher.

situs, the space proposed by Poincaré is also freed from a coordinate system. As explained by Heuser:

"Der Raum wird zunächst aufgelöst in eine Menge von Örten, deren Kongruenzbeziehungen zu einem fixen Punkt den unendlichen Raum ergeben. Die einzelnen geometrischen Figuren entstehen dadurch, dass bestimmte Punkte festgehelten werden, die zueinander eine konstante Abstandsbeziehung innehaben, während andere (variable) Punkte innerhalb dieser Konstellation als beweglich gedacht werden."[29]

Poincaré's theories are placed in a special scientific and social context of interest on the concept of space. In fact, as noted by Henderson, one of the most important philosophical bases developed by Kant in *Kritik der reinen Vernunft* is the distinction between synthetic and analytic judgments. Kant argued that there exist judgments that are synthetic *a priori* and demonstrated their existence by means of axioms of pure mathematics and geometry. Consequently, the *a priori* nature of the axioms governed Kant's definition of space as a pure form of sensibility. Thus, according to Kant there is no space with more than three dimensions. Kant's space corresponded to Euclidean space in that it accepted only three dimensions.[30] The philosophical questions derived from the development of non-Euclidean geometries, especially due to Kant's reflections about space, brought the subject of new geometries and the possible existence of more than three dimensions to the popular sphere. This was the case of Hermann Ludwig Ferdinand von Helmholtz (1821-1894) who tried to popularize the subject to an audience not familiar with mathematics. Helmholtz argued that geometrical axioms vary according to the kind of space inhabited.[31] He theorized the space curvature, from which derives a fourth dimension in space, as a property of the space that can be recognized only through analytical calculation.[32]

|Prop. XVII| The geometry that accompanied mankind through millennia was based on direct experience with nature; it reflected the space in which mankind lives. This

---

29 | Heuser M.-L. 2007, p. 188.

30 | See Henderson L.D. 1983.

31 | See Helmholtz H. 1876.

32 | See Helmholtz H. 1876. It is interesting to note that the popularization of non-Euclidean geometries was specially focused on the existence of a fourth dimension in space. Certainly, this subject was the most interesting for the public. In fact, it was perceived as a weakness of human senses from which derive a kind of illusion of the space in which humans live. In other words, it was understood as the human inability to see reality as well as the existence of an illusion generated by human cognition. Consequently, some literary works like *Flatland* (1884) by Edwin Abbott Abbott (1838-1926) acquired huge public interest as well as the interest of artists like Duchamp and some Cubists. Theories about a fourth dimension were also the source of many science fiction works, for example some H.G. Wells' tales. For further information about this subject, see Henderson L.D. 1983.

notwithstanding, geometry, in turn, is also a means of analysis of spaces invented by mankind and derived from abstractions of nature. In Poincaré's words: "(...) Nous avons créé l'espace qu'elle [geometry] étudie, mais en l'adaptant au monde où nous vivons."[33] Thus, thanks to Poincaré, the notion of dimension started to be understood as an instinctive concept built by our ancestors or somehow implanted in our childhood. In consequence, Poincaré could create a space that allowed him to question the universal determinacy: the universe seen as a clock. By using geometric imagination, Poincaré analyzed movement. Leibniz's influence is clear. Leibniz's *Analysis Situs* generates an interesting concept of movement. In fact, this geometric structure allows us to determine movement by the relationships of spaces, by the relationship between points, whose links determine movement.[34] Thanks to this particular approach, Poincaré noted the chaotic character of nature, even though he did not define it clearly.[35]

Poincaré attempted to create a space able to accept some phenomena that could not be accepted by the space governed by Euclidean geometry. One should remember that in that period, geometry was neglected and considered obsolete, but Poincaré created a new need for geometry and its language. Regarding geometry, he stated:

"Il nous permet donc encore de nous diriger dans cet espace qui est trop grand pour nous et que nous ne pouvons voir, en nous rappelant sans cesse l'espace visible qui n'en est qu'une image imparfaite sans doute, mais qui est encore une image. Ici encore, comme dans tous les exemples précédents, c'est l'analogie avec ce qui est simple qui nous permet de comprendre ce qui est complexe."[36]

|Prop. XXII| Poincaré encouraged the use of geometry in order to create an alternative space useful for analyzing complex phenomena. As noted above, this space emerged through the *Analysis Situs*, in which one finds the fundamental concepts of topology:[37] e.g. the principle of transformation, the disappearnce of the coordinates in the space and the principle of invariableness.[38]

In Euclidean geometry, two objects are equivalent when it is possible to transform one into the other by means of rotations or translations, that is to say transformations that keep the angle, the size, the area and the volume.

---

33 | Poincaré H. 1908, p. 121
34 | See Heuser M.-L. 2007.
35 | See Ekeland I. 1995.
36 | Poincaré H. 1908, p. 39.
37 | Note that Poincaré's work *Analysis Situs* derive from the study of the concepts of Algebraic Topology. This research in multiple volumes, the first of which was edited in 1892 in *Comptes-Rendus*, was completed by a paper of 1895 entitled *Analysis Situs*. Then, the notion of *Analysis Situs* was definitively completed in a series of papers edited between 1899 and 1905, these entitled *Compléments à l'Analysis Situs*.
38 | See Dieudonné J. 1989, p. 18.

|*Fig. 1.5*|

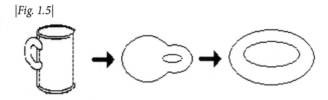

In the topological dimension (dT), the concept of transformation acquires a much wider definition. In the topological dimension, geometric properties of bodies remain unchanged after the transformations exerted on the body. This proprety of the objects in topology is know as homeomorphism (fig. 1.5).

The objects in the topological dimension are equivalent in a larger sense. The topology allows the object to bend, stretch, twist, etc… while remaining the same size; the object still denotes the same object.[39] An example that may help us to understand the usefulness of deformations is given by the plans of the public transport of cities. We are aware that these representations are not geometrically accurate. Neither the scale, the curves, nor the positions coincide with the objects represented. Certainly, these deformations are useful in maps, and it would be possible to argue that they transmit with high fidelity the needed information: the topological information.[40]

In addition, the difference between dT and dE is useful in measuring the disorder in a system. If dT = dE, there is order in the system. Conversely, if dT < dE, the system is highly disordered. This means that in the absence of irregularity the objects coincide in the two dimensions.

In 1914, Felix Hausdorff (1868-1942) provided the scientific world with his work *Grundzüge der Mengenlehre* in which he introduced some theoretical and topological notions of a dimension nowadays known by his name. Although there had been proposals of this kind, e.g. from Maurice Fréchet, it was Hausdorff who provided a comprehensive theory of topological spaces.[41] He offered the possibility of thinking and recognizing the existence of fractional dimensions. In other words, he not only recognized the irregularity in a space, but also the possibility to measure it. The theorization of this dimension placed scholars closer to the recognition of an irregular nature and, as a consequence, also influenced the way to represent nature.

---

39 | See Stewart I. 1975.

40 | It is interesting to note how the space represented by the topology found an interesting analogous in the space described by Merlau-Ponty from a phenomenological analysis. Borrowing from Merlau-Ponty, "L'espace est en soi, ou plutôt il est l'en soi par excellence, sa définition est d'être en soi. Chaque point de l'espace est et est pensé là où il est, l'un ici, l'autre là, l'espace est l'évidence du où. Orientation, polarité, enveloppement sont en lui des phénomènes dérivés, liés à ma présence. Lui repose absolument en soi, est partout égal à soi, homogène, et ses dimensions par exemple sont par définition substituables." (Merleau-Ponty M. 1964, p. 47.)

41 | In this regard see Dierkesmann M. – Lorentz G.G. – Bergmann G. – Bonnet H. 1967.

1.5 Some Words About Chaos

The universal non-determinacy was a recurrent idea, but neither science nor philosophy could clearly demonstrate it because of the lack of a solid theory that could displace the theory of the *universe-clock*.[1] There was a theory of a universal harmony, which allowed us to 'predict' and calculate an apparent universal order, mankind and society included.[2] In this regard, Poincaré pointed out in 1908 in his *Science et méthode*, and in particular in the first book entitled *Savant et la science*, that:

"N'est-ce pas là, pour nous autres mathématiciens, un procédé en quelque sorte professionnel ? Nous sommes accoutumés à *extrapoler*, ce qui est un moyen de déduire l'avenir du passé et du présent, et comme nous savons bien ce qu'il vaut, nous ne risquons pas de nous faire illusion sur la portée des résultats qu'il nous donne. Il y a eu autre fois des prophètes de malheur. Ils répétaient volontiers que tous les problèmes susceptibles d'être résolus l'avaient été déjà, et qu'après eux il n'y aurait plus qu'à glaner. Heureusement, l'exemple du passé nous rassure. Bien des fois déjà on a cru avoir fait l'inventaire de ceux qui comportent une solution. Et puis le sens du mot solution s'est élargi, les problèmes insolubles sont devenus les plus intéressants de tous et d'autres problèmes se sont posés auxquels on n'avait pas songé."[3]

Seventy years later, these same ideas were identified with chaos theory.

Chaos theory was born in a context of broad scientific research focused on incomprehensible phenomena, the so-called monsters of chaos.[4] One must wait until 1975 to see the materialization of this theory through the word 'chaos', put forward by the mathematician J. York. Science, at that time, underwent a serious crisis. Several scientists in the United States and Europe started looking for a way to recognize the chaotic world, and mankind started to recognize and identify the indeterminacy of nature. Deterministic thought, which was born with Newton in the seventeenth century and exalted by Laplace in the nineteenth century, was decisively abandoned during the 1970s thanks to the technical possibilities offered by the personal computer.

---

1 | In the Bible, chaos is synonymous with mix, disorder, elements not yet divided. The essence of the universe derives from a voluntary action of separating, dividing, ordering and then defining, in order to finish the original chaos. It is in this sense that the biblical passage where God separates light from darkness and named light "day" and darkness "night" has been read. It is important to note the lack of time in chaos. In the biblical passage, God, day by day, defined and separated elements. However, this chronology is imposed by the will of God and not by the chaotic state of universe. According to Leibniz, chaos is a set of possibilities, the non-coordination of individual essences. See Deleuze G. 1988.
2 | In this regard see Smith A. 1966 (1759).
3 | Poincaré H. 1908, pp. 19-20.
4 | See Aubin D. - Dalmedico A.D. 2002.

Chaos theory focuses on the analysis of movement: bifurcations,[5] attractors[6] and fractals unveiled a new way to analyze processes and movements. Some physicists argued that chaos was a science of process and not a science of state,[7] and it is understood as a dynamic phenomenon. "It occurs when the state of a system changes with time. There are regular changes, the stuff of classical dynamics, and chaotic ones, and no doubt worse, which we do not yet understand."[8]

Mankind believed for centuries that the solar system, and therefore everything, could be included in a cyclical action. Thanks to Poincaré, one began to observe that some systems could express a non-cyclical development and also that the position of a system is highly dependent on its initial data.

"The hallmark of chaos is that the motions diverge exponentially fast. Translated into a prediction problem, this means that any input error multiplies itself at an escalating rate as a function of prediction time, so that before long it engulfs the calculation, and all predictive power is lost."[9]

In the analysis of a system, a small error in the original data results in a completely different position after a while. It is this phenomenon of sensitivity to initial conditions that allowed the realization of chaos.[10] Recognizing the existence of chaotic systems allowed a new vision of the universe. From the moment that the chaotic nature of some movements was identified, chaos was recognized in many fields: fluids, weather, aircraft traffic, in our cities as well our cities themselves, politics and more.[11] The acknowledgment of irregular phenomena allows us to represent society under a new structure as well; a new structure that can be illustrated by a fractal object. In addition, the social space started to be described through topologic characteristics, it is to say, as a space built by the relationships between objects. In Foucault's words:

"L'espace dans lequel nous vivons, par lequel nous sommes attirés hors de nous-mêmes, dans lequel se déroule précisément l'érosion de notre vie, de notre temps et de notre histoire, cet espace qui nous ronge et nous ravine est en lui-même aussi un es-pace! hétérogène. Autrement dit, nous ne vivons pas dans une sorte de vide, à l'intérieur

---

5 | Bifurcations theory focuses on the mathematical study of qualitative changes in the topological structure. There is a bifurcation when a small variation of parameter values causes a qualitative or topologic change in the system, a change of its nature. These changes may generate a disaster.

6 | In the study of dynamical systems, an attractor is a set, a curve or a space to which a system evolves in an irreversible way in the absence of disturbances.

7 | See Browand F.K. 1986.

8 | Stewart I. 1992, p. 46.

9 | Davis P. 1992, p. 216.

10 | Martens M. – Nowicki T.J. 2003, p. 6.

11 | For a deeper discussion of this subject, see Musha T. – Higuci H. 1976.

duquel on pourrait situer des individus et des choses. Nous ne vivons pas à l'interieur d'un vide qui se colorerait de différents chatoiement, nous vivons à l'intérieur d'un ensemble de relations qui définissent des emplacements irréductibles les uns aux autres et absolument non superposables."[12]

Before the formulation of chaos theory, the movements that were subsequently approached through this new theory were analyzed through the deterministic laws of Newton.[13] This kind of approach was however imperfect, as clearly explained by M. Martens and T.J. Nowicki:

"When one deals with a system that is highly sensitive to initial conditions (think of turbulent flows or weather), it becomes very hard to calculate and predict the longer-term future. The surprising fact is that very long-term behavior can be understood much better. Moreover, in many practical systems the evolution that starts at any typical initial state will show this asymptotic behavior after a rather short period of time. This leads to the notion of an attractor."[14]

|**Prop. IV**| Since these movements were recognized, it became necessary to represent them in a space, that is, to place them into a space in order to study them.

|*Fig. 1.6*|

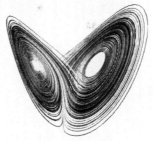

As we will see, fractal geometry became an important instrument for representing these phenomena. However, I would like to draw attention to the Strange Attractors,[15]– mainly to the Lorenz Attractor (fig. 1.6). To understand the Lorenz Attractor it is important to know the difference between dissipative dynamical systems and conservative dynamical systems.

The dissipative dynamical systems are systems with 'some sort of friction'; they are systems that manifest a loss of energy in its dynamics, a loss of energy that is continuous.[16]

The second kind of system, the conservative dynamical systems, maintain its energy; the motion of their objects is conserved and no energy is lost. Thus, in the first

---

12 | Foucault M. 1984, p. 47.

13 | See Mullin T. 1992.

14 | Martens M. – Nowicki T. J. 2003, p. 69.

15 | An attractor is a set that can dictate a dynamical system through a variable, a dynamical system that evolves over time. The attractors enable the representation of systems geometrically in n-dimensions.

16 | Peitgen H.O. – Jürgens H. – Saupe D. 1992, p. 655.

case, the system tends to be simple patterns of motion; in the second case, in the case of conservative dynamical systems, the system tends to the complex, to chaos. Consequently, strange attractors are fractals as geometrical patterns.[17]

The development of strange attractors, in particular the Lorenz Attractor, generated great hope in the social sciences as well as in the natural sciences. It could represent the instrument that helps us to understand such chaotic phenomena as turbulence, our planet's climate and human brain activity.[18] Theses chaotic systems, which were illustrated by the strange attractors, reached the larger public as the butterfly effect, after the title of a paper by Edward Lorenz, *Does the Flap of a Butterfly's Wings in Brazil Set Off a Tornado in Texas?*[19]

As we will see in what follows, nascent fractal geometry was able to take form within the research on chaotic phenomena undertaken during the Seventies. Chaos theory, like fractal geometry, consists of repetitive operations. Applying fractals to chaos theory is a special use of fractal geometry, as it not applied to real objects, but to mental ones.

Over time, fractal geometry started to extent beyond the scientific field. In a relatively short time, fractal objects came into our quotidian lives.

---

17 | See Peitgen H.O. – Jürgens H. – Saupe D. 1992.

18 | Peitgen H.O. – Jürgens H. – Saupe D. 1992, p. 656.

19 | See Wolfram S. 2002.

1.6 Fractus, Fracta, Fractum

In *Les objets fractals ; forme, hasard et dimension,* Benoit Mandelbrot carried out a study of nature and chaotic phenomena with the help of some geometric structures, which were considered an idea of an esoteric and unusable space, a pathology of mathematics. These geometric structures were fractal objects.[1] Fractal geometry used these 'pathological' structures and turned them into tools of science. Today, these structures, used in the development of fractal geometry, are called proto-fractals.[2] This new geometry of nature was born from a special interest in the shape of natural objects, called rough objects.

In nature, says Mandelbrot, rough forms prevail over soft shapes. To describe the process, which excluded the nature from mathematics, Mandelbrot observes that a prehistoric man saw some mild forms, the full moon, the pupil of the eye and some fruits. This notwithstanding, mathematics began to deal with simple shapes and then developed geometry, which became an exact science. Rough forms were in such a way moved into the field of arts.[3] Euclidean geometry is often described as a 'cold' and 'dry' geometry because it cannot describe the shape of a financial statement, of a cloud, a mountain or a tree. Only painters have ever taken into consideration these forms and realized that these rough forms were completely beyond geometrical analyses. Mandelbrot uses the words of Eugène Delacroix to show the consciousness of these kinds of forms by artists: "Everything is idealized by man. The straight line itself is his invention because it is nowhere in nature."[4]

|Prop. XX| Science showed its weakness: it was not able to recognize certain shapes. Although, geometry made big progresses toward the recognition of many forms and phenomena, there was still a 'weakness': geometry could not recognize roughness, fragmentation, irregularity, which were phenomena strongly present in nature.

Mandelbrot's challenge was to study and describe what geometry defined as formless or amorphous. His method was to apply and to study fractal objects, which can be mathematical or natural objects. These fractal objects are characterized by irregular, rough, porous and fragmented shapes, and above all, they have the same properties at all scales. Thanks to this last characteristic, the use of these particular objects ac-

---

1 | See Mandelbrot B. 1995.

2 | See Mandelbrot B. 1997.

3 | This phenomenon of alienation of science from nature was manifested by Merleau-Ponty as follows: "La science manipule les choses et renonce à les habiter. Elle s'en donne des modèles internes et, opérant sur ces indices ou variables les transformations permises par leur définition, ne se confronte que de loin en loin avec le monde actuel. Elle est, elle a toujours été, cette pensée admirablement active, ingénieuse, désinvolte, ce parti pris de traiter tout être comme "object en général", c'est-à-dire à la fois comme s'il ne nous était rien et se trouvait cependant prédestiné à nos artifices." (Merleau-Ponty M. 1964, p. 9.)

4 | Mandelbrot B. 1997, p. 31.

quired an important utility in Mandelbrot's research. They became the central thread of all his work. The idea was that some aspects of the world have the same structure at all scales, just the details change when one changes point of view. Thus, every little piece of an object contains the 'key' of the entire construction, just like in a fractal object.[5] The fractal character of nature, according to Mandelbrot, is directly reflected in the economy that nature applies in its structure. As Mandelbrot explains, nature never uses different DNA codes, or different structures to create a branch of broccoli. From the moment that a three-view system is created, nature generates branches periodically until it stops, as in the case of broccoli and the human lung. Ramification of ramifications of ramifications, such as with broccoli in nature and the lung within our body, the growth of a body is arranged with a simple code that can be defined as the repetition of the smallest structure. The continuous, related repetition is the basis of a fractal structure, simplicity within the complexity of nature.

This idea was first introduced to the scientific world by Poincaré in a work that became vital for Mandelbrot's research. In 1908, Poincaré highlighted this 'simplicity' of nature. He noted that thanks to this simplicity it is possible to conduct a study of nature. According to Poncaré, the most interesting phenomena are those that can be used multiple times because they can be renewed and applied to other circumstances. The simplicity of nature, a simplicity of absolute complexity because of its infinite possibilities of combination, is what allows the existence of science. He used as example the chemical elements. Assuming that the number of chemical elements was 60 billion, Poincaré states that science, in that case, would be almost useless because of the inability to gain experience. It would be impossible to compare the elements because each case would be almost unique:

"il y aurait une grande probabilité pour qu'il soit formé [un caillou] de quelque substance inconnue ; tout ce que nous saurions des autres cailloux ne vaudrait rien pour lui ; devant chaque objet nouveau nous serions comme l'enfant qui vient de naître ; comme lui nous ne pourrions qu'obéir à nos caprices ou à nos besoins ; dans un pareil monde, il n'y aurait pas de science ; peut-être la pensée et même la vie y seraient-elles impossibles, puisque l'évolution n'aurait pu y développer les instincts conservateurs."[6]

Poincaré was interested in the study of facts that can be repeated, namely simple facts that can create complex structures, even infinite structures. He noted that in a complex fact there are thousands of circumstances that meet by chance. As such, it was necessary to develop a method to analyze and understand complex facts. As in the case of a biologist who studies with more interest the single cell than the entire animal – because of the similarities that they have to the entire organism – the scientific world started to develop the concept of symmetry between scales. Symmetry was understood as the beauty of nature, as the universal harmony in chaos.

---

5 | Mandelbrot B. 1997, p. 36.

6 | Poincaré H. 1908, p. 10.

Mandelbrot's fractal geometry corresponds to a quest for universal harmony between scales. The analysis of irregular objects needed a new revolutionary concept that required a neologism: 'fractal object' and 'fractal'. These terms derive from the Latin adjective *fractus*, meaning 'irregular' or 'broken'.[7]

This story begins in 1953 when Mandelbrot went to Princeton, invited by John von Neumann, the father of computers.[8] Subsequently, in 1958, Mandelbrot began a close collaboration with the *avant-garde* of new technologies at IBM. In this center, he worked on economic movements and, there, he had his first contact with a fractal object. Mandelbrot's interest in economic movements allowed him to see, during a conference at Harvard, a diagram concerning the distribution of income, which in turn gave birth to his idea of fractal geometry.

Economists at that time could not measure price changes in accurate manner because of the intermittent nature of these movements.[9] They based their analyses on a dichotomy between small and large economical changes. They argued that the small economic changes, occurring during short periods, were not related to major variations derived from macroeconomic movements, economic crises, wars and so on. Economists perceived this difference as a dissimilarity between two phenomena: the first of an ordered type, the second of a chaotic type.[10] After seeing this pattern, on his return to the IBM research center, Mandelbrot began an in-depth analysis on changes in cotton prices since 1900.[11] Changes in the price of cotton became a quite useful study. The information on cotton prices, cotton being a centralized market, was accessible. Further, computer technology at that time was starting to emerge from the field of mathematics and physics and starting to become a tool of economists. This study led to the identification of a constant within these economic changes.[12] In fact, during a period of great economic turmoil – e.g. the economic crisis in 1929, the two world wars – there was a constant, a symmetry.[13]

Subsequently, Mandelbrot worked on communications interference. At that time, it was impossible to establish an average of these distortions because they did not show regularity. Mandelbrot introduced deeper temporal divisions between the times of 'clean' transmission and distortions. It could be an hour or twenty minutes of transmission; there would still be a geometric correspondence between clean moments and moments of noise. There was a harmony between the scales. By making the

---

7 | See Mandelbrot B. 1995.

8 | *Le Monde* 2 - 16 au 22 Mai 2004 Numéro 18, *Un génie né dans les choux; rencontre avec l'inventeur des fractales.*

9 | See Mandelbrot B. 1983.

10 | Fan L.T. – Neogi D. – Yashima M. 1991, especially *Change in Commodity Prices 4.1.*

11 | See Mandelbrot B. 1963a.

12 | It is interesting that Mandelbrot affirms that the search for symmetry is a common desire of both science and art, as he said "l'art et la science sont en quête constante d'une symétrie." See Mandelbrot B. – Lorenz E. – Peitgen H.O. 1990.

13 | See Gleick J. 1987.

scale smaller Mandelbrot was able to note the 'structure' of the distortions. By means of this 'deepening' he was able to find the proportion between the periods and its constant. He identified the symmetry in a chaotic field.[14]

|**Prop. II**| In this research, Mandelbrot applied an abstract model known among mathematicians as the *Cantor Set* or *Cantor Dust*, which is now considered the first example of a fractal object.[15] Among the family of 'monsters of mathematics' the *Cantor Set* is the most special, due to its role in contemporary mathematics as well as in fractal geometry. In fact, it is considered as the fundamental structure of many fractal objects.[16]

|*Fig. 1.7*|

"Construction of the Cantor Set: Start with the interval [0,1]. Now take away the (open) interval (1/3,2/3), i.e., remove the middle third from [0,1], but not the numbers 1/3 and 2/3. This leaves two intervals [0,1/3] and [2/3,1] of length 1/3 each and completes a basic construction step. Now we repeat, we look at the remaining intervals [0,1/3] and [2/3,1] and remove their middle thirds, which yields four intervals of length 1/9. Continue on in this way. In other words, there is a feedback process in which a sequence of (closed) intervals is generated: one after the first step, two after the second step, four after the third step, eight after the fourth step, etc."[17]

The main line contains all the points, which are unlimited. The derived lines are also infinite in number and they are sets that allow a one-to-one correspondence. In other words, in the *Cantor Set* the whole is in the part. Such space does not exist in classical geometry. Euclidean geometry dealt with lines, circles, triangles and cones that move geometry away from nature, from the 'real'. As Mandelbrot says, "Clouds are not spheres, mountains are not cones, coastlines are not circles, and bark is not smooth, nor does lightning travel in a straight line."[18] By means of the application of the *Cantor Set* to the problem of interferences, Mandelbrot discovered the application of the 'geometric monsters' to both irregular objects and chaotic movements. Consequently,

---

14 | See Mandelbrot B. 1963b.

15 | The *Cantor Set* has been published for the first time in 1883. See Cantor G. 1883.

16 | Peitgen H.O. - Jürgens H. - Saupe D. 1992, especially 2.1 *The Cantor Set*.

17 | Peitgen H.O. - Jürgens H. - Saupe D. 1992, p. 68.

18 | Mandelbrot B. 1983, p. 1.

Mandelbrot started researching the irregularity present in several phenomena and natural objects. He was particularly interested in the differences between the measurement of common borderlines between countries, for example between Spain and Portugal.

Why are the dimensions of the coasts different in some encyclopedias?

|**Prop. V**| Mandelbrot stated that the measurement changes according to the scale or according to the distance from which it is measured.[19] Each coastline is, in such a sense, infinite, that is, its measurement depends on the scale used: the smaller the scale, the longer the coast. This phenomenon is due to how much the shape of the coast is taken into consideration: its ribs, curves, bays and peninsulas. These irregularities cannot be fully covered nor measured with a large scale. If the measurement scale becomes smaller, the bays will exhibit sub-bays, the same for the peninsulas.[20] Euclidean notions of depth, length and width are unable to cover irregular shapes, which make up the greater part of nature. However, how does the coastline show its fractality? That is to say, how is a fractal object projected onto a coastline? To understand this process, it is necessary to look at this classic fractal made by Helge von Koch (1870-1924) in 1904. As noted above, in 1872, Karl Weierstraß demonstrated the existence of special curves, in particular curves that have no tangents. The *Koch Snowflake* was devised to convince the scientific world of the existence of a continuous curve that has nowhere a tangent. As one can see in the figure (Fig. 1.8), the *Koch Snowflake* is formed by angles, which are spread over the entire space.[21]

|*Fig. 1.8*|

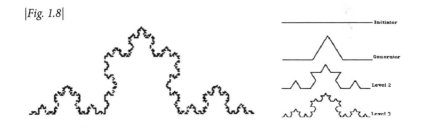

"Here is the simple geometric construction of the Koch curve. Begin with a straight line. This initial object is also called the initiator. Partition it into three equal parts. Then replace the middle third by an equilateral triangle and take away its base. This completes the basic construction step. A reduction of this figure, made of four parts, will be reused in the following stages. It is called the generator. Thus, we now repeat, taking each of the resulting line segments, partitioning them into three equal parts, and so on. Self-similarity is built into the construction process."[22]

---

19 | See Mandelbrot B. 1967.
20 | See Gleick J. 1987.
21 | Peitgen H.O. - Jürgens H. - Saupe D. 1992. See 2.4. *The Koch Curve*.
22 | Peitgen H.O. - Jürgens H. - Saupe D. 1992, p. 90.

Koch's curve has been described with these words: "such a Koch construction is defined by an initiator, which may be a collection of line segments, and generator, which is a polygonal line, composed of a number of connected line segments."[23]

Initiator and generator are two apparent states that determine a structure in becoming.[24] They organize the set. Their state is a state of constant becoming, inflection or infinite variation. According to Gilles Deleuze, the Koch curve derives from an act of rounding exerted on the angles, an action that meets the Baroque and consequently, Leibniz's self-similarity.[25] This curve passes through an infinite number of points, which do not admit tangents. It wraps an infinite cavernous or spongy world.

However, what is the relationship between this state of constant becoming, this endless repetition of the structure within itself, and the apparent infinity of a natural space like the coast of Great Britain? Initially, Mandelbrot's arguments seemed untenable. It was clear that the size of the coast changes depending on the scale of measurement. But this lack of precision was not tolerated by the scientific world and this caused some problems for Mandelbrot.[26] His vague notions like 'far' and 'near' caused some troubles. It is clear that between the notions of 'farer' and 'closer' there is an infinite distance that could not be defined. Due to this apparent weakness, the concept of the fractional dimension was developed. If the length of the coast was impossible to measure, its degree of roughness could, by means of the new concepts allowed by the notion of fractional dimension.

The similarities between the coastline and the *Koch Snowflake* became clear. First, it was necessary to recognize the shape of the coast, then to place it into a dimension that would accept its irregularities and its infinite nature. The *Koch Snowflake* represented a useful tool in that respect. In fact, like with the coast of Great Britain, in the Koch curve the line that defines the surface is infinite but the total dimension of the area is measurable and unchanging. From a topological point of view, the Koch curve has dimension 1 because it is assimilated as a single line. Accordingly, a circle and a coastline are the same and are equal to 1 in dT. They are recognized as lines without area.[27] dT does not recognize the complexity of fractal shapes, it does not measure the irregularity or the roughness. Thus, Mandelbrot developed the concept of the fractal dimension, denoted by a "D".

---

23 | Peitgen H.O. - Jürgens H. - Saupe D. 1992, p. 91.

24 | It is important to note that the development of topology transformed the idea of the set as a group of objects. In fact, the set started to be also understood as a web of connections between objects. Thus, the set started to be seen as an open entity due to the possibility of establishing relationships between objects as well as between different sets. This capacity allowed the identification of the state of continuous becoming of sets. Indeed, these relationships developed a kind of continuum. See Frahm L. 2010.

25 | See Deleuze G. 1988.

26 | See Mandelbrot B. 1967.

27 | See Fan L.T. - Neogi D. - Yashima M. 1991.

"Nombre qui quantifie le degré d'irrégularité et de fragmentation d'un ensemble géo métrique ou d'un objet naturel, et qui se réduit, dans le cas des objets de la géométrie usuelle d'Euclide, à leurs dimensions usuelles."[28]

|**Prop. XIX**| Let us look at this classic fractal, which is actually forty years younger than the *Cantor Set*: the *Sierpinski triangle*.

|*Fig. 1.9*|

"We begin with a triangle in the plane and then apply a repetitive scheme of operations to it (when we say triangle here, we mean a blackened, "filled-in" triangle). Pick the midpoints of its three sides. Together with the old vertices of the original triangle, these midpoints define four congruent triangles of which we drop the center one. This completes the basic construction step. In other words, after the first step we have three congruent triangles whose sides have exactly half the size of the original triangle and which touch at three points which are common vertices of two contiguous triangles."[29]

And its successive stage, the *Sierpinski Carpet*.

|*Fig. 1.10*|

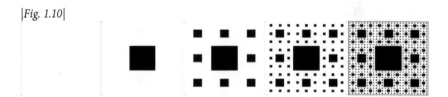

"We begin with a square in the plane. Subdivide into nine little congruent squares of which we drop the center one, and so on. The resulting object which remains if one carries out this process infinitely often can be seen as a generalization of the Cantor Set."[30]

Fractal objects achieve very complex shapes that dT and dE cannot recognize. By looking at an irregular object, one realizes that there exists in the dT and dE a forgotten degree: both dT and dE deny the existence of gray between black and white.

28 | Mandelbrot B. 1995, p. 255.

29 | Peitgen H.O. - Jürgens H. - Saupe D. 1992, p. 79.

30 | Peitgen H.O. - Jürgens H. - Saupe D. 1992, p. 81.

|*Fig. 1.11*|

Peitgen, Jürgens and Saupe show that a complicated object like the object in figure 1.11 would be of dimension 1 in the dT. By analyzing it from this point of view, it is possible to note the importance of fractal geometry. We can see just by looking at the object that, a fractal object allows a degree of complexity nonexistent in both dT and dE.

The concept of dimension used by scientists did not recognize the complex nature of some forms. To analyze the *Cantor Set* as a series of points, or the *Koch Curve* as a single line, means neglecting the complexity of an infinite structure.

|**Prop. XVIII**| A fractal set illustrates an object that possesses special qualities. If one analyzes in detail the *Sierpinski Carpet*, the object acquires a complexity that goes beyond the notion of dimension, and even of state. Let us look again at the *Sierpinski Carpet*, a proto-fractal which has no area because its holes are infinite. The construction of the *Sierpinski Carpet* is aimed at creating an object (*Super Object*) of universal character, that is, an object that contains an infinite number of objects. In this case, all the objects of topological dimension 1 on a plane:

|*Fig. 1.12*|

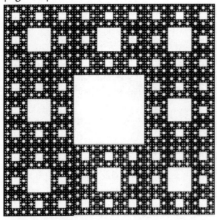

"**The House of One-dimensional Objects**: We are now prepared to get the idea of what Sierpinski was trying to accomplish when he invented the Carpet. We want to build a house or hotel for all one-dimensional objects. This house will be a kind of Super Object, which contains all possible one-dimensional objects in a topological sense. This means that a given object may be hidden in the super object not exactly as it appears independently, but rather as one of its topologically equivalent mutants."[31]

Therefore, the *Sierpinski Carpet* is a universal object; no matter the degree of complexity occurring in a curve, it can be included in this Super Object.[32] In other words, any one-dimensional (dT) object on a plane is present in the *Sierpinski Carpet*.

The perception of this fractal object is quite special. What is before our eyes is not actually there. Somehow, there are curves, lines, squares, and also several forms that

31 | Peitgen H.O. - Jürgens H. - Saupe D. 1992, p. 112.

32 | See Allouche J.P. - Shallit J. 2003, pp. 405-407.

we cannot see even though our intellect is able to project them. We can also consider the *Sierpinki Carper* as an open structure because of its ability to 'become', which is also the basis for its infiniteness.

|Fig. 1.13|

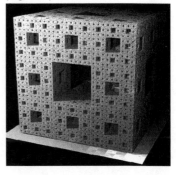

The problem arises when an object presenting some interceptions is represented in the *Carpet*. Not every curve keeps its topological dimension when it moves from the plane to the space. Therefore, the universality of the *Sierpinski Carpet* was valid only for one-dimensional objects on the plane, but not in the space. The mathematician Karl Menger (1902-1985) solved this problem by creating a Super Universal Object for curves in the space:[33] the *Menger Sponge*.[34]

In the early years of the twentieth century, scientists started to analyze objects that could contain an infinite number of shapes. Therefore, dimensions consisting of fractions, e.g. ½, were theorized.[35]

Thanks to Felix Hausdorff (1868-1942), scientists realized that creating a consistent notion of dimension was more difficult than they previously thought. According to Hausdorff, the dimension of a straight line is 1, and that of the *Cantor Set* is 0, because it consists of a series of disconnected points. On the contrary, the dimension of the *Koch Snowflake* is Log4/Log3=1.2619. The latter is a fractional number as in the case of the *Sierpinski Carpet*, whose dimension is equal to 1.892789.[36]

"Contrairement aux nombres de dimensions habituels, la dimension fractale peu très bien être une fraction simple, telle que 1/2 ou 5/3, et même un nombre irrationnel, tel que log4/ log3 ~ 1,2618... ou π. Ainsi, il est très utile de dire que certaines courbes planes très irrégulières que leur dimension fractale est entre 1 et 2, de dire de certaines surfaces très feuilletées et pleines de convolutions que leur dimension fractale est in-

33 | To better understand this process, I advise: Peitgen H.O. - Jürgens H. - Saupe D. 1992, Chapter 2.7 *The Universality of the Sierpinski Carpet*, pp. 112-121.

34 | These last proto-fractal objects allow us to deal with the concept of set from a different point of view. As already noted, one started to understand the set as a web articulating many heterogeneous entities developing a continuum, developing a topologic space in which one establishes geometric relationships between the objects, a space free from coordinates. As we will see in this text, these spaces started to be developed in the cinematographic narrative after the Second World War.

35 | Mandelbrot B. 1995, p. 12.

36 | Peitgen H.O. - Jürgens H. - Saupe D. 1992, p. 109.

termédiaire entre 2 et 3, et enfin de définir des poussières sur la ligne dont la dimension fractale est entre 0 et 1."[37]

In the next figure, one can see the recognition of irregularity developed by Mandelbrot, namely the irregularity forgotten by both Euclidean geometry and the topological dimension.

|*Fig. 1.14*|

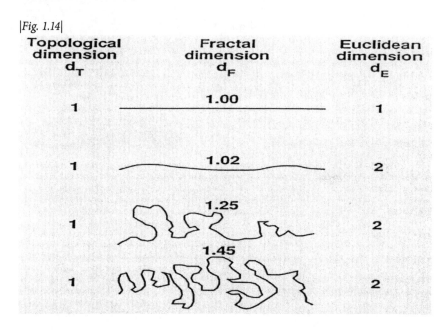

Topological dimension d_T	Fractal dimension d_F	Euclidean dimension d_E
1	1.00	1
1	1.02	2
1	1.25	2
1	1.45	2

Through the recognition of a fractional dimension, fractal geometry became 'the geometry of nature'.

37 | Mandelbrot B. 1995, p. 12.

1.7 Veritas Filia Temporis

Over the centuries, Euclidean geometry imposed important parameters aimed at the creation of an abstract image of natural phenomena, thus enabling intelligible representations of nature. Thanks to the capacity to 'adapt' itself to the visual experience of everyday life, Euclidean geometry *pre*arranged the mental process and cognitive structures. In this context, nature was perceived as a regular entity. But, technology's improvements created a bigger horizon highlighting irregular forms and phenomena present in nature. Hence, this created the necessity of new geometries to analyze these forms unrecognizable by Euclidean geometry. The necessity of these new geometries is established by the forms and phenomena *disclosed* through technology's improvements. Science improves technology, and technology allows for the perception of new structures.

Since Prometheus, the 'inventor of technology', nature was something unsurpassed by human action: "For Art (τέχνη) is weaker than Necessity."[1] Nature remained as a rule imposing insurmountable limits in which mankind constructed its perception, its knowledge, and its acts: mankind adapted itself to the natural laws. Poïesis (from ποιέω, 'to create') – that is to say, the capacity to produce and transform by imitating the generative process of nature – and praxis (πράξις) – the practical dimension, the capacity of act – took as a limit nature (physis, φύσις). Both poïesis and praxis can be described as the act of giving form to nature. It does not mean to change it, because nature was a limit, but it means to 'release the latent potentiality of nature.'[2] Both actions, poïesis and praxis, require science (episteme, ἐπιστήμη).

After the 'discovery' of the 'regularity' of natural processes, mankind is able, thanks to technology, to understand, through imitation, some natural processes (see *The Destruction of Space*). Under this logic, mankind is unable to dominate nature. Hence, mankind can just reveal its secrets and imitate its 'predicted' process. It is highly possible that this reasoning initiated the Greek conception of truth (*aletheia*, ἀλήθεια). The literal meaning of the word ἀλήθεια, truth, is 'the state of not being hidden, being evident.'[3] It follows that Greeks recognized the supremacy of theory over praxis; moreover, for their logic, only a perfect awareness of the immutable natural laws allowed for a correct political or technical action.[4]

---

1 | Aeschylus, *The Prometheus Bound*, 514. (Tranlation: Thomsom G. 1979.)

2 | Galimberti U. 2005, p. 278.

3 | For the translation of *aletheia* (ἀλήθεια) as 'Unverborgenheit', see Heidegger M. 1954 (1930).

4 | It is important to note that for Greek cosmology it was impossible to imaging the existence of technology's power on nature. In fact, nature, for the Greek knowledge, is not a God's or Human's creation, but something self-everlasting, without beginning and without end. This identity was also self-identify. Therefore, mankind, to understand some phenomena or ideas, did not use himself as measurement, but the *kósmos*. For example, the *lógos* derived from the *kósmos*, and not from man.

The only means to discover those laws and to find their regularity was the improvement of technology. Facing the impossibility to transform nature, philosophical knowledge was restricted to contemplate it.[5] One can find this conception in Cicero's words:

"Man himself however came into existence for the purpose of contemplating and imitating the world; he is by no means perfect, but he is 'a small fragment of that which is perfect."[6]

Plotinus shares the same opinion and describes praxis as an 'immobile' act of observation of the cosmos.[7] The limits imposed by the Greek idea of nature subordinate technology, and science, to the simple act of observing and analyzing nature.

The revolution in the conception of nature started by the Biblical religions can be remarked in the idea of Original Sin and in the belief that the universe is God's creation. Starting from this point, the meaning of nature changed. Nature was no longer an individual entity self-everlasting, without beginning and without end, but it was God's creation, and mainly, God's gift. For this reason, after this big revolution, the most important of mankind's relationships is not with nature but rather with God 'the creator'; as exemplified by St. Augustine's words, "amare mundum non est cognoscere Deum." The world became a place of expiation for human sin. Nature was no longer characterized by its everlasting existence; it became the place where mankind could reach salvation through work. Furthermore, the idea of an eternal nature disappeared because of the notion of the First Day – the day of God's creation – and that of Last Day – the day of redemption:[8]

"Because you listened to your wife and ate from the tree about which I commanded you, 'You must not eat of it,' Curse is the because of you; through painful toil you will eat of it all the days of your life. It will produce thorns and thistles for you, and you will eat the plants of the field. By the sweat of your brown you will eat your food until return to the ground, since from it you were taken; for dust you are and to dust you will return."[9]

---

5 | The act to 'contemplate' is the act through which mankind recognizes its place in the cosmic hierarchy, and, the limits of its acts derive from this acknowledgment. Through the contemplation, mankind can find the adaptation of its acts within the limits of the un-exceeded nature. The conception of contemplation was transported into the Latin thought, see Galimberti U. 2005, p. 279.

6 | Cicero, *De Natura Deorum*, II, 14. (Tranlation: Rackham H.M.A. 1933.)

7 | See Plotinus, *Enneads*, III, 8, 3.

8 | Notwithstanding, note the difference between the Old and the New Testament. In the Old Testament, the history is characterized by an idea of 'waiting', in the New testament by the idea of a 'participation' in the redemption.

9 | *Genesis*, 3, 17-19.

This temporal notion gave to the western culture a historical conscience that substituted the cosmological existence of Greek knowledge. This shift of paradigm represents the foundation of a 'turnover' in nature's conception. In fact, this change created a phenomenon of 'debasement' of nature in order to give the supremacy to man. Under the Christian logic, nature is the result of God's will; nature's meaning derives from the denotation that the human being assigns to it.[10] There is no longer the Greek man who observes the nature, it is to say, a man exceeded by nature's power. After the Christian revolution, Mankind has the nature in his hands, a nature at the mercy of God and, then, of man.

In the Modern Era, one can recognize a change of perspective. The scientific knowledge, that is, the *theoria* of the Greeks and the *contemplatio* of Latin knowledge, is no longer understood as *fine ultimo* to which *praxis* is subordinate. In fact, *theoria* and *contemplatio*, in the Modern Era, became an operative means. From this moment, man interpreted his presence in the world as a chance, almost a mission, to be the 'dominator' of nature. And man's supremacy over nature was expressed in his act of making truth. This truth is no longer the Greek *aletheia* (ἀλήθεια), but the Hebrew *'emet* (אמת) strongly related to the verb 'to do'.

The old idea of an untouchable and everlasting truth is now replaced. The human being acquires the capacity to 'act' upon nature thus establishing a continuous creation of truth. In other words, the difference between the Greek' and Hebraic truths consists of the fact that the first one is something the man 'knows' and the second stays in the sphere of 'what man practices.'[11] Then, under the Hebrew's conception of truth, there is something formed in time, something created in and by the period (*Zeitraum*).[12]

God's will dictates man's control on nature, and man's control on nature finds as only possibility technology's improvement. Thus, technology represents the possibility to create truth under the 'Will of the Lord'. In consequence, it is indispensable to learn 'nature's language' in order to obtain a real possibility to dominate the universe:[13] *regnum hominis* is born.

Since the man is the creator of his own 'truth' and his own world, he becomes the 'owner' of his future. In this case, the 'only foreign thing' to mankind is the 'di-

---

10 | It is interesting to quote Flusser in this regard. "Die Handlung abstrahiert das Subjekt aus der Lebenswelt, Klammert es aus ihr aus, und was übrigbleibt, ist das dreidimensionale Universum der zu fassenden Gegenstände, der zu lösenden Probleme. Dieses Universum der Objekte kann nun vom Subjekt umgeformt 'informiert' werden. Kultur is die Folge." (Flusser V. 1996, p. 12.)

11 | Galimberti U. 2005, pp. 293-304.

12 | On this point, see also Benjamin W. "Innerhalb großer geschichtlicher Zeiträumen verändert sich mit der gesamten Daseinsweise der menschlichen Kollektiva auch die Art und Weise ihrer Sinneswahrnehmung." (Benjamin W. 2002c (1939), p. 356.)

13 | Note that *theoria* proclaimed a deductive process. On the other hand, the modern notion of truth is formed by an inductive process.

vine energy' (*l'élan vital*) that sets in motion the universe and the life. The only way to overcome this lack is through mechanics. The mechanic transposition requires a special knowledge of numbers and weighs, and it needs to move and translate objects and phenomena from the nature into a space mathematically calculated. Thus, the 'truth' is created in the space where the intelligible abstractions can be placed, i.e. Euclidean space.

|Prop. XIV| Mankind must create its kingdom, and to do it, it must transport/translate nature into a *place* recognizable and analyzable by the human cognition.[14] Aiming to extend the *regnum hominis* – even on the God's kingdom – mankind accepts the 'weakness' of its senses. In fact, by using technology and science in order to start a considerable improvement of the visual media, mankind needed to transport nature and to reconfigure it into a recognizable dimension: mankind could extend its kingdom. Certainly, these visual media have a strong influence on mankind's sensory perception (*Sinneswahrnehmung*). Every epoch builds 'truth' by means of the analytical tools created by technology's developments.[15] One can maintain that our sensorial perception is, in some sense, 'formatted' by technology, especially by the visual media deriving from it. Technology modifies nature and also gives to man the instruments to analyze this modified nature. In fact, the visual media perform a translation of nature's complexity into our rational and recognizable universe; the *regnum hominis*.

---

14 | In regards to this subject, Morin affirms that information does not exist in nature but that mankind extracts it from nature. In his words, "nous transformons les éléments et événements en signes, nous arrachons l'information au bruit à partir des redondances." (Morin E. 2005, p. 145.)

15 | See also, on the same topic, Lyotard J.-F. 1979. Especially *La recherche et sa légitimation*.

2 The Geometrical Machine

-Papa, is the goat real?
-I don't know, my boy, you must ask Monsieur Daguerre.

2.1 PERSPECTIVE: THE GEOMETRY OF SIGHT

The fact that humanity could create its truth, implies mankind's tendency to prefer the representation to the 'real', the image instead of the thing. This phenomenon is completely embodied by perspective. Through perspective the pictorial representations concentrated their essence in rational principles, in geometrical principles.

"In a sense, perspective transforms psychophysiological space into mathematical space. It negates the differences between front and back, between right and left, between bodies and intervening space ('empty' space), so that the sum of all the parts of space and all its contents are absorbed into a single 'quantum continuum.'"[1]

During the Renaissance the intention to represent natural objects with a high degree of objectivity created a different relationship with nature. A kind of perception in which every natural object is perceived as pictorial, and every pictorial representation is constructed with a Euclidean geometrical organization. The Renaissance purpose was a construction of an image on a two-dimensional surface able to produce for the beholder an illusion of a three-dimensional object, a simulation of our perception of natural objects. The principal aim of perspective was to operate a perfect translation of nature in order to produce in the beholder, in Gombrich's words, an effect "akin to visual hallucination." Perspective aims to attain the correct equation in which the image must appear like the object and the object like the image. In fact, "exact perspectival construction is a systematic abstraction from the structure of this psychophysiological space."[2]

---

1 | Panofsky E. 2009⁵, p. 31.
2 | Panofsky E. 2009⁵, p. 31.

This system, based on previous studies on human perception, allowed the creation of images with a sort of scientific construction, thus accomplishing a 'real translation' of nature. It allows not only the act of depicting natural objects, but also the analysis of nature under a pictorial vision.

"A perspective system always implies the notion that reality is pictorial, and sets the goal of image making to be congruence between pictorial object as perceived and the same as pictured; all alike constructed out of a repertory of basic pictorial forms."[3]

|*Fig. 2.1*|

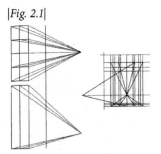

This mode of pictorial view and representation has, as a logical consequence, the search of an objective representation of the object, i.e. the perfect illusion, the *trompe l'œil*. Hence, perspective's aim is to represent the 'world as it appears' dealing with tangible and measurable relationships. However, every geometry imposes a particular point of view and also a specific way of interaction.

The so-called 'mathematical' or 'artificial' perspective developed by Leon Battista Alberti (1404-1472) – invented in all probability by Filippo Brunelleschi about 1420 and transmitted by Alberti – is in fact the materialization of the Renaissance's 'dream' to construct pictorial images.

The Renaissance represents a period rich in technical developments for the construction of spaces, the most important being perspective.[4] The geometrical construction of the mathematical perspective is based on two premises accepted as axiomatic in classical as well as mediaeval optics. The first one claims that the visual image, a product of 'visual rays' (these conceived as straight lines connecting the eye with the object seen), configures the 'visual pyramid' or 'visual cone'. In this first part of his treatise, Alberti describes the 'pyramid of visual rays' in order to explain the functioning of the sense of sight, it is to say, visual angles, the apparent quantities, etc. The second axiom, named '*intersegazione della piramide visiva*' by Alberti, determines the projection on a plane of all the points constituting the visual image. These points will intersect the 'visual pyramid.' Alberti uses the fundamental principle of Euclidean optics, and establishes the optical foundation of the pictorial diminution to a point, i.e. the basis of the new perspective system.[5] Consequently, the correct representation

---

3 | Heelan P.A. 1988, p. 102.
4 | It is interesting to note the analysis developed by Borsò and Görling about the techniques of the measurement of the two dimensional space of maps, such as the topology. See Borsò V. – Görling R. 2004.
5 | See Alberti L.B. 1950 (1435).

by means of the perspective is obtained by a central projection of the objects that must intersect the 'visual pyramid.'[6]

|*Fig. 2.2*|

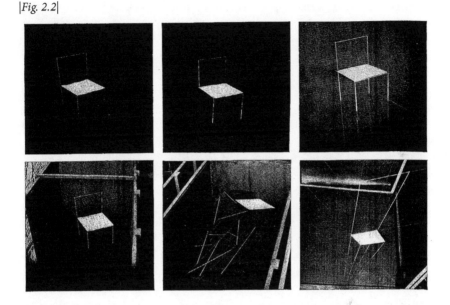

|**Prop. XXIII**| In front of a pictorial representation, the beholder always needs to "possess subjectively the embodied intentionality-structure necessary to perform the expected hermeneutic of experience; this in turn, involves the sharing of a common World."[7] Visual representations use natural objects as signs, but these natural objects cannot be translated or reproduced as such. Consequently, the translated objects set off a process in the visual imagination of the beholder. Therefore, according to Heelan:

"we recognize an image to be an image of something only if we have some prior acquaintance with the kind of thing that is being represented and are perceptually oriented to look for it in the image."[8]

---

6 | Note that the central projection is perfectly analogous to that produced in a photographic camera, and it derives from elementary geometrical methods. It is also interesting to see that the central perspective intricates a deformation of the normal shape of things. Paradoxically, this system, at the same time, offers the possibility to render optical spaces in the most realistic way. Quite interesting, those realistic images, derived from this 'translation tool,' suggest to mankind its daily visual experience. Aiming at simulating perfectly the human's visual experience, the central perspective must apply deformations to the object represented.

7 | Heelan P. A. 1988, p. 105.

8 | Heelan P. A. 1988, p. 105.

In Philostratus' words: "No one can understand the painted horse or bull unless he knows what such creatures are like."

The ambiguity is an intrinsic factor of the image. An image is essentially ambiguous because it could be the projection of any form from the family of three-dimensional Euclidean objects. The nature of the problem of the ambiguity may be demonstrated by the 'size-distance' relationship. We cannot judge the size of an object unless we know its distance, and *vice versa*.[9] For example, the beholder knows that a large human figure is meant to be closer by than a small house.[10] The ambiguity of the image imposes also a specific position for the beholder. In the action of 'recognizing pictorial representations', in order to determinate what can be perceived and what not, the beholder needs to appeal to both his knowledge about the object represented and its intentionality.[11]

Alberti's system of perspective supposes the canvas as a 'window' in which 'the object represented sends reflected rays to the beholder's eyes', simulating the rays transmitted through a real window. This flat space (the canvas) enables the creation of a geometrical composition generating a phenomenon of intersection between the plane in the canvas and the viewer's eye. The beholder, adopting the spatial position required by the geometrical composition of the picture, is able to 'reconstruct in his mind' the depicted object. 'Alberti's window' did not imply a 'merely record' of a visual experience, but it operates a 'perspective representation', it is to say, a representation responding to the 'imaginary' of a period. Alberti's perspective can be interpreted as a visual medium that 'translates' nature into the language of a whole social-period. Here it is quite interesting to quote Dürer's words about perspective: "Perspectiva ist ein lateinisch Wort, bedeutt ein Durchsehung."[12]

It follows that perspective representation is the product of the 'grammar and vocabulary' imposed by Euclidean geometry and applied in the translation of nature that responds to the *Zeitgeist*.

|Fig. 2.3|

---

9 | See Gombrich E. H. 1960[11], especially, VIII. *Ambiguities of the Third Dimension.*

10 | See Arnheim R. 1974, especially, *Application to painting,* pp. 234-239.

11 | This apparent imposition of the geometrical pictorial representation can be linked not only to the optical or physiological instance but also to the social convections or rules adopted by public agreement for the purpose of convenience.

12 | Lange K. – Fuhse F. 1970 (1893), p. 319.

"We see only one aspect of an object, and it is not very hard to work out exactly what this aspect will be from any given point. All you have to do is to draw straight lines to that point from any part of the object's surface. Those that will lie behind an opaque body will be hidden, those that have free passage will be seen. Moreover, the fact that we see only along straight lines is also sufficient to account for the diminution of the aspect at a distance."[13]

|**Prop. XX**| From the point of view of the pictorial process, perspective's invention generated a kind of 'autonomy achieved by the idea of space.' By using this method, artists create first space and then the solid objects of the pictured world are arranged within it in accordance with the rules of Euclidean optics. Before this great invention, normally, artists would extend space gradually outward from the nucleus of an individual solid object.[14] This new way of constructing space in pictorial art certainly introduced into the theory of the representational arts, "was what became the central concept of Renaissance aesthetics, the hoary principle of *convenienza* or *concinnitas*, perhaps best rendered by the word 'harmony.'"[15] These two principles represent 'just proportions' that introduce an extension of the rational organization of form, into the reproductive imitation of 'reality'. Certainly, the phenomenon of the assimilation of the painting as a window, theorized by Alberti, implies, for the artist, another approach to 'reality', another approach to the organization of the forms on the canvas.

|**Prop. VIII**| In the spatial organization of perspective representation, the implication of infinity – or its symbolization – becomes a strong factor of pictorial composition. The 'vanishing point', the essence of the perspective, generates the notion and sensation of infinity. Every line, regardless of location and direction, must converge there. This point symbolizes infinity because it represents literally the **point where parallels meet**. Certainly, the notion of infinity in perspective representation brings important philosophical questions into the art of painting.[16] As asserted by Arnheim, infinity and centrality had been contradictory ideas since antiquity. On the one hand, according to Aristotle, the conception of a centralized world appeals to a finite system of concentric shells. On the other hand, Democritus and Epicurus excluded the possibility of a center in an infinite world. In the context of painting, the problem stays more on a theological level. On the one hand, there is God as a unique infinite identity and on the other hand, there is nature – the world – that takes an infinite form under the special geometry of perspective.

---

13 | Gombrich E.H. 1960[11], p. 250.

14 | See White J. 1957.

15 | Panofsky E. 1969, p. 27.

16 | It was also the case of the iconoclasticism. According to Mondzain, Constantine's iconoclastic position were motivated by the impossibility of enclose the divine within a line. In other words, if the icon represents the figure of the divine, it is enclosing it within a line. Thus, it is enclosing the infinite. See Mondzain M.-J. 1998.

"Artists tend to hide the conflict by seeking to avoid spelling out the vanishing point. Its location is implied by the converging directions of the orthogonal lines and shapes, but their actual meeting place is usually kept under a cloud. Only in the ceiling paintings and landscapes of the Baroque do we receive the image of a frankly open world that goes on forever."[17]

Infinity embodied in these pictorial compositions derives not only from the explicit existence of the vanishing point representing the point where parallels meet, but also from the possibility to accomplish a recursive operation in the spatial organization of the pictorial composition. The recursivity can be remarked when, by using a series of magnitudes and by placing them in a sequence in depth, the painter applies a recursive formula of diminishing magnitudes separated by diminishing intervals. Through this process, the painter may create a constant degree of decreasing shapes that project the space toward an infinite point, creating the feeling of endless depth. In addition, the system of perspective creates an isotropic, homogeneous and infinite space by imposing stable relationships between sizes, distances and depths. Even if those spaces created by the geometrical order of perspective did not correspond with the irregular forms present in nature, perspective was accepted as a system – almost a machine – that translates natural objects 'objectively'. The 'realistic,' understood as a translation of nature on the canvas, is just a representation of nature following the logic of 'how things look.' Things can be represented in a realistic way in accordance with the rules of representation.[18]

However, a rigorous spatial organization that respects Euclidean geometry is not the only way to create illusion through pictorial representations. Nature is irregular, and all forms and phenomena cannot be contained in rigid forms and rules represented by an axiomatic system. In the Euclidean space of perspective representation, the object is seen as being closer to reality even if it does not follow the axioms imposed by mathematical perspective, i.e. by Euclidean geometry. Indeed, non-Euclidean structures and non-Euclidean objects can also create a feeling of full-illusion. Some images, although not linear, can be considered as a perfect illusion of a natural object; these last attain this effect by size, contrast, textural variations, and also by shading and coloring effects. Consider, for instance, the so-called atmospheric perspective. Since 'air' was no longer interpreted as a transparent substance, but as an agent that changes the object's perception by the variation of colors, tonalities and blurring objects, these same effects – 'produced by the air' – were used in order to create the illusion of depth, which is a good example of how the artist uses both Euclidean and non-Euclidean arrangements in order to create the perfect illusion. Indeed, the illusion of depth is created by the relationship between the figures on the plane, almost a topologic phenomenon.

Borrowing from Arnheim:

---

17 | Arnheim R. 1974, p. 298.
18 | See Wartofsky M. 1980.

"In the organization of the plane figures, it was found that subdivisions occurs when a combination of self-contained parts yields a structurally simpler pattern than the undivided whole. (...) Areas physically located in the same picture plane split apart in depth and assume a figure-ground configuration because simplicity increases when the one-sidedness of the contour is uncontested and when the ground can be seen as continuing beneath the figure without interruption."[19]

|*Fig. 2.4*|

The illusion of depth points out that sensory perception (*Sinneswahrnehmung*) is the product of a 'struggle' between the structures derived from Euclidean forms and the irregularities perceived everywhere in nature. There are two special intentionalties – Euclidean and non-Euclidean – which pose the question of their interaction within visual perception. Euclidean geometry and non-Euclidean geometries are both present in the representation of nature. Both are instruments aiming at representing our irregular universe, thus aiming at creating visual effects. This phenomenon can be linked to Mandelbrot's words about the perception of nature. He claims that mankind, over the centuries, constructed a geometry that shaped his perception of nature. This geometry does not accept the evident irregularity of nature and its irregular phenomena, even if they are strongly present everywhere. Notwithstanding, Euclidean geometry demonstrated to be the most useful means to represent and simulate our irregular universe.

History, culture, and education, maintains Poincaré, taught us how to use the rigid rules of Euclidean geometry in order to lead nature under a Euclidean structure, that is, Euclidean geometry imposes an adaptation – translation – through the use of a particular rule of congruence. However, the artist also uses 'irregularities' in order to *re*create the nature. Yet, curiously, these irregularities are also placed in a Euclidean arrangement. Therefore, artists use Euclidean axioms as functional tools able to create the illusion of depth in their pictorial representations.

As a perfect tool of vision, Euclidean geometry allows, in its regularity and its strict axiomatic language, an intelligible representation of nature's irregularities. Such is the case of ambiguous images (Fig. 2.4); to be in front of nature means to be in front of two *Gestalts*. In front of these images, it is indispensable to switch from one to the other in order to perceive the totality of the image, in order to 'grasp' the representation. Quite surprisingly, we are familiar with such multistable visual phenomena: some pictorial compositions and architectonical constructions are composed by irregular forms that are 'engraved' in an Euclidean composition.[20]

---

19 | Arnheim R. 1974, p. 245.

20 | This phenomenon was described by Merlau-Ponty as follows: "Les peintres, eux, savaient d'expérience qu'aucune des techniques de la perspective n'est une solution exacte,

These phenomena are not only in the field of chromatic effects, as is the case of aerial perspective. Some regular figures, – or Euclidean – can also create some effects of depth that can be interpreted as irregular spatial compositions. They are **mediated** by Euclidean geometry, e.g. the Müller-Lyer illusion (Fig. 2.5). This illusion produces the feeling of a 'more distant object' that can appear to be smaller in size than a 'near-by object' despite the fact that they are of equal angular size.

|*Fig. 2.5*|

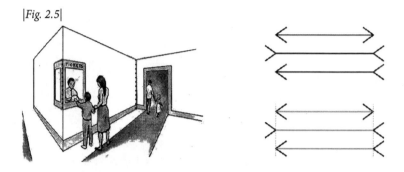

This phenomenon does not require a new configuration of the spatial parameters of Euclidean geometrical optics. It derives from the illusion that one can create in mathematical space by using geometrical constructions. The visual media – clearly Euclidean geometry and, consequently, the system of pictorial representation derived from it – are in some sense, systems that arrange, into an intelligible form the irregularity of nature. They codify natural objects into a Euclidean space, where mankind can develop a 'natural' perceptual process, and, can also analyze through forms natural phenomena.

The presence of some irregular forms in spatial representations shows that an optical field is not an input from which would derive a unique response. A variety of different functions may derive from the same optical stimulus producing a variety of different specific stimuli. It is possible to conclude that these stimuli are in some ways shaped by technology – visual media, which are derived from it – and by new geometries.

In pictorial representations, Euclidean geometry imposes the system of perspective in order to translate, following common cannons, the complexity and the irregularity of natural elements into an intelligible form. Even if those natural objects are unrecognizable or untranslatable under Euclidean axioms, our intellect uses this space and these axioms in order to create the phenomenon of full-illusion.

qu'il n'y a pas de projection du monde existant qui le respecte à tous égards et mérite de devenir la loi fondamentale de la peinture, et que la perspective linéaire est si peu un point d'arrivée qu'elle ouvre au contraire à la peinture plusieurs chemins : avec les Italiens celui de la représentation de l'objet, mais avec les peintres du Nord celui du Hochraum, du Nahraum, du Schrägraum..." (Merleau-Ponty M. 1964, p. 50.)

Since Euclidean geometry became the main mediation tool between human cognition and natural forms, mankind has been for search the mechanization of this system (Fig. 2.6). The Renaissance is not only the period when the perspective system of pictorial representations was refined but also the period when this technique became intuitive, almost mechanical. The space created by the perspective acquires more flexibility from the moment in which the irregularity of nature could be represented not just through mathematical compositions but also by using a more empirical method, for example, some arrangements and effects, such as chromatic effects.

|*Fig. 2.6*|

Pictorial representations are a question of illusion and this illusion must be represented in a Euclidean space, in a conventional plane that simulates natural perception.

The 'mechanization' of pictorial representations, brought by perspective, also generated a progressive phenomenon of 'externalization' of the process of the elaboration of pictorial composition. In fact, the mental process arranging the pictorial space under Euclidean's axioms could be transposed to a mechanical device: the camera obscura. The 'externalization' of this mental process starts a complex phenomenon of mediation that progressively excluded mankind from nature's representation.

2.2 THE CAMERA OBSCURA:
A PHENOMENON OF EXTERNALIZATION

The camera obscura replaced the complex geometrical constructions of perspective's theory. This mechanism dissociated the mathematical method that creates perspectival vision, giving the chance to fashion a perfect perspective and to reproduce a real place with an acceptable fidelity.[1] It is important to note that this mechanism materializes the phenomenon of 'externalization' highlighted in the previous part of this research. In addition, this mechanism is the first step of the process that makes the existence a rigorously mediated act.

The camera obscura was described by the Arabian scholar Hassan ibn Hassan (A.D. 965-1038).[2] In his most important work, *Book of Optics*, Alhazen corrected some misconceptions that had accompanied the scientific world over the centuries.[3] His work remained for the next five centuries the basis for every study about optics and the mechanism of sight. An important component in Alhazen's research is the way in which he supported his theories. In fact, he constructed devices to test his hypothesis: this is the case with the camera obscura. This trial represented a 'phenomenon of externalization' that allowed the scientist to understand how the sense of sight works.

Since Aristotle, sight represents the most important human sense because it is the 'first source of knowledge.' Certainly, understanding its functioning was a central point of interest. As we will see, the analysis of sight requires the study of the mind as a 'processor' of the information transmitted through the eyes. The understanding of this interaction between the human eye and the brain is clearly the principal 'inspiration' for project the camera obscura. As noted in the last chapter, perspective implies the reproduction – or translation – of natural objects under a Euclidean organization, it translates natural objects as 'they are seen in nature.' Consequently, the camera obscura is a translation device that combines the sense of sight in its totality and imposes a specific geometrical organization.[4]

---

1 | It is interesting at this point to quote Debray's words about the representation. In *Vie et mort de l'image* Debray maintains that "Représenter, c'est rendre présent l'absent. Ce n'est donc pas seulement évoquer mais remplacer." (Debray R. 1992, p. 49.)

2 | Generally known by the Medieval Latin version of his name, Alhazen.

3 | For example, many of the ancient Greeks believed that human beings were able to see because the eyes sent out rays that sensed objects. See Steffends B. 2007.

4 | The first analysis on Euclidean geometry, especially in optics, was started by al-Kindi, who produced a new understanding of the reflection of light. One can maintain that is the beginning of what became, in the European Renaissance, the laws of perspective.

|*Fig. 2.7*| |*Fig. 2.8*|

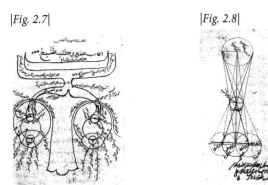

Alhazen considered the camera obscura to be a useful tool aimed at observing eclipses. He also stressed the significance of the relationship between the size of the aperture and the sharpness of the image.[5] However, Roger Bacon (1214/1220?-94) used this mechanism not only for the observation of eclipses but he also showed the possibility of viewing objects placed outside a darkened room.

"Mirrors may be so arranged that we may see whatever we desire and anything in the house or in the street, and everyone looking at those things will see them as if they were real, but when they go to the spot they will find nothing. For the mirrors are concealed [from the viewer] and so placed with respect to the objects, that the images are in the open and appear in the air at the junction of the visual rays with the perpendicular plane [cathetis]; therefore those looking will run to the image, and think that things appear there when there is nothing, but merely an apparition."[6]

In Bacon's optical writings he dedicated a big part for his treatise to the camera obscura.[7] There, he shows an especial interest in the life mediated by some visual media. In order to better understand the act of seeing, he analyzed the human eye as a 'machine.' Therefore, he started to give emphasis to the visual instruments that mediate the relationship between mankind and the Cosmos:

"We experience everything in the heavens and on earth. For celestial objects are observed by means of visual instruments, as Ptolemy and other astronomers teach, as are things generated in the air, such as comets, rainbows, and like; for their altitude above the horizon, their size, shape, and number, and everything in them are certified by means

---

5 | In photographic cameras it is regulated by a diaphragm.

6 | Bacon R. *Perspectiva* (Combach's edition, Frankfurt, 1614, p. 166) quoted by Gernsheim H. 1955, p. 2.

7 | See Part V of the *Opus maius*.

of vision aided by instruments. Through vision we also experience things here on earth, for concerning this world the blind can have no experience worthy of the name."[8]

The principal aim of ancient and medieval optical thought was to offer a theory of vision, especially of light – its propagation, its reflection, its refraction and its importance in the act of viewing. Bacon's interest in *perspectiva* was generated by his idea of the superiority of sight. He maintains that the only way to have an 'experientially test' is through vision.

In the last chapters of Bacon's *Prespectiva* ('sacred wisdom') he proposed a conciliation, which was truly revolutionary for the period, between science and God.[9] For Bacon, the knowledge of all the natural sciences is indispensable in order to attain the divine truth; and this science in turn depends on perspective explanation, clarification and certification.[10] Following this framework, *perspectiva* – therefore the mechanism of vision – takes an important place in Bacon's research. In fact, it can be applied in an important point of the scriptural exegesis and also, it brings humankind to 'natural truth', 'God's truth.'

In Bacon's oeuvre, through the allusion of the divine vision in the sacred Bible, it is possible to find many attempts to give a spiritual identity to the 'perfect vision' offered by *perspectiva*. For example, through this biblical passage:

"Preserve me, oh Lord, as the pupil of your eye"   [Psalm 17:8]

In Bacon's view, the impossibility to comprehend this biblical passage was caused by the human limitation from completely understanding God's creation. The question was 'how is the pupil preserved?' and, for Bacon, this question could be resolved by superseding the human understanding of God's creation by the improvement of the science of *perspectiva*.

|Prop. XVI| However, Bacon's revolution stays in his interest in 'how we see.' Therefore, he started his theory by studying the internal faculties of the *sensitive soul*, the latter being located in the brain.[11] He divided the brain into three cells; located in the first cell are the faculties of common sense and imagination. In the posterior cell Bacon locates the 'estimation' or estimative faculty and, in the middle cell of the brain,

---

8 | Bacon R. 1988 (1292) I 1.1.

9 | To note that in this point Bacon coincides with the Aristotle's idea of vision. In *Metaphysics*, Aristotle maintains, "All men naturally desire knowledge. An indication of this is our esteem for senses; for apart from their use we esteem them for their own sake, and most of all the sense of sight. Not only with a view to action, but even when no action is contemplated, we prefer sight, generally speaking, to all the other senses. The reason of this is that of all the senses sight best helps us to know things, and reveals many distinctions." (Aristotle, *Metaphysics*, 980a. 21-30. Translation: Apostle H.G. 1966.)

10 | Lindberg D.C. 1996, xxi.

11 | Lindberg D.C. 1996. xix.

there is the faculty of 'cogitation' – or cogitative faculty – this last one takes the place of reason.[12] From the brain, Bacon proceeds to the analysis of the optic nerves, which connect the brain to the eyes.

|*Fig. 2.9*|

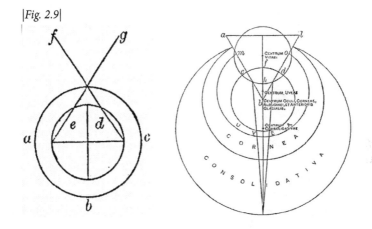

"Thus let ABC the skull, D the right side of the anterior cavity of the brain, and the left, enveloped by the pia mater, from the bottom of which let two nerves come forth on the right and left, meeting in the opening in the skull, and afterwards dividing, so that the nerve coming from right goes to the left eye, at F, and the nerve coming from the left goes to the right eye at G; and let them enter the openings of the concave bones, so that they spread out in that allow, as is show in the figure. But we must understand that just as the two nerves are derived from the pia mater, so are they also derived from the dura mater, and similarity from the lining of the skull, in which externally it is wrapped, and these three nerves are concave and meet in the opening, and one nerve is formed with three nerve coats, and this nerve so formed goes to each eye, and each eye has naturally a position similar with respect to the meeting of these nerves in the opening and at an equal distance from it, so that vision may be completed with greater certainty. (...) The whole eye, then, approaches the form of a sphere, and the coats likewise and the humors owing to the admirable qualities of the spherical form, because it is less subject to obstacles than a figure with angles, and is simpler than other figures and is mores spacious than other isoperimetric figures, as Alhazen, the author of Perspective, states."[13]

As we can see, in Bacon's view, the first reason for the eye's roundness is to make its swift movement possible, in order to be able to run from one visible object to another. Thus each object might be grasped with full certitude by such a swift motion. Bacon maintains also that:

12 | See Bacon R. 1996, Part 1 Chapter 2 and Part 2 Chapter 1.

13 | Bacon R. 1928, *Third distinction*, Chapter I. p. 432.

|*Fig. 2.10*|

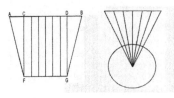

"if the surface of the eye were [a] plane, the impression [species] of an object larger than the eye could not fall perpendicularly on it, because perpendicular lines to a plane tend to different points and at right angles in each case, as shown in the figure."[14]

According to Bacon, judgment begins in the eyes and it is completed in the common nerve. Consequently, he conceives the visual act as a whole process generated by an undivided organism. In order to analyze the functioning of the organ of vision, he used some geometrical figures to describe the complex structure of the eyes and also the interaction between light, colors and eyes. For instance, the radiation incident on the eye can be conceived geometrically as an infinite set of cones or pyramids. In addition, Bacon did not conceive the image's formation on the surface of the lens, he theorized this phenomenon as a one-to-one correspondence between points in the visual field and points in the sensitive organ. He states that each visual field makes an impression on one point in the eye.[15] Bacon conceived of this one-to-one correspondence as an arrangement (*ordino*) put forth by the organ of vision in its totality – eyes and brain. Whatever the size of the external object, it must be arranged in the least amount of space, the latter represented by the organ of vision. Since every body and every magnitude is infinitely divisible, the act of seeing operates, according to Bacon, as an action of division and *re*-composition of form and size. The phenomenon of one-to-one correspondence analyzed by Bacon is clearly motivated by Aristotle's *Physics*, Book VI – especially VI. 1. 231[a] 21-32[a]22 – where Aristotle demonstrates the continuity of magnitude, time, and change, involving their illimitable divisibility by indivisible boundaries. Hence, Bacon posits "Therefore there are as many parts in a grain of millet as in the diameter of the world."[16]

Thanks to the analysis of Bacon and Alhazen, the act of vision becomes more a process than a simple contact between man and the external world. At that point, it is easy to understand Bacon's interest in the Camera Obscura. His conception of sight, as the only way to attain 'God's truth', could be developed just by an accurate study on vision's mechanism. The work of *perspectiva* means, for Bacon, an approach to this 'truth.' In Bacon's view, the understanding of the human sense of sight and its relationship with the external world must be derived from the field of the praxis; thus his interest in the camera obscura. Even if, since Bacon's analysis, scholars knew the

---

14 | Bacon R. 1928, Chapter IV. *fourth distinction*, p. 447.

15 | Bacon R. 1928, Chapter I. *sixth distinction*, p. 454.

16 | Bacon R. 1928, Chapter I. *sixth distinction*, p. 455.

possibility of seeing the external world within a darkened room, the camera obscura remained a technique to watch eclipses until the 16th century.[17]

|*Fig. 2.11*| |*Fig. 2.12*|

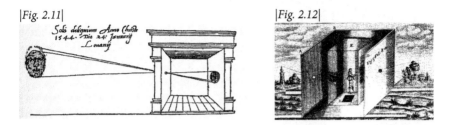

In the first half of 16th century this technique was assimilated into pictorial reproduction and quite surprisingly, was perceived as a writing technology. In a statement made by Vasari, Alberti was compared to Gutemberg. It was a misunderstanding in which Alberti was took, after Vasari's words, as the 'inventor' of a small camera obscura.[18] It is Leonardo da Vinci who gives a clear description of the camera obscura in his *Codex Atlanticus*, and in *Manuscript D.*[19]

In the second half of the 16th century the camera obscura underwent a transformation. Thanks to Girolamo Cardono's *De Subtilitate,* its French translation of Richard le Blanc (Paris 1556) '*La rotondité faicte de verre*', Daniel Barbaro's *La Pratica della perspettiva*[20] and the famous Giovanni Battista Porta's *Magiae naturalis* the use of the camera obscura was proposed in conjunction with convex lenses.[21]

---

17 | Consider for instance, John Peckhan (1230-1292) who wrote *Perspectiva communis*, where he notes its application to the observation of eclipses. Levi Ben Gershon (1288-1344), Erasmus Reinhold (1511-1553) and his pupil Gemma Frisius (1508-55) also were interested on the possibility of analyzing an eclipse through this device.

18 | After Gernsheim the apparatus referred by Vasari was the Alberti's 'intersector' an instrument for drawing by squares described in Alberti's Treatise on Painting.

19 | Da Vinci's notebooks remained unknown until Venturi deciphered and published them in 1797. Thus, the first published account of the camera obscura is contained in the first Italian version of Vitruvius's *De Architectura*.

20 | *La pratica della perspettiva* introduce the use of a diaphragm to sharpen the image, and also recommended the camera obscura as an aid to artists.

21 | Della Porta's *Magiae naturalis* presented in its first version (1558) four books in six editions, but it is the final version (1589) which is presented in twenty books and twenty-seven editions, both in Latin and translations into many languages, that introduced a completely new use for the camera obscura. Della Porta in 1589 added several pages proposing another use of the camera obscura transforming its concept of the mechanism into a real "entertainment machine." In fact, Della Porta hypothesizes a story-telling system that employs scenery, actors, and even a sound accompaniment. See Della Porta G.B. 1589. The excerpt concerned is quoted as an original image by Mannoni L.- Pesenti Campagnoni D.- Robinson D. 1995, pp. 48-52.

In Girolamo Cardano's *De Subtilitate* it is attested that:

"If you want to see the things which go in the street at [a] time when the sun shines brightly place in the window shutter a convex lens [*orbem e vitro*]. If you then close the window you will see images projected through the aperture on to the opposite wall, but with rather dull colours; but by placing a piece of white paper in the place where you see the images, you will attain the eagerly awaited result in a wonderful manner."[22]

The common miss-attribution of this invention to Giovanni Battista Porta is due to the fact that he was the first to suggest the use of the camera obscura for drawing. Thanks to Porta, the camera obscura became an aid for the artist. He proposed the mechanism to people who could not paint, and artists and scholars from diverse scientific fields focused on the improvement of this technique.

In the last years of the 16th century and the first half of the 17th century, the camera obscura, initially a darkened room in a house, became a portable apparatus.

|*Fig. 2.14*|

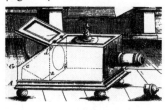

Friedrich Risner (ca. 1533-1580) was the first to propose a portable camera obscura in order to accomplish accurate delineations of topographical views. Subsequently, Johann Kepler (1571-1630) (Fig. 2.14), Christopher Scheiner (1575-1650) and Athanasius Kircher (1602-80) testified to the use of the portable camera obscura in science.[23]

The improvement that allowed this technology to become a widespread visual instrument is *the box camera*: a small portable camera. The reduction in mass started with Kaspar Schott's (1608-66) *Magia universalis naturae et artis*, published in 1657. In this work, he described the way to develop a little camera obscura consisting of two boxes (the type of camera that was used in the early years of photography). This apparatus be-

---

22 | Hieronymi Cardani, *De subtilitate libri xxi*, Nürnberg, 1550. In book iv, p.107. Quoted by Gernsheim H. 1955, p. 5.

23 | Sir Henry Wotton describes a portable tent camera obscura used by Kepler in a survey of Upper Austria. Kepler's tent camera obscura is a prototype between the darkened room and the box camera.

came a popular translation tool between nature and mankind.[24] In the last twenty years of the 17th century, the scientific field completed the camera's technology. The last step of this long process was given in 1676 by Johann Christoph Sturm (1635-1703) and it was fully realized in 1685 by Johann Zahn (1631-1707) when the camera obscura became a reflex camera (Fig. 2.15).

|*Fig. 2.15*|

"The reflex type illustrated in Fundamentum I consisted of a wooden box about 9 inches in height and breadth and about 2 feet in length, more or less, depending on the focal length of the lens combination to be used. The lens were arranged in an adjustable tube by means of which the image was focused on the oiled paper or opaque glass screen (the first published reference to the focusing-glass) on to which it was reflected, right way up, by a mirror set at an angle of 45°. To shade the image, the camera lid was provided with side flaps. The box and lens-tube were painted black inside to avoid internal reflections."[25]

This popular tool at the beginning of the eighteenth century was a mechanism ready for photographic technology. Some new prototypes were produced in the 18th century, – e.g. sedan chair cameras, table cameras, miniature cameras – but the camera obscura reached its full employment with the chemical developments of photosensitive substances, thus allowing for the creation of photographic technology. Even if this technique was used long before it was ever believed possible to fix images through a chemical process, just the act of using a 'seeing machine' produced the idea of subjugate the artist's vision to a mechanical imitation of nature; a 'lifeless imitation.'[26] This mechanism was perceived as a device that created a problem of dislodgment from the direct relationship between the artist and nature. In fact, the camera obscura re-composes natural objects into another plane, bringing out shadows and colors to the artist's eyes.

In Francesco Algarotti's *Saggio sulla Pittura* it is possible to feel his astonishment in regard to the potential offered by the camera obscura in pictorial representation. For Algarotti, the camera obscura is not only a mechanism that helps the artist to represent natural objects but also the camera obscura represents for him, the greatest tool for the analysis of the nature and, on the whole, more accurate than the human eye.

---

24 | Contrary to Mitry's affirmation, in which he argues that the camera obscura does not realize a tranlation of nature rather a direct recording, I consider that camera obscura realizes a translation of nature because it externalizes a mental process by applying Euclidean geometry. Thus it organizes space by means of the projection of Euclidean laws to a device. See Mitry J. 1987, p. 58.

25 | Gernsheim H. 1955, p. 14.

26 | See Scharf A. 1968, especially *The Camera obscura*, pp. 1-5.

Borrowing from Algarotti:

"Quell'uso che fanno gli astronomi del canocchiale, i fisici del microscopio, quell medesimo dovrebbon fare della Camera ottica i pittori. Conducono egualmente tutti cotesti ordigni a meglio conoscere e a rappresentar la Natura."[27]

A visual media like the camera obscura was indeed understood as a chance to penetrate the secrets of nature.

---

27 | Algarotti F. 1963 (1762), p. 87.

2.3 SELF-SIMILARITY: FOLD INTO FOLD
(LEIBNIZ AND THE MICROSCOPE)

Human weakness is clearly represented by Aeschylus' *Prometheus Bound*, in which the theft from the gods was a legitimate act, free of guilt. The imperative was clear, mankind must supplant, with technology, its sensorial weakness. Such is the case of the invention of the lens, which might remediate the impossibility to see farther and closer than the naked human eye. Sight was considered the most important sense of analysis[1] and was seen as a perfect 'tool' of investigation in 'an every day perspective'. Nevertheless, this sense is strongly limited when it comes to observing detailed information; in fact, the human eye proves to be a very poor tool for such purposes.

The universe, which was too distant – or too small – to be seen by even the sharpest eye, remained completely unknown, even unsuspected. After the European Renaissance, there arose a feeling of dissatisfaction in the scientific field caused by the poor resolution of the naked eye. After the Renaissance, many scientists focused their studies on the improvement of optical aids. Curiously, these improvements, first done in astronomy and mechanics, and soon disseminated to the biological and medical fields, were done after the final enhancement of mathematical perspective and the total assimilation of the camera obscura in pictorial representations. It might be possible to affirm that mankind, after reaching the technical possibility of reproducing its environment, focused its knowledge in order to explore nature from another point of view. Humankind identified in these visual media the unique solution for the weakness of its senses and, in consequence, the sole opportunity to analyze the world from an 'objective' point of view, the 'perfect' point of view of visual aids.

Even if the first written evidence of lenses date from the first century A.D. – Romans had experimented with different shapes of clear glass and discovered both proprieties to make an object appear larger and to focus the sun's rays in order to start a fire[2] – the first steps of the research of a real prosthesis for sight were done in the thirteenth century by spectacle makers, who produced eyeglasses in order to correct vision deficiencies. Notwithstanding, this research was accomplished after the Renaissance, when the scientific world was focused on the development of optical aids.[3]

---

1 | See Aristotle, *Metaphysics*, 980 a. 21-30 (Ed. by Apostle H.G. 1966.)

2 | Indeed, from the writings of Pliny we have good evidence about the use of clear glass in medical practice for the cauterization of wounds. Seneca also attested his awareness of the possibility of enlarging letters through a globe of glass.

3 | Evidently, the development of the camera obscura is strongly linked with the microscope. As noted in the last chapter, Alhazen's *Opticae Thesaurus Alhazeni Arabis*, Roger Bacon's *Opus Majus* (see Bacon R. 1928) and Giovanni Battista Della Porta's *Magia Naturalis* (especially *Of Strange Glasses*, see Della Porta 1589) analyzed some phenomena like refraction, magnification, etc. In particular, Alhazen is probably the first to have really appreciated the action of a lens of a convex form.

The monks – the only men who could read and write at the time – who wished to continue their work of writing and copying manuscripts into their older age, developed spectacles. The first evidence of such spectacles is found in a Florentine manuscript dated 1299:

"Mi trovo cosi gravoso di anni, che non abbia vallenza di leggiere e scrivere senza vetri appelati okiali, truovati novellamente per comodita delli poveri veki, quando affiebolano del vedere."[4]

It is stated that spectacles were invented by Salvano d'Armento degli Amati, a nobleman from Florence. Yet, this invention was popularized by Alessandro della Spina of Pisa. Spectacles became a common instrument in the first years of the fourteenth century. Even if this instrument represented an important aid to the human eye, it did not represent an instrument for the analysis of nature. Spectacles merely helped to reach the natural limit of human sight.

|*Fig. 2.16*|

The first revolutionary step that would change the human perspective of the universe was made by two Dutch spectacle makers: Zaccharias Janssen and his father, Hans.[5] During their experiments with lenses they mounted several lenses in a tube, producing greater magnification of images.[6] This invention is known as the 'compound microscope.' In this microscope, each lens is mounted in a drawtube, which can slide in the outer casing. It is possible to link the desire to improve the 'prosthesis' for the human eye to the superb anatomical studies of Andreas Vesalius' *De humani corporis fabrici*, published in 1543. Vesalius' work presents an accurate illustration of natural structures that can be observed without a visual tool. *De humani corporis fabrici* became an inspiration for future scientists. Vesalius began a detailed study of anatomical structures and in this way he focused the attention of the scientific world towards the representation of internal human anatomy, its true structure and its functioning. After that moment, the imperative was to develop an instrument that would allow for visual enlargement, in order to change the human point of view.[7]

The invention of the microscope was understood by some philosophers as an 'addition to the human senses;' such was the case for Robert Hooke (1635-1703) who pre-

---

4 | "I find myself so pressed by age that I can neither read nor write without those glasses they call spectacles, newly invented, for the great advantage of old men when their sight grows weak." Quoted by Court T.H. – Clay R.S. 1932, p. 5.

5 | See Wu Q. – Merchant F.A. – Castleman K.R. 2008.

6 | See Croft W.J. 2006.

7 |For further reading on the microscope's development see Court T.H. – Clay R.S. 1932 and Bradbury S. 1967.

sented the microscope as a **prosthetic device to revolutionize man's view of nature.**[8] The view offered by this new visual medium was perceived as a chance to penetrate a forbidden territory, 'to bring' to *regnum hominis* objects present in the deepest or furthest reaches of the universe; in order to be faithful to our text, to translate a deep structure of nature into a geometric organization.

Micrographia, the work of Hook, was enriched by copper-plate illustrations drawn with the aid of a microscope. In this book every sort of object or animal within was analyzed and represented with a high degree of technical acuity. The design of Hook's microscope – a design which remained the same for over a hundred years – consists of the combination of two convex lenses of a very short focal length, mounted in a cell with a pin-hole diaphragm close to the lens; the eye-piece consists of a large field-glass and an eye-lens; beyond the eye lens there is a cup to control the distance of the eye from the lens.[9]

|*Fig. 2.17*| |*Fig. 2.18*|

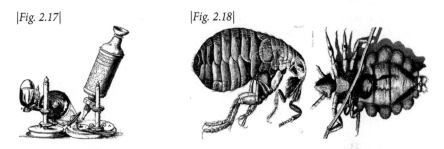

During Hooke's time there was no science of microscopy. Thus, the most trivial objects – Hooke's microscopic observations were focused on common objects – seen under magnifications of up to one hundred times were a captivating spectacle for both the scientific world and the greater public. Maybe the most significant observation made by Hooke was that of the structure of cork (2.19); "*Observation XVII: Of the schematism or texture of cork, and of the Cells or pores of some other such frothy Bodies.*"

Hooke remarks that these pores or cells are not very deep but they have many little boxes, which he calculated to be in the number of twelve hundred million per cubic inch. He also realized that these cells contain air, accounting for the reason cork floats in water.

---

8 | See Hooke R. 1961. (1665)

9 | Court T.H. – Clay R.S. 1932, p. 21. As stated by the authors, the introduction of the field lens has often been attributed to Hooke. Note however H. Monconys, who died in 1664, preceded him.

|*Fig. 2.19*|

The most important point in his note about the structure of cork is that Hooke used, for the first time in biology, the term "cell," a term of fundamental importance in the definition of the functional units of living organisms.[10] The examination of deeper structures by the means of such visual device represented a big problem for a conservative society. The ability to see those 'secrets' in nature through a prosthesis to the human eye was understood as a violent act against the laws of God, i.e. mankind forsook God's will by defying the natural limits imposed in its creation.[11]

This rejection of conservatism grew after the popularization of microscopic images. During the eighteenth-century, the splendid *Micrographias* became a popular object, almost an 'art product.' Several editions and translations in various languages spread the images of a micro-world in Europe. Consider for instance Henry Baker's *The Microscope Made Easy*, George Adams' *Micrographia illustrata*, and *Micrographia nova* by Benjamin Martin, who, before the publication of *Micrographia nova*, developed the first inexpensive pocket microscope.[12]

The theological problem was not the reproduction of objects or little animals like the famous Hooke's flea. The issue was born precisely when the borderlines of the 'visible' were extended.[13] A big debate developed from the new human capacity to regain one's lost unity with nature through the new extension of the sense of sight. This revolutionary change caused a big discussion in both the scientific and social sphere. In fact, Hooke's microscope, as a prosthetic device – a tool to regain the lost unity with nature – became an extension of sight into entirely new regions. The difference is clear, with the first advancement, mankind could observe in detail some animals and some natural objects, with the second one, mankind gained access to the wonders of the microcosmos,[14] to a new way to structure the geometrical vision of the universe.

---

10 | Bradbury S. 1967, p. 55.

11 | See Bradbury S. 1967.

12 | See Schickore J. 2007, especially *Pleasure and Information*.

13 | Every visual medium 'formats' the idea of 'truth.' Such is also the case of the microscope that uncovers the existence of a microcosmos. In fact, the ideas of the composition of many natural objects, and even the human body, changed radically with this instrument; that means both a new truth about nature and a new way to imagine structures in mechanics, as well as in society. This logic is already present in Baker's words when he claims in *The Microscope Made Easy* (2009, p. iii.) (1742): "nothing is really needful but good glasses, good Eyes, a little Practice, and a common Understanding, to distinguish what is seen; and a Love of Truth, to give a faithful Account thereof."

14 | Schickore J. 2007, p. 21.

The microscope became not only a tool that produces knowledge about nature but also of the self.[15] Mankind could, by means of the microscope and telescope, find a new universal order, a new hierarchy. As a consequence, the microscope became a tool for discovering metaphysical truths.[16] The first step of this conception of the universe can be identified in van Leeuwenhoek's works.

Antoine van Leeuwenhoek (1632-1723) was one of the most important Dutch natural scientists of his time, and his work, focused on microscopic observation, influenced many scientific and philosophical fields. Van Leeuwenhoek revealed a revolutionary way to conceive of nature and even fashioned improvements for microscopes with his own hands.[17] He became extremely skillful in the fabrication of polished bi-convex lenses. According to van der Star, who measured the resolution and magnification of several of van Leeuwenhoek's lenses, two of these microscopes, now in the Leyden Museum, magnify 79x and 126x and have resolutions of 3×5 microns. We can also find one of them, in the Utrecht Museum, that seems to be exceptional; its magnifying power is 275x.[18]

|*Fig. 2.20*|

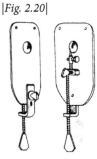

"The finished lenses were mounted between two plates of metal each containing a small hole; the plates were riveted together to hold the lens firmly in position between two holes. The objects were fixed upon a point which was then moved into the focus of the lens by a system of screws."[19]

---

15 | Schickore J. 2007, p. 23.

16 | It is interesting to see how the source of knowledge is focused in the eye and how after the invention of the microscope, the theory became strongly founded in the act of seeing through this scientific tool. This feeling is materialized through a strongly marked difference between van Leeuwenhoek's observations and his reflections. Snelder highlights van Leeuwenhoek's common use of the words *"ik verbeeld mij"*, *"ik imagineer mij"* (I imagine) at the moment, while elaborating upon his reflections. On the opposite side stays the observation, on which he attached absolute value, but as for his theoretical reflections, he was willing to drop them if they proved to be contradicted by later observations. See Snelders H.A.M. 1982, pp. 57-78.

17 | Van Leeuwenhoek's lenses were much better than those that were standard in this time (see Zuylen V.J. 1982.) Reiner Graf attested to the high performance of van Leeuwenhoek's microscopes in a letter sent in 1673 to Henry Oldenbug, secretary of the Royal Society; "a certain most ingenious person here, named Leeuwenhoek, has devised microscopes which far surpass those which we have hitherto seen, manufactured by Eustachio Divini and others." Quoted by Bradbury S. 1967, p. 75.

18 | Bradbury S. 1967, p. 79.

19 | Bradbury S. 1967, p. 78.

The substantial difference between van Leeuwenhoek's observation and that of previous microscopes resides in the matter of study. Van Leeuwenhoek's interest in the structures of natural objects led him to see through microscopes any kind of thing – liquids, animals, solids, minerals, and any natural object made part of his subject of study.[20] His interest in improving microscope shows clearly that he was a purely inductive researcher. He focused his research upon what he observed and, afterward, linked it with theories and personal reflections. It is from his observations through the microscope that he could build the idea of an encased world; an 'encased universal structure' which found its maximal expression after his analysis of crystallographic and globular structures. During his observations of crystals, van Leeuwenhoek attempted to describe with great precision the shape of plants, the crystals of urine, juices, vinegar, etc. He could see, by means of a saturated solution, that crystals maintain their shape.[21] Thus, van Leeuwenhoek supposed big crystals to be built up of small ones of the same shape. He even went further still, assuming that those small crystals are built up again of still smaller ones with the same shape. The very smallest particles of crystals still have the same shape but were invisible to his microscope.[22] Van Leeuwenhoek noted the same self-similar composition in common salt, but in this case, they are composed by cubical crystals, i.e. small cubes repeated until infinity.[23] Thanks to his depth of observation, van Leeuwenhoek concluded that crystal's molecules are polyhedrons having the same shape as the crystal itself. For van Leeuwenhoek, matter was built up of small spheres, or globules (*klootgens*).[24] Starting in 1674, he focused his studies on the presence of globules in milk and blood. In a successive step, he observed the presence of globules as a basic component also in common salt, earth, clay and many other substances. To his amazement he found that "the particles in all those biles [the bile of cow, calf, sucking-lamb, yearling sheep, and rabbit] resembled each other closely in size, as do all the particles that compose the bodies of animals as far as I have observed till now."[25]

Globules composed the whole; every object, animal, and substance, under his eyes, was an infinite set of globules.[26] His doctrine of globules was a kind of corpus-

---

20 | See what he recorded in his personal letters (van Leeuwenhoek 1939.)

21 | See the *Letter to the Royal Society*, 23 January 1685, quoted by Snelders H.A.M. 1982.

22 | Snelders H.A.M. 1982, pp. 57-78.

23 | See *Letter to the Royal Society*, 5 January 1682.

24 | Quoted by Snelders H.A.M. 1982, pp. 57-78.

25 | *Letter to the Royal Society*, 7 September 1674, quoted by Snelders H.A.M. 1982, pp. 57-78.

26 | We can see van Leeuwenhoek's near obsession with globules in a letter of Christian Huygens wrote on January, 1675, to Henry Oldenburg: "Je voudrois bienscavoir quelle foy on adjoute chez vous aux observations de notre Monsieur Leeuwenhoek qui convertit toute chose en petites boules. Pour moy après avoir en vain taschè de voir certaines choses qu'il voit, je doute fort, si ce ne sont pas des deceptions de sa vue, et encore

cular theory that created some disturbances in the scientific, as well as in the philo-sophical field. According to van Leeuwenhoek, globules are everywhere; he saw them in human muscles, in human teeth, in minerals, in plant matter, and in liquids. It is important to note that van Leeuwenhoek not only discovered the omnipresence of globules but also, by analyzing sperm (in fact, he is the first to observe spermatozoa), blood, muscles and capillaries he recognized the presence of the so-called *animalcules* which we know refer to as microorganisms.

The awareness of this microcosms populated by little animals creates two phe-nomena: a) consciousness of the limitation of human senses, now surpassed by tech-nology – even generating deep theological problems – b) the possibility to imagine another kind of structure in the world.

The influence of van Leeuwenhoek on Leibniz's theory of monadology is clear. As Leibniz claims, van Leeuwenhoeck's observations helped to form his ideas about the generation of beings. Leibniz considers van Leeuwenhoeck as one of the most excel-lent observers of his time, and thanks to him, he could note and validate his idea about universal structures. After van Leeuwenhoeck's microscopic observations, Leibniz was able to imagine the animal, as any other organized substance, under a precise encased (*emboîtée*) structure. Leibniz considers – it is clear the influence of the first vision of spermatozoa realized by van Leeuwenhoek – the generation of animals and organized substances as a 'development', a sort of augmentation.

"Cependant, pour revenir aux formes ordinaires, ou aux *Ames brutes*, cette durée qu'il leur faut attribuer, à la place de celle qu'on avoit attribuée aux atomes, pourroit faire douter si elles ne vont pas de corps en corps, ce qui seroit la *Metempsychose*, à peu près comme quelques philosophes ont crû la transmission du mouvement et celle des especes. Mais cette imagination est bien eloignée de la nature des choses. Il n'y a point de tel passage, et c'est icy où *les transformations* de Messieurs Swammerdam, Malpi-ghi et Leewenhoeck, qui sont des plus excellens observateurs de nostre temps, sont venues à mon secours, et m'ont fait admettre plus aisément, que l'animal et toute autre substance organisée ne commence point, lorsque nous le croyons, et que sa generation apparente n'est qu'un developpement, et une espece d'aumentation." [27]

|Prop. II| This physical phenomenon 'of development' allowed Leibniz to realize some metaphysical theories, which he elaborated upon in his younger age. Leibniz found it impossible to realize the principles of a true unity (*les principles d'une veritable unité*) in passive matter. In fact, according to Leibniz, the whole is a set (*collection ou amas*) of parts extending into infinity,[28] which implies some notions of inner dynamics.

---

plus, quand il pretend decouvrir les particules, dont l'eau, le vin et d'autres liqueurs sont composees, a quoy il a mandè a mon pere qu'il estoit occupè." Quoted by by Snelders H.A.M. 1982, pp. 57-78.

27 | Leibniz G.W. 1996b (1695), § 6.

28 | See Leibniz G.W. 1996b (1695).

Leibniz's theory presents, in different points, the concept of structure in its traditional meaning, it is to say, in the meaning of construction or organization.[29] In this way, he analyses the structure of inert and living bodies as well as the nature of thoughts.[30] According to Leibniz, it is impossible to think a simple notion in an isolated way. The essence of a thought resides in its possibility to be placed in reference to many others.[31] Following this logic, the essence of a notion or idea resides in its 'mediality'; in its capacity to link itself with other ideas.[32] Leibniz identified the character of the idea in its capacity to integrate itself in successive lines of reasoning derived from many others ideas, which are themselves linked. In such a system, a system that bases its order on the strong dichotomy between the simple and the composite, the idea of composition is privileged.[33] Nonetheless, the existence of simple and composite is strongly combined. In fact, the composites prove the existence of simples, because the composite is nothing other than a *mass* or *aggregate* (*aggregatum*) of simples.[34]

---

29 | It is interesting to quote Serres' words regarding the exact meaning of structure "C'est un ensemble de signification non définie, groupant des éléments en nombre quelconque (éléments dont on ne spécifie pas le contenu) et des relations, en nombre fini, dont on ne définit pas la nature, mais dont on définit la fonction quand aux éléments. On obtient un modèle (un paradigme) de cette structure si l'on spécifie le contenu des éléments et la nature des relations. L'ensemble de ces paradigmes ont en commun, analogiquement, la structure en question." (Serres M. 1968, p. 4.)

30 | See Serres M. 1968.

31 | See Leibniz G.W. 1996d (1768).

32 | For Leibniz, this kind of structure is also manifested in some animal instincts. In *Monadologie* § 26, Leibniz analyzes memory as a sort of succession (*consécution*) of souls imitating reason. According to Leibniz, memory works as a structure linking memories. In his words: "C'est que nous voyons que les animaux, ayant la perception de quelque chose qui les frappe et dont ils ont eu perception semblable auparavant, s'attendent par la représentation de leur mémoire à ce y a été joint dans cette perception précédente et sont portés à des sentiments semblables à ceux qu'ils avaient pris alors." (Leibniz G.W. 1996c (1714), § 26.)

33 | Leibniz developed a theory that opposes Newton's conception of space. In fact, for Newton, space and time is a single entity that has its own properties and is totally independent of whatever it contains. Thus, space represents an open field without limits and in which atoms are arranged and governed by gravity. In Newton's conception of space, there can exist an empty space, because space is totally independent of the object 'in it contained.' As we can see in this chapter, for Leibniz, space does not represent an independent entity. In fact, the world is constructed, according to him, through the relations between entities. These relations are explained through the existence of the Monad. Consequently, space represents relations between single entities; hence an empty space is inconceivable.

34 | It is possible to perceive a composite not only as an entity that possesses many parts, but one that is folded (*plié*) in many ways. On this topic see Deleuze G. 1988.

Rutherford analyzes Leibniz's argument as follows:

- There exist composites.
- Any composite is a mass or aggregate of simples.
- Therefore, there exist simples.[35]

|**Prop. VI**| At this point, it is important to note Leibniz's use of the term 'substance' and how it acquired a deeper meaning.[36] A substance, for Leibniz, is an entity capable of action. It can be simple or composite. A simple substance is one that has no parts and a composite substance is an 'assemblage' of simple substances, or monads.[37] Leibniz's technical meaning of 'aggregates' (*entia per aggregationem*) does not only denote a multitude, it denotes many things as one, highlighting the relationships among those things, in other words, a multitude is conceived as one, as a composite unity. In the 'aggregate' the monad is a simple substance that 'enters' into composites, and the entity of the monad is characterized by its simplicity and it is explained by the fact that it exists without parts.

"Mais en estant revenu, après bien des meditations, je m'apperceus, qu'il est impossible de trouver *les principes d'une veritable Unité* dans la matiere seule ou dans ce qui n'est que passif, puisque tout n'y est que coolection ou amas des parties jusqu'à l'infini. Or la multitude ne pouvant avoir sa realité que *des unités veritables* qui viennent d'ailleurs et sont tout autre chose que les points mathematiques qui ne sont que des extremités de l'étendu et des modifications dont il est constant, que le *continuum* ne sçauroit ester composé"[38]

Leibniz imposes the necessity to recognize this kind of atom that represents the totality of a being, 'its essence,' in the meaning of fundamental unity.[39] This indivisible

---

35 | Rutherford D. 2009, p. 37.

36 | "Quanti autem ista sint momenti, in primis apparebit ex notione substantiae, quam ego assigno, quae tam foecunda est, ut inde veritates primariae, etiam circa Deum et metes, et naturam corporum, eaeque partim cognitae, sed paum demostratae, partim hactenus ignotae, sed maximi per caeteras scientias usus futurae consequantur." (Leibniz G.W. 1996e, pp. 197-198.)

37 | It is important to remember that the term Monad was borrowed from Neoplatonism. For Neoplatonism this term designated a state; the state of One. The term Monad represented the unity that wraps a multiplicity and this multiplicity develops the One as a series. See Proclus, *Elements of Theology* § 21, 204.

38 | Leibniz G.W. 1996a (1765), p. 204.

39 | By explaining this concept of a minimal particle that envelops activity, Leibniz links the minimal particle to the soul (*Esprit*). Being that this minimal particle is the essence of beings, it is recognized in the human soul: "C'est qu'il faut donc dire que Dieu a creé d'abord l'ame, o toute autre unite reelle de telle sorte, que tout luy doit naistre de son

particle (*points metaphysiques ou de substance*) can be interpreted as the essence of the subject because its presence represents its true existence. Without those, it would be not real. The absence of those unities (*veritables unités*) leads to the impossibility of conceiving the multitude. As noted above, the multitude is composed of simples that have no parts:[40] *La Monade* is defined as a simple substance that enters into the composites (*Qui entre dans les composés*).[41] Thus, monads establish a relationship of 'every-totality' while bodies or composites are collectives that follow a relationship with others.[42]

In Leibniz's theory, matter conserves its character of infinite divisibility. The small parts of matter form 'whirls' (*tourbillons*), which create smaller 'whirls' and so on, to infinity. These 'whirls' of matter are in contact with the whole. Thus, matter presents an infinite porous texture, spongy or cavernous without the existence of a vacuum. In this conception of matter, every cavern lies within a cavern. In Deleuze's words:

"chaque corps, petit soit-il, contient un monde, entant qu'il est troué de passages irréguliers, environné et pénétré par un fluide de plus en plus subtil, l'ensemble de l'univers était semblable à 'un étang de matière dans lequel il y a des différents flots d'ondes."[43]

|Prop. XI| Leibniz considers monads as independent and perfect entities because they are the source of their self-inner actions.[44] He theorized the inexistence of an absolute vacuum as proof of his idea of continuous form in which the void represents just a human idea derived from the *horror vacui*. The absence of vacui and the idea that everything is connected makes this substance (the monad) an autonomic and universal link everywhere. Hence, Leibniz identifies a degree of divinity in this substance; "il n'y a qu'un Dieu, et ce Dieu suffit."[45] The monad became supreme, unique and indispensable, and its universal articulation, thanks to its links between simples, makes every

---

propre fonds, par une parfaite spontaneité à l'égard d'elle-même, et pourtant avec une parfaite conformité aux choses de dehors." (Leibniz G.W. 1996a (1765), p. 218.)

40 | It is important to remember that Leibniz assimilated the existence of Monads as a metaphysical point. The concept of monad implies some changes in the notion of thing (*chose*). In consequence, the concept of monad imposes some negations. "Von der Einfachheit der Monaden abgesehen beruhen auch die folgenden auf Negationen: Unteilbarkeit, Unzerstörbarkeit, Figurlosigkeit, Zeitlosigkeit, Unbeeinflussbarkeit und Fensterlosigkeit." (Poser H. 2009, p. 81.)

41 | Leibniz G.W. 1996c (1714), §1.

42 | Deleuze explains this relationship as follows "Les monades sont des unités distributives, suivant un rapport chacun-tout, tandis que les corps sont des collectifs, troupeaux ou agrégats, suivant un rapport les uns-les autres." (Deleuze G. 1988, p. 133.)

43 | Deleuze G. 1988, p. 8.

44 | It is important to remember the analogy created by Leibniz between monad and soul.

45 | Leibniz G.W. 1996c (1714), § 39.

action and movement dependent upon it (*doit être incapable de limites et contenir tout autant de réalité qu'il est possible*).[46] From this thought the infinite entity represented by this minimal particle, or substance, is derived and is itself put in relation to God's perfection – personified by its infinite nature because, for Leibniz, the absence of limits (*bornes*) characterized perfection. The absence of limits represents the possibility to include reality; therefore God is, for Leibniz, an entity of infinite perfection. Furthermore, in this system – or universal structure – imagined by Leibniz everything is linked. Every creature has some perfection derived from God's influence; from its connection with God. Therefore, imperfections are caused by the inability to be without limits (*elles ont leurs imperfections de leur nature propre, incapable d'être sans bornes*).[47] This fundamental difference makes creatures different from God. Indeed, the *Natural Inertia* of bodies causes a creature's original imperfections.[48]

Existence implies a link with the whole. Thus, it is understood as an arrangement (*accommodement*) among every created thing, where everything is linked with everything else and everyone is linked with all others. In this system, every simple substance shows a variety of connections able to express the way of interaction with the others and of the others, that is, of the entire system.

As noted in the first part of this text, these ideas were fundamental for a new conception of space, for the development of topology. In fact, such a system represents space as 'pure relationship between objects.' Therefore, the rapport between simple substances represents the activity and to a certain extent, the structure of the whole universe;[49] (*elle est par consequence un miroir vivat perpétuel de l'univers*).[50]

Every monad represents the universe; the corps represents the universe because of the connections of the matter; the soul represents the entire universe because it represents the body. This structure of the whole allows Leibniz to completely accept the idea of the universe as a divine machine or natural automaton, where the machines of nature, i.e. human bodies, are also machines in every piece of infinity. Thus, the antique and recurrent idea of the divisibility of matter found in Leibniz an eloquent voice.

"Et l'auteur de la nature a pu pratiquer cet artifice divin et infiniment merveilleux, parce que chaque portion de la matière n'est pas seulement divisible à l'infini comme les anciens ont reconnu, mais encore sous-divisée actuellement sans fin, chaque parti en

---

46 | Leibniz G.W. 1996c (1714), § 40.

47 | Leibniz G.W. 1996c (1714), § 42.

48 | Leibniz uses monadology in order to prove God's existence. In fact, the existence of an entity that has no borders, no negation and no contradiction, represents a way to know God's existence *a priori*. God is for Leibniz the primitive unity, the original substance, source of every monad, the place or production of every monad.

49 | According to Lyssy, Leibniz uses an old Neoplatonic metaphor, which maintains that the world is a mirror of God. See Lyssy A. 2009.

50 | Leibniz G.W. 1996c (1714) § 56.

parties, dont chacune a quelque mouvement propre, autrement il serait impossible, que chaque portion de la matière pût exprimer tout l'univers."[51]

Leibniz assumes self-similarity as the fundamental phenomenon of the structure of the universe; a self-similarity derived, of course, from a specular phenomenon. The phenomenon of self-similarity analized by Leibniz derives from his idea that every single substance is connected with the whole and also every piece of matter is conceived as a structure contained inside another, which presents the same form but in another dimension *ad infinitum*.[52]

"Chaque portion de la matière peut être conçue, comme un jardin plein de plantes, et comme un étang plein de poisons. Mais chaque rameau de la plante, chaque membre de l'animal, chaque goutte de ses humeurs es encore un tel jardin, ou un tel étang."[53]

It is clear the influence of van Leeuwenhoeck's observations. The encased (*emboîtée*) structure, a product of Leibniz's reflections about the universe, seems impossible to

---

51 | Leibniz G.W. 1996c (1714) § 65.

52 | Leibniz affirms that philosophers have many problems analyzing and theorizing the origin of forms in nature. These problems, for Leibniz, disappear thanks to the precise research realized through the microscope, on insects, animals and the many organic bodies in nature. These studies on nature allow Leibniz to affirm – in opposition to the idea in which the production of organisms was derived from chaos – that every organism is product of seeds (*semences*) which transport some pre-formations. For Leibniz the generation is a development of growth, and death is an envelopment of diminutions. This concept of generation is materialized for Leibniz in the process of maggots that become flies. The necessity of preformation in Leibniz's theories is clear. In fact, for Leibniz, every substance, organic or inorganic, made part of the infinite system, a system folded into infinity. Deleuze's theories of Folding, express this necessity as the inner fold inside every organism. In such a system as Leibniz's one, preformation becomes a necessity that is 'proven' with the microscope. Preformation, in fact, represents an inner determination that realizes the passage, fold by fold, that constitutes an infinite system. An organism, under this logic, is folded into a seed, and the seed is folded into another seed like a matryoshka. This idea of preformationism, seemingly confirmed by the microscope, was certainly abandoned because of the notion of evolution or development. In fact, the notion of evolution does not conceive of the preformed organism or *organism enboîtés*, but it theorizes the existence of epigenesis, it is to say, the formation of an organism is the product of another thing, an exterior one. In Deleuze's words "Le développement ne va pas du petit au grand, par croissance ou augmentation, mais du général au spécial, par différenciation d'un champ d'abord indifférencié, soit sous l'action du milieu extérieur, soit sous l'influence de forces internes qui sont directrices, directionnelles, et non constituantes ou préformantes." (Deleuze G. 1988, pp. 14-15.)

53 | Leibniz G.W. 1996c (1714) § 67.

realize without acknowledging van Leeuwenhoeck's animalcules. Leibniz's theory of monadology highlights the existence of a divine structure in which all is connected; all is inside of everything, producing relationships of similarity. This special spatial organization does not allow for the existence of sterility, death, confusion or chaos.

"Ainsi il n'y a rien d'inculte, de sterile, de mort dans l'univers, point de chaos, point de confusion qu'en apparence; à peu près comme il en paraîtrait dans un étang à une distance dans laquelle on verrait un mouvement confus et grouillement, pour ainsi dire, de poisons de l'étang, sans discerner les poisons memes."[54]

In some way, by means of the idea of encased structures, Leibniz recognizes the existence of harmony in chaos, harmony between the scales, a harmony that can be reached by means of the specular phenomenon, which is immanent in nature, and is personified by self-similarity.[55] Self-similarity makes natural variation coincide with change of scale.[56] The same phenomenon is clear in the Koch curve and in Mandelbrot's fractal dimension in which the concept of interdimensionality is fundamental. Like looking at the variation along a winding stretch of coastline, by widening or tightening focus, it is possible to find another fold inside the fold.

---

54 | Leibniz G.W. 1996c, § 69.
55 | See Foucault M. 1966, especially, chapter II *"La prose du monde."*
56 | Deleuze G. 1988, p. 23.

2.4 Self-Similarity as a Narrative Tool

|Prop. IV, V, VI, VIII| According to Leibniz, the world becomes a representation expressed by means of the spatial organization composed by monads, that is, an infinite organization within an infinity of folds, which are in continuous movement of 'folding' and 'unfolding.'[1] Therefore, Deleuze identified the inflection as the 'real atom' or 'essence of matter.' He considers the inflection as a genetic ideal element of the fold, which can be recognized in the active line of Klee, as well as in both Baroque style and Leibniz's writings.

The inflection-point can be recognized in a straight line thanks to its infinite character. In fact, in a straight line, it is possible to mark two points A and B. It does not matter if those points are near or far, it is always possible to insert one point between the points A and B: point C. The inflection point, in this case is represented by C, thus, C is the fold, the recognition of infinity. In the case of Koch's curve, the infinite variation is an intrinsic factor of the inflection.[2] This elastic point allows for the conception of an infinite structure in an everlasting movement. As noted above, Koch's curve is the product of an operation that rounds off angles, which are proliferated by means of a law of self-similarity. This curve crosses an infinite number of angular points and in no part does it admit a tangent. It is more than a line and less than a surface i.e. the everlasting movement and the flexibility of its essential point – the inflection point – organize an infinite structure, which has a fractal dimension. The point of inflection generates a dynamic effect in a recursive form. However, in this case the point is not a point in space, it is no longer a simple point on the curve, no longer the point of inflection where the tangent crosses the curve, but it is considered a *point of view* on a site. In these kinds of structures, the movement is not in the direction of point by point. It is fold by fold. In other words, site by site. The inflection, or fold, through its movement, organizes another kind of symmetry. In fact, in this *whirligig* movement that creates infinite structures, harmony exists between the scales.

The *principle of scaling,* manifested in Leibniz's idea of the structure of the whole, represents one of the most influential concepts of Mandelbrot's fractal geometry. This principle is defined as the same shape being present at all scales. The phenomenon is produced in some objects and phenomena of nature and is also manifested in some mathematical formulas and geometric objects, especially in the proto-fractal objects realized by Georg Cantor, Giuseppe Peano, David Hilbert, Helge von Koch, Wactaw Sierpinski, Gaston Julia and Felix Hausdorff.

Like Leibniz with the microscope, Mandelbrot used computers in order to analyze and theorize new structures in nature. He recognized the presence of harmony in chaos, harmony between the scales. By using proto-fractals, Mandelbrot acquired an important tool that allowed him to identify spatial organizations that are in many ways analogous with Leibniz's encased universe. Mandelbrot used proto-fractal ob-

---

1 | Deleuze G. 1988, p. 115.
2 | Deleuze G. 1988, p. 22.

jects in order to discover not only the harmony in chaotic movements, both natural and non-natural, but also in order to develop a geometry able to recognize irregularities in nature.[3] Proto-fractal objects were interpreted as 'mathematical monsters.' They were seen as shapes intended to demonstrate the deviation from the familiar, rather than to typify the normal. However, Mandelbrot, by using them, demonstrated that these early mathematical fractals have many features in common with shapes found in nature, for example, the *principle of scaling* and *self-similarity*.[4]

|*Fig. 2.21*|

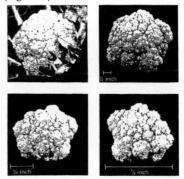

An object is self-similar if the whole can be divided into parts, each of which preserves its similitude with the whole. From a mathematical point of view, the reduction process can be repeated into infinity.[5] Thus, a mathematical self-similar object contains infinitesimal details.[6] The most used example to explain this phenomenon in nature is the shape of cauliflower. Its structure in branches presents, in every single part, the same shape of the whole, in smaller scale.

|**Prop. XIII**| A branch of a head of cauliflower is composed of smaller branches that manifest the same shape of the head. The self-similar structure of the cauliflower is perceptible down to four or five 'levels,' then the branches are too small. This is not

---

3 | Proto-fractal objects were created during the 19th century. Thus, many people remark that fractals and their descriptions go back to classical mathematics and mathematicians of the past like Geor Cantor (1872), Giuseppe Peano (1890), David Hilbert (1891), Helge von Koch (1904), Waclaw Sierpinski (1916), Gaston Julia (1918), and Felix Hausdorff (1919). It is true that the creations of these mathematicians played a fundamental role in Mandelbrot's concept of a new geometry. But, at the same time, it is true that they did not think of their creations as conceptual steps towards a new perception or a new geometry of nature like Mandelbrot has done. See Peitgen H.O. – Jürgens H. – Saupe D. 1992, p. 63.

4 | Curiously, the term 'self-similarity' is not older than 40-years-old.

5 | It is important to remember that the phenomenon of self-similarity is also present in the decimal system. Our notion of measurement uses self-similarity in different scales e.g. a meter is ten decimeters, or one hundred centimeters: a centimeter is ten millimeters. One meter was originally defined as $1/_{10,000,000}$ of the distance between the North Pole and Earth's equator as measured along the meridian passing through Paris. Now it is defined as the distance traveled by light in an absolute vacuum in $1/_{299,792,458}$ of a second.

6 | Mandelbrot B. 1997, p. 40.

the case with proto-fractal objects, like the *Cantor Set*. In mathematical objects the phenomenon of self-similarity can be infinite. The part corresponds to the shape of the whole and the whole can be contained within the part. In other words, each part represents the whole at another scale. Self-similarity means symmetry across scales, a harmony that implies a recursive form, a pattern inside the pattern, a fold that follows a fold.[7] Self-similarity is present everywhere in nature and in popular culture: in the infinitely deep reflection of a person standing between two mirrors, or in the cartoon depiction of a fish eating a smaller fish eating a smaller fish…[8]

Mandelbrot's interest in those geometrical objects was the research of an harmony in chaos. He could not only produce detail at a finer and finer scale, he could also produce detail with constant measurements.[9] Further, the phenomenon of self-similarity imposes a reflection on an elementary notion of geometry known as similarity. In geometry two objects are similar if they have the same shape, regardless of their size. Corresponding angles however must be equal, and corresponding line segments must all have the same factor of proportionality. According to Peitgen – Jürgens – Saupe:

"when a photo is enlarged, it is enlarged by the same factor in both horizontal and vertical directions. Even a oblique, i.e. non-horizontal, non-vertical, line segment between two points on the original will be enlarged by the same factor. We call this enlargement factor scaling factor. The transformation between the objects is called similarity transformation."[10]

If a photo is enlarged by a factor of three, the area of the resulting image is $3 \times 3 = 3^2 = 9$ times the area of the original. Thus, if we have an object with area A and the scaling factor s, then the resulting object will have an area which is $s \times s = s^2$ times the area A of the original. We can see that the area of the scaled-up object increases as the square of the scaling factor. In three-dimensional objects, if we take a cube and enlarge it by a scaling factor of 3, it becomes three times as long, three times as deep, and three times as high as the original. The area of each face of the enlarged cube is $3^2 = 9$ times as large as the face of the original cube. For objects of any shape whatsoever, the total surface area of a scaled-up object increases as the square of the scaling factor. The enlarged cube has three layers, each with $3 \times 3 = 9$ little cubes. Thus the total volume is $3 \times 3 \times 3 = 3^3 = 27$ times as much as the original cube. In general, the volume of a scaled-up object increases as the cube of the scaling factor.[11]

The same phenomenon is also present in nature. As remarked by Galileo in his *Dialogues Concerning Two New Sciences* (1638), the elementary observations present-

---

7 | See Gleick J. 1987.

8 | One can remark that the phenomenon of self-similarity is immediately related to the concept of limit. See Gleick J. 1987.

9 | See Mandelbrot B. 1997.

10 | Peitgen H.O. – Jürgens H. – Saupe D. 1992, p. 138.

11 | Peitgen H.O. – Jürgens H. – Saupe D. 1992, p. 139.

ed above have remarkable consequences. For example, the weight of a tree is proportional to its volume. "Scaling up a tree by a factor s means that its weight will be scaled by s^3. At the same time the cross-section of its stem will only be scaled by s^2. Thus, the pressure inside the stem would scale by $s^3/s^2 = s$. That means that if s increases beyond a certain limit, then the strength of wood will not be sufficient to bear the corresponding pressure."[12] The existing tension between area and volume also explains why mountains do not exceed a height of 7 miles.

|Fig. 2.22|

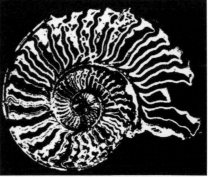

The growth of an ammonite also shows a phenomenon of similarity. An ammonite grows according to the law of similarity; i.e. it grows in such a way that its shape is preserved. The 'spiral' form of the ammonite allows for some reflections on mathematical forms and natural ones. "Spiral is a curve which, starting from a point of origin, continually diminishes in curvature as it recedes from that point; or, in other words, whose *radius of curvature* continually increases."[13]

On the one hand, this definition allows for the inclusion of a large number of different curves; on the other hand, it excludes a curve, which, in popular speech is a spiral, thus confusing the notion of a true spiral, for example, the shape of an ammonite, which is a *cylindrical helix* or *screw*. In helices and screws, there is not a definite origin or starting point and they do not change their curvature as they proceeds. Thus, the 'spirals' in nature are not, mathematically speaking, spirals at all, but *screws* or *helices*. They belong to a different family of curves.[14] In de la Goupillière's words, nature exhibits "un reflet des formes rigoureuses qu'étudie la géométrie." Geometrical spirals have fascinated mathematicians throughout the ages. Archimedes (287-212 B.C.) wrote a treatise on these forms and also created a spiral named for him.[15] The distinct quality of the Archimedean spiral is that the distance between its windings remains constant.

---

12 | Peitgen H.O. – Jürgens H. – Saupe D. 1992, p. 141.

13 | D'Arcy W. T. 1969, p. 172.

14 | In popular speech, spirals are traced by nature in the florets of a sunflower in a lock of hair, in a staple of wool, in the coil of an elephant's trunk, in the 'circling spires' of a snake, in a chameleon's tail, etc. See D'Arcy W.T. 1969.

15 | "In the elementary mathematics of a spiral, we speak of the point of origin as the pole (o); a straight line having its extremity in the pole, and revolving about it, is called the radius vector; and a point (P), traveling along the radius vector under definite conditions of velocity, will then describe our spiral curve." (D'Arcy W.T. 1969, p. 175.)

|*Fig. 2.23*|

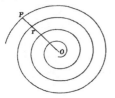

"If, while the radius vector revolves uniformly about the pole, a point (P) travels with uniform velocity along it, the curve described will be that called the equal spiral, or spiral of Archimedes."[16]

In contrast to the Archimedean spiral there is the equiangular, or logarithmic spiral, in which the whorls continually increase in breadth, and do so in a steady and unchanging ratio.[17]

|*Fig. 2.24*|

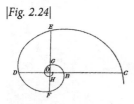

"If, instead of traveling with a uniform velocity, our point moves along the radius vector with a velocity increasing as its distance from the pole, then the path described is called an equiangular spiral."[18]

This last spiral is related to geometric sequences and also creates a system that goes to infinity through its self-similar particularity.[19] As remarked by Bernoulli, a scaling of the spiral with respect to its center has the same effect as simply rotating the spiral by some angle. However, most living things in nature grow by a different law; they are not self-similar. As noted by Peitgen – Jürgens – Saupe, "an adult is not simply a baby scaled up."[20] In the growth from baby to adult, different parts of the body scale up, each with a different scaling factor.

|*Fig. 2.25*| |*Fig. 2.26*|

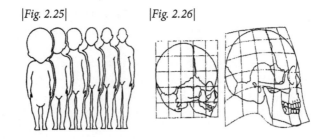

---

16 | D'Arcy W.T. 1969³, p. 73.

17 | This spiral was first recognized by Descartes and discussed in the year 1638 in his letters to Mersenne.

18 | D'Arcy W.T. 1969³, p. 73.

19 | The mathematician Jacob Bernoulli (1654-1705) devoted a treatise entitled *Spira Mirabilis* to the logarithmic spiral. He was impressed by the phenomenon of self-similarity presented in this spiral. Thus, he chose the inscription *Eadem Mutata Resurgo* (In spite of changes – resurrection of the same) for his tombstone in the Cathedral of Basel.

20 | Peitgen H.O. – Jürgens H. – Saupe D. 1992, p. 142.

The example of the ammonite clearly shows the existing difference between natural objects and its possible representation by means of geometrical forms. Geometrical forms are able to create infinite forms by applying recursive formulas. On the contrary, the perception of natural forms becomes just an allusion to the geometrical object and its proprieties, sometimes creating some confusion.[21]

In Nature (e.g. the romanesco cauliflower), in every physically existing object, self-similarity may hold only for a few orders of magnitude. Below a certain scale, matter breaks down into a collection of molecules, atoms, and going a bit further, elementary particles. Also it must be considered that in the example of the cauliflower the part can never be exactly equal to the whole.[22] Nevertheless, the phenomenon of self-similarity is totally different in fractal objects. As we can see, in the next figure, (Fig. 2.27) the Koch curve seems to be created by four identical parts.

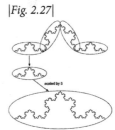

|*Fig. 2.27*|

If we chose one of these parts and observe it under a 'variable zoom lens' at exactly 3x magnification, the little piece seems to be identical to the entire curve. We can take one of these four pieces, and make the same operation again, and again, and again, into infinity, and each of them seems to be identical to the entire curve, even if we apply a magnification of 9x with our 'variable zoom lens.'

According to Peitgen – Jürgens – Saupe there are three different kinds of self-similar structures. The following three images are examples of these. Each contain small replicas of the whole. The first type of self-similarity identified by Peitgen – Jürgens – Saupe is called, by the authors, *Self-Similarity at a Point*:

"Consider for example a cover of a book that contains on it a picture of a hand holding that very book. Surprisingly, this somewhat innocent sounding description leads to a cover with a rather complex design. As we look deeper and deeper into the design, we see more and more of rectangular covers."[23]

---

21 | This phenomenon of allusion of natural objects to geometric ones is clearly described by Bergson in his first work *Essai sur les données immédiates de la conscience* where the philosopher argues that "les Phénomènes physiques qui se succèdent et sont perçus par nos sens distinguent par la qualité non moins que par sa quantité, de sorte qu'on aurait quelque peine à les déclarer d'abord équivalentes les uns aux autres. Mais, précisément parce que nos sens les perçoivent, rien n'empêche d'attribuer leurs différences qualitatives à l'impression qu'ils font sur nous, et de supposer, derrière l'hétérogénéité de nos sensations, un univers physique homogène." (Bergson H. 1889, p. 154.)

22 | See Peitgen H.O. – Jürgens H. – Saupe D. 1992.

23 | Peitgen H.O. – Jürgens H. – Saupe D. 1992, p. 146.

|*Fig. 2.28*|

In this case, the copies are arranged in one nested sequence, and clearly, a self-similar property can be found only at **one particular point.** This is the limit point at which the size of the copies tends toward zero.[24]

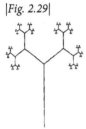

|*Fig. 2.29*|

The second figure corresponds to the *Self-Affinity*. As we can see, the complete tree is made up of the stem and two reduced copies of the whole. It is also possible to remark, that smaller and smaller copies of the whole tree are accumulated in its leaves. Thus, in this case, one may claim that the property of self-similarity is latent in the set of leaves. Although, the tree is not strictly self-similar, as the stem is not similar to the whole tree.

In this case, it is possible to interpret the stem as an affine copy of the whole, a copy that is compressed to a line.

|*Fig. 2.30*|

The last figure is the *Sierpinski Gasket*. As we know, it is a fractal, thus, we can find copies of the whole near every point of it. The Gasket is composed of smaller, but exact, copies of itself. In this case the authors have called this phenomenon *Strict Self-Similarity*.

These three different cases are normally called self-similar figures. Even if we know that just the *Koch Snowflake*, or the *Sierpinski Gasket*, are Strictly Self-Similar.

Taking into consideration these three kinds of self-similarity, to which category does the cauliflower belong? The cauliflower would be a "physical approximation of a self-similar, but not strict self-similar, object akin to the two-branch tree."[25] Like in the spiral's case, these forms exist in nature but they are not really similar to its mathematical representation. However, in common speech they are considered self-similar. It is important to remark that all these three different forms deal with recursivity, and all of them make allusion to infinity through the recursion of its shape repeated similarly in different scales.

---

24 | See Peitgen H.O. – Jürgens H. – Saupe D. 1992.

25 | Peitgen H.O. – Jürgens H. – Saupe D. 1992, p. 146.

|**Prop. IV, V, VI**| Recursion implies some inner dynamics. *Initiator* and *Generator* are both the essential conditions to follow a recursive formula that allows for the creation of an infinite space. For this reason, Mandelbrot tried to analyze chaotic phenomena through fractal objects. As noted in the chapter *Some Words About Chaos*, chaos is the result of dynamics; it occurs when the state of a system changes with time.[26] Therefore, chaos was defined as a science of process and not as a science of state. Aiming at analyzing chaotic movements, Mandelbrot used fractal objects and, through their recursivity, he was able to recognize some harmony between different scales. Some natural and non-natural objects present a self-similar structure and, in some of them, their dynamic process is not clearly manifested. Such is the case of a mountain or a tree, in that, apparently, their self-similar shape is not the result of the constant movement. In the case of the mountain, its self-similar structure is the consequence of erosion and telluric movements constantly produced over the course of millennia.[27]

|*Fig. 2.31*|

The structure of a mountain is the outcome of a simple process – plate tectonics, erosion, water – which generates a complex structure. Relatively small dynamics, over a great period of time, generate chaos. In the above image (Fig. 2.31), it is possible to observe a simulation of the dynamic process that simulates the formation of a mountain. As we can see, a simple triangle – a mathematical object that does not exist in nature – is transformed into a complex figure, which represents a mountain. In these five steps, we can recognize the long process of telluric movements that create the complex structure of a mountain, a structure that presents some self-similar characteristics. In the following image, it is possible to appreciate the self-similar form in the geometrical representation of a leaf (Fig. 2.32).

|*Fig. 2.32*|

Natural self-similar objects are the result of small repetitive dynamics and these continuous movements are imperceptible. Nevertheless, there are some non-natural self-similar forms that clearly manifest their dynamics. Such is the case of video-feedback phenomenon.

---

26 | See Stewart I. 1992.

27 | It is important to remember that those movements are chaotic; in consequence, they become a matter of study in fractal geometry.

Video feedback phenomenon was a matter of study in the eighties because it provided a readily available system useful for studying spatial and temporal dynamics. This phenomenon is the result of a moment in which the video camera frames its self-visual information on the monitor; in other words, the camera 'looks' at its own framed image.[28] Usually, video technology codifies optical information in electrical information then transfers them to the monitor. The movement of information from camera to monitor collapses when this movement starts to go round and round the camera-monitor loop, i.e. when some portion of the output signal is used as input.[29] In video feedback, the optical image on the monitor is converted by the camera into an electronic signal which is then converted by the monitor into an image on the screen. This image is converted into an electronic signal again *ad infinitum*. The continuous-time optical signal of the monitor collapses with the method of codification of the camera, which creates a set of *rasters* thirty times a second.

|*Fig. 2.33*|

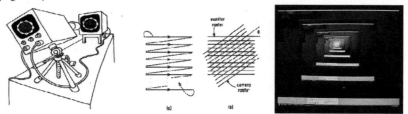

"Within each raster it spatially dissects the incoming picture into a number of horizontal scan lines. It then superimposes synchronizing pulses to the electronic signal representing the intensity variation along each scan line. This composite signal drives the monitor's electron beam to trace out in synchrony the raster on its phosphor screen and

---

28 | To note that, in his lectures in Bochum, Vilém Flusser shows his interest on the phenomena of reflection and speculation and their importance on philosophical thought since the classical period. These phenomena allow him to create an interesting analogy between the mirror and video technology, in which the creation of infinity through a specular effect becomes a useful tool aiming at analyzing nature by means of the conception of new spaces. However, Flusser highlights an important difference between the mirror and the video camera. He claims that the video monitor has some 'memory' (*Gedächtnis*), in consequence, the reflection phenomenon of the video monitor becomes a reflection of the point of view of another person. "Der Monitor beim Video hat ein Gedächtnis. Nicht nur ist der Monitor ein Spiegel, der die Seiten nicht umdreht, er ist ein Spiegel mit Gedächtnis. Was Sie im Monitor sehen, ist nicht Ihr eigener Blick, sondern der Blick der Kamera, des Kameramannes. Es ist ein Spiegel, der die Ansicht eines andern auf uns spiegelt." (Flusser V. 2008, p. 183.)

29 | See Crutchfield J.P. 1984.

so the image is reconstructed. The lens controls the amount of light, degree of spatial magnification, and focus, of the image represented to the camera."[30]

The evident dynamics on this phenomenon allowed some scientist during the eighties to study chaotic movements and attractors.[31] The dynamic of video feedback is a phenomenon that creates not only time-dependent behavior but also complex spatial patterns.[32] The space and time created, into infinity, through video feedback clearly shows a rich dynamic which generates – in real time – a self-similar object, an infinite structure created by means of the recursivity of a specular phenomenon.

|Prop. VIII, IX, X| As noted above, the recursive form always implies a generator element; in the straight line it was identified in the point, in the Koch curve it was the line, etc. *Initiator* and *Generator*, both in their nature allow for a successor and set in motion an infinite inner dynamic process that changes our knowledge of structure and our notion of infinity. A system that allows the operation $X + n$ allows for the creation of infinity. In these sorts of structures the dynamics are the essence. Continuous form implies generation and, in consequence – as claimed by Grassmann – it also implies some spatial notions defined as *Setzens* and *Verknüpfens*. Under this logic, infinity changes its sense. It is always potential but it is not defined by itself or by a 'limit' in a series; its definition can be recognized by a kind of law of order or continuity, which classifies the limits and transforms the series into a set (*ensemble*).[33]

|Prop. XI| An object placed in an infinite space – created in continuity by inner dynamics – changes the nature of the object. It becomes a part of an infinite set in eternal generation; its position (*Setzens*) and its relational-interaction (*Verknüpfens*) with the whole begin to make part of its natural condition, of its essence. This notion is clear in Leibniz's monadology. According to Leibniz, an object changes its character when it is placed in the space of constant an infinite movement; **the object becomes functional**.

In Leibniz's theory, the object is no longer defined by its essential form but by its functionality in the whole. This 'new kind of object' was recognized by Deleuze as an *objectil*.[34] An object is no longer an object when it is placed in a continuum,[35] i.e. its new status does not imply a spatial mold, a relationship of form to matter. The status of an *objectil* implies the notion of temporal modulation in which the continu-

---

30 | Crutchfield J.P. 1984, p. 192.

31 | Unbounded or divergent behavior can be interpreted as an attractor in infinity.

32 | See Crutchfield J.P. 1988.

33 | See Deleuze G. 1988.

34 | See Deleuze G. 1988.

35 | Deleuze recognized the condition of objectil as a modern conception of a technologic object. When the production of an object is placed in a continuum; i.e. when the production of material objects is organized by digital processes and no longer by deep-drawing.

ous variations of matter generate a continuous development of form.[36] According to Deleuze, in Leibniz's theory, the object is no longer essentialist; it becomes an *event* (*événement*).

An *objectil* cannot be interpreted as a point in space, it is a place, a position, a situs, and this transformation of object also imposes the radical transformation of subject. In Deleuze's words, the subject is no longer a sub-ject, it is a *"superject."*[37] Thus, the relationship between *objectil* and *superject* implies another notion, the notion of *point of view*.[38] When the object becomes an *objectil* – i.e. it follows a group of transformations – the subject becomes a *superject* – i.e. it becomes *point of view on a site*. The eternal movement of the object, its metamorphosis, transforms subject into *superject*, and the term of *superject* refers to the notion of *point of view* because it is a series of transformations to which the *objectil* is subordinated: it is a site. In other words, *point of view* is what allows the recognition of the passage from one form to another. The *superject* has a relationship with the infinite series of the *objectil*, and this relationship determines the *point of view, a situs*.[39] The *superject* is a witness of the *objectil's* dynamic, of its metamorphosis, i.e. of its passage from form to form.

|Prop. XII| The term metamorphosis denotes the link between forms, the passage from profile to another profile. **Thus, the superject, as a point of view, is an action of order.** It is the act that gives form to the event (the object), in order to understand its metamorphosis. As a consequence, the phenomena of metamorphosis and anamorphosis acquire extreme importance in Deleuze's thesis. If metamorphosis denotes the passage from form to form, anamorphosis, according to Deleuze, is the **act of taking form from the inform; it is the act of acquiring form.**[40]

The process of anamorphosis was understood as the fantastic and aberrant side of perspective. In Baltrušaitis words: "une perspective dépravée par une démonstration

---

36 | Deleuze G. 1988, p. 27.

37 | Deleuze G. 1988, p. 27.

38 | In this dynamic spatial organization the center does not refers to a point of view; it is the point of view that refers to the center. This substitution of point of view is highlighted in the substitution of geometry of a circle and sphere with the geometry of a cone. See Serres M. 1968.

39 | It is clear that the recursive form creates an eternal movement that generates the infinite structure of the whole. The whole, as an infinite structure, developed through folds. The central point posed an important discussion in the philosophical field. Is there a center in the infinity? According to Deleuze, this question was the central philosophical discussion during the seventeenth century. In fact, this question is strongly present in Leibniz's writings as well as in Pascal's ones. Serres and Deleuze found in the notion of *point of view* the solution to the question regarding of the center of infinity.

40 | According to Deleuze, the informal is not the negation of form; it is the form folded. "l'informel n'est pas négation de la forme: il pose la forme comme pliée, et n'existant que comme « paysage du mental », dans l'âme ou dans la tête, en hauteur ; il comprend donc aussi les plis immatériels." (Deleuze G. 1988, p. 50.)

logique de ses lois."[41] In Italy the process of anamorphosis became a matter of study. As quoted by Baltrušaitis, Dürer, in a letter to Pirkheimer, stated his interest in learning the technique. Therefore, Dürer traveled to Bologna aiming to learn "die kunst in geheimner Perspektive."[42]

|*Fig. 2.34*|

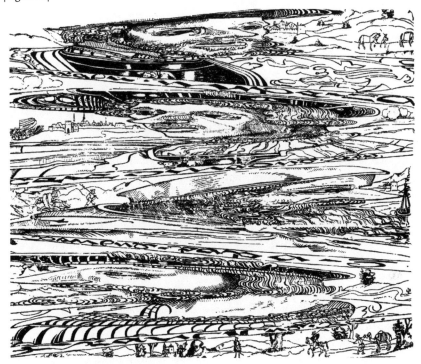

The interesting aspect of this technique, dating to the 11th century, is the appearing and disappearing effect that it generates. It is not a coincidence that Erhard Schön (1491-1542), a pupil of Dürer, entitled a work, (Fig. 2.34) realized by means of this technique, *Vexierbild* (paint with secret). When positioned in front of this piece, the beholder is unable to immediately interpret the representation. He must reach a predefined point of view in space. If viewed from one side, it is possible to perceive a transformation; the four trapezoid registers occupied by landscapes, animals and people, undergo a 'passage' from *in*form to form; four heads emerge from the frame.

---

41 | Baltrušaitis J. 1984, p. 5.

42 | In Italy, the process of deformation was perceived as a 'whim,' something funny for the artist. In opposition, North Europe interpreted this process as a dramatic tool of the painter, giving to the painter an extraordinary power. See Baltrušaitis J. 1984, p. 34.

|*Fig. 2.35*|

If the beholder observes this piece alternately from the left to the right side, he becomes aware of its 'transformations.' Four faces appear: Charles V, Ferdinand I, Pope Paul III and Francis I of France. In addition, from the correct point of view, the beholder can see Latin and German inscriptions which state the names of those depicted.

This work presents a high level of symbolism articulated in two dimensions, it is to say, the dimension in which landscapes, animals, and people are visible from a position in front of the work and the four faces, representing the pope and kings, which are visible from both lateral sides. Every anamorphic figure, visible from a precise point of view in space, in this case the face of an important personality, is placed within a scene that represents an important event in the life of the personality depicted by means of the anamorphosis' technique. Behind Charles V, a representation of a war scene; behind Ferdinand I, the Siege of Vienna (1529-1532); behind the Pope Paul III, God menacing a Turk and a war ship; behind François I, some oriental people and some camels representing his relationship with the Turks.[43] The narrative created by means of the superposition of dimensions generates the feeling of being in front of a magic representation.[44] The flat surface, i.e. the white canvas, undergoes a kind of 'fractalization' by acquiring a half dimension, like a dimension represented by a decimal number in which the possibility to recognize the forms, therein represented, is not allowed from all points of view in space. There is a kind of 'secret dimension' that can be perceived only if the subject admits its condition as *point of view* on an object.

Let us turn our attention to *The Ambassadors* (1533) by Hans Holbein the Younger (1498-1543), which is the most famous example of anamorphosis in painting (Fig. 2.36). This painting was made in England, where the artist lived since 1532. The two French ambassadors, Jean de Dinteville (1504-1565) and Georges de Selve (1509-1542) are represented in life size.[45] This wonderful oeuvre, rich in symbolism, required a particular installation.[46] The place that houses *The Ambassadors* should meet some particular requirements in order to make the whole pictorial composition readable. The painting was installed in the Castle of Polisy in a big room and was placed in front of one door and next to another. The painting was placed at the bottom of the

---

43 | See Baltrušaitis J. 1984.

44 | The anamorphosis and the *trompe l'oeil* borrow the same order of principles: fake proportions and the manipulation of reality.

45 | See Ferrier J.L. 1977.

46 | In order to get a deeper analysis of the piece, I recommended Baltrušaitis J. 1984. Of special note is the chapter *Les Ambassadeurs de Holbein*.

wall, slightly above the floor. Each door corresponded to the point of view required for 'creating' the form of both dimensions displayed on the canvas.[47] The way to interact with this painting clearly shows a different rapport between object and subject, thus, creating, in this specific case, a special narrative, a *mise en scène*. In fact, the special installation required by *The Ambassadors* divides its appreciation into two scenes:

|*Fig. 2.36*|

The first scene corresponds to the moment in which the viewer enters the room through the door located in front of the painting. In this scene the beholder is in front of a normal perspective pictorial composition – almost a *trompe l'oeil*. He can examine the symbolism in the oeuvre, the colors and the characters. As the beholder approaches, the white 'smudge' at the bottom of the image becomes more unrecognizable; the *inform* is present, the object, foreign to this point of view, becomes more abstract. At this moment the second scene begins.

He leaves the room in the direction of the side arranged in advance by the installation of the painting. Then, as he is approaching the door, he gives a look back to the inform object represented on the canvas. At this point in space, the beholder experiences a tunnel-vision which causes the scene of the ambassadors to disappear and

47 | See Panofsky E. 1954.

makes the 'smudge' appear, clearly represented and recognizable from this side, as a skull, a *memento mori* indicating the end.[48]

|*Fig. 2.37*|

In the anamorphosis, the *point of view* extracts a form from chaos. It is not a coincidence that there was an interest in this technique during the Baroque. Both, the notion of point of view as the center of infinity and the relation between *objectil* and *superject* had certainly influenced the interest in anamorphosis techniques during the seventeenth century. The anamorphosis materializes the transformation of both the object in *objectil* and the subject in *superject*. As noted above, between the variation and the *point of view* there is an essential relationship; every point of view is a *point of view* on a transformation. It is not the point of view that varies with the subject; it is, rather, the condition under which the subject grabs a variation (metamorphosis) or 'something,' which equals X (anamorphosis).[49] Further, it does not mean that there is a variation of truth generated by the subject, rather it is the condition under which the truth of one variation of the subject (metamorphosis) appears. According to Deleuze, it is precisely the idea of perspective during the Baroque, where the *point of view* on a variation replaces the center of one figure or spatial configuration.[50]

---

48 | See Baltrušaitis J. 1984.

49 | See Deleuze G. 1988.

50 | Deleuze explains this concept by using the famous example of cone, where the point of view is placed at its tip. In fact, from the point of the cone one can describe the circle, the ellipsis, the parable, the hyperbole, even the straight line and the point. Deleuze identifies the cone as an *objectil*, which describes (*qui decline*) a family of curves. Deleuze G. 1988, p. 29.

In Serres' words, it is "une architecture de la vision."[51]

The geometric organization of *The Ambassadors* allows us to start with a deep analysis of the *mise en abyme*. As we will see, the *mise en abyme* might also derive from a reflection phenomenon, which is also present in *The Ambassadors*. The sensation of the 'double,' highlighted by Baltrušaitis in the presence of the two dimensions analyzed above in Holbein's painting, is described as follows: "C'est comme s'il y avait non pas une, mais deux compositions, chacune avec sont point de vue, juxtaposées dans le même cadre."[52] By combining perspective and anamorphosis, the special organization of *The Ambassadors* splits the whole composition into two dimensions. As claimed by Hallyn, this piece spreads out two faces to the beholder. On the one hand, the first face corresponds to classic perspective, while the lateral point of view, on the other hand, corresponds to anamorphosis. By means of anamorphosis, the beholder is also divided through an asymmetric split that defies ordinary observation.[53] The simultaneity of these two different perspectives dissociates the point of view. In *The Ambassadors*, the skull, painted by means of the anamorphisis technique, occupies just a little part of the whole. It is positioned in another representation, this composed by means of another geometry. Hence, the skull is placed in *abyme*. It is a narration within a narration, a painting within a painting, a fold within a fold. *Mise en abyme* always splits the oeuvre in which it is contained. It creates a disorder in the unity of the systematic spatial organization and constructs an 'adding set' (*ensemble agrégatif*) of two different spaces which generate discontinuity, rupture, tear.[54]

---

51 | The conception of the point of view as a center allows Deleuze to analyze the event (object) as *One* in opposition to *Many*. According to Deleuze, chaos does not exist, it is just an abstraction; it is our impossibility to assimilate the point of view that creates the harmonic interaction between *objectil* and *superject*. Thus, he recognizes chaos as "*pure Many*" or "pure diversité disjunctive." The event, the object, is the opposite of chaos because it is something; it is a "*One.*" In this analysis, Deleuze accepts some interpretation of the notion of chaos in Leibniz's works. Form a cosmologic point of view, according to Leibniz, chaos is a set of possibilities, i.e. all the individual essences trying to exist on their own. From a physical point of view, chaos would be endless darkness. From a psychic point of view, chaos would be all possible perceptions together, a blackout.

52 | Baltrušaitis J. 1969, p. 104.

53 | Hallyn F. 1980a, p. 167.

54 | See Hallyn F. 1980b.

2.5 Mise en Abyme: Blazon Into Blazon

|Prop. VIII, IX, XIII| A recursive space can sometimes imply self-similarity, which is manifested in nature and in expressive arts. André Gide called this phenomenon of recursion in narrative arts '*le procédé du Blason*.'[1] The process consists of placing into an 'abyss' (*en abyme*)[2] a subject into another. It is the case of some paintings by Memling, Quenting Matsys and, the most famous, *Las Meninas* by Velásquez and *The Arnolfini Portrait* by Van Eyck. In literature, this phenomenon was identified by Gide in *Hamlet*, Wilhelm Meister and, of course, in his works, e.g. *Cahiers d'André Walter, Le traité du Narcise* and *La tentative amoureuse*.[3]

In order to better understand the process of 'placing something *en abyme*' it is important to spend some time going over the art of heraldry.

Considered as an archeological science, and still present in many European flags, stamps, coins and public monuments, heraldry is first made reference to starting in the eleventh[4] century.[5] Its long tradition makes heraldry an important tool for historians; it was called by Gérard de Nerval "the key of French history."[6]

---

1 | In heraldry's language, the notion of blazon into blazon is described as 'on the whole.' When this figure of blazon into blazon 'on the whole' creates a third level, the process is called 'on the whole of the whole.' Foras defined this process in his dictionary as: "*Sur le tout. – Se dit d'un écusson mis en cœur ou en abîme sur un écu contenant deux ou quatre ou plus grand nombre de quartiers.*" And for 'on the whole of the whole' Foras write: "*Sur le tout du tout. – Se dit d'un écusson placé sur celui qui est déjà sur le tout. Souvent ces deux écussons sont eux-mêmes écartelés ou partis.*" (Foras (de) A. 1883, p. 408.)

2 | It should be considered that the word can be writen in three different forms; "*en abyme*", "*en abysme*" and "*en abîme*". The last one is not so common.

3 | See Gide A. 1951.

4 | According to Van D'Elden, the evidence of heraldry before the twelfth century is recognized as "preheraldic." Van D'Elden S.C. 1976, p. 8.

5 | See Sorval (de) G. 1981.

6 | The origins of heraldry are not certain. Galdbreath suggests three possibilities: the derivation of arms from family and city signs, the adoption of arms through the Crusaders from the Orient or a derivation of Germanic runes (see Galbreath D.L. 1948.) The presence of some profane subjects, such as Mercury's serpent, Neptune's trident, Apollo's lyre, shield and helmets of the Egyptians and coins of Greek city-states in some coast of Arms, has made some scholars suppose that its origins could be linked to antiquity. These similar systems are not considered Armory because they "died away without posterity or traceable connexion (sic) with the heraldry of the Middle Ages." (Wagner A. R. 1939, p. 14.)

|*Fig. 2.38*|

As noted by Sorval, the first stylized graphics in heraldry were directly influenced by eastern Asian cultures, the Persian and the Byzantines. It is during the Crusades that these decorative themes began to be strongly present in heraldry. Then, the graphics of this art underwent the influence of Gothic art, of the Renaissance, etc. It is possible to see some transformations during these periods but, indeed, the meaning and expressions remain the same, e.g. the animals keep the same functions and attitude, always aggressive, highlighting claws, tongues and tails.[7] Lions seem to be flames; there are bicephalous eagles with arabesques tails, etc.[8]

Who had a blazon and how were these mysterious objects created?

The first condition to have a blazon was to belong to any estate of arms. Nevertheless, the blazon was a conquest. It was possible to acquire one's own blazon when proclaimed knight. When somebody receives a blazon, he obtains the pre-established blazon of arms to which the recipient belongs, it is to say, when somebody receives a blazon, he has the chance to insert his personal emblem into the blazon of his lineage. Over time, these modify the totality of the emblem, creating a recursive space, which represents linearly the evolution of a family, fiefdom, etc. Even if the emblem remains a personal[9] object, it enters into a changing process that creates infinite links with other families, fiefdoms and communities.[10] However, the spatial organization of the blazon was not an anarchic composition. According to Fox-Davies, armory is a science which dictates "the rules and laws that governed the use, display, meaning and knowledge of the pictured signs and emblems appertaining to shield, helmet or banner."[11] Some rules – almost a grammar – governed the personal adds into the emblem.[12] The

---

7 | See Franklyn J. – Tanner J. 1970.

8 | See Sorval G. 1981.

9 | It is possible to recognize these personal modifications in the blazons of French kings. In fact, Louis XII of France (1462-1515) created a blazon in which a porcupine bears the royal arms. During the reign of Francis I of France (1449-1547), king from 1515 until his death, a salamander bore the royal arms.

10 | See Sorval G. 1981.

11 | Fox-Davies A.C. 2006, p. 1.

12 | The colors were an important source of meaning in heraldry. An important study on heraldry is contained in the work of M. Antoine Court de Gébelin, within he analyzes the art of heraldry by dividing it into three parts: "Dans la premier Partie nous traiterons des Symboles Armoriaux en général, de leur origine, de leur droit, & en particulier du droit de Bouclier, du rapport de ces Symboles avec leur objet, &c. Dans la deuxiéme, des couleurs de ces Symboles, du droit d'Enseignes sur lesquelles elles se plaçoeint, des noms & de l'origine de ces couleurs, de leurs rapports avec leurs objects, sur-tout des

Royal Art dictated the norms that presided over the changes in the blazon and they were accepted by a superior authority, which varied on the basis of the field, for example family blazon, royal blazon, fief blazon. In England, heraldry was regulated by visitation. There were tours of inspections organized by officers of arms.[13] Thus, when the emblem was authenticated, it covered almost an institutional role. That is why it was something assumed and imposed respect. It is important to remember that the authenticated blazon was seen as a gift from heaven.[14] Blazons connoted knowledge, and they were also perceived as a language.[15] Its utility did not remain in the battle camp as an identifying emblem for the different armies at war. The personal dimension acquired by the emblem gave it a narrative function useful in relating the past and present of the owner, his ambitions, his ideas, and his feats. Thus, its importance was incommensurable. The relationship between a knight and his emblems was very close; a knight honored his arms, and an important arm brought honor to its bearer. As noted by Zips, the description of arms included the formula "als (sam) er (es) lebte" indicating the close relation between the bearer and his arm.[16]

It is possible to posit that a blazon develops a diegesis.[17] The changes or additions relate important events in the life of a knight, fiefdom or family. A blazon allows the beholder to identify important events in the life of the bearer of the blazon, permitting also important connections between historical texts and transformations into the emblem. Blazons relate historical events, myths and legends – or create them – by using a recursive form on a flat surface. Consider for instance, Wilfred the Hairy's case (?-897) quoted by Court de Gébelin.

Héraux qui en connoissoient. Dans la troisiéme, des Symboles relativement aux Monnoies, & en particulier du droit des Monnoies, de la nature des objects représentés sur les Monnoies antérieurs aux Rois Grecs & aux Empereurs Romains ; quand & comment on changea ces objets ; & de quelques Monnoies dont jusques ici on n'avoit pu par cette raison découvrir le Pays ou le Peuple auquel elles appartenoient." (Court de Gébelin 1782, p. 128.)

13 | See Van D'Elden S.C. 1976.

14 | Sorval G. 1981, p. 50.

15 | It is interesting to quote Sorval when he explains the linguistic character of the blazon: "Et de même que dans toute langue les signes graphiques constituant des mots son symboliques ou issus de symboles anciens, l'écriture héraldique se présente comme une calligraphie symbolique que l'on peut rapprocher des idéogrammes chinois ou des hiéroglyphes égyptiens." (Sorval G. 1981, p. 71.)

16 | Quoted by Van D'Elden S.C. 1976, p. 9.

17 | According to Court de Gébelin, there are some arms that were commonly called *Armes parlantes*. They were commonly Arms relative to people or fiefs.

|Fig. 2.39|

"Après la bataille de Saucour, au IXᵉ siècle, gagnée par Louis III sur les Normans, ce prince alla visiter, dit-on, Wiffrey *le Velu*, Comte de Barcelonne, qui avoit été blessé dans le combat : Louis, charmé de sa valeur ; de ses services, de ses vertus, l'assura de sa reconnoissance : le Comte se borna à lui demander des armes qui fissent connoître à la postérité ce qui venoit de se passer. A l'instant, le Roi trempe le doigt dans le sang de ses plaies, en trace quatre traits en forme de pals sur l'Ecu du Comte, qui étoit d'or, & lui dit, *Comte, ce seront ici désormais vos armes* : de-là, celles des Comtes de Barcelonne, & ensuite des Rois D'arragon, qui sont d'*or à quatre pals de gueules*. C'est à ce Wiffrey que commence la Génélogie héréditaire des Comtes de Barcelonne, & que remonte ainsi les Armoires de cette Province."[18]

The geometrical composition of the blazon is full of symbolism, indeed, the blazon was seen as the union between heaven and earth, a sacred space where a divine geometry could write the essence of a 'noble man,' a 'warrior of God.'[19] The virgin surface of the blazon was denoted as "table d'attente" or 'plan of manifestation' alluding to the sacred space above which the Holy Ghost glided at the beginning of the universe. In that virgin space, which makes allusion to the space where God creates all things, there is the possibility to express and to place a, theoretically, infinite number of geometrical figures and add new ones; this practice is called *marshalling*. In heraldry, recursivity is possible because the rules of blazons compose a space where new forms can be added or placed inside the original emblem; emblem into emblem, blazon into blazon.[20]

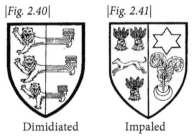

|Fig. 2.40| *|Fig. 2.41|*

Dimidiated   Impaled

---

18 | Court de Gébelin A. 1782, p. 130.

19 | See Sorval G. 1981.

20 | One of the methods used to divide the field is known as *party per fess*. It divides the field into halves by means of a horizontal division. Its opposite is known as *party per pale*, which divides the field into halves by using a vertical line. *Party per bend* and *party per bend sinister* divide the field by means of a diagonal line. *Party per salitre* is a division that partitions the field into four parts by using two diagonal lines like an X. See Fox-Davies A.C. 2006.

In armory there are many methods for adding new emblems, consider for instance, *quartering,*[21] *dimidiating,*[22] *impaling.*[23] As noted above, inheritance of emblems, division, modification and additions, cannot create an anarchic spatial organization. The purpose of these divisions is to express alliances, inheritances, occupations, etc.

The *dimidiated* method allows for the joining of two coats of arms. This method splits the coat down the middle; consequently, the coats that compose the new one lose half their sides. The *impaled* method allows the union of coats by keeping the entirety of each piece of the union. This technique keeps both coats intact by positioning them into a half space. The method of *quartering* allows for the joining of several coats of arms in a single escutcheon. *Quartering* implies the division of the escutcheon into equal parts. The first step of this technique consists of dividing a single escutcheon into four equal parts – *party per cross.*[24] One example of a *party per cross* is the coat of arms of the United Kingdom, (without the escutcheon of Hanover), in which England is repeated in the first and fourth quadrants and Scotland and Ireland occupy the second and third spots, respectively (see Fig. 2.42).

|*Fig. 2.42*|

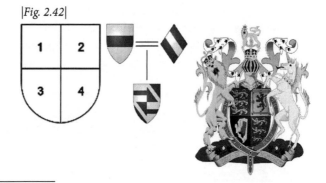

---

21 | The Encyclopaedic Dictionary of Heraldry of Franklyn and Tanner states, under *Quarterly*, "When blazoned without a specific fied number, '~ of four' is understood which is produced by a combination of party per pale with party per fess." (Franklyn J. – Tanner J. 1970, p. 270.)

22 | The Encyclopaedic Dictionary of Heraldry of Franklyn and Tanner states, under *Dimidiation*, "a primitive method of marshalling whereby the dexter half of the husband's shield (cut per pale) was displayed on one shield with the sinister half of the wife's. This method led to deceptive combinations, particularly when both fields were of the same colour; and also to the apparent creation of some very incongruous mixtures." (Franklyn J. – Tanner J. 1970, p. 106.)

23 | The Encyclopaedic Dictionary of Heraldry of Franklyn and Tanner states, under *Impalement*, "the marshalling of two coats of arms upon one shield palewise: most commonly employed in marital achievement when the arms of the husband are compressed into dexter half and those of the wife into sinister half of the combined display." (Franklyn J. – Tanner J. 1970, p. 180.)

24 | See Neubecker O. 1976.

In quartering, there is no limit in the number of division allowed. If a family possesses too many emblems, they are obliged to use just those that they consider the more significant.

|*Fig. 2.43*|

However, there are some coats of arms that present more than seven hundred quarterings. Such is the case of the emblem of the Temple-Nugent-Brydges-Chandos-Grenville family, which possesses 719 heraldic quarterings (Fig. 2.43). The method of *quartering* is a method that materializes the process of placing one image inside another, of creating – or alluding to – a space able to contain information *ad infinitum*, '*Blason dans le blason*'. In such a space, the subject suffers an inner duplication. In other words, there is a fold of the image inside itself.[25] Although, this method does not create a self-similar phenomenon; it generates some relations of similarity inside the whole.

In heraldry, the *abyme* or *fess-point* means the exact center of an escutcheon. 'To place something in abyme' means to depict something in the middle of the shield.[26]

|*Fig. 2.44*|

If we observe the bearing of King George III, we can see the arms of England, Scotland and Ireland (Fig. 2.44). The escutcheon of Hanover is in abyme, on which the crown of Charlemagne is also in abyme.

---

25 | It is interesting to note the importance of heraldry in the Middle Ages by quoting Van D'Elden in her analysis of the origin and symbolism of heraldry: "In the Middle Ages heraldry maintained an all encompassing position touching upon virtually every element of society. Its importance was not questioned; its significance was understood by all. Evidence of heraldry appear on the battlefield, at tournaments, on armor, weapons, shields, and flags, on the horses' bardings, on tents, in the crest, badge, and device, in the livery, in the battle cry, in military, ecclesiastical, and domestic architecture, on tapestries, illuminations, seals, jewelry, and clothing. A knowledge of heraldry formed part of a gentleman's education, and was recognized by the people in popular political songs." (Van D'Elden S.C. 1976, p. 6.)

26 | In a French dictionary of blazon, the word 'abyme' is defined as: "Abîme. – C'est le Coeur de l'écu. On dit qu'une figure est en abîme quand elle est avec d'autres figures au milieu de l'écu, mais sans toucher aucune de ces figures." (Foras de A. 1883, p. 6.)

Heraldry influenced Gide's concept of *mise en abyme*.[27] Gide's *Journal* displays the admiration of the author for the '*procédé du blazon*.' Nevertheless, his admiration for this process was focused on the 'reflection effect' to which it alludes.

"J'aime assez qu'en une œuvre d'art on retrouve ainsi transposé, à l'échelle des personnages, le sujet même de cette ouvre. Rien ne l'éclaire mieux et n'établit plus sûrement toutes les proportions de l'ensemble."[28]

The utility of the oeuvre 'being placed in *abyme*' is to manifest and to facilitate the intelligibility of its formal structure.[29] The *mise en abyme*, by means of a phenomenon of reflection, means the establishment of a phenomenon of similarity between the whole image and the part contained within. In addition, in Gide's quotation, it is possible to remark that his interest was not only on the mere encased image, or narrative, within the whole, but also on the specular phenomenon created by this process. In other words, he was more interested by self-similarity as narrative tool that informs the viewer, or reader, about the meaning of the whole and about the structure of the image, than by either the recursivity of this phenomenon and its capacity to contain an infinite amount of information upon a surface. The proceeding of depicting an object within itself was a very common practice in medieval texts and paintings. In some medieval texts it is possible to see representations of a book, which represents the book that contains it. In the next figure below (Fig. 2.45) we can see a 'self-portrait' of the scribe who placed the book in *abyme* that contains the image.[30]

|*Fig. 2.45*|

From this image arises the question about resemblance in *mise en abyme*. According to Whatling, who mentions this image as an example of resemblance in the process of *mise en abyme*, "there is a continuum of sorts, ranging from the purely generic (a type of object) to the very particular (a specific physical instance of that type which contains its own image.)"[31] Both possibilities allow the hypothesis that the object contained might reveal clues about the nature of the thing that contains it.

---

27 | As noted by Dällenbach, Gide's passion in heraldry is attested too by the correspondence with Paul Valéry in a letter dated the 15th November 1891, where Gide claims: "Je lis une plaquette de Hello sur le style. Et j'étudie le Blason ! C'est admirable. Jamais je n'avais regardé ça." (Dällenbach L. 1977, p. 17.)

28 | Gide A. 1951, p. 41.

29 | See Dällenbach L. 1977.

30 | Note that in this case, recognized as a case of *mise en abyme*, there is a distortion of the meaning of *mise en abyme* of heraldry.

31 | Whatling S. 2009, p. 4.

This idea shows some analogies with Leibniz's theory of monads and its connections with the whole. It also generates a debate about the relationship between Microcosm and Macrocosm.

Whatling also analyzes another example of *mise en abyme* that does not show self-similar characteristics. By analyzing this mosaic, (Fig. 2.46) Whatling highlights a double *mise en abyme*. The mosaic, placed in the southwestern entrance of Hagia Sophia in Istanbul, places in *abyme* both, Hagia Sophia itself and the city that houses the

mosaic. The figure to the left side is Justinian I offering Hagia Sophia to the Virgin. To the right side, Constantine the Great is offering the city of Istanbul.[32] From heraldry's notion of *abyme*, which describes just the center of the escutcheon, to the notion of *abyme* in these last examples, dating to the Middle Ages, the question of similarity and self-similarity arises. In both cases, the allusion to a space where huge quantities of information can be placed is clear. Both are structures that create an encased universe, like that described by Leibniz, and both are also narrative tools that deal with the notion of infinity by means of the creation of recursive spaces.

Mise en abyme is a process that imposes some reflection on the relationship between microcosms and macrocosms and its utility to human cognition. Some thoughts about microcosms can be useful too for understanding the role of similarity in the process of placing something in *abyme*.[33] According to Foucault, a microcosm is a theme (*thème*), the apparition of which can be explained inside a pattern (*schème*) of thought dominated by the research of similarity.[34] In this way, Foucault gives to microcosm the status of 'category of thought' (*catégorie de pensée*), a category that can be applied on all natural ambits. In Foucault's words:

"Comme *catégorie de pensée,* elle applique à tous les domaines de la nature le jeu des ressemblances redoublées; elle garantit à l'investigation que chaque chose trouvera sur une plus grande échelle son miroir et son assurance macrososmique ; elle affirme en retour que l'ordre visible des sphères les plus hautes viendra se mirer dans la profondeur plus sombre de la terre."[35]

---

32 | The same practice of placing the city into the city was performing by the Panoramas in the eighteenth century. See the chapter *The Panorama: An Example of 'Gigantomanie des Mediums'.*

33 | Whatling S. 2009, p. 4.

34 | See Foucault M. 1966. Of special note is chapter II, "*La prose du monde.*"

35 | Foucault M. 1966, p. 46.

Through Foucault's words it is possible to understand that the degree of *catégorie de pensée*, given by Foucault to microcosm, recalls a mirror phenomenon. Indeed, under this logic, **the world is an infinite mirror of itself.**[36]

"Jusqu'à la fin du XVIe siècle, la ressemblance a joué un rôle bâtisseur dans le savoir de la culture occidentale. C'est elle qui a conduit pour une grande part l'exégèse et l'interprétation des textes; c'est elle qui a organisé le jeu des symboles, permis la connaissance des choses visibles et invisibles, guidé l'art de les représenter. Le monde s'enroulait sur lui-même : la terre répétant dans le ciel, les visages se mirant dans les étoiles, et l'herbe enveloppant dans ses tiges les secrets qui servaient à l'homme. La peinture imitait l'espace. Et la représentation – qu'elle fût fête ou savoir – se donnait comme répétition : théâtre de la vie ou miroir du monde, c'était là le titre de tout langage, sa manière de s'annoncer et de formuler son droit à parler."[37]

Foucault conceived of the world as something covered by signs, which humankind must decipher, and these signs present some resemblances and some affinities, that is, the signs become forms of similarity. Hence, according to Foucault, knowledge means interpretation, and interpretation is based on exterior correspondences. Following this framework, humankind discovers everything by means of both signs and exterior correspondences, by means of similarity between the scales.[38] The described relationship between the macro- and microcosms join Poincaré in his idea of human conception of natural simplicity, thanks to which the sciences can analyze the complexity of nature. As noted in the chapter *Fractus, Fracta, Fractum*, Poincaré recognizes in the abridged number of the classification of chemical substances the possibility to analyze a huge quantity of substances present in nature. He does not understand this 'simplicity of nature' as a tool useful for classifying natural substances in order to make them 'readable' by human cognition. In his words, it is possible to recognize a specular phenomenon that creates an indispensable relationship between scales; the small quantity of chemical substances allows humankind to create a rapport with the infinity of nature. The specular phenomenon highlighted by Poincaré represents the possibility to create an infinite set by using a recursive form. Dällenbach recognized the same character in Gide's process; the creation of an infinite set by means of a recursive form created through a specular phenomenon.

---

36 | See Hallyn F. 1980b.

37 | Foucault M. 1966, p. 32.

38 | Therefore, Foucault claims that divination is in total part of knowledge because the interpretation of signs does not mean to discover hidden things since the phenomenon of resemblance. "C'est pourquoi les plantes qui représentent la tête, ou les yeux, ou le coeur, ou le foie auront efficacité sur un organe." (Foucault M. 1966, p. 48.)

Resemblances in the relationship between micro and macrocosmos can be generic or very particular, such as in the case of the exercise of the process of *mise en abyme*;[39] which fascinated Gide. His interest was focused upon the mirror effect, "*le récit spécu-laire.*" Through his *Journal*, one can note his curiosity in the 'split phenomenon' created by means of a mirror and then transported into his narrative structure.

"J'écris sur ce petit meuble d'Anna Shackleton qui, rue de Commailles, se trouvait dans ma chambre. C'était là que je travaillais ; je l'aimais, parce que dans la double glace du secrétaire, au-dessus de la tablette où j'écrivais, je me voyais écrire ; entre chaque phrase je me regardais ; mon image me parlait, m'écoutait, me tenait compagnie, me maintenait en état de ferveur."[40]

The 'specularization' of Gide's writing is the product of the specularization of his image. By writing, Gide sees himself as a writer; he asserts "Je me voyais écrire." This feeling is reflected in his work, especially in *La tentative amoureuse* (1893). In this work he deals with the relationship of a person to fiction.

"J'ai voulu indiquer, dans cette *Tentative amoureuse*, l'influence du livre sur celui qui l'écrit, et pendant cette écriture même. Car en sortant de nous, il nous change, il modifie la marche de notre vie ; comme l'on voit en physique ces vases mobiles suspendus, pleins de liquide, recevoir une impulsion, lorsqu'ils se vident, dans le sens opposé à celui de l'écoulement du liquide qu'ils contiennent. Nos actes ont sur nous une rétroaction. « Nos actions agissent sur nous autant que nous agissons sur elles », dit Georges Eliot."[41]

This established relationship between the person and fiction is exemplified in Gide's work *La tentative*, in the role of narrator attributed to a character in the fiction. For this reason, he creates a specular relationship between the '*je*' (I) and the '*lui*' (He) in

---

39 | As noted above, the process of *mis en abyme* creates different sorts of links between the objects, which are contained in the oeuvre. They can be generic (i.e. those that deals with the type of object, as is the case of the scribe's image mentioned above), or very particular and deal with a specific physical instance of that type which contains its own image (the case of Hagia Sophia's mosaic). They can be also strictly self-similar. Whatling analyzes these distinctions, appealing to the medieval concepts of *quidditas* and *haeccaetas*. The first term (quiddity form the Latin *quidditas*) was, in fact, a term to denote the essence of an object, translated literally in English whatness or what it is. It was useful in describing the properties of a particular substance, properties shared with other substances of its kind. This term was contrasted by haecceity, translated literally into English as this-ness. This denoted positive characteristics and always individuals of a substance. See Whatling S. 2009.

40 | Gide A. 1951, p. 252.

41 | Gide A. 1951, p. 40.

the piece. Dällenbach described this particular relationship as "rapports of rapports." In this rapport, the relationship between the narrator N with his narration R is homologous with that between the character-narrator n with his narration r.[42] According to Dällenbach, it is precisely this particular relationship that marks the difference with the other narrative process initiated by *One Thousand and One Nights* and used by *Le Roman comique* (1651-1657) as well as by the *Picaresque Novel*. In Gide's process, it is not a narration that contains narrations, like in *One Thousand and One Nights*. Gide constructs a narrative structure in which the second narrative reflects the first one. According to Dällenbach, the reflection created by the second narrative is needed in order to produce a retroaction, which creates the analogy between the situation of the character and that of the narrator.[43] This phenomenon generates a notable effect of similarity in Gide's work.[44] This specular effect is in fact the deeper difference and motive of agitated discussions, between Gide's *procédé du Blason*, and the *mise en abyme* in heraldry. As we have seen, heraldry does not create any specularization of the work. Heraldry generates a recursive space, where huge quantities of information can be contained. Hence, Gide's *procédé du Blason* was in fact a metaphor of the meaning of *abyme* in the art of heraldry.[45] Both methods recall the idea of infinity. Nevertheless, we can see that the metaphor of blazon into blazon, in Gide's process, was distorted.[46] Dällenbach identifies the source of this problem as the confusion created between the word *abyme*, a *terminus technicus*, and its metaphysical meaning which recalls more the mathematical self-similar structures, or video feedback phenomenon, than the action of 'placing something into the center' or placing the oeuvre into the oeuvre, for instance, the story within the story in Fellini's *8 1/2* (1963) or *One Thousand and One Nights*.[47]

---

42 | Dällenbach L. 1977, p. 30.

43 | See Dällenbach L. 1977.

44 | This theory, proposed by Dällenbach, was criticized by Angelet C. in « JOURNAL » ET « TENTATIVE AMOUREUSE ». The author argues that Gide's blazon process does not correspond to a specular phenomenon like that proposed by Dällenbach. The rapport explained by Dällenbach, in Angelet's thoughts was wrong because: "Il se trouve que le rapport établi par l'auteur n'est pas d'un récit majeur à un récit mineur, mais d'une fiction à une réalité ou, pour parler comme Gide, d'une réalité a une matérialité." (Angelet C. 1980, p. 16.) According to Angelet, in Gide's œuvre there is not a specular phenomenon rather the first subject – e.g. in *La Tentative Amoureuse* – is an "avatar" of the man who writes the story.

45 | See Dällenbach L. 1977.

46 | See Dällenbach L. 1977, especially *"Un Héritage critique."*

47 | One can find some analogies between the process analyzed by Dällenbach as *'récit speculaire'* and that analyzed by Genette, in his oeuvre *Palimpsestes* (1982), known as *'l'autopastiche'*, the example of which was found by Genette in *La recherché* by Proust. See Genette G. 1982, especially XXI.

In the *mise en abyme's* concept there is the same problem of the mathematical and natural spirals (see *Self-Similarity as a Narrative Tool*); the same self-similarity in nature and *strict self-similarity* of fractals. There is a big difference between placing something into *abyme*, in its real meaning, i.e. to place something into the center, and to reflect something by means of a specular phenomenon, duplicating it. The former creates an infinite place by means of a recursive formula of X + n which does not imply self-similarity, on the contrary, the latter phenomenon, by means of a specular phenomenon, creates a recursive formula of X + x where x represents a double, a reflection, implying self-similarity. Without a doubt, these two different methods are a source of infinity and both are important phenomena that are always present in our mediated relationship with nature.

It is interesting to see how Dällenbach analyzes different process like parallel mirrors, mathematic infinity, vertigo, Leibniz's theory of encased universes, monads, macrocosm-microcosm and the Matryoshka-doll effect. The author divides them into some groups, all different phenomena which are known as *mise en abyme*:

- "*Simple*" *reflection*, which is represented by the phenomena of blazon into blazon, microcosm and monad. Its examples in literature are *Ulysses* and *Un amour de Swan*.
- *Reflection until infinity* is also symbolized by monads and, especially, by its mathematical reference, the infinity of parallel mirrors, the box of *Quaker Oats*. As a literary example Dällenbach gives Huxley.[48]

There is in fact a generalization of the process of *mise en abyme* due to the metaphor *speculaire*, which joins the heraldry form. For this reason, Dällenbach highlights the existing differences by calling Gide's process 'specular.'

In conclusion, *Mise en abyme* is a term that groups many different phenomena – from the simple *reduplication* to *reduplication into infinity* – dealing always with the concept of reflection, recursion, and, logically, infinity.

"Je dois mon premier contact précis avec la notion d'infini à une boîte de cacao de marque hollandaise, matière première de mes petits déjeuners. L'un des côtés de cette boîte était orné d'une image représentant une paysanne en coiffe de dentelle qui tenait dans sa main gauche une boîte identique, orné de la même image, et, rose et fraîche, la montrait en souriant. Je demeurais saisi d'une espèce de vertige en imaginant cette infinie série d'une identique image reproduisant une nombre illimité de fois la même jeune Hollandaise qui, théoriquement rapetissé de plus en plus sans jamais disparaître, me regardait d'un air moqueur et me faisait voir sa propre effigie peinte sur une boîte de cacao identique à celle sur la quelle elle-même était peinte. Je ne suis pas éloigné de croire qu'il se mêlait à cette première notion de l'infini, acquise vers l'âge de dix ans (?), un élément d'ordre assez trouble : caractère hallucinant et proprement insaisissable

---

48 | Dällenbach L. 1977, p. 38.

de la jeune Hollandaise, répété à l'infini comme peuvent être indéfiniment multipliées, au moyen des jeux de glace d'un boudoir savamment agencé, les visions libertines."[49]

|*Fig. 2.47*|

Some authors recognize *mise en abyme* in similarity, self-similarity, to place in *abyme* – in the meaning of heraldry process – to include a narration within a narration, etc. Indeed, this vast concept represents just a space governed by a recursive form that generates a space where the objects contained within establish a special relationship between them, a relationship that displays some phenomena of similarity. In popular speech, Leibniz's theory can be understood as *mise en abyme* because it recognizes an encased world that continues on into infinity, a macro world that contains a micro world that contains a micro world etc. It is a phenomenon that recalls some self-similar shapes, e.g. a Matryoshka-doll, which is identified as both the simple reflection and the reflection into infinity, phenomena highlighted by Dällenbach.[50] As noted by Dällenbach "(...)la mise en abyme est une réalité structurée malgré la variété et l'accidentalité apparente de ses manifestations effectives."[51]

Mise en abyme responds to many examples that impede its understanding. However, the essence of this concept can be identified in the character shared by these different phenomena, i.e. recursivity. The matter of this unclear concept is recursion as a means of creating, or imagining, an infinite space, a space where the infinity of nature – of the universe – can be contained in order to become an indispensable narrative tool. Furthermore, *mise en abyme* is a narrative instrument that changes the classical notion of plot, in which the plot has a beginning and end. This last particularity opposes plot to real world. *Mise en abyme* creates a narrative in which its recursive form generates a kind of life-without-end.[52]

---

49 | Leiris M. 1946, p. 37.

50 | For further reading on the role of the 'specular phenomenon' in both pictorial expressions and theater, I suggest Hartlaub G.F. - Weißenfeld F. 1958. and Schmenling M. 1977.

51 | Dällenbach L. 1977, p. 210.

52 | In Metz words, "constructions « en abyme » dans lesquelles la fin de l'événement-raconté explicite et établit les conditions d'apparition de l'instance-raconté, dénuements en forme de vis-sans-fin." (Metz C. 1968, p. 26.)

2.6 THE PANORAMA: AN EXAMPLE OF 'GIGANTOMANIE DES MEDIUMS'

|Prop. XIV| The strengthening of the *virtual gaze* started in the Paris Exposition Universelle of 1900. All the devices aimed at the constructions of a 'new space' converged there. At the 'Exposition,' one could not only find the cinematographic machine, but also the 'preceding steps' of the Lumière Brothers' *chef d'oeuvre*. In this great exhibition a wide variety of instruments able to extend the 'field of the visible' were shown:[1] the French Universal Exposition was the exposition of the visual reproduction machines.

The arrival of the mobilized machines – trains, escalators and elevators – brought to mankind a new perception of space and corporal movement. In this context, the photographic technology coincides with a new human perception of space created by the stores, the exhibition halls, the museums and the *passages*. The coincidence of these diverse spaces and the different ways of interaction that they involve, created in the 19th and 20th centuries, a phenomenon of juxtaposition between the *mobilized gaze* – brought by the new technologies in transport, urban planning and architecture – and the *virtual gaze* – brought by photographic technology.[2] Both architecture and visual apparatuses gave a new conception of space. The new character of space developed in the 18th and 19th centuries could be derived from the 'visual constructions' that governed at that time, e.g. the Panopticon, conceived in 1791 and the Panorama in 1792.

Robert Barker patented the Panorama in Edinburgh on June 17, 1787 – but the first completely circular Panorama was shown in London in 1792 – and in 1785 Jeremy Bentham designed the Panopticon.[3] These apparatuses share several characteristics that in some ways embodied the *zeitgeist* of the beginning of the nineteenth century. Both constructions – the Panorama and Panopticon – light the peripheral area of the spatial composition and place the beholder in the dark. Both are circular constructions and both share the concept of the 'observation-platform' with the aim of seeing the peripheral area clearly. Both are architectonic designs that express another relationship between objects in space.[4] Both spatial organizations are disciplinary methods of observation and both reply to the same phenomenon of '*dilatazione dello sguardo*.'[5] "Panopticon and Panorama, two words with identical meaning; *Allschau* (all-embracing vision)."[6]

---

1 | See Freidberg A. 1994.

2 | See Freidberg A. 1994.

3 | See Oettermann S. 1980.

4 | See Günzel's analysis on Foucault's concept of diagram. Günzel S. 2007, pp. 20-21.

5 | Bordini S. 1984, p. 43.

6 | Oettermann S. 1980, p. 35.

In the Panopticon's case, we can see a phenomenon of dislocation of the pair *voir - être vu*.[7] This structure provides a dissymmetry of vision thanks to its particular geometry. In consequence, the Panopticon can be understood as an optical machine that enables a **shift of the point of view**. The Panopticon was considered as "catalyctic agent inducing human goodness or reformation as part of a purely mechanical operation."[8] This structure allows organizing the space where subject and object move to another plan in which the actions of 'to see' and of 'to be seen' change their character. This architectural mechanism establishes a strong control over the prisoner(s), it translates the *'régime panoptique'* – a social and political control – into the simple act of seen, bringing the disciplinary space to our private lives. It also creates the illusion that power is always present monitoring us. As stated by Bentham, this spatial organization 'extends to night the security of the day.'

Since the first schema projected by Bentham it is possible to identify the central points of this particular spatial organization, i.e. light and order. The construction foresees the lighting of the cells leaving in darkness the guard, this last one, placed in the center of the rotunda. Both spatial organization and the lighting effect allow the warden to have a panoramic series of small peepholes through which he could spy out not only the inmates but also his subordinates. "Thus a hierarchy of three stages was designed for, a secular simile of God, angels and man."[9] Through the Panopticon, Bentham promoted a radical secularization of the divine *Allschau*. He proposed a kind of 'democratization' of the divine gaze through a phenomenon of internalization.[10] The Panopticon can be understood as a clear example of spatial organization aimed at conveying a specific idea of society; in Bentham's words, "Morals reformed–health preserved–industry invigorated–instruction diffused–public burden lightened....all by a simple idea in architecture."[11]

With the Panorama the phenomenon of 'translation' appears between rural and urban spaces. This pictorial representation creates a 'dilatation' of the city and transports the countryside, or the far spaces, into the life of the townspeople.[12]

At the beginning, Baker's invention was called 'La Nature à Coup d'œil.'[13] The name Panorama – from the Greek *pan* and *orao* translated as a 'view of the entirety'– is attested in German for the first time in 1795 (*Journal des Luxus und der Moden*)

---

7 | Foucault M. 1975, p. 235.

8 | Evans R. 1971, p. 21.

9 | Evans R. 1971, p. 22.

10 | Oettermann S. 1980, p. 35.

11 | Bowring J. 1843, p. 39.

12 | See Benjamin W. 2002a. (1935.)

13 | It is interesting how Robert Barker presents his invention in the British patent: "An entiere new contrivance or apparatus, which I call La Nature à coup d'oeil, for the purpose of displaying views of nature at large by oil painting, fresco, water colours, crayons or any other mode of paintings or drawing." (Rober Barker, *British Patent* no. 1612, 19 June 1787. Quoted by Mannoni L.- Pesenti Campagnoni D.- Robinson D. 1995, p. 157.)

and in English in 1801 (*Encyclopedia Britannica*).[14] When this particular technique reached Paris it was called '*Tableau sans bornes*.'[15]

"By the Invention called La Nature à Coup d'Oeil, is intended, by drawing and painting a proper disposition of the whole, to perfect an entire view of any country or situation as it appears to an observer turning quite round; to produce which effect the painter or drawer must fix his station, and delineate correctly and connectedly every object which presents itself to his view as he turns round, concluding his drawing by a connection with where he begun."[16]

The phenomenon of translation generated by this pictorial representation entails also a new search for objectivity in pictorial compositions; its goal is the creation of a 'real' space, a perfect translation of natural spaces into another dimension.[17] In this process of translation of nature, the illusion was reinforced by a phenomenon defined as 'Gigantomanie des Mediums' useful to simulate the infinity of the landscape.[18]

The Panorama, in the 19th century, does not represent a new technique for the reproduction of images – i.e. it was used before anamorphosis and *trompe l'œil* –, but a new technique for showing images and also a new way to see the world, a new way to represent nature. The revolution of the Panorama's technique resides, on the one hand, in the research of an objective translation (with a scientific aim) of one natural object to another plane; on the other hand, in the search of the full-immersion (obtained by the huge circular composition) of the viewer to the pictorial representation.[19] This new form of image's representation requires a new conception of perspective, of the scale, and of the lighting, in other words, a special way of image projection that clearly determines the parts of blackness and those of brightness. The 360° spatial

---

14 | Oettermann S. 1980, p. 8.

15 | Bordini S. 1984, p. 20.

16 | Barker R. *British Patent no. 1612*, 19 June 1787. Quoted by Mannoni L.- Pesenti Campagnoni D.- Robinson D. 1995, p. 157.

17 | In Larousse of XIX century Panorama stated for give a definition of 'total illusion'. J. FR. Michaud, Biographie Universelle Ancienne et Moderne, 1811-1862, the Panorama stay under the voice "Prévost Pierre"; "toujours fidèle imitateur de la nature, c'est sur les lieux mêmes qu'il allait copier les tableaux, qu'il rendait ensuite avec une si rare perfection, et il devait être doué à bien haut degré de la mémoire des yeux, puisqu'il se contentait de prendre sur les lieux de simples croquis, d'une grand exactitude linéaire, il est vrai, et que tous les détailles existaient dans sa mémoire." And about his Panoramas he wrote "Jamais l'illusion n'avait été poussée aussi loin." (Michaud J.Fr. – Michaud L.G. 1968 (1811-1962), vol. 34, pp. 332-333.)

18 | Hick U. 1999, p. 244.

19 | On this subject see Zglinicki F.V. 1979, especially: *4. Kapitel Die Zauberlaterne entfaltet ihre Macht- Phantasmagorien und Nebelbilder*, pp. 55-79.

organization imposes also a singular point of view. The beholder has to be in the central point of the architectural composition that houses the pictorial representation.

In the development of this technique, the most significant problem to solve was the creation of a procedure able to build a *trompe l'oeil* with the particular distortion of a horizon line of 360°. The procedure that allows the illusion is clearly explained in Barker's patent:

"He must observe the lights and shadows how they fall, and perfect his piece to the best of his abilities. There must be a circular building or framing erected, on which this drawing or painting may be performed; or the same may be done on canvas or other materials, and fixed or suspended on the same building or framing to answer the purpose complete. It must be lighted entirely from the top, either by a glazed dome or otherwise, as the artist may think proper. There must be an inclosure within the said circular building or framing, which shall prevent an observer going too near the drawing or painting, so as it may, from all parts it can be viewed, have its proper effect. This enclosure may represent a room or platform, or any other situation, and may be any form thought most convenient, but the circular form is particularly recommended, of whatever extend this inside enclosure may be. There must be over it, supported from the bottom or suspended from the top, a shade or roof, which in all directions should project so far beyond this inclosure as to prevent an observer seeing above the drawing or painting, when looking up. And there must be without this inclosure another interception to represent a wall, paling, or other interception, as the natural objects represented, or fancy may direct, so as effectually to prevent the observer from seeing below the bottom of the drawing or painting; by means of which interception nothing can be seen on the outer circle but the drawing or painting intended to represent nature. The entrance to the inner enclosure must be from below, proper building or framing being erected for that purpose, so that no door or other interruption may disturb the circle on which the view is to be represented. And there should be below the painting or drawing proper ventilators fixed, so as to render a current circulation of air through the whole, and that inner inclosure may be elevated at the will of an artist, so as to make observers, on whatever situation he may wish they should imagine themselves, feel as if really on the very spot."[20]

It was really difficult to translate the geometrical space of the sketch (a flat space) to the cylindrical Panorama's composition. The horizon and the objects represented in a flat surface undergo a change of proportion and form at the time of the transfer onto a cylindrical space. The solution to the problem of the distortion was proposed by Barker by means of a system of curved lines adapted to the concave surface, which seemed like straight lines from the central viewing platform. In time this procedure became more empirical.[21] The first method used by Barker was similar to the *Quadra-*

---

20 | Barker R. *British Patent no. 1612*, 19 June 1787. Quoted by Mannoni L.- Pesenti Campagnoni D.- Robinson D. 1995.

21 | See Bordini S. 1984, *Modalità di sposizione*, pp. 69-82.

tura and *Graticolatura*,[22] techniques previously used in ancient Roman art and in the anamorphosis process.[23] Afterwards, in order to shape the indispensable distortion, the projection of shadows was used and, at a later period, the projection of photographic plates onto the cylindrical surface.[24]

The idea of the collage of images, aimed at creating a bigger horizon, was used even before Barker's invention. Barker's innovation was based on the multiplication of drawings in order to connect them in a cylindrical structure. Some scholars, especially topographers, cartographers, geologists and geographers, use a similar technique.[25] Analogous procedures were employed for the purpose of analyzing, from a graphic point of view, the Alps.[26]

The first scientific illustration of the Alps in 180° became an object of popular interest. These images, once used by the scientific community, were appreciated by the tourists as a souvenir of their journeys in the mountains.

|Fig. 2.48|

---

22 | *Quadratura* was a type of illusionistic decoration in which architectural elements are painted on walls and/or ceilings in such a way that they appear to be an extension of the real architecture of the room into an imaginary space. See *The Oxford Dictionary of Art.*

23 | When Daniel Barbaro (1559) analyzes the camera obscura he includes a section dedicated to "a beautiful and secret practice of perspective, which does not allow the painted things to be seen, except from a certain and determined point, beyond which it is not possible to distinguish that which is painted." It is a system already noted by Leonardo Davinci and also quoted by Della Porta. The term 'anamorphosis' first appears in the 17th century used by Schott 1657 indicates the technique that develops images, constructed according to geometrical laws, overthrowing the ordinary laws of perspective. These images regain their logical sense only when observed from a determined point of view. See *Self-Similarity as a Narrative Tool.*

24 | The photographic plates method usually pursues the following steps: picture-projection-draw-painting. Note that this process of photographic plates drifts apart, in a certain sense, the reality of the landscape and takes as the real object the image created on the photographic image. See Scharft A. 1968.

25 | See Bordini S. 1984, p. 30.

26 | See Solar G. 1979.

In *Voyages dans les Alpes*, Horce-Bénédict de Saussure (Fig. 2.48) drew the mountain range in a complete tour of the horizon. Those pictorial compositions, used with a scientific goal, moved the panoramic representations away from artistic tradition. The purpose of these works was to create a special geometrical order aimed at translating one precise place in its totality. In consequence, this translation imposes a kind of composition rich in details, which was useful for scientific research. In this technique of image reproduction, the scientific constituent generates a phenomenon that can be described as: 'denuding of the aesthetic components of graphic compositions.' These images enjoin a new type of relationship between the beholder and the image and also, between the designer and his composition. The designer, in order to give an exact reproduction of the geographic and topologic information, leaves aside aesthetic intentions, the canons of conventional landscape painting and any type of allegorical idealization, symbolic or personal stylistic expression.[27] From the viewer's perspective, these images require a special effort to recreate and recompose the 360° representation in a mental-image.

The Panorama, as 'optical simulator,' conveys through its mechanisms the vision of a modern form of both society and nature.[28] It creates a new notion of movement forcing the spectator to change the way he analyzes these pictorial representations, that is why the Panorama was defined as a 'visual-trip.'[29]

|*Fig. 2.49*|

In the Panorama, the object manifests evident distortions (Fig. 2.49). The pictorial composition in this special space is projected, as in the case of anomorphosis, to be observed from a precise point in space. From this point, the illusion can be created and the distortion shaped by the cylindrical space is avoided. The precise point of observation, imposed by this technique, corresponds with the position in which the

---

27 | See Bordini S. 1984, especially *Disegno scientifico e veduta a trecentosessanta gradi.*

28 | Oettermann S. 1980, pp. 9-12.

29 | de Valenciens P.H. 1820 (1800), p. 343.

drawer composes the image; therefore, the Panorama represents a particular phenomenon of translation. The drawer literally transports his complete vision into 360°. The translation of those far spaces into a spatial organization of 360° also imposes the development of an appropriate architectonical space aimed at housing the pictorial representation. Consider for instance, Robert Fulton's and Prévost's rotundas in Paris at the end of 18th century, like in Rome and Berlin.[30] There, the isolation of the Panorama's images was an essential requirement to create the artificial conditions necessary to give the perfect full-immersion to the beholder. The full-immersion in a 360° perspective was founded on the Panorama's special arrangement that isolates the representation in order to create an artificial atmosphere.[31] From one part, Barker's invention follows the logic of the theater in which the architectonic space is understood as a preordained space. From the other part, the Panorama – especially the moving Panorama – develops a bigger interaction between the show and the edifice. In fact, the edifice is built in function of the show and it is used as the medium that allows the combination of the mobilized gaze – by using railway, moving platforms, etc. – and the virtual movement allowed by the mobilized pictorial compositions. Their interaction creates a phenomenon of periodicity of the image that gives the Panorama a notion of *spectaculum*. In fact, the Panorama represents a strong symptom of the irruption of the marketing logic in art production; it represents the industrialization of creative production.[32] As mass audience medium, the Panorama starts with a new compromise inside creative production. It was an innovative form of art and merchandise that provokes not only interest in the bourgeois class but also in the popular classes.[33] For the first time, a portion of the public without a special interest in art gave life to an art market that in a short amount of time had a wide circulation. Due to the commodification of the image, the existence of the Panorama becomes totally dependent upon the public. The *spectaculum* encourages the improvement of the technique necessary to create a perfect illusion, which is easier consumable. Thus, the Panorama, as popular phenomenon, creates the necessity of novelty. The spectators, in a sort of 'binge' upon the panoramic image, impose a special speed of consumption. In this crossroad of art, science and market, the panorama developed a deep revolution inside spatial representations. Like a pictorial oeuvre, scenic show, architectonical space and communication tool, the Panorama's phenomenon creates an agreement between

---

30 | Zglinicki F.V. 1979, pp. 94-95.

31 | When the technique of panorama acquires its popularity, these constructions were present in all big capitals around the world. The mode of 'ama' starts with the big success of the Panorama. Some mechanisms that simulated the panorama were created and they were characterized by the same termination in its name 'ama,' e.g. Diorama and Dellorama –through image's brightness - Georama - used a Balloon - Neorama - used a building - Myriorama - scenic kaleidoscop - Cyklorama - presents draw rivers - Pleorama - simulating a water ride - etc. See Zglinicki F.V. 1979, p. 97.

32 | See Hick U. 1999, especially, *Die Omnipotenz des privilegierten Blicks*, pp. 235-250.

33 | Bordini S. 1984, especially, *L'invenzione del Panorama*.

aesthetic pretensions and topographic precision;[34] these last offered by the mechanical component obtainable by means of a special camera obscura.[35] The spatial compositions created by means of this mechanical technique caused the impression of translating the objects from nature to another dimension with a strong component of objectivity. Spectators and art critics declared, regarding the illusion created by the Panorama's pictorial compositions, that it was the same arrangement on the canvas as on the human eye. They perceived the representation like the original object.

The illusion created by the Panorama requires not only the precise point of view imposed upon the beholder, but also the impossibility of having references to real space: hence, the 'Tableau sans bornes.' A pictorial composition without borders creates in the beholder the inability to compare the difference between the real place and its representation. In that period, some thesis about image reproduction and perception upheld that the camera obscura creates a better illusion through its faculty to 'detach' the lone objects from the complexity of natural space.[36] In fact, the camera obscura imposes an *isolated* vision of the element that will be represented. During that period some artists argued that the human perception of things is conditioned by the relationship with other objects around them. Algarotti expressed this idea with these words:

"Né punto da stupirsi che con tale ordigno, [the camera obscura] quello arriviamo a scernere che altrimenti non faremmo. Quando noi volgiam l'occhio ad un oggetto per considerarlo, tanti altri ce ne sono dattorno, i quail raggiano ad un tempo medesimo nell'occhio nostro, che non ci lasciano ben distinguere le modulazioni tutte del colore e del lume che è in quello, o almeno ce le mostrano mortificate e più perdute, quasi tra il vedi e il non vedi. Dove per contrario nella Camera ottica la potenza visiva è tutta intesa al solo oggetto che le è innanzi; e tace ogni altro lume che sia."[37]

Following this framework, the perception of an object is not only determined by itself, but also, its appearance is the product of the relationship of the elements around it.[38] With the use of the camera obscura, the perception of the natural objects changes because it erases the 'disturbance' of the objects around the object that would be represented. Thus, by using the camera obscura, our perception – under this idea – is

---

34 | Hick U. 1999, p. 239.

35 | Daniel Schwenter (1585-1636) invented this special mechanism. His camera obscura was posed upon a rotating axis that enable a translation of a 360° landscape. See Oetterman S. 1980, p. 239.

36 | See Lavin I. 1980.

37 | Algarotti F. 1963 (1762), p. 86.

38 | It is important to note in these reflections on the spatial composition in pictorial arts the analogies with the space proposed by topology and the flexibility of objects.

focused on the 'essence' and the human eye is able to perceive the object in its totality without the influence of the other objects around it.[39]

The same phenomenon was appreciated in dramatic art. In theater, some directors asserted that the dramatic power would be stronger if the scene isolated the dramatic center with fewer objects around the action. Several objects in the stage meant the dispersion of the spectator's attention.[40]

In Barker's 'tableau sans bornes' the spectator becomes an actor of the silent composition. There, the human presence is understood as an object between other objects, a representation among representations.[41] This last phenomenon is the outcome of the disappearance of the physical division between stage and stalls on which the theatrical spatial organization was subjected. The division between the stalls and the space of the illusion – represented by the stage – disappears in the Panorama; it becomes a unique space. In order to create the phenomenon of full-illusion in the spectator, a preparatory place for the immersion was used in some Panoramas.[42] By means of a dark-corridor placed before the access to the Panorama's central platform, the spectator's eyes lose the possibility of perceiving the difference between the natural light and the artificial light that illuminates the pictorial composition. In the Panorama, the primary ground of the illusion, and in consequence the spectator's full-immersion, is the impossibility to compare a well-defined pictorial space with another spatial organization around it, i.e. to create the 'dormancy effect.' The infinite horizon and the composition in 360° in the Panorama eliminates the picture frame and creates a space

---

39 | It is interesting to note that the cinematographic camera was also understood as an engine that constructs the narrative space using this phenomenon of isolation. For example, Pudovkin compares the change of shot in cinematography to the "natural transference of attention of an imaginary observer." (Pudovkin V.I. 1970, p. 70-71.) Thus the camera, as a prosthesis, was also provided with a kind of consciousness ('imaginary observer') able to isolate important objects in order to construct a narrative and capture the attention of the audience like the human sight naturally does.

40 | The influence of the spatial organization of the Panaroma's building had some repercussions on the theatre. Some attempts had tried to import the circular spatiality of the panorama in the theater's scenic composition. See Bapst G. 1899, pp. 588-590.

41 | Bordini S. 1984, p. 88.

42 | It is interesting to remark that every representation impose particular conditions in order to create in the beholder a 'dormancy effect'. As in Plato's 'Allegory of the cave' the 'dormancy effect' becomes indispensable to make of the prisoner a 'victim' of one illusion of reality, in Baudry's words "(...) une hallucination à l'état de veille et une rêve dans le sommeil." As we know, the cinematograph creates this effect by means of the darkness in the room, "sorte de démure souterraine en forme de caverne possédant une entrée du côté du jour." (Baudry J.-L. 1975, p, 59.) This subject will be better analyzed in the chapter dedicated to the cinematograph.

where there is no possibility to compare. Hence, the Panorama's spatial organization becomes self-referenced.[43]

The self-referencing phenomenon, thanks to the high degree of illusion enabled by this technique, creates the possibility to manipulate 'several dimensions.' Some Panoramas use real people or material objects coordinated in perspective and color with the pictorial representation. Consider for instance, the *Panorama of Spithead* that presented some material waves and the central platform of observation was a representation of a frigate. Another example of the coordination between dimensions are Charles Langlois's Panoramas, in which, the central platform was not a simulation of the frigate, but a real part of an old frigate ('*La Bataille de Navarin*' – 1830). The real frigate was completely inserted into the pictorial composition. The platform of observation was in the extremity of a real frigate and it was joined to the pictorial composition by using perspective. The representation of the warship was half material half pictorial and these two different dimensions were indiscernible.[44] The same phenomenon had been presented in the scenes of war where real cannons were accompanied by a group of artillery soldiers in the pictorial space, even the soldiers, sometimes, were represented by material shapes e.g. paper board.[45]

The Panorama's spectator is not in front of the real object, and neither he is in front of its mere representation. Thanks to the endless horizon and the composition in 360°, the pictorial composition allows the beholder to navigate an infinite space; like he does in nature. As Bordini maintains, the Panorma's viewer has the sensation to see "il mondo nella sua incalzante riduzione ad immagini."[46] Both, endless horizon and panoramic view, gave to mankind the illusion to be able to enclose nature in one image, to watch the universe from one point of view, from God's point of view.

As noted above, the Panorama – like the Panopticon – favors one point in space where the possibility to have a global view is offered. The necessity of *Allschau* is clearly present in both mechanisms. Presumably, this necessity might have been created by the new horizon shaped by the hot-air balloon on June 5th, 1783.[47] It was the first time that mankind could see the earth from another angle; from God's angle. A new notion of the horizon is born when a different point of view was attained. After the invention of the hot-air balloon, the word 'horizon' expanded its connotation of per-

---

43 | The frame as we know it today was developed during the Renaissance. Its function of emancipation of the pictorial space from the wall is an useful tool in order to create deep vistas. "This world came to be conceived as boundless–not only in depth, but also laterally–so that the edges of the picture designated the end of the composition, but not the end of the represented space. The frame was thought of as a window, through which the observer peeped into an outer world, confined by the opening of the peephole but unbounded in itself." (Arnheim R. 1974, p. 239.)

44 | Bapst G. 1891, p. 24.

45 | Bordini S. 1984, p. 97.

46 | Bordini S. 1984, p. 52.

47 | Oettermann S. 1980, p. 13.

spective both in the geographical field and in the astronomic one. In the artistic field, the word 'horizon' acquires the connotation of *'lointain*.[48] In the new connotation of 'horizon', the classical perspective's geometrical order was not the only issue aimed at creating an infinite vision. In fact, the classical geometrical order needed the aid of human sensibility. In order to do it, the artist took into account more factors like the chromatic features derived from both distance and atmospheric conditions (aerial perspective).[49] The colors of the never-ending heavens were useful instruments to create the sensation of infinity. As testimony to this phenomenon we have the oeuvre of Caspar David Friedrich.

|*Fig. 2.50*|

The work of this romantic master of painting recreates the universal infinity and places man in front of both the never–ending nature and mankind's endless soul. Since his first exposition in Berlin in 1810, Friedrich presents his oeuvres as a manifest of a new type of pictorial landscape representation, especially with *Mönch am Meer*.[50] His method of pictorial composition was inspired basically as another way to observe nature. "Nicht die treue Darstellung von Luft, Wasser, Felsen und Bäumen ist die Aufgabe des Bildners, sondern seine Seele, seine Empfindung soll sich darin widerspiegeln."[51] Often, Friedrich organizes the space through a close forefront, opened to an infinite landscape, toward an endless horizon.[52]

In his compositions, he produces a sense of embodiment between the viewer and the characters. Frequently his oeuvres present in the forefront a person observed from behind. The viewer incarnates himself in those characters in front of the infinite horizon, watching the endless universe ahead of them. He uses often a re-framing method

---

48 | Bordini S. 1984, p. 45.

49 | See Bordini S. 1984, especially *L'impero Della visione*.

50 | See Börsch-Supan H. 1960.

51 | Hinz S. 1974, p. 101.

52 | The freedom expressed through these compositions has been linked with the social movement started by the French revolution. According Fleischer I. – Hinz B. – Schipper I. – Mattausch R., Friedrich's compositions represents the sentiment of freedom and subjectivity created by the end of the feudalism in the new concept of *'citoyen'*. See Fleischer I. – Hinz B. – Schipper I. – Mattausch R. 1974. Also, the phenomenon is perceived in the study of Vaughan W. 1979.

of painting a figure in front of a window watching the infinite horizon. In his oeuvre, we can feel the attempt to create an infinite space through a recursive operation, established by the relationship between the viewer, the oeuvre's frame, the figure and the window's frame.[53] In this *mise en abyme*, both the viewer and the figure in the pictorial composition are in front of an infinite space.

---

53 | See Börsch-Supan H. – Jähnig K.W. 1973.

2.7 PANORAMA AND MOVING PANORAMA AS PROTO-FRACTAL SPACES

The early nineteenth century saw the development of Moving Panoramas. This new technique replaced the phenomenon of *Allschau* by both a stronger immersion of the beholder in the graphic representations through more realistic images and the huge accumulation of information in the same space, through the articulated rotundas. The accumulation of images was obtained by means of very long painting-moving rollers aimed at creating a sequence of scenes.[1] The reduction of the image's size and the disappearance of the 360° composition also entails the loss of the anamorphosis technique changing the concept of the unique point of view.

|*Fig. 2.51*|

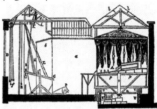

In the Moving Panoramas the building housing the pictorial representation was more articulated. If the Panorama requires a circular structure to represent a 360° space, in the case of the Moving Panorama (e.g. Diorama) the building must be articulated inside. These articulations were useful in shaping a narrative by means of showing the image in sequence. Via the moving rolls, the images obtain a temporal component that creates an 'editing' phenomenon.

The movement of the images was sometimes coordinated with the movement of the viewer by means of rails. Thus, the architectonic space in the Moving Panoramas was built with an aim towards organizing the space in such a way as to combine the mobilized gaze – operated by physical motion by means of the transporting technique (in this case the railways) – the visual gaze – operated by a geometrical arrangement of perspective, lighting and moving rolls – and the virtual movement, this last one created by a unique diegetic time derived from the interaction between the mobilized gaze and the visual gaze. Further, the Moving Panoramas improved the 'encyclopedic logic' already intrinsic in the first Panoramas.

|Prop. XIII| The first Panorama presented by Barker, the year after he took out a patent on his invention, was called *A View of Edinburg* and it was presented in this city. Then, Barker started similar exhibitions in Glasgow and London. When Robert Fulton became an associate of Barker, he introduced the invention to France. In June 1800 the first Panorama in Paris was displayed in a rotunda on the boulevard Montmartre; *View of Paris*. This Panorama represented a view from the roof of the Tuileries.[2] These Panoramas were instruments aimed at *re*-configuring the city's space and to display it under a different spatial organization. Furthermore, they represented an attempt to *re*create and display the physical space laying outside of the rotunda. The

---

1 | See Herbert S. 2000.
2 | See Dickinson H.W. 2009.

act of recomposing the space of the city and then showing it in a rotunda of seventeen or thirty-five meters in diameter is an attempt to insert the totality within the piece: the whole city inside the city. It is possible that the odd sensation that the spectators had in those Panoramas was created by the phenomenon of *Myse en abyme* produced by the spatial relationship established between the city and the Panorama.

|Prop. XVIII| The narrative space created by the Moving Panoramas offers the possibility to store bigger quantities of information and present it under a special spatial organization. This characteristic is an attempt to make the Panorama a 'universal object,' an object able to acquire an infinity of information. Consider, for instance, the Panorama *L'histoire du siècle* (1889). On this occasion, for the centenary of the French Revolution, the Panorama *L'histoire du siècle* proposed to the public a large quantity of images, these coordinate by editing it in the temporal extension. The Moving Panorama was able to contain and present the images of the country's history within a chronologic order. For example, some portraits of historic personalities who had participated in important historic moments; like the *Hohenzollern Gallerie* (1892). This Panorama intended to create a chronologic sequence of 250 years about the history of the dynasty.[3] Further, these Panoramas use the spatial organization in order to give a privileged gaze, and so creating some symbolic formation often used by nationalisms.

In the 1900 'Paris Exposition', the central attraction was the technique of pictorial reproduction in 360°. Even if this technique of image reproduction was an old technique, it gained the public's curiosity. This 'geometry,' thanks to its juxtaposition of spaces – and time – was the big attraction during the colonialist period.[4] The interest of the European population in the conquered countries encoureged the 'geometers' to bring those far spaces to the capital of the 19th century.[5] Before this big event in Paris, the entire city was adapted with some circular buildings aimed at housing the special panoramic images. Those big buildings were the spatial points where the Panorama's geometry could have expressed its great narrative.[6] It was the case of the Moving Panorama *Le tour du Monde*. In this building, the spectator could 'travel' to some exotic ports proposed by the people of the Messageries Maritimes.[7] But the Panorama *Le tour du Monde* was not the only one presenting exotic places, for instance, the magnificent travel through the North African coast offered by the Stereorama *Poetry of the Sea*. This presents a special phenomenon of 'harmonization' of dimensions. *Poetry of the Sea* combines the physical – or material – space with the imaginary space of the pictorial composition, for example, some metal sheets represented waves in the imaginary ocean, this in *trompe-l'oeil*. Both spaces shape a special geometrical order where

---

3 | Hick U. 1999, p. 248.

4 | The same 'colonialist feeling' accompanied the first steps of the cinematographic narrative, especially in the documental film. See Sadoul G. 1949. This topic will be better analyzed in the chapter dedicated to the cinematography.

5 | See Sternberger D. 1955.

6 | See Kraemer H. 1985 (1900).

7 | Zielinski S. 1999, p. 24.

the movement of the traveler – created by a hydraulic system applied on a steamship – inside the Sterorama was combined with the movement of the waves presented in 'real dimension.' The physical structure of this Stereorama foresees the synchronic movement of the steamer where the spectator 'travels' the imaginary place and the physical structure.[8] Some armatures achieved colossal dimensions like the Mareorama *Illusion of a Trip in the Sea*. It reached 7.500 meters long and twelve meters high, in which, the pictorial composition was rolled. Aimed at creating the illusion of movement, the roll turned on, showing the image in sequence. The performance was coordinated with the movement of the steamship able to simulate a storm at sea.[9] The same phenomenon of *re*-combination was offered by the Panorama *Trans-Siberian Express* in which the spectator was accommodated in a luxurious compartment. The movement was created by means of the image-rolls, posed in front of the windows, simulating a travel from Moscow to Beijing. In this last case, the image-rolls created the movement showing an image at 300 meters/minute.[10] The travel, of forty-five minutes, was across Moscow, Omsk, Irkutsk, the Baikal shores, the Great Wall of China, and Beijing.[11]

Some panoramas mixed the pictorial representation with live performance, like the famous M. Dumoulin's Panorama, in which the material component of the architectural place entered into symbiosis with the totality of the Panorama's representation. Dumoulin's Panoramas created a special geometrical place where the landscapes of the far colonized lands were represented as well as the people from these lands. The figures were real people from these colonized countries, acting out a performance, and wearing their traditional costumes. The tendency was to create longer stories and travels better articulated in diegetic time. Such is the case of the Pleorama that promoted a magnificent tour in the Bay of Naples and also down the Rihne from Mainz to St. Goar.

The research of a diegesis manifested in the Pleorama is interesting. This travel showed a complete day's journey. During one hour, the 'passenger' might see the moving roll showing the painted canvases: coast, landscapes, bays, small towns, etc., changing according to the sun's movement; sunrise, half day, sunset. The instance of the Padorama offers the same diegetic temporality. It was a 'mechanical-pictorial show' that simulated a train trip covering Liverpool to Manchester.[12]

---

8 | Friedberg highlights an interesting coincidence between the development of the machines of the Diorama, Panorama and cinema – which she considers machines of visual transport – and the development of new mobility in architecture and urban planning brought about by machines of transport. See Friedberg A. 1994.

9 | Vries L (de) 1975, p. 93.

10 | Vries L (de) 1975, p. 93.

11 | Bordini S. 1984, p. 320.

12 | To note that the line Liverpool-Manchester is the first English train line, and had been inaugurated just four years before the presentation of the Padorama *Liverpool-Manchester*.

The lighting technique was another factor that developed a better-articulated narrative. Like in the Eidophusikon (1781), the Diaphanorama (1815) and the Diorama (Greek *dia* through, *horama* view) (1823) the lighting was an important component able to create a special diegetic time. Through the lighting, the scene acquired a special shade and reproduces the atmosphere of sunset or noon thanks to the chromatic effect produced by the lighting shining through a colored glass.

Nikolaus König opened his *Exposition du Diaphorama de la Suisse* in 1815; eight landscapes, made in watercolor in a half-greaseproof, half-scraped paper aimed at creating different tonalities of color and degrees of transparency. The lighting of the canvas was the most important factor of this technique. The pictures were illuminated with both direct and indirect light and also form the backside.[13] It is possible that the Diaphorama was the inspiration of Daguerre's Diorama.[14] The term Diorama, before employed with the meaning of a miniature model scene, in Daguerre's meaning describes a translucent image.[15] The Diorama's spatial technique was characterized by both the use of translucent materials and the special disposition of shutters and curtains. The avant-gardist's use of gas lighting and the special technique of *recto - verso* lighting on the canvas, created special effects in the pictorial representations that were perceived by the public like magical effects.[16] The method used by Daguerre (1787-1851) in his Diorama was as follows:

"The first effect was painted on the *front* side of transparent white calico, which had to be as free from joins as possible, and which was prepared on both sides with two coats of parchment size. The colours were ground in oil but applied to the calico with turpentine, and in single strokes, to avoid causing opacity. The second effect was painted on the *verso* of the calico by transmitted light, so that the artist could judge where to preserve and where to paint over the transparent parts of the first effect; this was done with opaque grey paint, the gradiation of tones being produced by variation in the opacity of the paint. When this general effect of light and shade was obtained, the picture was coloured in transparent tints. In conjunction with coloured screens, Daguerre then achieved what he termed "The decomposition form", on the principle that if a green and a red part of the painting are illuminated by red light, the red object will be vanish while the green one will be appear black, and *vice versa*. In this way astonishing changes could be brought about in the picture, and figures which had not been visible in the first effect appeared one by one in the second effect."[17]

The attraction exerted by this technique on the public did not depend upon the articulation between two dimensions – e.g. in the Diorama *View of the Mont Blanc taken*

---

13 | Bordini S. 1984, p. 296.

14 | Gernsheim H. - Gernsheim A. 1956, pp. 13-45.

15 | See Herbert S. 2000.

16 | Mannoni L.- Pesenti Campagnoni D. - Robinson D. 1995, p. 177.

17 | Gernsheim H. – Gernsheim A. 1956, p. 32.

from the Valley of Chamonix of 1831 where Daguerre placed a living goat in the composition – but from the light game coordinated with the transparency of the canvas. Like Daguerre's English patent of Diorama specifies "an improved Mode of publicly exhibiting Pictures or Painted Scenery of every Description and of distributing or directing the Day Light upon or through them, so as to produce many beautiful Effects of Light and Shade."[18]

Daguerre focused on the lighting effects created by means of the coordination of the light projection and the tonalities shaped by the translucency.[19] Three years after the *View of Mont Blanc taken from the Valley of Chamonix*, Daguerre improved his technique with the Diorama 'à double effet;' *Diorama del Porto di Grand*. This technique consists in composing a pictorial representation with different images placed on both sides of the canvas.[20] These images are superimposed only on a few points of the canvas. Thanks to both the double-side lighting and the chromatic light, the Diorama was able to create temporal and spatial ellipsis without appealing to the spectator's physical movement. That means, two different images on the same plane, two different spatial and temporal notions represented on the same dimension, for instance, *A midnight Mass at Saint-Etienne-du-Mont* (1834).

|*Fig. 2.52*|

In this Diorama not only was the passage from day to night more realistic, but the temporal ellipses were accompanied by the gradual appearance of the faithful inside the realistic church, which had previously been empty.[21] *A midnight Mass at Saint-Etienne-du-Mont* is a Diorama that represents a huge improvement in the illusion of

---

18 | An extract of Daguerre's English patent form Gernsheim H. – Gernsheim A. 1956, p. 13.

19 | We can consider this technique as the first step of the Daguerrotype.

20 | The *Diorama à double effet* can be compared to the technique created in the 19th in England called 'Dissolving views.' This technique consists in the use of two or more lanterns to project accurately superimposed views on the same screen allowing sophisticated effects of transformations. See Mannoni L.- Pesenti Campagnoni D.- Robinson D. 1995, pp. 134-141.

21 | Bordini S. 1984, p. 299.

movement. The narrative flexibility offered by the coordination of lights dictated the disappearance of the real objects present in the performances. Some newspapers of the epoch testify to the enormous curiosity of the public. They wrote about the Diorama, calling it "(…) a new conquest, a happy application of the principles of optics and catoptics to the effects of painting. The results are magic and justify the naïve expression of a child who exclaimed that 'it was more beautiful than nature!'"[22] In addition to this, 'Le journal des artistes' presents further proof of the big event in form of verse:

"Son obscure foret, chef-d'œuvre de peinture,
Trompe les yeux du peintre, égale la nature,
Et ce savant tableau, si plein de vérité,
Par son aspect fait croire à la réalité."[23]

However, Daguerre was criticized for his way of coordinating art and technique, and also for the use of material elements (even live animals) in his pictorial representations. As a testimony of the heated debate provoked by Daguerre's way of making art, one can quote Daguerre himself:

"It is just for this mixture of nature and art that many art critics blame me; they say that my live goat, my chalet and my real fir trees are illegitimate aids for the painter. That may be well be so! My only aim was to produce the most complete illusion; I wanted to rob nature, and therefore had to become a thief. If you visit the Valley of Chamonix you will find everything as it is here: this chalet with projecting eaves, and the tools you see here, even the goat down there, I brought back from Chamonix."[24]

The temporal and the spatial ellipsis created by means of the Diorama's technique initiated the definitive reduction of the visual camp in the technique of the Panorama. The 360° spatial organization used by the Panorama disappears with the Diorama's coming. In fact, the Diorama initiated a 'cut-out' phenomenon, able to isolate a fragment of the panoramic vision. In consequence, the public definitively replaces the 360° vision with the new temporal and spatial component of the pictorial composition.

The space created by the pictorial representation acquires some flexibility. The central point of vision imposed by both the 360° spatial organization and the particular horizon that imposed the anamorphosis technique disappear. The spectator lost the interest of the full-immersion as a feeling – procured by the chromatic horizon and the impossibility of comparing the representation with the represented object – and gain an interest on the object's representation as an act of objectivity, as a real translation of nature.

---

22 | La Quotidienne, 4 August 1822, from Gernsheim H. – Gernsheim A. 1956, p. 17.
23 | Gernsheim H. – Gernsheim A. 1956, p. 34.
24 | Gernsheim H. – Gernsheim A. 1956, p. 30.

The phenomenon of 'no-reference' in the Diorama's case was created through light and not through colossal dimensions. As noted above, 'Le tableau sans bornes' was indispensable in creating the full-immersion and the idea of depth. The 360° composition of the Panorama erased the picture frame, thus creating the idea of infinite depth and the phenomenon of total vision. The Diorama creates this sensation by means of both, the dark side, intended to impede the vision of the image's frame and, the half-light conditions of the observation platform. In such space, the spectator was unable to see the borders of the image because of the architectonical organization of the space.

|*Fig. 2.53*|

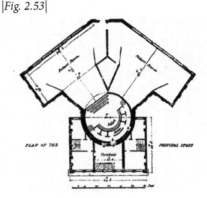

"The auditorium – a light wooden construction 12 meters (39 ft.) diameter and 7 meters 75cm. (25 ft. 2½ in.) high – was supported by a strong wooden framework which turned round upon a pivot, its circumference resting on struts with rollers which revolved on a circular rail. The ingenious mechanism could be worked by one man, who at the sound of a bell turned a crank until the proscenium (7meters 50 wide X 6 meters 50 high-24 ft. 4½ in.) came to rest opposite the second picture, which adjoined the first."[25]

In the Diorama, the canvas' dimension was 22m X 14m and the platform of observation always kept the distance of 13m from the canvas. The public was forced to watch the picture through a tunnel of 15 or 20m in length. This tunnel was very useful in erasing the limits of pictorial representation. The walls of the tunnel created, by hiding the image's frame, both the perception of infinity and the feeling of full-immersion.[26]

First, the movement was created by means of chromatic effects – e.g. the passage from the morning to the evening – subsequently, the research aimed at creating the illusion of movement used both the movement of the architectural structure and the light projection on the canvas.[27] In the Diorama's technique, the sensation of movement becomes the field of the images via its inner movement using the transparency and lighting. The Diorama 'à double effet' offered an abstract idea of succession that clearly shows the logic that will be followed by the cinematographic technology some years later. This technique initiated a rupture in the discontinuous form of the painted image in succession. The Diorama 'à double effet' uses the logic of the *coupes immo-*

25 | Daguerre L.J.M. *Histoire et description des procedés du Daguerrotype et du Diorama*, Paris 1839. Quoted by Gernsheim H. – Gernsheim A. 1956, p. 18.

26 | It is interesting to see the role played by the darkened room on a phenomenological level as analyzed by Baudry. See Baudry J.-L. 1975.

27 | Vries L (de) 1975, p. 94.

biles that could be joined to the space (position) or to the time (moment) and places it in one immobile plane. It is also possible to identify both the immobility of the plane and the dislodgment of the movement. Both phenomena are characteristic of the cinematographic technology and can be recognized by the immobility of the screen and in the act of the image's projection. Further, one can recognize in the Diorama 'à double effet' some fluttering effect aimed at creating the artifice of movement, this effect is analogous to the cinematograph, it is to say, the movie projector's shutter that interrupts periodically the luminous flux of the lantern.[28] It would be possible to link the Diorama's logic of light, shadow and the chromatic variations to the temporal ellipsis used in the cinema by means of editing effects as: fade out, fade in or even dissolve. The Diorama developed a logic that was followed in the search of a narrative using the images in sequence.

---

28 | Fihman G. 1999, pp. 62-85.

2.8 Photographic Technology: A Translation Tool of Nature's Shadows

The space developed by the Diorama 'à double effet' incited a research aimed at improving photographic technology, and it is Daguerre who carried out this study. Daguerre wrote to Niépce who was the heir of a tradition started in 1725 by Johann Heinrich Schulze (1687-1744). In fact, Schulze was the first to produce images by means of light on nitrate of silver.[1] He was the first to distinguish the action of light and heat on silver salts.

In 1725 Schulze was trying to make phosphorus by using nitric acid and silver and he performed the experiment at an open window into which the sun was shining brightly. The side exposed to the sunlight turned purple and the other side, turned away from the light, remained white. He published in 1727 the details of his experiment under the title *Scotophorus pro Phosphoro Inventus*.[2] Paradoxically, Schulze was searching, through chemistry, for a light-producing substance – Phosphorous from the Greek φώς ('light') and φόρος ('bearer') 'bringer of light' – and he found a substance that produces darkness – Scotophorus 'bringer of darkness.'

Like Thales of Milethus, Schulze began the acknowledgment of a space that admits the 'transport' of nature through shadows. He invented a mechanism that 'trans-

---

1 | Gernsheim H., analyzes the historical process that allowed mankind to fix an image by using the chemistry. He maintains that the blackening of silver salts by light was really unknown to the alchemists of the Middle Age and Renaissance. In fact, Albertus Magnus (1193-1280) mentioned coloring effect on the skin by means of nitrate silver but he did not understand this effect as caused by the light exposure. Greorgius Agricola (1490-1555) did not make reference to the nitrat. Georgius Fabricius (1516- 1571) describes for the first time the silver chloride and recognized its capacity to change of color. But this phenomenon was linked to a thermic phenomenon not to the tendency of change color in light. Johan Rudolf Glauber (1604-1668) testifies that the nitrate of silver was used in order to stained the hard-woods, but he was also unaware of the cause of the change of color. According to the same Gernsheim H. the only two experiments before Schulze who attributed the darkening of silver salts to the sun were Angelo Sala (1576-1637) and Wilhelm Homberg (1652-1715). In 1612 Sala wrote 'When you expose powered silver nitrate (lapis lunearis) to the sun, it turns black as ink' (Angelo Sala, *Septem Planetarium terrestrium spagirica recensio*, 1614. Also incorpored in his collected works *Opera medico-chymica*, 1647.) And Homberg on 4 September 1694 exhibited to the Académie Royale des Sciences in Paris among other things a small marbled box made of beef-bone. Having dipped the bone in a solution of nitrate of silver and blackened it by exposure to the sun. Gernsheim H. 1955, p. 20.

2 | Schulze communicated the experiment in Acta physico-medica Academiae Caesariae, Nürnberg, 1727, vol.i, p. 528. Observatio 233. English translation R.B. Litchfield in *The Photographic Journal*, 30 Nov. 1898.

lates' and forms an object – under another relationship of proportion and form – into another plan.

It is possible to claim that Schulz's invention represents the birth of photography, if we literally translate the term: 'Light-writing'. However, this new dimension founded by Schulz needed two essential complements. First, the ground where the translation of objects would be fixed and second, a mechanism, which would translate a natural object reconfiguring it into a geometrical order, it is to say, a Euclidean arrangement. The mechanism was the camera obscura. Nevertheless, the impossibility to fix the 'translated' image remained the obstacle.

As noted in the last chapters, there were many techniques of image 'translation' and visual tools, but these last, were 'limited by the presence of the artist's hand.' Due to the demand of the middle class to create less expensive methods of preserving likenesses of themselves, painters were focused on miniature sizes aimed at reducing prices and also in the development of a technology that allowed for image *r*eproduction. Étienne de Silhouette satisfied this mass demand (Fig. 2.54). Traced from the shadow cast by a lamp, (Fig. 2.55) Silhouette's method allowed the painter to create a figure in a short amount of time and for a reasonable price for the middle class.[3]

|*Fig. 2.54*| |*Fig. 2.55*|

These silhouettes became a highly popular object in the early 18th century. Nevertheless Silhouette's technique posed the problem of *r*eproduction. By using this technique of 'shadow tracing', the artist was able to compose a portrait – always painted in black – in a short time, but the copies took the same time, and the cost were as much as the original portrait. Even when, in the end of the 18th century, a system for producing multiple copies of a portrait was invented,[4] those methods were unable to produce, and reproduce, an image rich in details and color like the real artistic oeuvres of the miniature painters.

The intervention of the artist's hand – even if some critics understood the presence of a mechanism that not only translated the object into a perspective order (the camera obscura), but also fixed the image on a ground, (the photographic procedure)

---

3 | Coe B. 1976, p. 9.

4 | Gilles Louis Chrétien invented this system in 1786. For more details about this system see Coe B. 1976, p. 8.

as usurping the artist's functions[5] – was understood as an obstacle of the technique of translating a natural object to another plane in proportion and size.

Could light directly produce an image marketable to the middle class without the special skills of the artist?

On the one hand, the scientific field was focused on chemistry's developments in order to create a surface capable of receiving and fixing the translation of natural objects by means of an optical mechanism. On the other hand, the artistic field was interested in a technology that not only allowed fot the transport of a natural object in scale within a perspective composition, but their interest was also focused on the image's production and reproduction without special skills. This last interest was in response to the necessity for a mechanical mass reproduction of the oeuvre.[6]

The first attempts to improve Schulze's invention were focused upon the research of the surface where the image could be fixed. The question was, where could one 'write' by means of light and by using chemistry? In this research an odd phenomenon was manifested. Why was this action of transport – or translation – of a natural object into another plane immediately assimilated and connected to writing technology? Why was this technique not assimilated as a technique of spatial organization, as geometry?

In 1737 Jean Hellot (1685-1766) published a work under the title *Sur une nouvelle encre sympathique*, dealing with the method of the application of silver nitrate onto paper.[7] This title attests the assimilation of photographic technology as a writing technology. The following attempts to improve Schulze's invention were focused on the improvement of this 'ink' and how to fix it upon a surface. This was Scheele's situation. Carl Wilhelm Scheele (1742-1786) analyzed the action of light on silver chloride[8] and discovered that the chloride becomes insoluble in ammonia.[9] Another important finding of Scheele's is that the violet rays of the solar spectrum have a greater and more rapid darkening effect on silver chloride than the other wavelengths.[10] Nevertheless, the problem of fixing images on a surface remained.

---

5 | Scharf A. 1968, p. 7.

6 | These motivations might be the starting point of the big discussion about the artistic character of the photography. The close relationship between the photography (or even with the preceding techniques of image creation e.g. the miniatures, or Silhouettes) and the market logic of mass production created the direct connotation of the images reproduction by means of the chemical or optical process as a sole production without artistic attempts. See Benjamin W. 2002b (1936), p. 334.

7 | Annual proceedings of the Histoire de l'Accadémie Royale des Sciences, année 1737, 1766, Paris.

8 | Giacomo Battista Bancaria discovered in 1757 the light-sensitivity of silver chloride. See Comentarii of the institute and academy of science and arts of Bologna, vol. IV, Bologna, 1757. Also Gernsheim H. 1955, p. 22.

9 | See Scheele C. W. 1777.

10 | Gernsheim H. 1965[3], p. 7.

In an important piece of research, Thomas Wedgwood (1771-1805) conduced the first experiments in making images on paper by means of the chemical reaction offered by silver salts.[11] Thomas Wedgwood is considered the first person to have recorded an image with a camera by means of the action of light.

In order to solve some problems connected with light, Wedgwood used silver prepared differently, and his observations thereon led to the invention of what was termed 'silvered ware,' namely a pattern of dead or burnished silver upon a black earthenware body.[12] Wedgwood started some experiments in the production of light from different bodies by heat and attrition and he found that with the paper moistened by a solution of silver nitrate, it would pass through different shades of grey and brown and, at length, become nearly black with exposure to daylight.[13]

|*Fig. 2.56*|

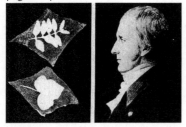

Wedgwood's first attempts at forming a negative image were by means of blocking the light from reaching the paper.[14] He made various attempts at fixing the copies, it is to say, to prevent the uncolored side of the copy from reacting with light. Nevertheless, all his trials were unsuccessful. He was forced to preserve his copies in a darkened place, and they could be viewed by the candlelight, otherwise the surface would blacken.[15]

Wedgwood's interest was in translating an object (its shadow) directly onto another surface, another dimension. The conception of this new dimension was useful in order to understand and prove a new idea of human perception. Even if Wedgewood's technique was rich in writing connotations his theories about human perception let us to distinguish a depth idea about spatial organization and multidimensionality. His cognitive approach to vision generated the necessity to idealize another dimension where objects – the real objects translated by means of photographic technology – could be observed in another relationship of distance and space. Wedgwood was trying to understand, through his metaphysical research, the insightful concept of *idea* and its relationship with sensorial perception, i.e. perceptual learning. His interest in the interaction between *ideas* and perception allowed him to state: "The two acts or states of mind, called perception and idea, have a common nature"[16] and "every perception of the object leaves behind it an idea which instantly coalesces

---

11 | See Wedgwood T. – Davy H. 1802.

12 | According to Wedgwood's correspondence to Byerly, Februar 1791. Quoted by Meteyard E. 1970 (1866), vol ii.

13 | See Newhall B. 1982, p. 13.

14 | This technique is called today 'contact printing.' Wade N.J. 2005, p. 514.

15 | Goldberg V. 1988, p. 53.

16 | Quoted by Wade N.J. 2005, p. 516.

with the subsequent perception."[17] He also posits: "perception becomes a language, of which the chief use is to excite the correspondent series of thought, and the senses are seldom intensely and long employed but in the examination of new objects."[18] The examination of these 'new objects' might be the motivation for his research on the photosensitive substance, thus, the transport of the natural objects into another plane.[19] His most important aim was to find the means of interaction with 'new objects.' To be in front of a 'new object' was important in order to better understand the human perception.

Wedgwood's interest in 'new objects' can be linked to Sartre's analysis of perception. According to Sartre, when I am in front of an object, although it enters (*entrer*) in its totality into my perception, it is only presented (*donné*) one side to me. The perception of a cube (in Sartre's example) is always something that appeals to the multiplication of its possible points of view. In consequence, I have to learn (*apprendre*) about the object.

"Je ne puis savoir que c'est un cube tant que je n'ai pas appréhendé ses six faces; je puis à la rigueur en voir trois à la fois, mais jamais plus. Il faut donc que je les appréhende successivement. Et lorsque je passe, par exemple, de l'appréhension des faces ABC à celle des faces BCD, il reste toujours une possibilité pour que la face A se soit anéantie durant mon changement de position."[20]

|Prop. XII| Following this framework, Sartre can maintain: "L'objet lui-même est la synthèse de toutes ces apparitions."[21] However, when I think about the concrete concept of a cube, I find myself 'in front of' its six faces and it's eight angles at the same time. Thus, my thought could be perceived as a complete act where it is not necessary to 'complete' the form or fully grasp the object, as in the case of perception. This dissimilarity characterizes the different natures of the act of perception and the act of thinking (*pensée*). Hence, Sartre claims that it is impossible to think a perception and perceive a thought.[22] Perception is not a passive action for the mind, and this action is tightly linked with the 'idea' – in Wedgwood's theory, or '*conscience*'[23] in Sartre's meaning – thus, a 'new object' was an important point of Wedgwood's research. For Wedgwood, a 'new object' represents the possibility to individualize the mind's pro-

---

17 | Quoted by Wade N.J. 2005, p. 516.

18 | Quoted by Wade N.J. 2005, p. 516.

19 | Note that Wedgwood's scientific and intellectual life is developed while Lambert's theories were published and just some years before the big revolution started by Gauss in the field of geometry.

20 | Sartre J.-P. 1940, p. 23.

21 | Sartre J.-P. 1940, p. 23.

22 | Sartre J.-P. 1940, p. 24.

23 | Closer meaning of the German word: *Bewusstsein*.

cess of recognition, how objects are perceived when their awareness is not yet 'mechanized' by some geometrical influence.

Berkeley's *An Essay towards a new Theory of Vision*, represents an important contribution for Wedgwood's research.[24] In fact, the concept of *superficial distance*, introduced by Berkeley, can be understood as the inspiration of Wedgwood's theory on the perception of depth.

An Essay towards a new Theory of Vision starts with an exhaustive analysis of mankind's perception of distance. Berkeley claims that "distance is in its own nature imperceptible, and yet it is perceived by sight."[25] He allows distance's analysis as a notion merely brought into view by means of some other idea, "that is it self immediately perceived in the act of vision."[26] The 'some other idea' was certainly in reference to the 'mechanism' implanted by geometry, in this case, expressed in optical science. At that point, his investigation gave the opportunity to analyze the perception of distance from another point of view. Those lines and angles used by optics in order to explain the perception of distance "are themselves not at all perceived, nor are they in truth ever thought of by those unskillful in optics."[27] With these words, Berkeley rejects the geometrical constructed doctrine of mathematics and optics in the phenomenon of perception.

"Every one is himself the best judge of what he perceives, and what not. In vain shall any man tell me that I perceive certain lines and angles which introduce into my mind the various ideas of distance, so long as I my self am conscious of no such thing."[28]

|Prop. XVIII| In order to highlight the mind's process in the act of perception, Berkeley analyzes Isaac Barrow's (1630-1677) optical lectures (1667). By using a geometrical analysis, Berkley shows a contradiction in Barrow's work with which Berkeley could posit that the eye – or the mind – perceives "only the confusion" caused by the convergering and divergering rays at different distances.[29] Distance, as noted by Berkeley, is not only particular to sight; it involves all the human senses. Distance can be only analyzed or perceived by taking into consideration a specific object and the knowledge that the beholder has about it, thus, implying a subjective dimension, in consequence, a mental process unique for every single person. However, his conclusion about distance imposes the analysis of another important notion that became the fundamental point of Wedgwood's research: the magnitude of the object. For Berkeley, magnitudes are notions that apply to all senses, as well. When we do not perceive the magnitudes

---

24 | For more specific information about the philosophical influence of Berkeley on Wedgwood's thesis, see Clark D.M. (ed.) 2008.
25 | Berkeley G. 1964 (1709), p. 173.
26 | Berkeley G. 1964 (1709), p. 173.
27 | Berkeley G. 1964 (1709), p. 173.
28 | Berkeley G. 1964 (1709), p. 173.
29 | Berkeley G. 1964 (1709), p. 184.

of objects immediately by sight, we do perceive them by the mediation of "any thing which has a necessary connection with them."[30] Thus, the analysis of an object's magnitudes applies to the 'idea.' By utilizing other senses, mankind's cognition is able to create a notion of the magnitude of a determinate object.

"Those ideas that now suggest unto us the various magnitudes of external objects before we touch them, might possibly suggested no such thing: Or they might have signified them in a direct contrary manner: so that the very same ideas, on the perception whereof we judge an object to be small, might as well have served to make us conclude it great. *Those ideas being in their own nature equally fitted to bring into our minds the idea of small or great, or no size at all of outward objects; Just as the words of any language are in their own nature indifferent to signify this or that thing or nothing at all."*[31]

The distance, as with the magnitude, utilizes the same senses and sets off the same course in mankind's cognitive process. Certainly, our perception of the magnitude of an object implies the notion of distance. This examination allows Berkeley to maintain that:

"All which visible objects are only in the mind, nor do they suggest ought external, whether distance or magnitude, otherwise than by habitual connexion as words do things."[32]

These 'connections' are something that one acquires and afterwards they become mechanical actions. This example clearly shows Wedgwood's interest in the creation of 'new objects' and the interaction with them.

"A man born blind and made to see would, at first opening of his eyes, make a very different judgment of the magnitude of object intromitted by them from what others do. He would not consider the ideas of sight with reference to, or as having any connexion with, the idea of touch: His view of them being entirely terminated within themselves, he can no otherwise judge them great or small than as they contain a greater or lesser number of visible points."[33]

Wedgwood's principal aim was the development of a photosensitive substance. In fact, such a technique represented the possibility to analyze mankind's process of cognition in front of 'new objects' and new perspectives. Wedgwood's interest goes beyond the perception of a simple object. His search for distance and magnitude perception created the necessity to understand the illusion of depth. He maintains that, the perception of depth – or the projective aspect of vision – could be created by means of

---

30 | Berkeley G. 1964 (1709), p. 195.
31 | Berkeley G. 1964 (1709), p. 195.
32 | Berkeley G. 1964 (1709), p. 202.
33 | Berkeley G. 1964 (1709), p. 203.

many associated points of view.[34] Different dissociated views of the same object could be used to create – or *re*-create – the sensation of depth. Under Wedgwood's thesis, the perception of the form of a whole object can be 're-built' in its totality by a mental-spatial process using separated views of the same object.

It is possible to imagine what kind of perception the scientist had regarding the first objects he translated onto paper by means of the superposition. The leaves and glass paintings, exposed for six or eight hours, traced the silhouette that in the budding dimension could be understood as an objective translation of a natural object. The profiles and silhouettes of those translated objects could be interpreted not as a reproduction – because they are poor in detail and less realistic than the painting – but as the transport of a natural object into a new dimension where it was possible to *re*-build the totality of the form by using a mental process. In conclusion, these translations of nature were the only ways to understand how our perception functions when it is 'free' of Euclidean impositions. Further, those translations created a strong felling of objectivity in the beholder. Nevertheless, this felling was not the product of the high degree of resemblance with the object represented. The objectivity of those translations was created by the silhouette's implication that the object represented really exists.

It is impossible to know how Wedgwood's impressions were of these images. Due to his premature death – thirty-four years old – he could not resume his photographic research and summarize his work in details. The extant contemporary documentation does not allow understanding the real – or deep – reason for Wedgwood and Davy's work. It is clear that the imperative was to fix the image upon a surface. It is attested in Davy's observations, after using the chloride in microscopic images, "Nothing but a method of preventing the unshaded parts of the delineation from being coloured (darkened) by exposure to the day is wanting, to render the process as useful as it is elegant."[35]

---

34 | It is possible to compare these new objects to the introduction of ideal elements in geometry. Further, as one can see, Wedgwood's research on photographic technology shows a philosophical aim that could allow a new way of representing space, a way of seeing space as the relationship between objects, in other words, a topologic space.
35 | Quoted by Gernsheim H. 1955, p. 33.

2.9 Stereoscopic Vision

|**Prop. XXIII**| For centuries, philosophers and scientists speculated about the relationship between the external world and the human eye. The Renaissance 'imposed' the idea of an ideal eye that undergoes, like a passive organ for recording, the inputs of information which issue from the external world.

Since the beginning of the camera obscura, there were many questions about human sight. Being the camera obscura a mechanism that simulated the organ of vision in its totality, i.e. the eyes and the mind process of perception, the scientists analyzed the process of vision in the same way. Thus, the first question raised by the camera obscura was focused on the inverted image produced by this optical system. Why is our perception of the world not inverted? According to some scientist the radiations passing through the cornea and the crystalline lens give *inverted images* of any illuminated external objects upon the retina of the eye. Some authors have attributed the correction to an operation of the mind, and others contend that it functions upon purely optical principles. Another important question is raised by the consideration of the fact that we have two eyes at a certain distance from each other. Therefore, both images formed on the retina cannot be exactly similar, nevertheless, we see a single object.[1] Consequently, binocular vision became an important phenomenon to try to understand.[2] The question that sprang up of this phenomenon was focused on the effect created by the brain activity in which the mind combined two dissimilar images in order to create one.

Sir Charles Wheatstone presented the stereoscope (1838), highlighting the sensation of depth created by the mechanism. (Fig. 2.57) His experiments suggested that stereoscopic vision creates, by the action of the body, a fusion of a three dimensional image by means of two-dimensional projections.[3] Wheatstone's experiments suggested another kind of rapport between mankind and space.

"By inducing the illusion of solidity with only binocular cues, and prompting the experience of solidity where no depth actually existed, the stereoscope called into doubt the alleged subordination of vision to touch, an assumption predicated on the belief in a self-present world 'out there.'"[4]

The notion of the eye as a passive organ disappears and also the idea that vision can be represented geometrically, i.e. the paradigm created by the Renaissance's perspective.

---

1 | See Hunt R. 1839.

2 | Leonardo da Vinci in his *Trattato della Pittura* analyzing some peculiarities of vision bear on the phenomenon of the stereoscope.

3 | See Schiavo L.B. 2003.

4 | Schiavo L.B. 2003, p. 116.

|*Fig. 2.57*|

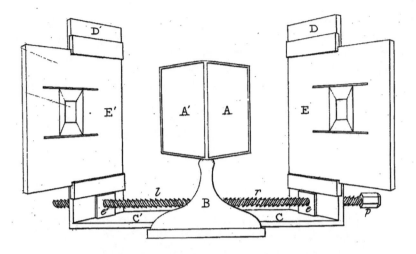

"The instrument consists essentially of two plane mirrors, so adjusted that their backs forth an angle of ninety degrees with each other. These mirrors are fixed by their common edge upon a horizontal board, in such a manner that, upon binging it close to the face, each eye sees the image in a different mirror. At either end of the board there are panels, in which the drawings are placed. The two reflected images coincide at the intersection of the optic axes, and form an image of the same apparent magnitude as each of the component pictures."[5]

Binocular vision reinforces the 'destruction' of the paradigm that maintained the rigid idea of geometry as the only tool able to translate nature. This analysis can be completed with Merleau-Ponty's interpretation about binocularity. In fact, Merleau-Ponty qualifies this phenomenon as an 'intentional' act that follows some intentional goals in order to share the common world.[6]

The discussion generated by the invention of the stereoscope was focused on the 'arbitrariness between stimulus and sensations.' Corresponding more to an illusion than to a rigid geometrical construction, the idea of depth was understood as a sensation derived from a more empirical spatial organization than from a Euclidean structure.[7]

---

5 | See Hunt R. 1839.

6 | See Merleau-Ponty M. 1945.

7 | The neurophysiological point of view about the binocularity of human vision posits that "The two images are not 'fused' not 'suppressed,' but instead the incoming barrage of neural data from each eye may be thought of as contributing to a common pool of information that leads to the emergence of a percept of a single object in depth." (Uttal W. 1978, p. 432.)

The irregularities of vision were the central point of interest for scientists and philosophers. Mankind understood that every sensorial phenomenon, in order to be studied, like in the case of geometry, requires its own special 'point of view.'

The visual devices, as tools for translating nature, generated spaces in which man could place forms, objects and phenomena in order to examine them. However, with the stereoscopy, one started to theorize a new way to understand the space. In the stereoscope's case – like for the others apparatuses of vision – its matter moves to the marketing field.[8] Nevertheless, even when this particular technique became a popular source of recreation, it conserved its character as an 'objective translation tool' useful for the scientific world, as attested in the next quotation:

"You may learn more, young American, of the difference between your civilization and that of the Old World by one look at this than from an average lyceum-lecture an hour long" claimed Holmes concerning the stereoscope.[9] This quotation shows some commercial – or political – interest in the stereoscope's technique, and also expresses the phenomenon of 'replacement' of the objects generated by a visual tool.

---

8 | Schiavo L. 2003, p. 118.

9 | See Holmes O.W. 1861.

2.10 PHOTOGRAPHIC TECHNOLOGY: A NATURE'S PENCIL

Since the Renaissance, the main purpose of the artist was to represent nature 'as it is'. The artistic expression, after the fifteenth century, depended on the imitation of the external world. Reality had to be represented at the highest degree of 'objectivity'. Since then, the impossibility to reconfigure reality on a canvas was perceived as a shortcoming. Nevertheless, quite surprisingly, this last point did not represent the central aim of the research on photo-sensibility carried out since Schulze's time. Moreover, even the work of Joseph Nicéphore Niépce,[1] who succeeded in leaving a permanent image on a surface by means of both the optical mechanism (camera obscura) and the chemical process (bitumen of Judea), did not aim at reconfiguring nature. In Niépce's view, photographic technology was not a tool aimed at translating a natural object into another dimension. His first goal was simply to improve upon new lithographical techniques; what he called *"a sort of gravure."*[2]

The natural *iter* of an image's reproduction by means of chemistry converged with the camera obscura.[3] As already noted, this mechanism was omnipresent in image reproduction. The problem to solve was how to 'remove the artist's hand' from the process of pictorial reproduction; to find a substance able to fix the image formed on the 'darkness.'

|Fig. 2.58|

After Niépce's first trials in the lithographic field, he observed two factors of this technology that could be improved in order to develop a technology of image reproduction. The first was the improvement of the sharpness of the image, its transfer to positive, and the image's fixing. The second was the improvement of photogravure's technique. In fact, the solution to the problem of fixing the image could be offered by this technique and also, the possibility to create an infinite number of copies of the same frame.[4]

Unable to draw, Niépce improved upon a technique that allowed him to copy drawings. His first Heliograph by superposition was accomplished in July 1822. The Heliograph of Pope Pius VII is his first successful and permanent heliographic copy

---

1 | His baptism register, made in the parish of Chalon-sur-Saône, attested as his real name Joseph Niépce. It may be possible that the name of Nicéphore is just a nickname.
2 | See Jay P. 1976.
3 | Niépce called the camera obscura "un point de vue d'après nature."
4 | See Jay P. 1983.

of an engraving by means of bitumen of Judea[5] on glass.[6] It was then that Niépce's aim changed completely. He looked towards, after the improvement of the heliography, permanently fixing an image of nature and to reproduce it in mass quantities through a device. In order to make a copy of nature, it was indispensable to accomplish the same act as Thales of Miletus, it is to say, a transport – or translation – of an object in relation to its size and scale by means of the shadow and light projected by the exposure of this object in sunlight. The aim was to create a system that accomplished this translation within fixed parameters in order to achieve an intelligible act, i.e. to fix a Euclidean arrangement of nature by means of the camera obscura.

|*Fig. 2.59*|

5 | Niépce was also interested in botanic and chemistry. In 1806 Niépce, with his brother Claude, planned a reciprocating engine functioning by means of Lycopodium powder (a vegetable). Their project was to build a ship functioning with this fuel. It was a revolutionary idea because the highest technique used at that time was the Steam Engine. After this idea Niépce turn his interest to the Petroleum oil and also into the Asphalt, it means the Bitumen of Judea, an important substance for the heliography.

6 | "The Bitumen of Judea process: In this process bitumen was dissolved in white petroleum, and a thin layer spread on a glass plate, on which Niepce superimposed an engraving made transparent by oiling. When exposed to light for 2 or 3 hours the bitumen under the white parts of the engraving became hard, whilst that under the dark lines remained soluble and could be washed away with a solvent consisting of oil of lavender and white petroleum. The resulting picture was unalterable by light." (Gernsheim H. 1955, p. 38.) On this subject see also Potonniée G. 1925, p. 108.

In 1826 or 1827, Niépce succeeded in recording an image on a bituminized pewter plate in a camera obscura.[7] Eight-hours of exposure was enough to produce a faint but identifiable image of the view from his window[8] (Niépce's house in Saint-Loup-de-Varenes, Fig. 2.59)[9] The latent image was visible by dissolving bitumen parts. The result was a permanent positive image where the light was represented by the bitumen and the shadows by the bare metal.[10] The long exposure time made this technique unable to realize photographic pictures, and that is why it remained in the production of plates for printing, his original aim.

Niépce's last attempts were not longer focused on the research of a special 'ink'. From the correspondence between the Niépce brothers – Claude and Joseph – we can read that they understood those trials as a "means to **engrave** on stone, on copper and on glass."[11] For Claude Niépce, the engraving of nature's views was "one of the most useful and most brilliant discoveries of the century, and I am sure, and I desire with all my heart, that it will be infinitely productive."[12]

This productivity represented Daguerre's central point of interest. Daguerre was accustomed to using the camera obscura as an aid to the perspective composition used in Panoramas, especially in topographical views. His employment of the camera obscura became systematic for the preparatory sketches necessary for each Panorama. For Daguerre, who usually employed real objects in his Dioramas, a technique that allowed him to imprint natural images themselves in a durable way was a central point in his research.

The Dioramas and Daguerre's luminous substances impressed Niépce. That is why he accepted the offer to work with Daguerre on the research of photographic technology.[13] After a long collaboration with Niépce, and later, with Niépce's son Isidore, Daguerre was able to reproduce and fix a clear image in the first half of 1837; the Daguerreotype was introduced with its first successful still-life.

---

7 | After Barthes, the first photography was made by Niépce in 1922, 'La table mise', see Barthes R. 1980, pp. 133-139.

8 | Coe B. 1976, p. 14.

9 | The long duration of exposure is also identifiable in the lighting of this picture, the first in the history. In fact, one can see the different points of lighting produced by the movement of the sun during the long exposure time. It is interesting to note that Gaudreault identifies in this image a kind of interesting set. In fact, he affirms that an image is in fact a series of superimposed images (thus, plural). In his words, "È un'immagine che ne contiene altre cento in maniera non discreta: non si possono separare le une dalle altre. Non si tratta propriamente di un *singleton*, ma di un conglomerato di *singleton* indifferenziati e sovrapposti." (Gaudreault A. 2002, p. 30.)

10 | Gernsheim H. – Gernsheim A. 1956, p. 51.

11 | For more information see Jay P. 1988.

12 | Quoted by Gernsheim H. 1955, p. 40.

13 | See Gernsheim H. – Gernsheim A. 1956, Chap. III *The invention of Photography*.

|*Fig. 2.60*|

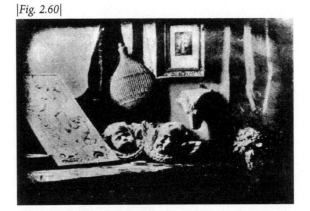

Daguerreotype's process of exploit was very long because of the legal problem of royalties. In fact, the Daguerreotype could be understood as an improvement of the heliographic process of which Niépce is the inventor.[14] Daguerre felt that the improvement upon Niépce's technique which Daguerre had realized on his own, were sufficient to call his discoveries by his name alone. However, this long process was the witness to a new paradigm in the relationship between mankind and nature. This technology of image reproduction was no longer understood as an '*encre sypmathique*' or an useful means in the process of lithography. The Daguerreotype was the first tool that perfectly combined the action of the translation of an image, its reconfiguration and its fixation onto a surface.[15]

During the next months after his discovery, Daguerre attracted publicity by driving around Paris with the apparatus on a truck, photographing monuments and public buildings. First, he tried to take advantage of the phenomenon of 'images-overindulgence' created by the illusionist representations to the public. His Diorama represented the proof that a large public was seeking new ways of interaction with images.

The 'Diorama à double effet' confirmed the social necessity of the perfect illusion in pictorial compositions, a 'perfect' translation of nature. His apparatus was also the answer to the economic necessity of image production. However, he failed in his goal of creating a market with his new apparatus. Towards the end of 1838, Daguerre re-

---

14 | See Niépce I. 1841.

15 | "At the Conservatoire des Arts et Métiers the inventor himself gave weekly demonstrations of the process. After the silvered copper plate had been thoroughly cleaned and polished, it was sensitized by vapour of iodine in an iodizing-box, forming a thin layer of silver iodide on its surface. After exposure the latent image was developed by vapour of mercury heated over a spirit-lamp, the mercury attaching itself to those parts of the silver iodide which had been affected by light. The picture was then fixed with hyposulphite of soda (before March 1839 this was done with common salt), washed with distilled water, and gently dried over a flame." (Gernsheim H. 1955, pp. 56.)

introduced the photographic technology to the milieu of its provenance, the scientific world. After his failure, and searching for economic support, Daguerre presented his Daguerreotype to a number of scientists, including J.B Dumas, Biot, Humboldt, and Argo, with the purpose of interesting the government.[16] The Daguerreotype was introduced by François Dominique Argo to the Chamber of Deputies as an instrument that:

"does not demand a single manipulation which is not perfectly easy to every person. It requires no knowledge of drawing, and does not depend upon a manual dexterity. By observing a few very simple directions, any one may succeed with the same certainty and perform as well as the author of the invention."[17]

The French political class understood the photographic engraving process as a means able of "represent[ing] inanimate nature with a degree of perfection unattainable by the ordinary processes of drawing and painting –a perfection equal to that of nature herself."[18] Paul Delaroche exclaimed hysterically, "From today painting is dead."[19] Obviously, the debate in the Chamber of Deputies meant the strengthening of Daguerre's fame.[20]

Instead of reorganizing nature under a specific order like in the Panorama, photographic technology assigned to the lens the faculty to **discover** elements in nature.[21] The goal was no longer to simulate nature but to transport/translate it into a new dimension in order to be studied under another point of view. This technique lost its calligraphic association, and took on a drawing connotation. The *Magazine of Science and School of Arts* called this new technology: "Photogenic or photographic Drawing."[22] On the one hand, this indicated the difficulty in assimilating a technology that translates nature, in absence of an artist's hand, as a translation device performing an act of spatial organization. On the other hand, its drawing connotation placed photographic technology in the field of art.

It is interesting how H. Fox Talbot testified to the arrival of this technology in England. He claimed that photographic technology (the Daguerreotype) – in English art known as Photogenic Drawing or the Calotype – were simultaneous inventions in both countries. Presenting his plates, Talbot clarified that his works "are Pictures themselves, obtained by the action of light, and not engravings in imitation of them."[23]

---

16 | Gernsheim H. 1955, p. 52.

17 | Quoted by Gernsheim H. 1955, p. 54.

18 | Gay-Lassac, in the French Upper Chamber, quoted by Gernsheim H. 1955, p. 54.

19 | Quoted by Gernsheim H. 1955, p. 54.

20 | See Pfau L. 1877, pp. 115-17.

21 | See Benjamin W. 2002a (1935.)

22 | See The Magazine of Science, and School of Arts, Saturday, April 20, 1839.

23 | *The Pencil of Nature* is the first book illustrated with photographic images and the first mass production of photographs.

Curiously, this explanation was necessary because, as Talbot affirms, in France many well-executed engravings were published in imitation of photographic images.[24] Talbot used – since 1834 – light sensitive paper, obtained by bathing it first with common salt (sodium chloride) and then with silver nitrate. In 1835 he was able to fix these images by rendering unaltered silver chloride relatively insensitive through bathing the paper in a strong solution of common salt. The first difference between Talbot's method and the Daguerreotype was that Talbot, with his process, obtained a negative picture. After the 'translation' of the natural object, he had to place freshly sensitized paper in contact with the negative and expose it to light, so he could obtain a positive print.[25] Additionaly, in Daguerre's technique, each picture was unique because they were fixed upon polished silver plates.[26]

|Fig. 2.61|

At that time, photographic technology became a source of interest for creating representations of architecture and also tried to develop into a portraiture technique.

Even if this technique, after Daguere's improvements, started to be interpreted more as an action of 'translation' or spatial organization than as 'writing technology,' it was still influenced by its calligraphic and lithographic connotations.

Another phenomenon generated by the photographic technology was the downfall of the Panorama which, started in the second half of the nineteenth century. The arrival of photographic technology took place when the Moving Panorama was at its

---

24 | Talbot H.F. 1969, pp. 3. The first edition of *The pencil of Nature* was published in London between 1844 and 1846 in six separated fascicles. A single design appeared on the covers of all fascicles.

25 | Talbot H.F. 1969. See *The introduction of The Pencil of Nature*, by Beaumont Newhall.

26 | Talbot's method – Calotype – created the notions in photographic technology – he used these words – of 'negative' and 'positive'. See, Talbot. H. F, *The process of Calotype Photogenic Drawing*, Communicated to the Royal Society, June 10th, 1841.

most popular period. The narrative developed by the Panorama was forgotten and replaced by the objectivity of the photographic re-production of images. Photographic technology reinforced the illusion of objectivity because it was a technique that assured the existence of the framed object; as Talbot maintained: "They are impressed by Nature's hand; and what they want as yet of delicacy and finish of execution arises chiefly from our want of sufficient knowledge of her laws."[27] With photography, one was obliged to believe in to the existence of the object represented:

"effectivement re-présenté, c'est-à-dire rendu présent dans le temps et dans l'espace. La photographie bénéficie d'un transfert de la réalité de la chose sur sa reproduction."[28]

Photographic technology arrived not many years after the Panorama and, being both contemporary methods, photography was used for some of the Panorama's construction. The first time that photographic technology was used in the Panorama was during the Crimean War (1853-1856).[29] The spatial representation of the battlefield had a scientific and a military goal. These images were useful as a document about the military actions and as a source of topographic information.[30] Like the Panorama, before being a popular event in European capital cities, photographic technology was an answer to some scientific necessities.

The Daguerreotype determined without a doubt the end of the rotunda and its 360° spatial organization. Even though the 360° pictorial compositions were shown around the world for over another half-century, the public perceived them as an old medium. *Daguerreotypomania* was everywhere, eclipsing the Panorama. Since the Daguerreotype first publicized, the old goals of the Panorama were re-elaborated by the 'Daguerreotypists.' Some serial publications – e.g. N.P. Lerebours' *Excursions daguérriennes* – invaded Paris.

The 1840s meant the arrival to Paris of distant places already presented by the Panorama. Guatier's *Voyage en Espagne*, and Girault de Prangey's *Monuments Arabes d'Egypte, de Syrie et d'Asie Mineure* brought to the French public these farway spaces, proving that they 'really exist.'

---

27 | Talbot H.F. 1969, p. 2.

28 | Bazin A. 2008 (1975), p. 13.

29 | The photographic technology researched a panoramic sensation before this war. In the first half of XIX century there were several attempts to create a panoramic horizon by means of the photographic technology. The first examples of this research were made with the Daguerreotype and usually they were composed by a series of pictures placed side by side aimed at creating the panoramic horizon. This 'side by side' method was used to prepare the pictorial composition of the panorama. They were also some attempts to create a photographic machine able to compose a panoramic image in one shot by means of some technical arrangements of the Daguerrotype.

30 | Bordini S. 1984, p. 60.

The firsts 'translations' operated by means of the Daguerreotype were focused on historical monuments, Parisian streets and landscapes. The long exposure time – 20 minutes in full sunlight – made this technology unable to compose pictures of people. This problem was partially solved by Johanes Baptist Insering (1796-1860). First, he decided to paint over the image and scratched in on the silvered plate – especially the pupils of the eyes – in order to correct the unsharpness caused by the movement. Although the problem concerned the milieu of chemistry. It was a process of a chemical acceleration which could offer the solution. Franz Kratochwila published, in *Wiener Zeitung*, the chemical process that allowed Insering to create the famous *Five-Minute Portraits* (1841).[31] In order to halt any movement of the body, a device was invented to prepare the figure for transition into immobile composition. Photographic technology transformed the subject into an object and, in this context, becoming an object was almost a surgical suffering.[32]

The headrest was the tool that shaped the body's position like the pedestal of the immobilized image (Fig. 2.62, 2.63). The plan developed by this technology was not only a dimension where it was possible to accomplish an objective translation of natural objects, but it was also a space that allowed mankind's projection into eternity.

|*Fig. 2.62*| |*Fig. 2.63*|

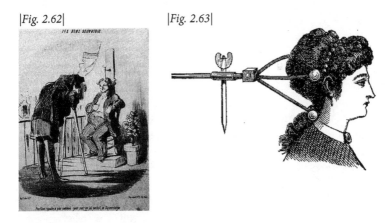

Photographic technology also means the defense against time. There is no longer death because in photography's space time does not exist. As maintained by André Bazin, concerning the 'clearing of the plastic arts of its magical functions', the plastics arts, in its parallel evolution with civilization, sublimates the incoercible requirement to exorcize time. Even so, with artistic representations, people do not believe in the ontological identity of the model and of the portrait, any more. They accept the *memento*, created by the representation, which impersonates the real: "celui-ci nous aide à nous souvenir de celui-là."[33] This *memento* institutes a complex phenomenon

---

31 | Gernsheim H. 1955, p. 56.
32 | Barthes R. 1980, p. 29.
33 | Bazin A. 2008 (1975), p. 10.

of dematerialization and of the creation of a space where the matter is no longer the survival of the man. The high level of objectivity in photographic technology initiated the creation of a space gifted with temporal autonomy.

After the fifteenth century, the balance created in pictorial art, between the symbolism and the realism of forms, started to lean toward the quest for an imitation, more or less complete of nature. Certainly, the scientific constituent (almost mechanical) brought by perspective was a decisive element. The illusion of three-dimensional space offered by the camera obscura – Da Vinci's prefigured Niépce's – allowed the artist to create a dimension where man could place object's representations with a high level of resemblance with the 'real', like man's direct perception of the world. The dimension created by the photographic technology started the phenomenon of replacement of the real, reconfiguring the forms into another plan.

|Prop. XXVI| As already noted, the arrival of the camera obscura encouraged the study of space, its re-elaboration and representation into another plan conserving the relationship of scale and proportion. Like in Thales' case, the idea was to transport/translate an object in accurate proportions. In fact, Thales' search was to translate the concrete and essential meaning of the object, of the world. From this operation – or mechanism – a meaning that represents the object translated into another plane must be derived.[34] Certainly, Thales' aim was not to reproduce an object in realistic terms, like the *trompe l'oeil* technique. His geometric operation and abstract process, aimed at translating the Egyptian pyramids, looked for the creation of a system that would allow mankind to translate an object into abstract forms. This action of 'translation' may be perceived as a *pars pro toto*. From this mechanism came a meaning that had to be translated from one system of signs to another. The interpretation was indispensable for understanding the object translated into the other plane. At this point, it is possible to understand Bazin's statement "la perspective fut le péché originel de la peinture occidentale."[35] The real aim of perspective and the camera obscura was not to obtain a *trompe l'œil* but to attain an equal level of symbolism and realism in pictorial representations.

Painting was placed between two different ambitions: an aesthetic one, in which the painting wanted to express spiritual realities transcended by the symbolism; and a psychological one, that manifested the desire 'to oust' the external world with its representation. 'Sin' – represented by the irruption of the *mechanism* in artistic expression – is recognizable since painting started a pursuit towards a technology able to respond to psychological necessity, forgetting the spiritual need of the symbolism in art. Realism, at some point in this long process, is understood to no longer be a necessity in concretely expressing the significant and essential of the world, but as a *trompe l'oeil* – *trompe-l'esprit* as Bazin maintains – in order to respond to the mere illusion of forms.

---

34 | "Meaning" as "traduzione di un segno in un altro sistema di segni." (Eco. U. 2003, p. 277.)

35 | Bazin A. 2008 (1975), p. 12.

Photographic technology satisfied the artist's obsession with the search for objectivity. Even if photographic technology was perceived as an inferior art, maybe due to the lack of color, this technology created the feeling of the perfect illusion formed by a mechanical reproduction from which the human hand is excluded. In this space the distinction between the imaginary and the real disappears creating a phenomenon that makes an object of each image and an image of each object. This phenomenon is clearly explained by Barthes when he analyzes the portrait as a moment where the person photographed is neither a subject, nor an object, but rather a subject that feels that he becomes an object: then he has a 'micro-experience of death (of parenthesis): he becomes a true *spectrum*.[36]

---

36 | Barthes. R. 1980, p. 30.

2.11 A NEW SPACE WHICH ACCEPTS MOVEMENT

|Prop. XXVII| Photographic technology opened the possibility to reproduce nature with a high degree of objectivity. This notion of objectivity was strongly supported by the notion of the real existence of the represented object. By means of photographic technology, mankind acquired a new geometrical space where nature could be analyzed from another point of view, but also a space where movement could be decomposed in order to be analyzed.

In the second half of the nineteenth century, the mechanical reproduction of images gave to the beholder the sensation of high objectivity and relief; nature in the "space of death," described by Barthes, acquired, at that point, the notion of 'reality.' The last step to give 'the true sensation of life' through the photographic technique was represented by the achievement of the technique of 'photographic moving pictures.' In other words, mankind would, by means of photographic technology, 'reproduce nature as it is.' It was not enough for the mechanical reproduction of a tree, in that reproduction, to be in accord with nature; the tree must bend at the will of the wind. The dimension realized by means of the photographic technology imposed again a new human aim, which was personified by a system that would permit the viewing of pictures in movement and in relief.

The natural *iter* of the research of the dimension of movement in photographic space was through animation. In fact, during the 1860s, the British Henry Cook and the Italian Gaetano Bonelli developed and perfected the photobioscope, which was a viewer of stroboscopic discs with microscopic and stereoscopic images.[1] The limit of this technique was represented by the photographic technology, which at that time used daguerreotype plates that were unable to capture ten, much less twenty images a second, the necessary speed to reproduce natural movement. The photographic technology of that time was also not sensitive enough for this aim. The sensitivity of the plate's surface was the limit to the attempts by Henry Dumont, creator of the photographic camera with successive plates (1861), and Louis Ducos du Hauron, inventor of the reversible camera with 290 lenses.[2]

It was during the year 1874 when documenting the dimension of movement became possible in photographic technology. Thanks to the French astronomer Pierre-Jules-César Janssen, the possibility to give this new dimension to photographic technology, a technology still influenced by Daguerre's plates, became real.

The passage of Venus across the sun is a rare phenomenon (it occurs only twice in a century) and it was of a great importance for astronomers around the world. Janssen's *photographic revolver* [3] was in fact created with the aim to make a rapid succes-

---

1 | See Mannoni L. – Pesenti Campagnoni D. – Robinson D. 1995.

2 | See Mannoni L. – Pesenti Campagnoni D. – Robinson D. 1995.

3 | It is important to remember that Janssen's revolver was not the first attempt that followed the 'revolver' form. In fact, the first machines that attempted to capture life from nature and not to recreate it by means of animation were conceived of as revolvers.

sion of photographs of the passage of Venus across the sun. The invention, presented on March 1873, was able to capture 48 successive images in 72 seconds. The surface where the image was fixed was a photosensitive disc of 18.5cm in diameter. The time of exposition was determined by the machine (*automoteur*) and could also be imposed by the user.[4]

The vision of the great astronomical phenomenon was scheduled in Japan, and there, Janssen's revolver would be tested. First in Yokohama and then, because of the weather, in Nagasaki, on December 9th the disc could be exposed. Even if the quality of the images was not really good, this machine, as Janssen claimed, was "encouraging for the future."[5] Indeed, Janssen's photographic revolver acquired a great importance not only because it opened up many possibilities for analyzing natural phenomena – Janseen recognized the importance of his invention especially in the astronomical and biological fields – but also because his machine represents the first step of the process that gave to mankind a new dimension in the spatial organization produced by means of photographic technology; the dimension of movement.

As stated in the last chapters, the notion of motion was an important point of the development of visual media as well as techniques of visual illusions. Before analyzing the experiments of Muybridge, it is important to remember that a long period of 'popular toys' using drawings preceded the real research on motion as a time-spatial dimension allowed by photographic technology. It is possible to identify the first step of the temporal dimension in photographic spatial organization in Archer's introduction of the wet-collodion process, which opened a real possibility of attaining the era of instantaneity and radically changed the panorama of the creation of the illusion of motion. Indeed, thanks to technical possibility of the instantaneity, photographic

---

Such is the case of the first model, manufactured by Eugène Deschiens, which functioned by a spring action and caused vibrations that damaged the photographic image. It is also important to remember that the use of the word 'revolver' was borrowed from Colt's 1840 handgun, not because of its cylinder but because of its manageability. This was also the case of Jonte's photo-revolver (1872), which was composed of two stock stores, one for the virgin plates, and the other for impressed ones. Enjalbert's revolver followed the same principle of Jonte's photo-revolver. The first ancestor of Marey's fusil can be recognized in Briois' revolver (1862), in fact, this last one impressed a rotating plate. Marey's fusil creates, of course, a long line of descent, consider for instance, Sand and Hunter's fusil (1885), the *photo-éclair* of Fetter (1886) and also the most recent Mamiya's revolver for 35mm film (1954).

4 | Janssen describes his invention, in particular the automatism of the machine, as follows: "L'instrument est automoteur, il donne de lui-même, et sans aucune intervention de l'opérateur, la série d'images à produire." (Pierre-Jules-César Janssen, *Presentation du revolver photographique et épreuves obtenues avec cet instrument, 1876,* in Oeuvres scientifiques, Paris 1929.)

5 | See Pierre-Jules-César Janssen, *Presentation du revolver photographique et épreuves obtenues avec cet instrument, 1876,* in *Oeuvres scientifiques,* Paris 1929.

technology could be able to (at least to imagine) capture movements in nature and decompose it in a series of fixed photograms.

Before 1878, the year in which Muybridge realized the technique of serial photographs, some techniques were already developed. Consider, for instance, Antoine Claudet and Jules Duboscq who set in motion stereoscopic photograph; Henry Mayhew produced a stereoscopic phenakistoscope also using stereoscopic photography and Coleman Sellers patented a "motion-picture" machine that he called the Kinematoscope.[6] This new dimension acquired by photographic technology was used in order to analyze the movement of animals, early on. It is important to remark that at that point this research was no longer focused on the achievement of the representation of movement in nature, but was clearly focused on the analysis of those movements by means of their decomposition. Thus, it was no longer a *trompe l'oeil*, it is to say, the creation of the feeling of movement by means of animation; it became a new dimension that allowed mankind a new analysis of space and time: a new dimension in the geometry derived from photographic technology.[7] This new dimension created a convergence phenomenon between the physiologist, who attempts to comprehend animals' movements and the artist who equated truth of nature with art.

|*Fig. 2.64*|

It is the case of Muybridge's research. Eadweard Muybridge (1830-1904)[8] was commissioned (1872) by Leland Stanford to take photographs of a running horse.[9] Five years latter, the commission changed, he asked Muybridge to take a series of views of the step of the horse in all its stages.[10] The research was aimed at discovering precisely the movement of the horse's legs while running. Thanks to an improved chemical formula and special equipment – twelve Scoville cameras, equipped with 'fast' stereo lenses and an electrically controlled mechanism for operating the cameras' specially constructed double-slide shutters[11] – in early June 1878, Muybridge made the first successful serial photographs of fast motion.

6 | The Kinematoscope was in fact a machine where were mounted static poses on a rotating drum. See Muybridge E. 1979.

7 | See Reis M. 2007.

8 | He was born as Edgard James Muggeridge, and then modified his name to Eadweard Muybridge.

9 | This commission was made by Leland Standford former governor of California and president of the Central Pacific Railroad Company.

10 | See Muybridge E. 1979.

11 | See Muybridge E. 1979, p. xvii, introduction by Mozley A.V.

During that month, he realized more tests and published them in various newspapers entitled *The Horse in Motion*. In the following summer, Muybridge expanded his experimental setup: he used 24 cameras set at intervals of twelve inches.[12] This last experiment applied a technique that he could elaborate at the university of Pennsylvania. The results were called *Studies of foreshortenings*.

|*Fig. 2.65*|

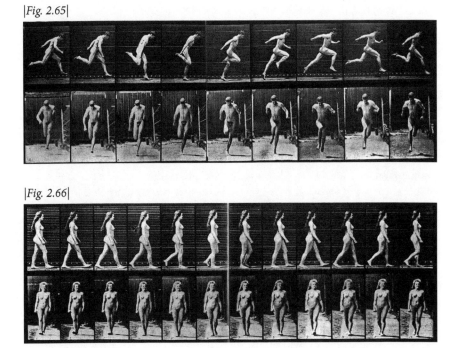

|*Fig. 2.66*|

In 1881 Muybridge published the result of his early photographic investigation of motion entitled *The Attitudes of Animals in Motion, A Series of Photographs Illustrating the Consecutive Positions Assumed by Animals in Performing Various Movements*. In this last edition, Muybridge explains the mechanisms used to achieve his experiments. It is important to note that he introduced a mechanism called a 'clock-work apparatus' which was used to make exposures at regulated intervals of time rather than distance. Time acquired its spatial notion in the photographic field and became an important dimension in the spatial organization realized by means of the photographic camera. Muybridge's principal aim was the 'translation' of time in terms of space.

The decomposition of movement, by means of photographic technology was extremely important in analyzing some pathologies that affect natural muscular movement. Some of Muybridge's plates depict patients suffering from locomotor ataxia,

---

12 | See Muybridge E. 1979.

lateral sclerosis, epilepsy, muscular atrophy, etc.[13] The field of plastic arts also demonstrated a notable interest in the decomposition of movement. In fact, the artist's
perception of movement changed thanks to the precision of the analysis offered by
Muybridge's instrument. The stop-motion photograph showed the animal in a position impossible to be perceived by the naked human eye and the artistic debate starts
when the precision of the natural movement of the locomotion of the animal demonstrates "what is optically true, is not necessarily, pictorially true."[14]

Even if Etienne-Jules Marey (1830-1904) was a contemporary of Muybridge, and
their investigations were focused on the subject of time, their results were completely
different. The most important difference between Marey and Muybridge is that for
Marey movement was a moment to synthesize by keeping the notion of one point of
view. In other words, Marey was interested in keeping the 'unity' of the movement.
Thus, he used a single point of view, i.e. a single camera. This is clear in his analysis
on avian flight. In that experiment, his aim was the analysis and the synthetization of
flight in order to 'condense it in time'. In contrast, Muybridge captured on each plate
the representation of one snapshot of the movement. On the one hand, Muybridge reproduced on the plate – every plate was different of the next one – the decomposition
in successive moments of one movement; on the other hand, Marey created a synthesis of the movement that generates an artificial representation in three dimensions.[15]
Marey reproduced "motion as a spatio-temporal continuum. Condensed through the
lens of a single camera."[16] With Marey's method time becomes a 'sculpture.' The dimension of time developed by Marey show the elasticity of the body in movement
through a flexible space. In these two different methods it is possible to see an important conceptual opposition analyzed by Merleau-Ponty. On the one hand, there is the
reproduction of movement understood as the passage of the object through different
spaces: in Merleau-Ponty's words, "une reverie zénonienne sur le movement." In this
movement's reproduction the viewer sees a rigid body covering a distance. On the
other hand, one is bringing the method of the sculpture in the line with the movement. Borrowing from Merleau-Ponty:

"Le cinéma donne le mouvement, *mais comment* ? Est-ce, comme on croit, en copiant
de plus près le changement de lieu ? On peut présumer que non, puisque le ralenti
donne un corps flottant entre les objets comme une algue, et qui ne se meut pas. Ce
qui donne le mouvement, dit Rodin, c'est une image où les bras, les jambes, le tronc, la
tête sont pris chacun à un autre instant, qui donc figure le corps dans une attitude qu'il
n'a eue à aucun moment, et impose entre ses parties des raccords fictifs, comme si cet

---

13 | See Rondinella L.F. 1929.
14 | Muybridge E. 1979. Quoted by Mozley A.V.
15 | See Hulten P. 1977.
16 | Zielinski S. 1999, p. 58.

affrontement d'imcompossibles pouvait et pouvait seul faire sourdre dans le bronze et sur la toile la transition et la durée."[17]

Muybridge's relation with the medical field was totally different from Marey's. As noted above, Muybridge's invention was used in the medical field because some doctors found in his stop-motion camera an important tool for analyzing some pathologies. Marey's case is totally the opposite. In fact, Marey went to Paris in 1849 to study medicine and ten years later obtained his doctorate degree with a thesis on the circulation of blood.[18] Thus, he became a well known physiologist (*un ingénieur de la vie*). His main idea about animals – of course also humans – was that they must be analyzed as a machine.[19] This conception of life – not so different from Bacon's idea that allowed for the exteriorization of sight by means of the camera obscura – allowed Marey to start research on inner movements of humans and animals by means of some machines, which translated natural movement into mechanical concepts. His aim was to achieve, with physics-like precision, an analysis of biological phenomena, primarily movement, as he defined it "the most important act." According to Marey, movement was a translation of all phenomena of life and its analysis implied its comprehension in time. In other words, life was a coordination of functions that could be analyzed as a multifarious mechanical apparatus coordinated in harmony. Thus, Marey's idea of physiology was based on the comprehension of successive states of the body in time. Hence, photographic technology became an important instrument for Marey's research.

|*Fig. 2.67*|

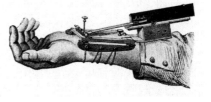

First, he studied the movement of animals – specially blood's circulation; his first research at the university – by using pre-existing apparatuses that he adapted or improved, e.g. the *Sphygmographe* by Vierordt used to read precisely blood's pulse.

He later began the analysis of locomotion of both horses and humans by using his *chronographe*, which was a drum with a lever and a cylinder. By placing rubber-tubes on each leg of the horse, the machine was able to record on a cylinder the force applied with each step (Fig. 2.69).

---

17 | Merleau-Ponty M. 1964, p. 79.
18 | His first publication in 1863 was influenced by his studies at the university on blood's circulation. See Marey E.J. 1863.
19 | See Marey E.J. 1873.

|Fig. 2.68| |Fig. 2.69| |Fig. 2.70|

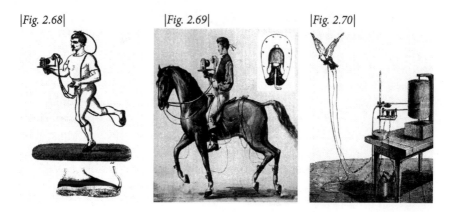

In the case of humans, a rubber sensor was placed in their shoes (Fig. 2.68). In the area of air locomotion, he was attempting to record the bird's wing beats (duration and frequency) and the simulation of flight (Fig. 2.70). As noted above, photographic technology arrived some years latter in Marey's works, precisely in 1882. Photographic technology represented just a means, which allows the improvement of his earlier works.[20] The influence of Muybridge's works is clear. In fact, in 1881 Marey met Muybridge in Paris and he asked him to obtain some photographs of birds. Marey was disappointed with Muybridge photos and at that moment he decided to obtain them himself. The success of Janssen's revolver inspired Marey to improve upon the photographic revolver used to watch the passage of Venus some years before. Marey's aim was clearly to take a photograph of the movement of the wings of a flying bird, it is to say, not only the animal accomplishing the aerial movement but also to divide the beat of the wings.[21] The use of the fusil photographique was already an old idea of Marey. In a letter to Muybridge of December 18, 1878, Marey advised the development of a photographic revolver in order to achieve the analysis of aerial movement. When Marey decided to work on the improvement of Jansenn's revolver, he aimed at the invention of a portable machine able to take a series of instantaneous pictures divided by short

---

20 | As a supplement of his work *Méthode graphique* he published in 1885 *Développemen de la méthode graphique par l'emploi de la photographie*. In this supplement he explained his interest on photographic technology: "J'ai cherché dans l'emploi de la photographie la solution de certains problèmes qui échappaient aux procédés d'inscription mécanique des mouvements."

21 | Or in Gaudreault's words "andare del multiplo all'uno." That is to say, the mechanism of translation aimed at capturing one image of the many virtual images of natural movements. Thus, Gaudreault posits that photographic technology attempts to "far sorgere l'unità dal complesso." (Gaudreault A. 2002, pp. 29-30.)

intervals.[22] The development of Marey's *fusil photographique* is attested in a letter to his mother on the February 3, 1882 during his yearly period in Naples:

"J'ai un fusil photographique qui n'a rien de meurtrier, et qui prend l'image d'un oiseau qui vole, ou d'un animal qui court en un temps moindre de 1/500 de seconde. Je ne sais si tu te représentes bien cette rapidité, mais c'est quelque chose de surprenant."

|*Fig. 2.71*|

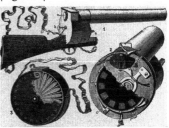

Designed as a real gun, the device was engineered with a lens in the barrel and a cylinder head on which turned the photographic plate when one pressed the trigger. The rotating plate was round or octagonal covered by gelatin silver bromide. The plate could stop 12 times per second in front of the lens, while the shutter let light cross through at 1/720 of a second per shot. The focus was adjusted by extending or shortening the barrel.

|*Fig. 2.72*|

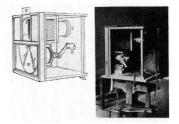

The same year he developed the *chronographe à plaque fixe*, in order to better capture on the same plate a series of successive images representing the different positions of a human or animal in locomotion. The outcomes of the experience with the *fusil photographique* did not achieve Marey's expectations. In fact, the images were not focused enough and were also too small; thus the subject – in that case the bird – has no volume or shape.

The problem of speed remained, it is to say, it was impossible to capture the wings' beat and divide it into multiple images. It is important to remember that Marey always tried to keep the use of stationary point-of-view in order to capture the decomposition of movement with a single vanishing point.

The method utilized by Marey during his first attempts with the *fusil photographique* was limited by the sensitivity of the emulsion. His invention was composed of one objective and a rotary shutter, which exposes the plate at every revolution. In order to obtain an intelligible image, it was necessary to operate the machine

---

22 | "Il fallait donc modifier la méthode et construire un appareil simple, portatif, au moyen duquel on pût, sur un oiseau volant en liberté, prendre une série d'images photographiques instantanées, à des intervalles de temps assez courts pour que plusieurs images consécutives correspondissent aux phases successives d'un même battement d'aile." (Marey E.J. 1890, p. 132.)

in front of a black background, which is not exposed upon the plate. Logically, it was necessary for the subject, in that case, men and horses, to be in white (Fig. 2.73). The first proofs, realized on October 1882 were made with a speed of 10 images/second. One year later, Marey developed the method of *Chronophotographies partielles ou géométriques*.

|*Fig. 2.73*|

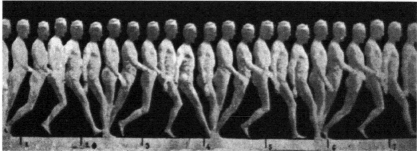

The interest of that method was the decomposition of the movement of slow subjects e.g. men. In fact, the flight of the bird was fast enough to be decomposed upon the plate without double exposures. This was not the case of the movement of a man walking. The speed of the human walk was not great enough to create a clear decomposition of movement, it is to say, the photographical space was collapsed at the same point with more than two images of the same object.[23] Marey resolved that problem by using two different methods. The first one consisted of special clothing, half white and half black, worn by the subject. That clothing allowed for the capturing of just one side of the subject – one leg, one arm, etc – thus improving the analysis of locomotion by avoiding the confusion of too many images at the same space on the plate (Fig. 2.73). The second method consisted of a black outfit, which covered the entire subject. This clothing had metal bands on the arms, legs and feet that were captured by the plate, showing both directions and positions of the bones (Fig. 2.74). These 'geometrical pictures' (*photographies géométriques*) were realized in June 1883. The most famous geometrical picture (Fig. 2.75) is *La course de l'homme en costume noir* (1883).

|*Fig. 2.74*| |*Fig. 2.75*|

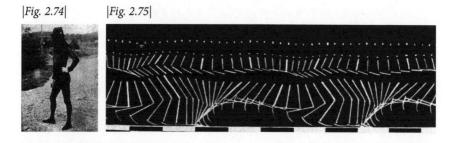

23 | See L'Herbier M. 1946.

Marey's physiological interest and his idea to photo-graph from one point of view allowed him to develop many others techniques like *la chronophotographie avec miroir tournant* (1888), *la chronophotographie sur bande de papier sensible mobile* (1888), *la chronophotographie sur pellicule mobile* (Fig. 2.76) (1890), *le projecteur chronophotographique* (1892-1893) and *le chronophotographe réversible* (1896-1897).[24] It is important to note that the projector he developed to visualize his work was not intended for public display but only for scientific interest, in order to improve the analysis of his images in movement.[25]

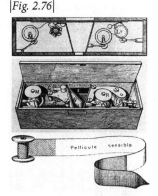

|*Fig. 2.76*|

His inventions during the last years of the 1880s clearly gave form to cinematographic technology. Starting in 1883, Marey became interested in the development of transferring film. He created a mobile plate in 1887 and the first mobile photographic strip was realized in October 1888 with *Le chronophotographe à pellicule mobile* (Fig. 2.76). In that apparatus it is possible to recognize the basis of the cinematograph.

During Marey's photographic period, his research was focused on avian flight; insect flight; human locomotion and movement; animal locomotion (especially the horse; it was his main subject in *La machine animale* of 1873);[26] the movement of objects, in order to improve the studies of both fields ballistic and acceleration of speed; stereoscopy, or the study of objects that create space through their movements, like the hyperboloid;[27] (Fig. 2.77) hydrodynamics and aerodynamics. These last subjects of study were developed in the late 1880s

|*Fig. 2.77*|

---

24 | See Hulten P. 1977.

25 | Marey's projector was developed in 1892 and it was supposed to be presented to *l'Académie des Sciences* in May. He never presented his projector because it remains some problems of flickering of the images. His mechanism of projection consisted in a rubberized linen strip where he stuck the series of images obtained by means of the *chronophotographe*.

26 | It was until 1888 that Marey could made a study on fishes, reptiles and small mammals. Thanks to both fusil with rotating mirror and mobile film, he was able to shoot on the bottom of water, thus he realized some chronophotographies about the movement of eels, fishes, snakes, rays, etc. These films were published between 1890 and 1891.

27 | The hyperboloid is a geometric object generated by means of the movement of rotation on its axis of a Hyperbola.

and 1900 and were published on *Le mouvement* 1894. It is important to remark that the objectivity offered by Marey's *fusil photographique* inspired scientists to deal with natural irregular shapes and chaotic movements.

|*Fig. 2.78*| |*Fig. 2.79*|

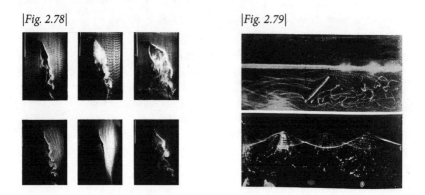

|**Prop. VI**| These studies in chaotic movements highlight the geometrical character of Marey's technique. In fact, his interest in chaotic movements and the method of analyzing it gave a new scientific character to his photographic technique. Like a new geometrical dimension, his views recognize irregular shapes and materialize chaotic movements like that of water and smoke (Fig. 2.78, 2.79).

His approach to natural movements was strongly influenced by the assumption that claimed the *Clockwork Universe Theory*. However, the image (Fig. 2.79) of the chronophotographie *Mouvements d'un liquide à la rencontre d'un obstacle plan* (1893), materializes some of Poincaré's thoughts. Both scientists' work coincided during the same period, the nineteen and first half twentieth century,[28] and placed Marey's visual instruments on the middle of the scientific revolution generated by Mandelbrot almost a century later. Marey's works converge also with Bergson's thoughts on positive metaphysic (*métaphysique positive*) in which Bergson – also a contemporary of Marey – proposes a metaphysics based on both the imitation and analysis of "Sciences of life"; in Bergson words, *"une théorie tout saturée d'expérience."*[29] In the philosophical field, Bergson placed his theory on the acknowledgment of the irregularity of natural movements thus, the bergsonism is defined as the awareness of a new situation in the history of the sciences.[30] However, the recognition of natural irregularity passes through all of human experience, it is to say, through the perpetual analysis of nature and its improvement allowed by other scientific fields. According to Bergson, every-

---

28 | It is important to note also that after 1896, maybe due to the collaboration with Lucien Bull or some Lumière's influence, Marey realized some views of cinematographically character; e.g. views of Paris of Pont de l'Alma, Pont d'Iéna, Place de la Concorde, etc.

29 | See *Bulletin de la Société française de philosophie*, 2 Mai, 1901, p. 59.

30 | Bergson H. 1889, *La durée réelle et la casualité*, pp. 150-163.

thing changes when sciences drive the intellect to other kinds of experiences.[31] In fact, the decomposition and the analysis of movement, allowed first by Muybridge's and then by Marey's experiences, gave another topic to the analysis of nature and natural movements.

Bergson's thoughts are clearly influenced by the improvements of motion picture techniques.[32] In his first work, *Essais sur les données immédiates de la conscience* (1889), Bergson begins his complex analysis of movement.[33] The first theory of time and space proposed by Bergson in 1889 needed scientific support of the human perception of time and its relationship with spatial notions. According to Bergson, matter and number, in the meaning of quantity and group, always undergoes, through human analysis, a 'translation' or juxtaposition into spatial terms. As a consequence, the notion of time also undergoes a juxtaposition with spatial notions.[34] Thus, Muybridge and Marey's works became extremely important to Bergson's notion of duration (*durée*) as a theory of time and consciousness. It is possible to claim that the analysis of time in spatial terms, started by Muybridge (his clock-work apparatus) and continued by Marey, allowed for Bergson's concept of duration, in which he constructs a difference between 'the time of mechanics' and the time of 'natural things.' In order to avoid confusion between these two different concepts, Bergson posits that the concept of duration is in opposition of time. His main concept grows from the apparent homogeneity of time. In other words, mankind's notion of time corresponds to a homogeneous space.

"Or remarquons que, lorsque nous parlons du temps, nous pensons le plus souvent à un milieu homogène où nos faits de conscience s'alignent, se juxtaposent comme dans l'espace, et réussissent à former une multiplicité distincte."[35]

By means of this theory, Bergson highlights the philosophical and cognitive confusion of the assimilation of time in spatial terms, from which the interpretation of movement as a covered space is derived and not as an action unique and indivisible.

---

31 | In an interview published in 1914, Bergson expressed the importance of cinematographic technique on philosophical field. "Il est évident que cette invention, complètement de la photographie instantanée, peut suggérer des idées nouvelles au philosophe." (Georges-Michel M. 1914, *Henri Bergson nous parle du cinéma, Le journal*, 20 février.)

32 | For Bergson, the cinematographic machine represents an exact point, which links science and metaphysic. See Fihman G. 1999.

33 | It is important to note that when Bergson published his first work, the studies in motion photography by Muybridge and Marey were in their advanced states. Indeed, Marey's had already accomplished his studies in animal locomotion and he was researching at improving *le chronographe à pellicule mobile*.

34 | See Bergson H. 1889, *Multiplicité numérique et space*, pp. 56-69.

35 | Bergson H. 1889, p. 67.

"Car si le temps, tel que se le représente la conscience se succèdent distinctement de manière à pouvoir se compter, et si, d'autre part, notre conception du nombre abouti à éparpiller dans l'espace tout ce qui se compte directement, il est à présumer que le temps, entendu au sens d'un milieu où l'on distingue et où l'on compte, n'est que de l'espace."[36]

According to Bergson, time conceived of as a homogenous entity could be just an illegitimate idea caused by the intrusion of some spatial notions. Time conceived as an homogenous undefined field proves the specter of space in the human cognition of time. Instead, time is an independent entity indivisible in eternal becoming.[37] According to Bergson, in order to divide time, a change of its nature is necessary.[38] Thus, the utility in the concept of duration,[39] in which duration personifies the illusory shape of a homogeneous field product of the intersection between time and space. At that point it was possible to analyze the concept of movement under another point of view. According to Bergson, movement is the personification (*symbole vivant*) of an apparently homogenous duration. One used to say that a movement is accomplished in space. Thus, movement is assimilated also as a homogenous and divisible entity, it is to say, movement is assimilating to the space covered by the object in motion. Zeno's paradoxes also became useful to support Bergson's theories. In fact, Bergson proposes an interesting analysis of the paradox of Achilles and the tortoise through which his analysis of movement found a clear example of mankind's conception of time. According to Bergson, the negation of Achilles' movement in that paradox was the negation of what the senses perceive of movement. Zeno takes the reason beyond the rational and brings to the extreme mankind's analysis of time under spatial terms. Achilles and the tortoise personifies Bergson's analysis in which the movement, understood as a homogenous duration, is developed **in the space**, thus the tendency to also comprehend the movement as a homogenous and divisible entity. In fact, the reasoning is linked to the covered distance confounding it with the pure movement.

"Or, en y réfléchissant davantage, on verra que les positions successives du mobile occupent bien en effet de l'espace, mais que l'opération par laquelle il passe d'une position à l'autre, opération qui occupe de la durée et qui n'a de réalité que pour un spectateur conscient, échappe à l'espace."[40]

---

36 | Bergson H. 1889, p. 68.

37 | It is possible to remark the same conception in Leibniz's theory of monadology. In fact, the established harmony of each monad and their relationship in the arrangement is the product of the action of an absolute and universal time on which the perfect concordance of monads can be expressed. See Bachelard G. 1932.

38 | Deleuze G. 1966, p. 32.

39 | Duration, in Deleuze's words, is a 'passage' a 'change', a 'becoming', it is a becoming that is prolonged. See Deleuze G. 1966.

40 | Bergson H. 1889, p. 82.

Movement is more than a thing; it is a progression. The human analysis of movement from a point A to a point B is just a mental synthesis. Humans lend to movement the same divisibility of space, forgetting that it is possible to divide a thing, but not an action.[41] Space and interval in Zeno's paradoxes become one, in other words, the space, infinitely divisible, imposes a pattern on the analysis of intervals. If the movement was composed of by parts infinitely divisible, the interval would never be covered. However, reality is that every step of Achilles is an action, an indivisible action, which, when placed in succession, brings Achilles to his goal. Zeno's 'mistake' is that he applied the same divisibility of space in order to reconstruct the movement of Achilles in its totality. However the reconstruction of Achilles' steps is made by using the steps of the tortoise, i.e. the paradox presents 'two tortoises' predestined to follow the same simultaneous act in order to never reach their goal. The reality is that Achilles overtakes the tortoise because the steps are indivisible as movements and present different quantities in space. Thus, the accumulation of Achilles' steps will give a higher magnitude to his movement.[42]

The last analysis elaborated upon by Bergson shows clearly that humanity projects time upon space. Therefore, the examination of time is based on a geometrical figure derived from that projection. The problem arises from when that geometrical figure represents a **thing** and not a **progression**.[43] In fact, when time is up, it is possible to represent the successive moments as external to each other and think of a line through space. However, it is understood that that line represents not the flow of time but its expiration. This line, which creates some spatial notions in the analysis of time, is just a symbol of time and is unable to manifest the state of becoming. Hence, time can be represented in space but just as time expired, time flowing cannot be represented in space.[44] Bergson concludes that a mathematical symbol able to express the essence of movement does not exist because these symbols, always intended to measure, are only able to express distances. Certainly, these thoughts were influenced by the vision of 'decomposed movement' generated by means of Muybridge and Marey's techniques.

The photographic fusil allowed for a new perception of movement and also highlighted humanity's process of perception of time and movement. The series of images

---

41 | See Bergson H. 1889.

42 | Bergson H. 1889, p. 84.

43 | As noted in the first part of this text, through topology the figures acquire a flexibility such that they could be seen as a progression of forms. It is interesting to see that some cinematic experiences attempted to show this phenomenon by means of the flexible qualities of represented objects. For instance, Emile Cohl's Fantasmagorie (1908) in which the line is in constant inflection. The line that constructs the figures in this stop-motion film present some topological properties that make it an object in constant metamorphosis. Consequently, it is a geometrical figure, due to its topological character, that represents a progression. For an in-depth analysis of Fantasmagorie, see Cubitt. S. 2004, especially *Graphical Film: The Vector*.

44 | See Bergson H. 1896, p. 213.

generated by the photographic fusil amalgamates time and space because each frame corresponds to a precise 'time', which is strictly correlated to a precise spatial notion. Thus, this technology was understood as an engine able to 'freeze' a succession of time, a 'portion of reality'. It is also possible to link this idea of 'frozen moment' to Bergson's analysis of *images-souvenirs* and *images-perception* and his analysis of human memory in which the memory is not only an act of observing past stock images but also an act of prolongation of its useful effects to the present.[45]

|**Prop. XXI**| In order to create an important distinction between the cinematograph and the human function of reminiscence, Bergson created three concepts that cannot be dissociated; pure memory (*souvenir pur*), image-remembrance (*souvenir-image*) and perception (*la perception*). According to Bergson, perception is not a mere contact between the spirit and the object; it is always heavily influenced by *souvenir-images,* which in turn is influenced by the *souvenir pur.*

"La perception n'est jamais un simple contact de l'esprit avec l'objet présent ; elle est tout imprégnée des souvenirs-images qui la complètent en l'interprétant. Le souvenir-image, à son tour, participe du « souvenir pur » qu'il commence à matérialiser, et de la perception où il tend à s'incarner : envisagé de ce dernier point de vue, il se définirait une perception naissante. Enfin le souvenir pur, indépendant sans doute en droit, ne se manifeste normalement que dans l'image colorée et vivante qui le révèle."[46]

According to Bergson, memory is a *sui generis* act through which humanity possesses conscience and through which mankind is able to break loose of present time in order to be placed on some region in the past. Memory, for Bergson, is an act of groping around in the past and he considers this human act as the act of putting an image into focus in a photographic camera.[47] These analyses allow Bergson to highlight the difference between memory and perception for the purpose of then analyzing time as a becoming entity through the notions of past, present and future. Under Bergson's logic, humanity believes that perception is a pure connection between the spirit and the object. In that case, memory would work following the same process but with the object in *absentia*. Bergson places perception into the present, memory into the past, because perception moves memory onto an earlier time. However, memory can also exist in the present, it can be placed on the time of becoming, in this instance of *hic et nunc* which is in perpetual becoming. Under Bergson's logic, "my present" (*mon présent*) is a perception of my immediate past and also a determination of the immediate future.[48] That is why he repeated that the progress of memory consists in

---

45 | See Bergson H. 1896.
46 | Bergson H. 1896, p. 147.
47 | See Bergson H. 1896, Chap. III, *De la survivance des images. La mémoire et l'esprit.*
48 | It is interesting at this point to quote Condé's words about Bergsons theories. Acoording to Condé, "L'oeuvre d'Henri Bergson a comme objet la fractalité de la mémoire et de la matière." (Condé S. 1993, p. 95.)

materializing itself, that is, in being placed in the present time, an analogous process of cinematography.[49]

Bergson's approach to cinema became stronger in his work *L'évolution créatrice*, published on 1907. His analysis of cinematography, presented in this work, was developed when cinematographic narrative was in still young, and its analysis, based on linguistic terms, came some years later. In fact, cinematographic narrative was an embryo when Bergson published his work. It is important to remember that D. W. Griffith started his cinematographic career in 1908 and his masterpiece, *The Birth of the Nation*, was realized in 1915, a film considered as the first exponent that used an extremely elaborate cinematographic narrative range from which the narrative of film could be erroneously compared to a language losing its geometrical connotations.

In *L'évolution créatrice* Bergson analyses cinematographic technology in geometrical terms. In this Bergson's work, it is possible to see that the cinematographic camera is analyzed as a tool able to construct a new spatial conception. According to Bergson, this apparatus simulates not only the physiologic mechanism of sight but also the mechanism of the human spatial perception and its relationship with sensations and memory. However, the simulation generated by the cinematographic camera gave him the possibility to highlight the existence of irregularity in nature and a different essence of time. While Bergson places the functioning of the cinematographic camera equal to the human operation of intelligence, he also highlights the analogy between physiological spatial analysis and that realized by means of the cinematograph in geometrical terms. According to Bergson, human intelligence finds in geometry its perfect completion because geometry, even in its incapacity to reconstruct the natural space, is able to create a different intelligible space where humans can develop their intelligence. Therefore, Bergson claims that reality is arranged (*ordonnée*) to the extent that it meets human thought.[50] Bergson deals again with Zeno's paradoxes in order to explain his concept of becoming, of movement. In his analysis he argues that the thoughts about movement elaborated upon by Zeno in his paradoxes are very similar to the cinematographic mechanism. In fact, both cinematographic technology and Zeno's paradoxes analyze movement by using immobility (*coupes immobiles*), i.e. positions in space or instants in time. According to Bergson, both methods imply the "absurd" idea that movement is composed of many immobile states, by an abstract idea of succession derived from the act of putting together positions or instants in an indivisible and heterogeneous entity, i.e in time.[51] Muybridge and Marey's experiences with moving pictures shows clearly that the human analysis of movement uses the same abstract idea of succession by applying a homogenous and universal mechani-

---

49 | See Bergson H. 1896.

50 | See Bergson H. 1907, *Chapitre III De la signification de la vie, l'ordre de la nature et la forme de l'intelligence.*

51 | Bergson H. 1907.

cal time influenced by spatial notions.[52] However, Bergson argues that movement is unique; it is a whole action from point A to point B. If it were possible to mark a point C between A and B it would no longer be a unique movement but two movements.[53] Therefore, Bergson claims that moving pictures creates the same denaturalization of the real entity of movement of that Zeno created in his paradoxes. Instantaneous photography, according to Bergson, isolates a moment of a whole movement in order to put a single photogram (*coupe immobile*) in a series. Science as well as cinematographic technique, according to Bergson, "accentuates" the rhythm of nature's flow, while not attempting to be inserted into it. Thus, cinematographic technology is so natural for human intelligence; it is adjusted to the requirements of science as well as to human perception.[54] In other words, the human perception of becoming is, according to Bergson, analogous to the cinematographic mechanism.[55] It is possible to note in Bergson's writings that the cinematographic camera acquires a complete status as a geometrical tool by means of its strong similarity to human perception, in Bergson's words, by means of the simulation that that mechanism creates of human intelligence. However, it remains an instrument that creates a Euclidean spatial organization even in its development of time. Unlike cartoons, cinematographic technology does not create an image in continuous creation. Cinema presents a completed image hence, cartoons correspond more to a Cartesian geometry while the cinematographic image is totally Euclidean.[56] In front of a moving picture the beholder misses the movement, while in reality the movement exists between the *coupes immobiles*.

|Prop. II, VI| Another interesting analysis carried out by Bergson in *L'évolution Créatrice* is of the Whole (*le Tout*). Bergson defined the Whole by means of the relationship between objects. According to Begrson, the relationship is not a property of the object; it is an exterior phenomenon. Hence, the capacity to be linked does not belong to the object but to the Whole. Begrson argues that the movement of a single object transforms the whole set by means of the relationships existing between every single object in the set, a set understood as a topologic space, as a web of relationships between objects.[57] From this point of view, the Whole is in constant change; it is pure becoming. This entity does not undergo a state; its state is the perpetual becoming.

---

52 | See Deleuze G. 1983, Chapter I, *Thèse sur le mouvement. Premier commentaire de Bergson.*

53 | Bergson H. 1907, p. 309.

54 | On the contrary, Deleuze claims that cinematographic technology does not present just a *coupe immobile* but a *coupe mobile*. He argues that the direct result of the projection is an image-movement and not a coupe immobile + abstract movement. See Deleuze G. 1983.

55 | Bergson H. 1907, p. 346.

56 | Deleuze G. 1983, p. 14.

57 | It is important to remark that the sets are not enclosed, because the Whole is open and linked with every single object. Therefore, Deleuze affirms that a closed set is just an artificial notion. See Deleuze G. 1983.

Thus, if we consider the *coupes immobiles* to be an object, because they make part of a set, we can claim that movement exists between the *coupes immobiles* and movement also reflects every object in a unique duration, to the Whole in becoming. These objects or *coupes immobiles* are in fact witnesses of the becoming of the Whole. In its 'fixity', put in a series, the *coupes immobiles* manifest the existence of the movement; a movement hidden by themselves.

Some time after the invention of cinema by the Lumière Brothers – an invention that did not respond to an artistic urge but to the technical perfection of a new technique[58] – the theories of Bergson were, in some ways, eclipsed in that field. Of course, the status of geometry that Bergson gave to the spatial construction of moving pictures was in opposition with the assimilation as a language that critics gave to cinematographic narrative. Maybe the strong influence of theater and literature on the cinematographic art created the research of a grammar in film narrative instead of a geodesy in the narrative space of film. Nevertheless, some authors used Bergson's thoughts on film analysis. Such is the case of Jean Epstein who published in 1946 his work *L'intelligence d'une machine*. In this work, he analyzes cinematography from a particular point of view, which allows for the understanding of cinematographic art as a spatial organization directly derived from the geometrical imposition of the camera. In Epstein's thoughts, the camera, endowed with its own intelligence,[59] creates a particular space, which the author unfastened from the "hierarchy" of natural things. This phenomenon is clearly shown in the short documentary film *Demolishing and Building Up the Star Theatre* (1901). In this film, movement is seen via the transformation of the space itself, not by an object covering a distance in space. Time and space of cinematography is, in Epstein's words, a "disarticulation of nature."[60] He describes this new space by using these words:

"Les chevaux planent au-dessus de l'obstacle ; les plantes gesticulent ; les cristaux s'accouplent, se reproduisent, cicatrisent leurs plaies ; la lave rampe ; l'eau devient huile, gomme, pois arborescent ; l'homme acquiert la densité d'un nuage, la consistance d'une vapeur ; il est un pur animal gazeux, d'une grâce féline, d'une adresse simiesque. Tous les systèmes compartimentés de la nature se trouvent désarticulés. Il ne reste plus qu'un règne : la vie."[61]

The capacity of the cinematographic camera to destroy the dogma of the irreversibility of life was for Epstein an important factor that required a long analysis and placed the analysis of film narrative more in spatial terms than in linguistic ones. According

---

58 | See Panofsky E. 1974.

59 | As it will be analyzed in the next chapters, the idea that the cinematographic camera posses its own intelligence was borrow also by Vertov who realized this concept on the screen.

60 | Epstein J. 1946. p. 6.

61 | Epstein J. 1946, p. 6.

to Epstein, the inexistence of entropy in film space becomes not only a special narrative instrument but also a different way to analyze life, to bring about some new phenomenological inputs and confront mankind with them. Hence, he criticized the way of perceiving cinematographic art as a machine "to reform and to popularize the theater."[62] According to Epstein, cinematographic art, is a philosophical instrument that offers a new way for humans to analyze the world, including society.

From the moment the cinematographic camera acquired its connotation as an artistic tool, the conservative wing of art found in this invention a dangerous enemy. In fact, cinematography was labeled as a "hobby of analphabets, miserable creatures…a machine to become stupid…"[63] The attacks made against film from the artistic field are well known. It is important to think about the period when cinematography created an irruption on the world stage. In fact, it was an irruption from the point of view of society because, this technique left the scientific sphere in order to invade the popular one in a few years; from the popularization of Edison's Kinematoscope (1891) to the Lumières' Cinématographe (1895) there was only a short period of time. Cinematography arrived in a social context where art and people where strongly divided, and cinematography proposed an interesting link between the two, thanks to its dependency on economic factors. It is also important to remember the tragedy of the Bazar de la charité (1897), which moved cinematography away from the bourgeoisie to the countryside and to the lower social classes from the beginning of this art form. However, some poets, writers, and painters found in cinematography a new way to interpret the world. This was the case of Guillaume Apollinaire, among others, who claimed, after the viewing of a Méliès' movie; "Monsieur Méliès et moi faisons à peu près le même métier: nous enchantons la matière vulgaire."[64] Of course the image perceived on the screen took on a magical connotation due to its similarity with reality, the particular time of its spatial organization that allowed some effects developed by Méliès himself, the nature of the objects represented, etc. 'La matière vulgaire', the nature, the life on the screen definitely changed its nature. However, some years later, when cinematography underwent some technical improvements, such as sound, and it was assimilated as a popular show, its analysis through linguistic terms was imposed. It could be the frenetic research of a grammar in this spatial organization that eclipses in such a way its analysis through geometrical terms. Nevertheless, this technique created a new way to analyze nature and society; it generated a new space where nature could be translated in order to be observed from another point of view. The flexibility of this new geometry allowed mankind to develop an infinite number of philosophical and artistic thoughts. It became a narrative instrument.

However, is the cinema a language?

---

62 | Epstein J. 1946, p. 9.

63 | Quoted by L'Herbier M. 1946, p. 27.

64 | Quoted by L'Herbier M. 1946, p. 16.

3 Film As Spatial Organization

On dit qu'a force d'ascèse certains bouddhistes parvi-
ennent à voir tout un paysage dans un fève.[1]

3.1 Visualizing Multidimensional Spaces

As noted in the first part of this text, the development of non-Euclidean geometries gave rise to some philosophical and scientific discussions about the existence of multiple dimensions of space. As Euclidean geometry was accepted as a geometry that perfectly simulates the human perception of space, so non-Euclidean geometries represented in consequence the incertitude of our perception of space. In other words, the existence of non-Euclidean geometries was seen as a sign of the human incapacity to perceive a hypothetical fourth dimension existing in space. Of course, technological improvements in visual media could not recognize the existence of that fourth dimension because they were mere extensions of the human senses. They were non-biological copies of a biological mechanism. Additionally, every visual medium was governed by Euclidean rules (See *The Camera Obscura: A Phenomenon of Externalization*).

|Prop. XVII| From the moment non-Euclidean geometries emerged from the scientific field and irrupted into the public sphere, multidimensional spaces became an interesting subject for the general public. Artistic expression started to represent the world in a space possessing more than the three dimensions theorized and imposed by Euclidean geometry. The popular belief can be summarized by the idea that only three dimensions can be perceived by the human brain. Human sight was in consequence considered as subjugated to Euclidean geometry, which lets us see that we are able to see, even if the space in which we live has many more dimensions.[2] Hence,

---

1 | Barthes R. 1970, p. 9.
2 | See Leadbeater C.W. 1910.

the general public and the artists interpreted non-Euclidean geometries as a tool to expand human perception.[3]

The first steps in the popularization of non-Euclidean geometries and multidimensional spaces were taken in the literary field. Authors like H.G. Wells and G. de Pawlowski represent an important step in the popularization of non-Euclidean geometries. In particular, Wells was very famous in France, a country that embraced in that period a frenetic interest in science fiction and also the country in which Poincaré developed the theories that became a popular subject.[4]

It was the concept of the *fourth dimension*, derived from non-Euclidean geometries, that embodied the engine of a new representation of space in the arts. In other words, the destruction of the Euclidean space was embodied by the existence of a hypothetical *fourth dimension*, which represented, in Albert Gleizes' words, "the figuration of space, the measure of the infinite."[5] Apollinaire's thoughts converged with this idea. According to him, the term *fourth dimension* characterizes the new possibilities of spatial measurement through which the immensity of space could be represented. In addition, he understood the *fourth dimension* as a dimension engendered by the three known dimensions. In his words:

"la quatrième dimension serait engendrée par les trois mesures connues : elle figure l'immensité de l'espace s'éternisant dans toutes les directions à un moment déterminé. Elle est l'espace même, la dimension de l'infini ; c'est elle qui doue de plasticité les objects. Elle leur donne les propostions qu'ils méritent dans l'œuvre, tandis que l'art grec par exemple, un rythme en quelque sorte mécanique détruit sans cesse les proportions."[6]

The connections between the theories popularized by Poincaré in France and the new space developed by painters are clear.[7] As noted in the second part of this text, Euclidean geometry governed the spatial organization of pictorial representation. Borrowing from Apollinaire, "on peut dire que la géométrie est aux arts plastiques ce que la grammaire est à l'art de l'écrivain."[8] However, after the development of non-

---

3 | See Henderson L. 1983, esp. *Paris 1900-1912: The fourth Dimension and Non-Euclidean Geometry in Popular literature.*

4 | Henderson notes the influence of Poincaré's thoughts on the first cubist exponents like Gleizes, Metzinger, Juan Gris and also Duchamp. See Henderson L. 1983.

5 | Quoted by André Tudesq, "Du Cubisme et de ses détracteurs: Une Querelle autour de quelques toiles," Paris-Midi, 4 Oct. 1912.

6 | Apollinaire G. 1965, p. 52.

7 | For example, Max Weber, who was in contact with Matisse, Metzinger, Apollinaire and Picasso, high exponents of the influence of non-Euclidean geometries in art. Note that Weber published in 1910 a work focusing on this phenomenon: *The Fourth Dimension From Plastic Point of View.* See Henderson L. 1983, p. 60.

8 | Apollinaire G. 1965, p. 51.

Euclidean geometries, pictorial representation started to free itself from Euclid's three dimensions. According to Apollinaire, the three dimensions of Euclidean geometry were no longer enough. He also posited that Euclidean geometry 'limited' the artist in the representation of infinity:

"Jusqu' présent, les trois dimensions de la géométrie euclidienne suffisaient aux inquié-tudes que le sentiment de l'infinie met dans l'âme des grands artistes."[9]

The new ideal, the new perfection within this new conception of space, was the infinite universe: a new search for infinity. But the infinite universe was embodied by the destruction of the classical space – its fractalization – and the destruction of the Euclidean *ordino* that guided the laws of perspective.[10] Further, this new space was perceived as the representation of a reality that was formerly 'hidden' by the three dimensions imposed by Euclidean geometry. In other words, to represent the world following non-Euclidean geometries was seen as an attempt to conceive a reality. According to Apollinaire, this is the most important aspect of the differentiation between the ancient painting and the cubist painting. He states that:

"Ce qui différence le cubisme de l'ancienne peinture, c'est qu'il n'est pas un art d'imitation, mais un art de conception qui tend a s'élever jusqu'à la création. En repré-sentant la réalité-conçue ou la réalité-créée, le peintre peut donner l'apparence de trois dimensions, peut en quelque sorte cubiquer. Il ne pourrait pas en rendant simplement la réalité-vue, à moins de faire du trompe-l'œil en raccourci ou en perspective, ce qui déformerait la qualité de la forme conçue ou crée."[11]

The new sense of freedom in the arts was based on the capacity to recognize the so-called *fourth dimension*. Indeed, to recognize the *fourth dimension* meant to be free from the classical perception imposed by Euclid and, consequently, to set the mind free from the Greek conception of beauty in which man is the measure of perfection. The *fourth dimension* places beauty in the infiniteness of the universe. Thus, some of Poincaré's theories, mainly his analysis of visual space developed in *La science et*

---

9 | Apollinaire G. 1965, p. 51.

10 | It is interesting to note how Schuster descrives the inmateriality of the space of the image and its multidemensionality. According to him "Die Ebene des Bild-Trägers, als Leinwand oder Bildschrim, flach oder gewölbt, besitzt Ränder als Begrenzungen, ein gewises Format, das sich präsize getreu dem metrischen System bestimmen lässt, eine bestimmte Farbe, eine Oberflächenbeschaffenheit – alles Eingeschaften innerhalb eines Austellungsraums, die, sobald die Projektion beginnt, sich immaterialisieren zu einem Raum für Erscheinungen unterschiedlicher Dimensionen, Lichter, Farben und Tex-turen, das heißt sich im Wahrgenommen werden öffnen zu einem Darstellungsraum." (Schuster M. 2000, p. 123.)

11 | Apollinaire G. 1965, pp. 56-57.

l'hypothèse, started to represent an important theoretical tool in the representation of the infiniteness of the universe on the canvas. The differentiation between perception and the logical process (or between *doxa* and *logos*) constitutes an important factor in representing space.[12] According to Poincaré, one must analyze the perception of visual space on two different levels. The first, the pure visual space, corresponds to the two dimensional image formed on the retina. The second, the complete visual space, corresponds to the first level of perception of a third dimension. However, he posits that human perception is more complete than the articulation of these two kinds of visual perceptions. Consequently, he adds new types of perceptual spaces – Tactile Space and Motor Space – through which he could identify the genesis of the notion of space not only in terms of sight and the sense of touch. For example, the motor space was the association of ideas derived from the 'feeling of direction' (*Le sentiment de la direction*). Hence, the muscular system, according to Poincaré, plays an important role in the notion of space.[13] As we can see, Poincaré's theories represent a clear attempt to displace perception from *doxa* to *logos*, a process applied by cubists and summarized by Picasso in one famous sentence: "I paint objects as I think them, not as I see them." Without doubt, cubists painters were influenced by the general interest in non-Euclidean geometries at that time. However, there is another influence that played a central role in the development of cubist art, mainly in Picasso's *Analytical Cubism*, and that is African art.

Picasso introduced African art into the process that some years latter would become Cubism, making Cubism an important converging point of scientific theories about non-Euclidean geometries and African artistic expressions.[14] African art represented an important way to visualize how non-Euclidean spaces were developed in the artistic field and also demonstrated how other cultures developed a fractal aesthetic.[15]

In *Les Demoiselles d'Avignon* (1907), (Fig. 3.1) it is possible to see how Picasso uses African styles in order to set the pictorial representation free from Euclidean laws. The two figures on the right side of the canvas are clearly depicted as African masks, anthropomorphic representations of "creative – and not merely imitative – applications of geometrical thinking."[16] African art represents in reality the possibility to see, in artistic spatial organizations, what non-Euclidean geometries theorized.

---

12 | See the chapter *Photographic Technology: A Translation Tool of Nature's Shadows*, especially Wedwoods's concepts of perception and idea in the human cognitive process, as well as Sartre's analysis of perception analyzed in the same chapter. See also the chapter *Stereoscopic Vision*.

13 | See Poincaré H. 1902, Chapitre IV *L'Espace et la Géométrie*.

14 | See Rubin W. – Fluegel J. 1980.

15 | See Eglash R. 2005.

16 | Eglash R. 2005, p. 65.

|*Fig. 3.1*|

African cultures developed a particular aesthetic characterized by the presentation of recursion, self-similarity, fractal dimensions and the allusion to infinite forms that recall Mandelbrot's fractal geometry. This aesthetic influenced architecture, jewelry, hairdressing, clothing, numeric systems, divination systems and so on.

In the image bellow, we can see an aerial view of the village of Labbezanga in Mali (Fig. 3.2) and a fractal graphic (Fig. 3.3). These images, analyzed by Eglash, show how some circular forms in African architecture do not have a single focus even if they present self-similarity.[17] These architectural forms share some properties with fractals, in particular, in this specific case, decentralized swirls of circular buildings showing scaling symmetry.

---

17 | Eglash R. 2005, pp. 31-32.

|*Fig. 3.2*| |*Fig. 3.3*|

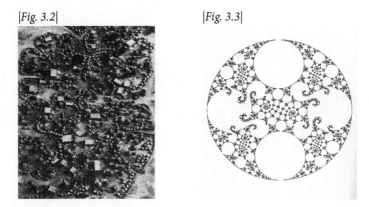

It is interesting to note that the African fractal aesthetic seems to be opposed to the western use of fractal forms. As posited by Eglash, western cultures' use of fractal design is based on a mimicking of nature; the awareness of the irregular shapes in nature demands the use of fractal forms to represent it. Conversely, African cultures' use of fractals comes from the realm of their culture.[18] Some stylization of forms, following recursive patterns that are more than abstract forms, provide evidence of the artistic interest in scaling proprieties that developed different geometric designs free from Euclidean conventions.

|*Fig. 3.4*| |*Fig. 3.5*| |*Fig. 3.6*| |*Fig. 3.7*|

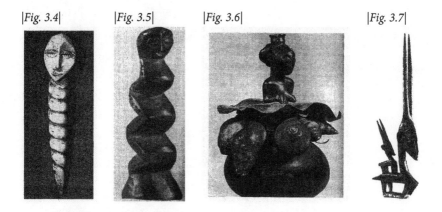

The stylization of some forms played an allegorical function. As noted by Eglash with regard to the shapes in some Bamara sculptures, (Fig. 3.6, 3.7) self-similar forms express in those sculptures the transformation in an interactive loop of human beings: "the child becomes a mother, who has a child, who becomes a mother, and so on."[19] Infinity, in the African arts, was commonly represented through snail shells, as well as in spiral forms (recalling the logarithmic spiral, see, *Self-Similarity: Fold Into Fold*),

---

18 | Eglash R. 2005, p. 51.
19 | Eglash R. 2005, p. 51.

which establish geometric sequences that develop a system able to generate an infinite structure due to its self-similar particularity (fig. 3.4, 3.5).

|*Fig. 3.8*|

Further, some recursive forms of African styles, for example in some textiles, attempt to represent a kind of passage from order to disorder. In other words, represented in those textiles is a kind of fractalization of the space in a multidimensional plane that contains Euclidean as well as non-Euclidean forms.

Perhaps Picasso saw in African art the possibility to conceive pictorial representations away from the Euclidean logic. In this sense, this art represented for Picasso the possibility to 'escape' from the western tradition of perspective imposed since the Renaissance. The irruption of African art in Picasso's *Les Demoiselles d'Avignon* (1907) marks the beginning of a rapid process that brought him to *Analytic Cubism*, e.g. the *Portrait of Ambroise Vollard* (1910).

|*Fig. 3.9*|

In this work, there is a rejection of perspective, thereby leading to a deformation of the object. Further, as the representative act is based on how the artist thinks the object and not on the mere perception of it, there is an attempt to represent the object – Ambroise Vollard – in its totality, that is to say, to represent all its faces. Hence, the process of the object's representation was based on the breaking up of the figure into facets in order to create a perspective of multiple viewpoints. This process is evident in Metzinger's image below (Fig. 3.10)

|*Fig. 3.10*|

The progressive destruction of the use of perspective initiated by Picasso and inspired by both African art and scientific theories about non-Euclidean geometries generated a new spatial organization based on the multiplication of viewpoints. In fact, its multiplication allowed the representation of the complexity of an object placed in a non-Euclidean multidimensional space, a space composed by more than three dimensions.[20] Further, the space produced by the multiplication of viewpoints on the canvas allowed the conception of the canvas itself as a flexible space, as a pure, multidimensional plan.

This phenomenon is clearly exposed in *The Clarinet* (1913). In this Braque's oeuvre, we can see how the artist completely destroyed the perspective (Fig. 3.11).

---

20 | It was theorized that the simple possibility of technical reproduction in art offered by photographic technology set the discipline of painting free from the search for an objective reproduction of nature. The influence of the theories of non-Euclidean geometries in arts movements, like cubism, shows that it was not only the appearance of photography that allowed artists to represent the world free from the Euclidean rules, especially the laws of perspective. As we can see, the artists started to represent the world designed by scientific improvements in geometry. Science and art started to recognize the irregularity of nature as well as the existence of dimensions that cannot be perceived by the human eye. Thus, it would be appropriate to recognize some forms of artistic expression or pictorial representations, like cubism, not merely as products of technological improvements, that is to say, as the product of the capacity to reproduce nature with the high degree of objectivity offered by photographic technology. It is possible to theorize that non-Euclidean geometries generated another meaning of objectivity that some forms of artistic expression, e.g. cubism, strived to reach.

|*Fig. 3.11*|

The multidimensional space created by the artist allowed him to present the texture of the objects. Further, this multidimensional space allows the creation of an organic unity in a space where each object is independent and placed in a defined dimension. The coexistence of many textures and unities in the same multidimensional plane – n-dimensional plane – generates a special analysis of *simultaneity*[21] as well as a concept of space-time in the image. The multiplication of viewpoints produces the coexistence of different entities in a homogenous space and also gives a hint about movement and time. According to Gleizes, the desire to register the total image generates a kind of dynamism. Gleizes highlights this phenomenon through Metzinger's oeuvres: "To purely objective truth he [Metzinger] wishes to add a new truth, born from what his intelligence will have allowed him to know. As he himself says, to space he will add time (*la durée*)."[22]

|**Prop. XX**| The multiplication of viewpoints was understood as the reconstruction of the object in time. However, it is important to remember that *durée* for cubists did not represent the *fourth dimension*. In Henderson's words:

"cubism's durée was simply the temporal means that enabled the artist to gather and synthesize information about the fourth dimension of space. As in n-dimensional geometry, time in Cubist painting plays only a supporting role, allowing the artist or geometer to

---

21 | Note that the word simultaneity was first used by Futurists in the context of painting. Futurists were interested in the simultaneity of states of mind as a product of the speed and complexity of modern life. See Henderson L. 1983, p. 91.

22 | Gleizes, "Jean Metzinger," Revue Indépendante, no. 46 (Sept 1911), pp. 165-166.

accomplish the physical or mental movement necessary to form an idea of an object's total dimensionality."[23]

Thus, time, in painting, also represented a way to impose a non-Euclidean organization on the pictorial space. In fact, the notion of time developed by the multiplication of viewpoints was the result of the rejection of Euclid's postulate about the indeformability of figures in movement. As we can see, indeformability for cubists became a rule in the higher dimensionality of space. Further, they not only theorized the deformability of the object though movement but also applied some properties of topological spaces in which the objects acquire an important flexibility and in which the graphical code, borrowing Cubbit, "works on the basis of likenesses that shift constantly with our perspective on them(…)"[24] In this multidimensional space:

"Les formes que l'on y situe ressortissent à un dynamisme que nous assumons de dominer. Pour que notre intelligence le possède, exerçons d'abord notre sensibilité. Il n'est que nuances. La forme apparaît douée de propriétés identiques à celles de la couleur. Elle se tempère ou s'avive au contact d'une autre forme, se brise ou s'épanouit, se multiplie ou disparaît. Il arrive qu'une ellipse se change en circonférence parce qu'on l'inscrit dans une polygone. Il arrive qu'une forme, plus affirmée que celles qui l'entourent, gouverne tout le tableau, y frappe toute chose à sa propre effigie."[25]

Again, in these words we can find the influence of Poincaré's *Analysis Situs*.[26] As quoted in the chapter *Toward Fractality*, Euclid's postulate posits that "things which coincide with one another are equal to one other." This postulate was dealt with by Hilbert in his research. In particular, the German mathematician developed a set of new axioms that allowed the development of topology. Hilbert's axioms and curved spaces opened up the possibility to represent the world without Euclidean rules, as in Metzinger's Cubist Landscape of 1911. This oeuvre from Metzinger represents in painting what Poincaré posited about axioms in geometry. According to Poincaré, axioms of geometry do not correspond to judgments or experimental facts. He affirmed that axioms are merely conventions, and that was what Cubism developed: new conventions, or new axioms of pictorial representation.

---

23 | Henderson L. 1983, p. 91.

24 | Cubbit S. 2004, p. 72.

25 | Gleizes A. – Metzinger J. 1993, p. 33.

26 | It is interesting to quote Poincaré's words: "Cette géométrie à plus de trois dimensions n'est pas une simple géométrie analytique, elle n'est pas purement quantitative, elle est aussi qualitative et c'est par là surtout qu'elle devient intéressante. Il y a une science qu'on appelle l'Analysis Situs et qui a pour objet l'étude des relations de positions des divers éléments d'une figure, asbtraction (sic) faite de leurs grandeurs." (Poincaré H. 1908, p. 40.)

|*Fig. 3.12*|

However, Cubism seemed to have adopted conventions that seem to be inconvenient for the representation of natural objects. As mentioned above, Euclid's geometry is certainly the most adequate geometry to describe the space of experience. But the aim of Cubism was to describe a higher reality, a reality that belongs more to *logos* and less to *doxa*. The Cubists attempted to bring about a new development of the human mind. This phenomenon was described by Gleizes and Metzinger as follows:

"Discerner une forme, cela implique, outre la fonction visuelle et la faculté de se mouvoir, un certain développement de l'esprit ; le monde extérieur est amorphe aux yeux de la plupart."[27]

Different from Futurists, who found in the machine and its rhythm the possibility to represent the world, Cubists focused on a new kind of perception in which the human cognitive process was free from cultural imposition and, particularly, free from the Euclidean *ordino*. The machine, as a prosthesis that improves the human analysis of nature, was rejected in order to liberate mankind from Euclidean spatial organization. Within Cubism, reasoning took the place of perception, and the eternal relationship between eye and brain started to be governed by a 'certain development of the mind.'

---

27 | Gleizes A. – Metzinger J. 1993, p. 30.

The concept of a higher reality represented a fundamental point for Cubism and at the beginning of the twentieth century it became a fundamental research subject in many forms of artistic expression. It is not a coincidence that Apollinaire, who identified the presence of the *fourth dimension* in Cubist painting, thereby identifying non-Euclidean geometries in art, also created the neologism 'surrealism' during the 1917 presentation of Jean Cocteau and Erik Satie's ballet *Parrade*, the costumes and sets of which were designed by Picasso. According to Apollinaire, this ballet evoked a kind of *esprit nouveau* whose aim was to modify the basis of art and lifestyle.[28] The word *surréalisme* (from the French *sur* – beyond + *realism* – realism) certainly recalls the *fourth dimension* in which the human cognitive process was trying to show a higher reality hidden by the imposition of Euclidean geometry and the conventions developed over centuries. The development of the mind theorized by cubist painters found an interesting way to liberate other arts through the *Manifest du surréalisme* written by Breton. From the first lines of his *Manifest du surréalisme* (1924), Breton theorizes the possibility to see beyond the established reality. In his words:

"Tant va la croyance à la vie, à ce que la vie a de plus précaire, la vie réelle s'entend, qu'à la fin cette croyance se perd. L'homme, ce rêveur définitif, de jour en jour plus mécontent de son sort, fait avec peine le tour des objets dont il a été amené à faire usage, et que lui a livrés sa nonchalance, ou son effort, son effort presque toujours, car il a consenti à travailler, tout au moins il n'a pas répugné a jouer sa chance (ce qu'il appelle sa chance !)."[29]

And

"Là, l'absence de toute rigueur connue lui laisse la perspective de plusieurs vies menées à la fois ; il s'enracine dans cette illusion ; il ne veut plus connaître que la facilité momentanée, extrême, de toutes choses."[30]

On the one hand, Poincaré criticized Euclidean geometry because it imposes a single way to analyze and represent the world, thus preventing us from visualizing the hyperreality. On the other hand, Breton criticized reason because it represented a cage for mankind in which the 'kingdom' of logic forces the human mind to live according to its parameters, thus limiting human experiences, which is even worse. In Breton's words:

"Inutile d'ajouter que l'expérience même s'est vu assigner des limites. Elle tourne dans une cage d'où il est de plus en plus difficile de la faire sortir. Elle s'appuie, elle aussi, sur l'utilité immédiate, et elle est gardée par le bon sens. Sous couleur de civilisation, sous prétexte de progrès, on est parvenu à bannir de l'esprit tout ce qui peut taxer à tort ou à

---

28 | See La quinzaine littéraire n° 977, 1er octobre 2008.
29 | Breton A. 1985 (1924), p. 13.
30 | Breton A. 1985 (1924), p. 13.

raison de superstition, de chimère ; à proscrire tout mode de recherche de la vérité qui n'est pas conforme à l'usage."[31]

|**Prop. XXIII**| Like the liberation of the eye from Euclidean rules (See *Perspective: The Geometry of Sight*) theorized by Poincaré and by the Cubists, Breton stimulates the liberation of thought, the freedom of the unconscious in artistic expression. Both forms of artistic expression, in Gleizes words, "impliquent les deux modes vivants d'une seule et même idée : la redécouverte de l'homme."[32]

In this regard, I would like to draw attention to a surrealist practice, developed by Salvador Dalí, known as *el método paranoico crítico*. This method is defined by Dalì as "actividad paranoico-crítica: método espontáneo de conocimiento irracional basado en la asociación interpretativa-crítica de los fenómenos delirantes."[33] Through this surrealist practice it is possible to see how signs, signifiers and signifieds interact under a "tyrannical generation of meaning which takes place in the human psyche."[34] As A. Ross remarked, their interaction can be illustrated as many particles suspended in a turbulent medium whose connections with one another develop a chaotic order determined by the individual's personality and experiences. As we may suppose, the number of the semiotic chains is infinite. Thus, to recognize an image means to reject the infinite number of links and interpretations contained in the same pictorial composition, or represented in the topologic space.

|*Fig. 3.13*|

The mind finds and creates a series of links – a process of association – that makes the image intelligible or generates a series of interpretations. This process is represented by the *Rorschach Test*, (Fig. 3.13) in which the patient is confronted with a series of ambiguous images thereby allowing the analyst to examine the characteristics of the patient's personality.

Dalí's method foresees both uncontrolled associations and a production of unconscious images (*delirium*). Then he applies a rational analysis to this irrational material and renders it intelligible. In Dalí's words:

---

31 | Breton A. 1985 (1924), p. 20.
32 | Gleizes A. 1969, p. 271.
33 | Dalí S. 1977, p. 23.
34 | Ross A. 1991.

"la actividad crítica interviene únicamente como líquido revelador de imágenes, asocia-
ciones, coherencias y sutilezas sistemáticas graves y ya existentes en el minuto en que
se produce la instantaneidad delirante."[35]

From a clinical point of view, patients affected by paranoia project thoughts and fears
onto somebody or something in order to pull out the 'inner reality' of their mind. In
this way, the paranoiacs construct an external reality. Thus the world of fears in which
the paranoiacs live is a world generated by the projections of their mind. Through
theses projections, the paranoiacs give symbolic significance to the objects around
them.[36] Further, the symbolic signifiers given by the paranoiacs are able to construct
a rational reality, a real world, the existence of which is founded on an obsessive idea.
The world constructed by the paranoid mind is very logical; it corresponds to the
perfect calculation of cause and effect laws. Thus, the world created by the paranoiac
can be shared. In fact, paranoia constructs intelligible and plausible events through
the significance given to objects. Hence, Dalí's images could be shared with other
persons. They originated through a signifying process that made these images intelligible. According to Dalí, the intelligibility of the paranoia derives from the technique
known as *imagen doble*, which, according to him, is:

"la représentation d'un objet qui, sans la moindre modification figurative ou anatomique,
soit en même temps la représentation d'un autre objet absolument différent, dénuée
elle aussi de tout genre de déformation ou anormalité qui pourrait déceler quelque
arrangement."[37]

|*Fig. 3.14*|

35 | Dalí S. 1977, p. 23.
36 | The effects of this pathology were described by Freud as follows: "Alles, was er an
den anderen bemerkt, ist bedeutungsvoll, alles ist deutbar. Wie kommt er nur dazu? Er
projiziert wahrscheinlich in das Seelenleben der anderen, was im eigenen unbewusst
vorhanden ist, hier wie in so vielen ähnlichen Fällen." (Freud S. 1904, p. 50.)
37 | Dalí S. 1930, p. 10.

For Dalí, the images derived from this method represented an important tool to systematizing the confusion, the chaos. For him, his technique is aimed at "systématiser la confusion et de contribuer au discrédit total du monde de la réalité."[38] Reality, in this case, is replaced by a second image, an image derived from the violence of the paranoid thought. This second image is, according to Dalí, the expression of the obsessive idea (*idée obsédante*). The chaos to which Dalí alludes is most definitely the infinity of possibilities allowed by the signifying, the many links generated by the intellect. Additionally, this double image allows a recursive operation described by Dalí as follows:

"L'image double (dont l'exemple peut être celui de l'image d'un cheval qui est en même temps l'image d'une femme) peut se prolonger, continuant le processus paranoïaque, l'existence d'une autre idée obsédante étant alors suffisante pour qu'une troisième image apparaisse (l'image d'un lion, par exemple) et ainsi de suite jusqu'à concurrence d'un nombre d'images limité uniquement par le degré de capacité paranoïaque de la pensée."[39]

Through this practice, Dalí highlights the complex nature of the sign(s) and assigns to painting the same nature as the poetic message, whose main feature is, following the ideas of Eco, the fact of being "strutturato come un messaggio ma di costituire in realtà una sorgente di messaggi."[40] In fact, the many possibilities of interpretation opened up by Dalí made possible the representation of a world free from a unique geometry. With Dalí, reality started to become chaotic and the chaos of nature acquired the very same essence as the chaos described by Leibniz. In other words, chaos became a synonym for an infinite set of possibilities of choice. Dalí's paranoiac-critical method represents a way to escape from the code, from the convention. It represents a stairway to the higher reality.

The surrealist method completely destroys the positivist hope of grabbing reality. Further, with surrealism, the *déchirure* of the image represents also a *déchirure* within reason. Dalí's paranoiac-critical method accentuates the virtual value of the image. Through this process it is possible to develop another analysis of the image in which the image is seen in its state of *figure figurante* and not just in its state of *figure figurée*. Thus, the image can be understood as a process in which the image as *figure figurante* represents, in Didi-Huberman's words:

"le chemin, la question en acte, faite couleurs, fait volumes : la question encore ouverte de savoir ce qui pourrait bien, dans une telle surface peinte ou dans un tel repli de la pierre, devenir visible."[41]

---

38 | Dalí S. 1930, p. 10.
39 | Dalí S. 1930, p. 10.
40 | Eco U. 2005⁸, p. 96.
41 | Didi-Huberman G. 1990, p. 173.

The image ceases to be a mere copy, a second thing that replaces the object. The image starts to be more than a second thing because it can be many things at the same time.[42]

The multidimensionality that the image acquires thanks to non-Euclidean geometries generated the split of the image itself and of its structure, a phenomenon that can be clearly seen using Dalí's paranoiac-critical method. Dalí's method generates a chaotic system in which logic is necessary in order to organize the many parts of the jigsaw puzzle, which is interpreted, according to Dalí, by the degree of the paranoia of the unconscious mind of the viewer. Thus, the degree of paranoia establishes the degree of presentation of the image. In other words, the image is a *materia informis* that takes shape simply through the mental process of the viewer. As Didi-Huberman remarked, quoting Freud's *Die Traumdeutung*, the interpretation of images, due to its rupture, requires more the knowledge (*Kenntnis*) than the science (*Wissenschaft*). Thus, the method of the interpretation of dreams developed by Freud became an important tool for the analysis of images. Didi-Huberman's primary interest in Freud's *Die Traumdeutung* was the dream's value of deformation (*Entstellung*) and the logic deriving from it. The image, like the dream, is like a rebus that presents many meanings.[43] Didi-Huberman's interest in Freud's *Die Traumdeutung* resides in the dreamlike image and its process, from which derives many similarities. Through the process of resemblance generated by the dream-related activity, the similarity between objects do not represent a formal unity (*unité formelle*) but a process. In other words, resemblance is no longer an intelligible characteristic of the object due to the rupture or fractalization of its representation.

In this context, in Didi-Huberman's words, "Il n'y a donc plus de « termes » qui vaillent, mais seulement des relations nouées, des passages qui se cristallisent."[44] Thus, like in the dream, images use resemblance as a degree of deformation (*Entstellung*) in order to be intelligible at first gaze and in this way they acquire a topologic quality. Certainly, without the influence of non-Euclidean geometries on artistic expression and their analysis, particularly on pictorial forms of expression like Cubism, the theorization of such images like the images produced through Dalí's Paranoic-critical method would have been analyzed as mere optical illusions belonging to a kind of magical field. Further, because of non-Euclidean geometries and fractal geometry, it has become possible to understand the virtual character of the image, its split, as the recognition of a fractional dimension in the representative space. In other words, the phenomenon of the harmony between the scales used by fractal geometry finds an analogy in the double image of the practice of critical paranoia. The image establishes a process of analysis similar to that established by Chaos Theory and its use of fractal geometry to the study of chaotic movements. Chaos theory is a science of movement, a science that recognizes the state of becoming. Both methods of analysis, the image

---

42 | See Merleau-Ponty M. 1964.

43 | It is interesting to remember the German word for rebus *Bilderrätsel*, 'an image enigma'.

44 | Didi-Huberman G. 1990, p. 184.

as *figure figurante* and fractal geometry in chaotic movements, recognize the 'potential to become' of the phenomenon, and both recognize the possibility of being something that is not at a defined state.

As mentioned above, the influence of non-Euclidean geometries played an important role in the development of Cubism. Apollinaire's ideas about a fourth dimension were in fact a way to identify the space composed by more than three dimensions as developed by some artists. To compose an n-dimensional space represented a way to go beyond the established reality and a way to present, through images, a higher reality. The same phenomenon was proposed by surrealism through the emancipation of the reason and the end of 'logic.' The surrealists attempted to reach this aim through a variety of methods, especially through *automatic writing*.[45]

The influence of non-Euclidean geometries on the audiovisual field could not be expressed in the same way as with painting. In fact, the cinematographic medium was in a sense enclosed in an Euclidean *ordino*. The cinematographic camera imposed a

---

45 | In his first surrealist manifest, Breton gives a kind of guideline to surrealist expression entitled *Secrets de l'art magique surréaliste*. The first paragraph, dedicated to surrealist writing, (Composition surrealist écrite, ou premier et dernier jet) recalls Kardec's spiritist method used by mediums to communicate, through writing, with spirits. I think it is important to quote Breton's paragraph about automatic writing: "Faites-vous apporter de quoi écrire, après vous être établi en un lieu aussi favorable que possible à la concentration de votre esprit sur lui-même. Placez-vous dans l'état le plus passif, ou réceptif, que vous pourrez. Faites abstraction de votre génie, de vos talents et de ceux de tous les autres. Dites-vous bien que la littérature est un de plus tristes chemins qui mènent à tout. Écrivez vite sans sujet préconçu, assez vite pour ne pas retenir et ne pas être tenté de vous relire. La première phrase viendra tout seule, tant il est vrai qu'à chaque seconde il est une phrase étrangère à notre pensée consciente qui ne demande qu'à s'extérioriser. Il est assez difficile de se prononcer sur le cas de la phrase suivante ; elle participe sans doute à la fois de notre activité consciente et de l'autre, si l'on admet que le fait d'avoir écrit la première entraîne un minimum de perception. Peu doit vous importer, d'ailleurs ; c'est en cela que réside, pour la plus grande part, l'intérêt du jeu surréaliste. Toujours est-il que la ponctuation s'oppose sans doute à la continuité absolue de la coulée qui nos occupe, bien qu'elle paraisse aussi nécessaire que la distribution des nœuds sur une corde vibrante. Continuez autant qu'il vous plaire. Fiez-vous au caractère inépuisable du murmure. Si le silence menace de s'établir pour peu que vous ayez commis une faute : une faute, peut-on dire, d'inattention, rompez sans hésiter avec une ligne trop claire. A la suite du mot dont l'origine vous semble suspecte, posez une lettre quelconque, la lettre l par exemple, toujours la lettre l, et ramenez l'arbitraire en imposant cette lettre pour initiale au mot qui suivra." (Breton A. 1985 (1924), pp. 41-42). As we can see, for Breton, this method of writing represented a kind of link with a higher world, like a form of spiritual communication that uses the hand of the writer to write a dictated text; "Continuez autant qu'il vous plaire. Fiez-vous au caractère inépuisable du murmure."

geometrical *ordino* that corresponded directly to an Euclidean geometry. Thus, the destruction of the Euclidean space was achieved by the filmic image in different ways.

The cinematic image could not perfectly follow non-Euclidean geometries. However, some attempts were made to allude to the existence of a 'fourth dimension' in cinematographic narrative. They were influenced by Futurist ideas about time as a dimension in the multidimensional space. An example of this is the Kinoki manifest, which admired the Futurist manifest and theorized a filmic expression guided exclusively by the cinematographic camera, by the 'consciousness' of the machine. The sense of objectivity given by the cinematographic camera, following the idea of the supremacy of the machine theorized by the Futurists, developed, through Vertov's genius, a new cinematographic narrative. For Vertov, the narrative was composed of the three Euclidean dimensions inherited by the camera obscura plus the dimension of time. Clearly influenced by the Futurists, Vertov developed a kind of adoration for the machine. He worshiped mechanics, the beauty of chemical processes and the machine as a supreme masterwork.[46] However, cinematography was not only influenced by Futurism; Cubism also had some influence on the spatial organization of the cinematographic narrative.[47] In fact, cinematography adopted the multiplication of viewpoints as a way to give form to the higher reality theorized by Cubists. This phenomenon can be seen in some of Eisenstein's works, like his masterpiece *The Battleship Potemkin* (1925), during the scene in the kitchen where the mutiny starts.

|*Fig. 3.15*|

In the image above, (Fig. 3.15) we can see ten pictures corresponding to ten seconds of the kitchen scene. As we can see, a lot of shots compose this short scene. Although in this case the multiplication of viewpoints does not attempt to reconstruct a 360° view of the event, Eisenstein multiplied the viewpoints using a series of jump-cuts that create a fractional space as well as a fractional time. It is possible to see in this scene that the jump-cut represents an inflection point in the image, recalling some proto-fractal objects.

---

46 | See Vertov D. 2011.
47 | See Lawder S. 1975.

In the soviet cinema of this period, the phenomenon of the multiplication of view-points was usually used in scenes rich in pathos. Another exponent of the multiplica-tion of viewpoints in soviet film is Dimitri Kirsanoff, especially in his *Ménilmontant* (1926). However, the attempts of cinematography to express the fourth dimension theorized by cubism were not only focused on the multiplication of viewpoints. In Fernand Léger's Ballet mécanique (1924), we can see in the cinematography a clear example of the theories developed by Cubists. This film is considered the clearest example of the cubist influence on cinema, most likely because it was realized by a French painter who adopted the cubist style in 1909.

The cubist forms and the spherical spaces in this film were created by means of optical distortions, for instance, the use of kaleidoscopes and the inversion of im-ages. In the first part of this film Léger shows the camera to the audience; he shows the instrument that composes the space of the narrative. However, the reflection of the camera is cast by a crystal ball, which recalls the spherical geometry of Riemann. After this shot, the director makes a series of takes in which a crystal ball is multiplied by a prismatic view. This optical effect multiplies the objects represented and destroys the Euclidean order imposed by the camera, generating a self-similar phenomenon.

|*Fig. 3.16*|

In this film, Léger alludes to the creation of a new space through spherical geometry as well as the impossibility of the camera to catch the higher reality. He also proposes a series of geometrical figures – a circle, a triangle – in rapid succession.

|*Fig. 3.17*|

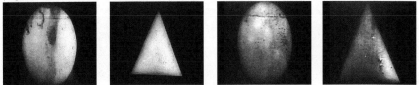

These figures, due to the speed of the changes, are almost unrecognizable. In the se-quence, the geometrical figures presented lose their rigid nature; they become flexible and unclear objects that recall the topological dimension. However, I would like to draw attention to the presentation of this film. In my opinion, it is in that aspect that the director shows the influence of non-Euclidean geometries on cinematography. The film's opening credits read:

"Le "BALLET MÉCANIQUE" a été composé par le peintre Fernand Léger en 1924. C'est le premier film sans scénario. Il a été présenté dans toutes les capitales d'Europe et plusieurs fois à New-York."

The limits of the cinematographic camera with respect to presenting the higher reality proposed by Cubism were overcome in the organization of the narrative. That is to say, cinematographic narrative started to be organized in a way that does not follow the linearity of the plot. This absence of script represents a new way to organize the narrative space, a way to create a space free from literary conventions, free from the traditions of theater brought by Méliès to the cinematographic art.[48] It is interesting to remember that the same proposition – a cinematographic narrative space free from scenario – was developed by Vertov during the same period.

It is possible to theorize that non–Euclidean geometries, the concept of the *fourth dimension* in painting, surrealism, Dalí's paranoiac-critical method and so on, in filmic images represented a change in the spatial organization of the pure narrative. It represented a new way to organize the interaction between paradigm and syntagm, a new *ordino* that recognizes fractal dimensions, that is, intermediate dimensions between the two well defined spaces, the spaces of things in *absentia* and things in *presentia*.

---

48 | See Sadoul G. 1949, Chapitre III *La mise en scène: Georges Méliès*.

3.2 A Geodesy of Film Narrative

In the first part of this text I analyzed the process of translation of nature that transformed life into a mediated act. In the same way, the evolution of visual media, which technologically allowed the birth of cinematography, was investigated from a historical point of view. In particular, the process through which each of the technical instruments considered moved from the scientific sphere to other fields of application was highlighted. Of course, the instruments analyzed above do not include all the media that allowed the creation of cinematography. My choice was based on two reasons: firstly, these instruments represent an important point for the analysis of cinematography as instruments of translation, thus of spatial organization; and secondly, they show the influence of technical improvements on the representation of space.

Let us briefly focus our attention on what I have pointed out in the previous chapters.

As noted in the previous chapters, mankind undergoes the necessity to mediate its relationship with nature in order to overcome the weakness of its senses. Hence, the focus on the improvement of technology, which allows the creation of spaces aimed at translating nature with a high degree of 'objectivity.' This historical survey on the development of visual media allows us to highlight the fact that media are not just the 'transporters' of messages, but that they also exert an extraordinary force on mankind's cognitive activities through their status as 'translators' of our environment.[1] Even if the instruments we are dealing with are the direct heirs of Euclidean geometry, which does not recognize irregularities in nature, they attempt to make out irregular forms and phenomena in order to translate them into a specific spatial organization.

The fundamental act of translating nature generates a recurrent will to manage huge quantities of information and organize them in a space, which becomes both an infinite and a narrative one. Thus, in the second part of this text, the change that each visual medium analyzed underwent from the scientific field – where its purpose was the improvement of the analysis of nature by means of the creation of a space in which natural objects and phenomena could be translated – to the artistic one was highlighted. Further, these instruments attempted to create an infinite narrative space (or at least its allusion), which implies the use of recursive formulas in order to create a particular spatial organization. For instance, in the case of perspective, this becomes clear through the recursive formula of diminishing magnitudes separated by diminishing intervals used by the painter to create a constant degree of decreasing shapes, which in turn projects the space toward an infinite point and creates the feeling of depth. The same phenomenon is also evident in the encased world theorized by Leibniz under the influence of contemporary technical improvements in the field of microscopy. In particular, the encased world discovered by means of the microscope, which broadens the borders of the visible by improving human sight, demonstrates the important role of similarity in the conception of space. In fact, by means of the

---

1 | For a deeper discussion of this subject, see Krämer S. 1998.

existence of analogies at different scales, it became possible to imagine the 'Whole,' namely, to represent it by the shape of the part. This phenomenon, as we have seen, is present in nature, in some mathematical formulas and geometric objects (proto-fractal objects and fractal geometry), as well as in some Panoramas (see chapters *Self-Similarity: Fold Into Fold* and *The Panorama: An Example of 'Gigantomanie des Mediums*). We have also seen (chapter *Mise en Abyme: blazon into blazon*) that recursivity also became an important narrative instrument known as *myse en abyme*.

Every visual instrument is aimed at the recognition of new objects, phenomena and shapes, thus every visual instrument allows a new conception of space and a new idea of structure. In particular, in the chapter dedicated to cinematographic technology, the process that moves this technology from the physiological field to the philosophical and artistic ones was investigated.[2] At that point, it was possible to consider film narrative as the result of the spatial organization created by the photographic technology. However, cinematographic technology generates its own spatial organization and develops a new concept of infinity. As noted above, photographic technology represented regular and irregular phenomena by means of the Euclidean space that it inherited from the externalization of the perspective to a device embodied by the camera obscura. Conversely, the cinematographic camera, besides sharing this characteristic inherited from the photographic technology, through its narrative component, is able to develop in time a kind of endlessness. It establishes, through the sequence of images, the continuum of physical existence.[3] It follows that it can be considered as a unique geometry from which, thanks to technological improvements (sound, video-technology or digital-technology), many other ways to organize the narrative space can be derived. Therefore, Deleuze, in his fundamental work *Cinéma 1. L'image-mouvement* published in 1983, claims that the cinematographic technique

---

2 | It is interesting in this regard to mention the analysis proposed by Curi on the philosophical role of cinematography. Curi argues that it is a mistake to think that the only way of expression of philosophy is the logical argument, that is, a *logos* free from *pathos*. Through Plato's Protagoras, Curi highlights the importance of the plot in philosophical reasoning. Protagoras, in order to explain the art of politics, asked his interlocutors if they prefer that he argues by using a story (*mythos*) or by means of reasoning (*logos*). According to Protagoras there are in fact two different ways to guide a demonstration. The first one, and the most widely known, is through the *logos*, associated with the concept of 'demonstration' and related in turn to the notions of abstract reasoning and computation. The second one is the *mythos*, that is, a narration, a story, the content of which can be truth or false. The difference highlighted by Protagoras is that the *mythos* is 'full of grace' (*charis*) and is more joyful. *Mythos* is also an instrument to demonstrate, just as *logos* is. By means of the *mythos*, the reasoning is imbued with pleasantness unknown to *logos*. See Curi U. 2009.

3 | See Kracauer S. 1997, p. 63. In fact, Kracauer found this will and also this possibility intrinsic to film in Leger's idea of the 'Monster film,' a film that would be twenty-four consecutive hours of the life of a couple.

finds its pre-history not in photographic technology, but rather in instantaneous photography, in particular in the equidistance of the snapshots materialized by the film as a surface and the mechanism that drives the images (= Lumière's invention of claws).[4] In Deleuze's theorization cinema creates a new spatial organization, which makes possible a new conception of space that does not adhere to an Euclidean *ordino*. He breaks in some ways with previous analyses of cinematographic technology. In fact, he conceived the film as a medium able to develop a space in becoming due to its capacity to generate non-Euclidean spaces. For Deleuze, cinematographic technology is a particular instrument that creates its own spatial organization and from which both a new conception of spatial structure and time derive.

Analyzing the bases of film spatial organization, Deleuze argues that Pasolini and Jackobson's viewpoint on framing is analyzed by means of linguistic terms that Deleuze considers unnecessary. He places the analysis of framing closer to informatics systems than to linguistic ones. According to Deleuze, saturation and refraction are fundamental concepts in understanding film narrative space, and these concepts come from informatics.[5] Further, by defining cinema as a pure spatial organization and by likening film narrative to informatics systems, he eclipses the frenetic search for a grammar in film narrative particular to the French formalist heritage.

The attempt to compare film narrative to language was in fact natural.[6] As noted in the second part of this text, every visual medium was associated, at its beginning, with the writing technique. It was the case for photographic technology, discovered within the lithographic field. The discovery of a chemical substance sensitive to light was even catalogued as 'ink.'[7] Cinematography underwent the same process. Further, its capacity to develop images in time sequences and to construct a plot directly related this technique to linguistics.[8]

It seems that the impossibility to create a perfect parallel between film narrative and linguistics resided in the impression of reality, which was the central point of film analysis before the Second World War.[9] Certainly, if compared with photography, film accentuates the impression of reality.[10] Movement was of course one of the factors that

---

4 | Deleuze G. 1983, p. 14.

5 | See Deleuze G. 1983, *Chapitre 2. Cadre et plan, cadrage et découpage*.

6 | See Brodwell D. 1985.

7 | On this topic see also Debray R. 1992. The author points out that, over millennia, images create in human cognition many systems of symbolic correspondences; it could be of cosmic order, social order, and also pure communication. It was many centuries before linear writing could 'format' human sensations and cognitive processes.

8 | Cinema was for the first time referenced as a writing technique by Victor Perrot in 1919, but it was during the late 40s that it started to be studied through linguistic analyses. On this topic see Mitry J. 1987, p. 33.

9 | See Laffay A. 1964.

10 | It is interesting to note how Barthes (Barthes R. 1964.) highlights the new categories of space and time derived from photographic technology. He qualifies the creation

accentuates the impression of reality in film.[11] Time was itself perceived as a perspective that sculpts the object in a kind of 'casting' (*moulage*) in becoming.[12] The impression of reality was also perceived as a factor deriving from the spatial composition of framing developed in time.[13] According to Morin, movement also creates the shape of objects, that is the image acquires volume by means of movement. Movement gives relief to the objects present in the image, and relief give life.[14] Movement was considered an important factor for the impression of reality because it shapes forms in the image.[15] Certainly, movement simulates the natural human perception of the objects represented.[16] Thus, movement makes it impossible to compare the linguistic articula-

---

of this new space like an illogical conjunction of 'here' and 'formerly,' thus, the 'unreal realism' generated by means of that technology, in which its real side corresponds to 'formerly': what is shown in the picture really existed. Its side of unreality is represented by the temporal balance in which things represented in the picture were *like that* but they are no longer *like that*. Another important difference between photographic and cinematographic technology is that the former produces a sense denoted only by means of its automatic process of photo-chemical duplication. This denotation in photography is just a copy of human perception, which is not codified and does not present its own organization, while cinema denotes, because of its temporal component: it must articulate the filmic space.

11 | See Morin E. 1956. Further, I would like to call attention to the fact that Metz, in order to make the distinction between the photographic image and the cinematographic one, used narrative instead of movement. In fact, Metz stated that the passage from one fixed image to two images represents the passage from image to language.

12 | See Bazin A. 2008 (1975).

13 | It is interesting to note that the impression of reality of the cinematographic image represents a problem impossible to solve if one attempts to create a perfect analogy between cinematographic image and language. This was Pasolini's argument. In fact, Pasolini refuted the impression of reality by arguing that cinema represents the reality. Pasolini theorized cinema as a language that presents double articulation. Thus, the shot was understood as a moneme and the objects present in the frame were understood as cinemes, equivalent to phonemes. Pasolini attempted to highlight cinema as a universal language, as an Esperanto; 'the language of reality.' On this topic see Pasolini P.P. 2000.

14 | See Michotte Van Den Berk A. 1948.

15 | The phenomenon is analyzed by Metz (Metz C. 1968) as *stéréocinétique*. See also Arnheim R. 1932.

16 | According to Epstein, time represents a kind of perspective or relief. It is interesting to note that he highlights this phenomenon also in Fernand Léger's paintings. Epstein posits that Léger, by means of the fragmentation of the space of the image, creates a multidimensional space that collides with the perspective of the natural human sight and from which derives a perspective constructed by the dynamics of the inner structure of that multidimensional space. In his words: "Ce qui orne la peinture de Léger de cette vie presque truculente, c'est d'abord le fractionnement. L'aspect des choses, pour lui,

tion of the plot in writing to the narrative spatial organization created through cinematographic technology. In fact, in film, actions are always actual, even if they recall past events, for example in flashbacks.[17] This important feature creates a fundamental distinction between cinematographic technology and both photographic technology and linguistic processes. In addition, it modifies Barthes' idea of the photographic impression of reality. The conjunction of real and unreal theorized by Barthes and obtained by photographic technology, where the real is represented by the real existence of the object translated into photographic dimension and the unreal by its *absentia* confirmed by the representation, loses its unreal component. This happens by means of the movement accomplished in front of the beholder: movement puts the object that is in *absentia* into *presentia*. While an image covers a space into a space (signifier-space --- signified-space), film, thanks to its temporal component, cannot only cover a space into a space by means of the image, but can also cover a space into time, for example a description by means of many shots of a space (signifier-space --- signified-time). In addition, it can cover time into time, for example a narration by means of many successive shots of an action into space (signifier-time --- signified-time). Film's capacity to develop a series of images in time allows it to create a system of temporal transformation and to develop a series of events in chronological order, whereas photography simply represents a technology that capture an image, a *punctum temporis*.[18] Paradoxically, the capacity to develop a series of images in time was also the reason why cinema was likened to language, and, under the formalist logic, was analyzed by using linguistic terms.[19] However, as we will see, the impres-

---

est un aspect par fragments. Toutes les surfaces se divisent, se tronquent, se décomposent, se brisent, comme on imagine qu'elles font dans l'œil à mille facettes de l'insecte. Géométrie descriptive dont la toile est le plan de bout. Au lieu de subir la perspective, ce peintre la fend, entre en elle, l'analyse et la dénoue, illusion par illusion. À la perspective du dehors il subsiste ainsi la perspective du dedans, une perspective multiple, chatoyante, onduleuse, variable et contractile comme un cheveu hygromètre." (Epstein J. 1974, p. 115.)

17 | With regard to this argument, it is interesting to remember Mitry's thoughts about the inexistence of indefinite articles in film narrative. See Mitry J. 1987, p. 44-45.

18 | Metz C. 1968, p. 27. It is also interesting to see that Couchot theorized that moment derives in such sens from movement. In his words; "Il apparaît (le temps) sous l'aspect indirect du *moment*, une sorte de condensation du mouvement des choses et des êtres en devenir que le peintre veut saisir. Condensation analogue au mot '*moment*' lui-même (*momentum*, conrtaction de *movimentum*, mouvement), comme si l'instant marqué par le moment ne pouvait découler que du mouvement, comme si la durée était première, l'instant second." (Couchout E. 2007, p. 26.)

19 | Debray claims that the first requirement to making an analysis of image is that one must avoid the confusion that image generates between 'thought and language'. He argues that image makes think by means of many other means that by means of signs. See Debray R. 1992.

sion of reality represented the main problem to the comprehension of film narrative as a language.

In his *Sémantique structurale*, Algirdas Julius Greimas notes that the minimal structure of every signification is defined by the presence of two terms linked to each other in a univocal relation. The signification presupposes the perception of both terms and their relationship. The same phenomenon was perceived in film narrative, which contrary to photography, passes from one image to many images and through editing, creates meaning by means of the links established between them.[20] As already observed by Eisenstein, "two film pieces of any kind, placed together, inevitably combine into a new concept, a new quality, arising out of that juxtaposition."[21]

Free from structuralist ideas, this statement by Eisenstein could be understood as the first quality of the complexity as defined by Morin. Borrowing from him, "Un tout est plus que la somme des parties qui la constituent."[22] Therefore, the essence of film narrative was perceived through editing, which found its scientific guarantee in the Kuleshov effect.[23] It is from the juxtaposition of images that associations of ideas are derived and by means of them – and through them – the beholder recognizes, or finds, an experience of life, a meaning. Using the words of Mitry:

|Fig. 3.18|

"Les images filmiques et leurs relations sont autant de stimulis qui « actualisent » des idées ou des émotions en rappelant à notre conscience des effets relatives à quelque expérience vécue."[24]

Hence, Mitry argues that the experience of Kuleshov of *the girl on the sofa* (Fig. 3.18) has no meaning if the beholder is a child who does not know sexual desire yet.[25] By means of this experience, it was possible to demonstrate that, as the girl does not express anything, what the beholder saw was not real. In other words, the viewer, in

---

20 | "Passer d'une image à deux images, c'est passer de l'image au langage." (Metz C. 1968, p. 53.)

21 | Eisenstein S.M. 1943, p. 14.

22 | Morin E. 2005, p. 114.

23 | See Balázs B. 2001.

24 | Mitry J. 1963b, p. 284.

25 | Mitry J. 1963b, p. 283.

front of a succession of frames, links the series of successive perceptions and brings each one of them to an 'organic whole.' Then, he builds logical relations and attributes expressions (or meanings) to what should be expressed or, in that case, to what she should have expressed. The girl on the sofa imposes a relation, man looking – girl looked, that recalls and signifies the idea of desire.

The Kuleshov effect was understood as the basis of cinematographic 'language.' It was the enlightenment of the mechanism creating meaning in moving pictures. Through the Kuleshov effect, a number of theories attempted to establish some automatisms in the relation: image – beholder. Following Bonitzer, these automatisms attempted to create an imaginary "healing" of the fractionated space through editing.[26] The Kuleshov effect demonstrated a kind of necessity, on the part of the beholder, for continuity and unity of the space; in other words, a need for homogeneity in the heterogeneous succession of different shots. As a consequence editing became the most important element of cinematographic art.[27]

According to Pasolini, editing governs this narrative instrument because it organizes the narrative, chooses the 'significant moments,' and can also transform a current (= present) image into a 'past sentence.' To be precise, editing can transform present into past but, at the same time, this past remains present because of the nature of the image, which is always actual. However, editing creates a succession of images respecting the linearity imposed by both the film as a carrier and the plot construction, which follows the canons imposed by Aristotle's *poetics*. Therefore, the act of editing was analyzed by means of linguistic terms even though the impression of reality raised some doubts on the comparison between film narrative and the functioning of a language.[28] This notwithstanding, image was equated to language and was analyzed as a formal system of signs governed by grammatical rules.

It is possible to highlight the influence of Greimas on the analysis of film narrative. The framework followed was clear. The combination of two terms, namely, in the case of film, the combination of two images, had to follow some 'natural rules.' Thus a tracking shot, a pan, or even the size of shots were perceived as governed by what was called a syntax.[29] This term was not understood in its pure Greek meaning of 'arrangement'[30] (σύνταξις), rather in its meaning of rules or principles governing the structure of a language.

---

26 | Bonitzer P. 1982, p. 28.

27 | See Mitry J. 1963a.

28 | The fact that the cinematographic image is always a real image (actual image) also raises some problems in comparing film narrative with linguistic structures. According to Balázs (Balázs B. 2001, p. 44.), due to the nature of the real image (actual image), the cinematographic image cannot be conjugated.

29 | Consider that, in a sequence, the change of the size of a shot was governed by a rule that limits the drastic and sudden change of shot size. For example a panoramic shot could not be followed by a close-up.

30 | From *syn* (σύν) "together", and *táxis* (τάξις) "an ordering".

The comparison between film narrative and linguistics was applied particularly during the period of silent film when it was easy to define cinema as a non-verbal language. This idea was recurrent during the silent period: the image was equated to a word,[31] a sequence shot to a sentence, and some effects, like cross dissolving or fading, to punctuation marks.[32] Cinema was in some sense understood as a kind of Esperanto,[33] and in consequence, the attempts to develop a cinematographic grammar were multiplied. However, cinema has not always been understood as a language.[34] Before becoming the means of expression that we know, cinema was perceived as a mechanical process of recording, archiving and reproducing visual shows, for example theater or even life it self. Malraux defined it a 'moyen de reproduction.' The problem of semiotics and the comparison between cinema and language grows after the first decade of the 20th century (1910-1915) when cinema started attempting to develop a complex plot. Some authors like C. Metz, among others, take this date as the birth of cinema. Certainly, the first attempts of the pioneers of cinematographic narrative were not directed at the development of a grammar. The goal of these pioneers was to tell a story by means of both moving pictures and the analogy with reality as embodied by the object represented. Some important and complex spatial constructions of film narrative, especially effects, which create spatial and temporal ellipses, were in fact developed by chance.[35] During the period before 1915, film narrative simply reproduced reality and narrative articulations were not aimed at creating a precise narrative. Think, for example, of Alexandre Promio's 'tracking shot' in *The Grand Canal of Venice* (1897), or Edwin Porter's reverse shot in his documentary film

---

31 | The idea that an image could correspond to a word was a mistake. In fact, as we know, objects translated by means of photographic technology undergo first a spatial arrangement. Thus, image is a geometrical form and it corresponds to a connotation, an iconic connotation, while the word corresponds to a denotation. The attempt developed by Eisenstein makes the same mistake. In fact, in his concept of cinedialectic, he uses the structure of linguistics and just uses the form of ideograms. On this subject see among others, Mitry J. 1987 and Aristarco G. 1977.

32 | Metz, in his analysis on the semiotic questions of cinema tried to solve the problem of whether cinema is *langue* or *langage*. Using Buyssens's concept of 'substance' to describe the semantic content of a shot, Metz argues that an image is not a word but rather a sentence and a sequence shot corresponds to a complex segment of discourse. See Metz J. 1968, especially *Langue ou langage?*

33 | It is interesting to note that Eisenstein contrasted cinematic narrative to "totally regulated languages as Esperanto" not because they have a fixed grammar and a fixed relationship signifying-signified but just because of their "sterility of expression" due to its "artificial" nature. See Eisenstein S. 1949 (especially *A dialectic Approach to Film Form*).

34 | Some examples of this vision of cinema are Béla Balázs, Marcel L'Herbier, Edgar Morin and Jean Mitry.

35 | See Sadoul G. 1949, especially *Mise en scène de Georges Méliès*.

Panoramic Views (1901),[36] that can be concider the ancescters of our feature films.[37] The creation of film narrative was developed by means of the repetition of particular ways of assembling images. To be exact, the image being a free creation (differing from words), its assemblage by means of editing was only focused on the creation of an intelligible linear suite.[38] In this suite, every single image is totally different to the previous one as well as to the successive one. It is governed by logic and not by grammar.[39] Thus, the ways to assemble images was developed only following the sensation produced for the beholder. In fact, film narrative is something in perpetual creation, without fixed laws. As noted by Panofsky, at that stage of the cinematographic narrative one was dynamizing the space and spatializing time.[40]

"Lorsque Griffith réalisa la première métaphore filmique, il ne s'est pas demandé comment il devait s'y prendre pour obtenir l'équivalent d'une métaphore verbale. Il assembla simplement ses images de façon à suggérer une relation instinctivement ressentie. Cela étant, il fut remarquable que c'était une métaphore. Mais, s'il a obtenu l'équivalent d'une forme linguistique, il n'est point parti de cette forme pour en proposer une éventuelle traduction."[41]

This phenomenon can be recognized in the development of *parallel editing* and *alternant editing* (called by Metzt *syntagme alternant* and *sytagme parallèle*), in which the alternation of shots defines the signifier. For example in a scene pursuer – pursued, where the viewer understands both chronological series as contemporary moments. In other words, the viewer understands that scene 1 continues while scene 2 is screening. On the contrary, in the *syntagme parallèle*, there is no possibility of dating, no temporal relation of shots.

Without doubt, the assemblage of images is part of the field of semiotics. Thus, its analysis was directly influenced by Saussure's thoughts and linguistic terms. Even though, according to Saussure, linguistics was a part of semiotics and the formalist influence made semiotics a part of linguistics. As a result, it was impossible to separate semiotics, even in its non-linguistic form, from the structures of language. When the 'taxonomy' of camera movements, effects, size of shot, and so on started, it was natural to find in every movement, effect, and size of shot an analogy with language and even with some figures of speech. For example, the series of shots was denoted as syntagme, a shot was understood as the equivalent of many sentences, and a close-up represented a synecdoche.[42]

---

36 | Mitry J. 1963b, pp. 157-165.
37 | See Panofsky E. 1974.
38 | On this topic, see Mitry J. 1963b, *Les débuts du montage*, pp. 267-285.
39 | See Mitry J. 1987, especially *De la sytagmatique*.
40 | See Panofsky E. 1974.
41 | Mitry J. 1987, p. 165.
42 | See Mitry J. 1987.

The strong influence exerted by the formalist tradition started to be eclipsed during the late 60s and completely disappeared during the 80s. As a consequence, some authors, who developed their works during the period influenced by French formalism, radically changed their mind. A particular case is that of Jean Mitry, who maintains during all his intellectual activity a certain distance from the analogy between film and language. However, he only rejected the idea that film could be as a language with its own grammar. Nevertheless, in his analysis, he used linguistic terminology and some linguistic logics.

After the so-called formalistic phase, during the late 70s, film narrative started to be comprehended as a narrative that places the beholder in front of a sequence of signals whose meaning was based on the combination of some non-singular cinematographic patterns with extra-cinematographic ones that are shared with other arts or cultural productions. The linguistic inspiration starts to be separated and moved by an analysis that recognizes kinds of intelligibility (*types d'intellibilité*). As mentioned above, the image is concrete but the relations created by means of editing between many images develop many intelligible webs (*réseaux intelligibles*).[43] It is possible to theorize that during this period the influence of Eco theorizations in the field of semiotics was paramount for both film analysis and the terminological changes in film semiotics. This is the case for Metz who, during the first phase of his work, attempted to create a perfect analogy between film and language and develop a cinematographic grammar, but was later influenced by Eco's theories. In *Langage et cinema*, Metz adopted Eco's notion of code instead of that of sign. This simply consists of a terminological change and not in a structural change of analysis. In fact, the notion of code used by Metz also foresees a fixed meaning in some cinematographic effects. His aim was no longer to find how and why cinema is a language. Metz started to wonder under which conditions cinema could be considered a language. Thus, he started to consider semiotics and forgetting linguistics, in other words, he started to define cinema as a language in the French meaning of *langage*, and not as a *langue*.

Following Deleuze's definition, cinema could be defined as part of those "langages sans langue (sémies), qui comprends le cinéma non moins que le langage gestuel, vestimentaire ou même musical..."[44] Hence, the frenetic research into linguistics in cinema loses its meaning, and, for example, the search for a double articulation in moving pictures was forgotten. At that point, the legitimate and extensive research developed by formalists seemed to find its limit in how film uses reality to construct narrative.

The study of signification in film narrative does not imply an analysis using syntactical structures in order to understand the functioning of a type of textual organization. Both editing and the significant structures constructed through it do not propose a fixed signified to the beholder. Images play with reality – thanks to analogies – and organize actual sequences in a narrative space from which meaning originates. Then, the beholder perceives these sequences as a discourse. Consequently, the

---

43 | See Metz C. 1977, especially, *Sémiologie audio-visuelle et linguistique generative.*
44 | Deleuze G. 1985, p. 38.

cinematographic image was equated to a sentence. In order to integrate the cinematographic image into a sentence it was necessary to find a way to equate the cinematographic image, as an analogy, into a sentence and then codify these analogical signs
in order to discover a structure (a non-analogical structure).[45] However, the images
in a film sequence are not reality. Framing, angle, shot size, etc. construct a kind of
reality. Placed in sequence, they are a kind of symbolic representation. As claimed by
Eisenstein, the meaning was in the collision of shots, their 'conflict,' which represents
to the beholder the 'birth' of concepts.[46] Attempting to find a universal grammar of
film narrative through the instruments of linguistics was a formalistic error, which
became clear with the development of informatics systems and their way to organize
space through the interface and its interaction with the database.

   During the 80s, the linguistic model applied to film narrative was overcome. The
most important exponent of that departure is Deleuze, who in 1983, the same year of
the publication of *Cinéma 1. L'image-mouvement*, claimed that:

"La référence au modèle linguistique finit toujours par montrer que le cinéma est autre
chose, et que, si c'est un langage, c'est un langage analogique ou de modulation. On
peut dès lors croire que la référence au modèle linguistique est un détour dont il est
souhaitable de se passer."[47]

Let us start our analysis with Deleuze's studies of Pierce. Pierce's studies were mainly
focused on the development of a formal doctrine of signs. Deleuze uses Pierce's studies on semiotics in order to bring film semiotics closer to Bergson's thought and, in
doing so, he took a position opposite to Metz's theories. In fact, Deleuze emphasizes
Pierce's conception of semiotics, which envisages the signs as a product of images and
their combination, and not as a product of linguistic determinations.[48] Further, this
approach to Pierce also allows him to elaborate an opposition to both Pasolini's idea
of universal language and Metz's idea of the language of cinematographic images. Following Pierce's definition of signs – in which the sign can be understood as a genesis
– Deleuze alienates the cinematographic image from the enunciation and the utter-
ance. Thus, image becomes an *énonçable*,[49] "une masse plastique, une matière a-signi-

---

45 | See Deleuze G. 1985, especially *Récapitulation des images et des signes*.

46 | Eisenstein S. 1943 and 1949, especially *The Structure of the Film*.

47 | Interview with Gilles Deleuze conducted by Pascal Bonitzer et Jean Narboni. Pub-
lished in *Les cahiers du cinéma* n° 352, October 1983.

48 | See Deleuze G. 1985, especially, *Récapitulations des images et des signes*.

49 | According to Vandenbunder, Deleuze's approach to Pierce is imprecise and De-
leuze's semiotics is more influenced by Bergson's *Matière et Mémoire*. He analyzes
Deleuze's theories on semiotics in some brief comments from which the Bergsonian
basis of Deleuze's work becomes clearer. According to Vandenbunder, both Bergson and
Deleuze conceived in the same way the terms image, object and perceived object. They
also share the idea of perception as the beginning of the semiotic process and the defini-

fiante et a-syntaxique, une matière non linguistiquement formée, bien qu'elle ne soit pas amorphe et soi formée sémiotiquement, esthétiquement, pragmatiquement."[50] According to Deleuze, narrative spatial organization of film establishes relationships between images from which meaning derives. This interaction acts on the whole structure that is between the space in *presentia* and the space in *absentia* – this latter represented by the *hors-cadre* –, the *paradigm* and the *syntagm*, or, to use a contemporary term from informatics, between interface and database. For Deleuze, even though the birth of cinema lies in the editing, editing does not allow the creation of a plot equating film narrative to language.[51] For Deleuze, editing gives to cinema the possibility to articulate the narrative space of moving pictures, thus to become a geometry. Editing becomes the essence of the spatial composition because it governs the 'layout' (*agencement*) of *images-movement*, which, in turn, creates a direct link with the Whole; with Time. Even though Deleuze highlights four fundamental kinds of editing[52] – organic, dialectical, extensive and intensive – he attests that the essence of editing – it does not matter what kind – is the act of putting the cinematographic image in relation with the Whole, that is, to link a single object to universal time. The space derived from cinematographic technology becomes, for Deleuze, a layered spatial organization, almost a palimpsest, governed by its own geometrical laws that recall some topologic qualities.[53] Thus, all his historical analysis is based on the classification of images and signs of film; he developed a synchronic description of images.[54] Deleuze's analysis is focused on the evolution of this geometry (cinematic narrative), the spatial organization deriving from it and the notion of structure that it generates.[55]

In order to develop his theory, Deleuze needed to start with changing the understanding of the basis of cinematography. He starts by defining the fundamental cin-

---

tion of perception as something that incorporates all the senses. Further, both theorize man as the center of indetermination and affection as the interval between the inducement to act and the action. See Vandenbunder A. 1999, pp. 87-88.

50 | Deleuze G. 1985, p. 44.

51 | The birth of cinema as a means of expression (and not as mean of reproduction) can be dated to the 'destruction of the defined space,' that is, when this medium started to 'imagine' and record a succession of instants, when the sizes of shots changed, and when it started to be considered less a theatrical art. See Malraux A. 1940 and 1946.

52 | See Deleuze 1983, especially *Chapitre 3 Montage*.

53 | With regard to this subject, Genette analyzes the palimpsest structure in literature by means of some 'deformations' that characterize his concept of hypertext. On the same subject, see also Ropars-Wuilleumier M.-C. 1999.

54 | See Fahle O. 1999, p. 115.

55 | Maybe, that is the reason why Deleuze did not conduct an in-depth analysis of cinema at its beginning when the camera was fixed and there was no editing, meaning that the movement was accomplished just in the inner structure of the frame by means of the movement of actors and objects, in other words, when it excluded a communication between the sets. On this topic, see Fahle O. 1999, pp. 117-118.

ematographic notions, and, since the beginning, we see that his conception of cinema is strongly related to his former work *Mille Plateaux*, published together with Guattari in 1980. The idea of rizhomatic structure developed in *Mille Plateaux* influences his conception of the space generated by cinematographic technology. Starting from the more basic notion of film spatial construction, i.e. framing, Deleuze shows not only his opposition to linguistic terms. He denotes framing as the determination of a relatively enclosed system.[56] He bases his analysis on the theories developed by Bonitzer in *Le champ aveugle*. According to Bonitzer, the action of framing represents a delimitation of space.[57] The film narrative space is composed and decomposed in a series of shots in which the single image acquires its differential unity.[58] In Deleuze's words:

"On appelle cadrage la détermination d'un système clos, relativement clos, qui comprend tout ce qui est présent dans l'image."[59]

In this conception of the enclosed system derived through the action of framing, Deleuze also highlights a layered spatial composition, which is constituted by sets (*ensembles*) and sub-sets (*sous-ensembles*). According to Bonitzer, who shares this theory, an image contains infinite virtual images. The use of the zoom lens highlights this composition.[60] The system of the image was also described using spatial terms by Gardies, through the difference he marked between *lieu* (place) and *espace* (space), in which *lieu* is seen as a fragment of *espace* and, consequently, the *espace* is seen as a set of *lieux*.

---

56 | It is interesting to note that following this framework, framing can be summarized as the action of showing, from a particular point of view, a relatively closed system, which is seen by the viewer as a space in becoming. In other words, to frame means to chose a point of view on a site, which Gardies analyses as *"mise en situation."* See Gardies A. 1993.

57 | It is important to remember that in French there is a semantic confusion between the size of shot, which is determined by the distance of the camera, and the take, the number in the succession or chronological measurement. In fact, in French, the word *plan* determines both shot and take. For example, a *gros plan* is a close-up and a *planséquence* is a long take. The same word determines a concept of both duration and space. It is true that the problem arose when the camera acquired mobility, e.g. the fixed shots of the pre-Griffith era and even Griffith's montage of multiplying points of view. However, distinguishing spatial and temporal notion by means of a semantic difference, as with the English words *shot* and *take*, became a necessity when the narrative gamut of movements was expanded with track shots, panoramic, camera Dolly, and so on. These movements refute the homothetic construction of the image. See, in more details, Mitry J. 1963a.

58 | Bonitzer P. 1982, p. 16.

59 | Deleuze G. 1983, p. 23.

60 | Bonitzer P. 1982, p. 17.

"Si le lieu est un fragment d'espace, il suffirait alors de recoller minutieusement, comme les pièces innombrables d'un puzzle, les divers morceaux pour reconstituer cette sorte de totalité idéale que l'on appellerait espace. De cette manière, on obtiendrait une double définition, en miroir, tautologique: le lieu est un fragment d'espace et l'espace un ensemble de lieux."[61]

Further, the difference between *espace* and *lieu* allow us to recognize space not only as a place (*endroit*) with three dimensions where the objects are arranged, but the space also acquires the possibility to be thought of as a web (*réseau*) of relationships between lines. This fragmentation in the understanding of the space allows to conceive the space from a prespective "d'une plus grande abstraction de type structurel."[62] As one can note, the analysis of frame becomes a geodesic art,[63] a survey into a geometrical system that is multidimensional.[64] This system presents some particular dynamics that can be identified in both the inner relationship of the different spaces composing the layered space of the frame and in the processes that put the sequence in relation to the Whole.[65] This is clear, for example, in the interaction between different spaces in the frame, especially in a frame composed with a large depth of field or in some special geometrical constructions that create an enclosed system of frames into a frame by means of decor (e.g. a space divided by a window or a door). [66]

---

61 | Gardies A. 1993, p. 69.

62 | Gardies A. 1993, p. 70.

63 | At this point I would like to quote Baudry's words about the dispositif in which dispositif means a "relation métaphorique entre des lieux ou d'une relation entre des lieux métaphoriques." (Baudry J.-L. 1975, p. 56.) Thus, it is a topic.

64 | Risholm develops an interesting link between cinematographic technology and the change in the conception of space produced during the nineteenth century. "Film, so lassen sich die bisherigen Ausführungen zusammenfassen, ist gekennzeichnet durch eine Dynamisierung des Raums, die durch spezifische Inszenierungsweise und Aufnahmetechniken realisiert wird, wobei sich in die Inszenierungen des filmischen Raums die verschiedenen Dimensionen und Aspekte der Raumpraktiken einschreiben und durch die filmischen Räume reproduziert, aber auch modifiziert werden." (Risholm E. 2001, p. 271.)

65 | The depth of field is perceived as a narrative tool that can create a substitution of the scene. Bazin highlights this phenomenon analyzing Renoir's films. In fact, Bazin finds in Renoir's composition a tendency toward the deep image, which partially eliminates the role of editing. It also creates continuity in the images and brings them closer to reality. See Bazin A. 2008, p. 74. Conversely, according to Deleuze, the depth of image does not assure the feeling of reality in the image. He finds in the depth of field a means of 'absorption of the real' to transport the space into the virtuality. See Deleuze G. 1985, p. 113.

66 | The analysis developed in the present study imposes another notion of depth of field. In fact, in the photographic image, the depth of field is known as the distance between the nearest and farthest object that are in focus. This phenomenon derives

|*Fig. 3.19*|

... Le plan, qui est autre chose que l'image...

These dynamics are strongly connected with the notion of *hors-cadre*, which attests to the divisibility of the frame, the enclosed system that recalls the 'folded' structure that will be analyzed by Deleuze in *Le Pli* some years later. However, the character of divisibility highlighted by Deleuze in the analysis of *hors-cadre* is equated with the analysis of matter. As for the divisibility of matter, from which derives a notion of a space composed of heterogeneous sets that are divided into sub-sets to infinity and which creates an enclosed system, but also a communicating system – recalling Gardies' description of space, "l'espace pouvait être composé d'un ensemble de traits particuliers, eux-mêmes saisis au sein d'un réseau relationel; qu'il s'opposait en outre au lieu comme le virtuel à l'actuel."[67] – the *hors-cadre* embodies a system that is divided and contained in another, which is also contained in another one to infinity.[68]

---

from the optical mechanism. In our text, depth of field, even if it also derives from the optical phenomenon imposed by the lens, is understood as a set of planes in the cinematographic image, from which derives a relational system between objects present in a single image, or, using Gardies' terminology, between '*lieux*' in the space. See Gardies A. 1993, especially pp. 112-115.

67 | Gardies A. 1993, p. 70. In addition, Gardies posits that "Par opposition au caractère amorphe de l'étendue, l'espace offre une propriété essentielle, celle de sa mise en forme. Et c'est l'homme qui en est l'opérateur." (Gardies A. 1993, p. 70.)

68 | Bonitzer argues that the *hors-champ* is the product of the material structure of the screen. He states that film narrative always plays with hidden objects. Thus, *hors-cadre*

In Deleuze's words:

"un ensemble étant cadré, donc vu, il y a toujours un plus grand ensemble, ou un autre avec lequel le premier en forme un plus grand, et qui peut être vu à son tour, à condition de susciter un nouveau hors-champ, etc."[69]

The set of all these sub-sets creates an infinite homogeneous entity. Here, once again, it is possible to recognize the influence of Bergson in the Deleuzian idea of film narrative. By admitting that no system – in this specific case the frame and its *hors-cadre* – is ever absolutely enclosed, Deleuze applies the notion of *fil ténu* developed by Bergson in *L'évolution Créatrice*, where Bergson deals with the organization of bodies:

"Nous verrons que la matière a une tendance à constituer des systèmes isolables, qui se puissent traiter géométriquement. C'est même par cette tendance que nous la définirons. Mais ce n'est qu'une tendance. La matière ne va pas jusqu'au bout, et l'isolement n'est jamais complet. Si la science va jusqu'au bout et isole complètement, c'est pour la commodité de l'étude. Elle sous-entend que le système, dit isolé, reste soumis à certains influences extérieurs."[70]

|Prop. XVII| The *hors-cadre* plays a fundamental role in the spatial structure created by film narrative.[71] In this regard, Bazin states that when an actor leaves the visual field of the camera, he still exist in another place, in another space of the film that is hidden. Through this analysis, he demonstrates that film narrative uses the continuity of the *hors-cadre* as a dramatic tool. Conversely, the analogy of the *hors-cadre* theorized by Deleuze with Bergson's conception of matter is based on the fact that both design an enclosed system that refers to another space, another (invisible) set. When this 'invisible' (*in absentia*) set becomes visible (*in presentia*), it also refers to its *hors-cadre*, and so on to infinity. The infinity referred to by Deleuze corresponds to Bergson's idea of universal time, which is not visible, is not a set and is present in the entire universe. *Hors-cadre* testifies to both the existence of sets present *elsewhere* and the existence of a space outside of the homogeneous space and time.[72] Consequently, the frame acquires a new geometric nature. This layered space, extending infinitely by means of *hors-cadre*, also places the single frame in an infinite and complex spatial organization. Hence the shot moves away from its linguistic connotation (as a sentence) and

---

plays an important role in this narrative. See Bonitzer P. 1982, especially *Bobines ou: le labyrinthe et la question du visage*.

69 | Deleuze G. 1983, p. 29.

70 | Bergson H. 1907, p. 503 (10).

71 | See Burch N. 1969, especially, « *Nana » ou les deux espaces*. In this Analysis of Renoir's Nana (1926) Burch exposes an interesting theory about the rhythm that the *hors-champ* give to cinematographic narrative.

72 | See Deleuze G. 1983.

starts to be strongly linked to the notion of movement as generator of space. The shot is the setting of the movement accomplished not only in the inner enclosed system of a frame, but also in the parts of the set. In such a structure established by the frame and *hors-cadre*, the shot modifies the whole system by means of the infinite links created between entities in *presentia* and entities in *absentia*, designing a topologic space. Thus, Deleuze claims that movement expresses a change of the Whole. In his words, movement is the "rapport entre parties, et il est affection du tout."[73] Hence, the shot modifies the space of the set and of the sub-set of the frame in *presentia* and, at the same time, it expresses changes in the whole composition, i.e. in the sets in *absentia*. The shot assures the state of becoming of this system: it is a conversion, movement and transformation of the Whole.[74] Deleuze defines the shot as *image-mouvement*, and this last is linked with the Whole in its perpetual changing, in becoming.[75] Consequently, the *image-movement* presents a double face. The first one is related to the position of the objects in the frame and the second one is the connection of the objects to the Whole. It deals with the position in the space, and the transformation of the Whole in time.[76]

Within this framework, the *image-mouvement*, if understood as a shot, represents, in its first state, the framing, the first face, that is, the spatial notion. Its second face, that is, the temporal notion, is developed by means of editing. Hence, Deleuze qualifies the fixed shot as a 'pure *image-movement*' that can be articulated by means of both the movement of the camera and editing. Thus, the notion of take is for Deleuze a fixed spatial notion; "une tranche d'espace." Sharing Mitry's critic of the expression *plan-séquence* (long take), Deleuze posits that a long take or a track shot is not a long shot but a sequence of many shots. This spatial conception of the shot represents a layered space in which the unity, the single, undergoes transformations depending on the multiplicity that it contains. For that reason Deleuze's admiration for tracks shots. Indeed, the camera in movement becomes a *general equivalent* of all means of loco-

---

73 | Deleuze G. 1983, p. 32.

74 | According to Deleuze, the shot can be understood as awareness (*conscience*) because it is able to divide and bond spaces. However, he posits that this awareness comes from the cinematographic camera, which is sometimes human, sometimes inhuman or superhuman. Deleuze G. 1983, p. 34.

75 | It is interesting to note how Deleuze compares the movement generated by the relation between the frames (editing) and the movement developed by the single image (frame) to Descartes's relative quantification of movement of variable sets and the quantification of absolute movement in the universe. Deleuze argues that cinema is analogous with Descartes's analysis. According to Deleuze, on the one hand, the shot, composed of framed sets, introduces into its elements a maximum of relative movement; on the other hand, the shot also participates in the continual transformation of the Whole, whose changes are expressed in a maximum absolute of movement. See Deleuze G. 1983, p. 68.

76 | Deleuze G. 1985, p. 50.

motion. The *image-mouvement* extracts the essence from the means of locomotion.[77] During a track shot, the camera undertakes a *coupe mobile* of movements. The shot, in this case, creates variations of the objects that are present in the set (in the image), of its parts, of dimensions, of lengths, and of positions. In a long take with a high depth of field, it is possible to find a complex spatial set that contains all the existing sizes of shot, from the close-up to the panoramic.[78] The nature of this spatial composition is special: it is a unity but at the same time it contains a multiplicity.[79]

The notion of shot described above allows the understanding of the assertion that editing is the determination of the Whole. Editing is the operation that creates the reflection of Time, that is, of the Whole. We can say that it creates the image of Time.[80] However, it is possible to identify editing in the single shot. As mentioned above, framing is the action of creating a well-defined spatial organization composed of sub-sets that interact with the Whole and from which meaning derives. We can note that this system of interactions between sub-sets established by the cinematographic narrative presents some analogies with Gardies' concept of space. As noted above, according to Gardies, the space, understood as a set of *lieux*, allows the coexistence of different *lieux* in the encased structure of the space. Thus, the plurality of *lieux* in

---

77 | Deleuze G. 1983, p. 37.

78 | Deleuze compares the spatial organization of the long take or the track shot with high depth of field to the spatial composition generated in painting during the 16th and 17th centuries. In fact, during that period, one can find the tendency towards a kind of superposition of plans. There was a kind of homogeny in a heterogeneous field. See Deleuze G. 1983.

79 | Note the distinction of depth of field realized by Deleuze through the analysis of paintings by Wölfflin. Deleuze showed that at the beginning the depth in the cinematographic image was the product of a juxtaposition of independent plans, a succession of parallel plans in the image. In order to show this kind of depth, Deleuze uses as an example the conquest of Babylon in *Intolerance* (1916) by Griffith. The other kind of depth of field is highlighted in Welles' *Citizen Kane* (1941). This one is defined by Deleuze as an image crossed by a diagonal that also crosses all the planes, putting the element of each plan in relation to each other and creating a direct link between the first plan and the last one. The comparison between the depth of the image in film and in painting, based on Wölffin, brings Deleuze to affirm that the depth of field elaborated by Welles can be recognized as baroque because of its analogy with the spatial composition governing painting during the 17th century. Deleuze claimed that the continuum created by this kind of spatial organization is developed in time and not in space, thus it creates a 'region in the time.' See Deleuze G. 1985, p. 141.

80 | This conception of the narrative space derived from the image in movement finds its most important influence in Bergson's *Matière et mémoire*. According to Bergson, everything, and thus every image, represents a 'path' that crosses the modifications that are spread to the infinite universe.

the space allows the organization of a "véritable système producteur de sens."[81] In the system described by Gardies, *lieu* becomes "la parole de l'espace-langue."[82]

The organization created by means of editing can be compared to the composition of an organism, the composition of an organic unity. This organism presents actions and reactions between its parts, which undergo a conflict that in turn modulates the rhythm and elaborates the narrative.[83] This conception is not in total opposition to Eisenstein's idea of collision montage in which the shot is also analyzed in biological terms and is seen as an organism. According to Eisenstein, the shot is not an element of editing, it is a cell:

"The shot is by no means an *element* of montage. The shot is a montage *cell*. Just as cells in their division form a phenomenon of another order, the organism or embryo, so, on the other side of the dialectical leap from the shot, there is montage. By what, then, is montage characterized and, consequently, its cell-the shot? By collision. By the conflict of two pieces in opposition to each other. By conflict. By collision."[84]

|Prop. IV| Eisenstein focused his research on montage and, in particular, on the following problem: how does *One* become *Two* in order to produce a new unity, and how does this process suggest that of a biological organism.[85] This *image-mouvement*, or image cell, is essentially divisible in the elements that it groups into sets. The interaction between these elements is based on the contrast between their components, that is, on the 'shock of images.'

The shock is the form of communication of the image movement.[86] Opposition – or contrast – is an important instrument in the spatial organization proposed by film narrative and this phenomenon is present in the set created by editing as well as in the layered composition of the frame. The link created by collision, according to Deleuze, is a 'bridge' that transports the pathos and has a direct effect on the spirit. It enables the act of thinking in the beholder. The pathos, indeed, realizes and concretizes the totality, a totality where the development of a part is determined by the remaining

---

81 | Gardies A. 1993, p. 78.

82 | Gardies A. 1993, p. 71.

83 | Deleuze highlights three main figures of editing. The first one is the *montage alterné parallèle*, which creates a one-to-one relation in which the images of a part succeed another part, following the rhythm. In this succession, the whole set establishes a relation with the parts in succession. The second figure is represented by *the insertion of the close-up*, which creates both a miniaturization of the set and a reduction of the scene, and endows the objective set with a kind of subjectivity. The third is the *montage encourant ou convergent*, in which there is an alternation of actions, of moments that then converge. See Deleuze G. 1983.

84 | Eisenstein S. 1949, p. 37.

85 | Deleuze G. 1983, p. 246.

86 | Deleuze G. 1985, p. 205.

parts, and the whole set is reproduced into the parts that compose it. Namely, through the pathos, the totality of the sets is no longer a group that subsumes independent parts. By means of pathos, the totality of the set becomes a concrete and existing totality. In such a system, each single part of the set is the product of the other parts that compose the set, and the whole is generated in the parts.[87] Every single frame varies in function to the others, and this variation is exerted on every single part of the image. In such an organization, action and reaction do not follow a direct or hierarchical order. Action, in such a sense, activates a reaction in some other point in space, that is, in the universe. That is to say, there is a correlation between two images that are not consecutive.[88] Thus, this space is in perpetual becoming and reflects the state of becoming of societies, of feelings, of life. Such a system recalls a chaotic phenomenon as well as a topologic space.[89]

This theory is far removed from the field of linguistics. For example, even if Deleuze accepts the existence of an analogy between the figures of speech described by Fontanier, he highlights that the spatial organization created by film narrative has its owns figures and that these figures only correspond to four kinds of figures theorized by Fontanier.[90] However, this conception of film narrative squarely refuses any correlation to linguistic terms. While under formalistic influence, the close-up was equated to a synecdoche, Deleuze adopts Balazs' theory in which the close-up is considered an abstraction of the spatio-temporal coordinates, recalling a fundamental principle of the topology.[91] The close-up in the film narrative space represents a change of dimension, which implies an absolute change of the spatial notions of the image. In

---

87 | Deleuze G. 1983, p. 57.

88 | Through this framework Deleuze traces a well defined difference between classic film and modern film, in which the modern film develops a new narrative form 'destroying' the sequence of events, designed by Deleuze with the formula S-A-S. Borrowing from Fahle, dealing with the classic film, "Diese Form der Erzählung ist kommunikativ, das heißt, sie versteckt keine andere Realität hinter den Bilder. Sie sagt das, was sie zeigt und zeigt das, was sie sagt. Die Handlungen der Protagonisten folgen dem Prinzip der Kasualität. Hinzu kommt, dass die wichtigsten Charaktere psychologisch klar definiert sind. Die Handlung durchläuft verschiedene Zustände, zum Beispiel Störung einer bestimmten (Ausgangs-) Situation, Kampf zur Beseitigung der Störung und Etablierung eines neuen stabilen Zustands." (Fahle O. 2005, pp. 12-13.)

89 | With regard to these sentences, it is important to remember that Godard posits that in cinema a description is the observation of mutations. See Godard J.-L. 1985.

90 | Deleuze G. 1983, p. 250.

91 | It is important to remember that Balázs gave more importance to the space created with a close-up of a human face: "Dem Gesicht gegenüber befindet wir uns nicht mehr im Raum. Eine neue Dimension öffnet sich uns: die *Physionomie*. Daß die Augen oben, der Mund unten, dass diese Falten Rechts, jene links liegen, hat keine räumliche Bedeutung mehr. Denn wir sehen nur *einen* Ausdruck." (Balázs B. 2001, p. 17.)

Deleuze's words, it is a mutation of the movement, which ceases to be translation and becomes expression.[92]

|**Prop. XXIV**| Although a close-up extracts the object from any spatio-temporal coordinate, it can generate its own space-time.[93] It is also possible that a mid shot exerts the spatial organization of a close-up by negating the perspective or the depth of field.[94] This fragmentary, or fractal space – because it recognizes a fractional dimension in the composition – is an important narrative tool that creates an enclosed infinite reality.[95]

It is interesting to note that Bonitzer, who influenced Deleuze's theories on cinema, also theorized the cinematographic image as a layered space.

|*Fig. 3.20*|

Bonitzer states that a mid shot contains sub-sets that can be represented by smaller sizes of shot, for example medium close shot and close-up. Through the analysis of Lumière's *L'arrivée d'un train à la Ciotat* (1895), (Fig. 3.20) Bonitzer argues that in this fixed shot are contained all the shot sizes. However, he does not recognize a close-up in the last seconds of the film when the train is very close to the camera. He states in fact that the point of view of the beholder at that time corresponds to a fixed point of view. As a consequence, this scene was 'rigid,' and therefore the close-up of the train

---

92 | In Panofsky's reflections on the film we can note how he analyzes movement in film, recalling a space of topologic nature. In the film, posits Panofsky, "Not only bodies move in space, but space itself does, approaching, receding, turning, dissolving and recrystallizing as it appears through the controlled locomotion and focusing of the camera and through the cutting and editing of the various shots – not to mention such special effects as visions, transformations, disappearances, slow-motion and fast-motion shots, reversals and trick films." (Panofsky E. 1974, p. 155.) Through this reflection one can see how the narrative space in film presents some analogies to topologic spaces. We can also see how movement in this complex space can be manifested in many different ways and how these different manifestations of movement can be highly expressive.

93 | It is important to remember that for Eisenstein the close-up also generates its own space-time dimension. See Eisenstein S.M. 1943.

94 | Merleau-Ponty argues that cinematographic screen does not have a horizon. Rather, it develops, according to Merleau-Ponty, an image that is organized under a different perspective. Merleau-Ponty M. 1945, p. 82.

95 | On the narrative role of fragmentation see also Bresson: "**De la fragmentation:** Elle est indispensable si on ne veut pas tomber dans la représentation. Voir les êtres et les choses dans leurs parties séparables. Isoler ces parties. Les rendre indépendantes afin de leur donner une nouvelle dépendance." (Bresson R. 1975, p. 95.)

is just a product of the layered space. In other words, the apparent close-up in this film by Lumière is more space than expression.[96] Like Bonitzer, Deleuze also argues that a close-up erases the depth of field and, by means of this phenomenon, generated by the space of the close-up, it is possible to identify the existence of shots free from any imaginary connection with the space, in other words, shots can be perceived as a pure surface.[97] Through this fragmentary space, Deleuze, by using Auger's terminology, highlights the existence and the role of the *espace quelconque* (any-space-whatever) in film spatial narrative construction.[98] The *espace quelconque* can be understood as a space that does not appear at first sight as a real field. Deleuze states that these first fractionary spaces were done by using the contrast of the image, the complex spatial constructions of the frame generated by means of the shadows.

The clearest exponent of the construction of such spaces has been identified with Expressionism. Expressionism is characterized by the use of shadows, which erase the borders of the spatial composition. The object placed in such a dimension loses its individuality and creates an unlimited space. In other words, the shades extend the image to infinity. Deleuze recognizes the *espace quelconque* also in the unlinked space and in the empty space. He argues that an example of this kind of space is recurrent in Italian neo-realism as well as in *L'eclisse* (1962) by Antonioni, especially in the scenes of the stock exchange (Fig. 3.21) and of the airport.[99]

|*Fig. 3.21*|

The *espace quelconque* embodies the space of the possible, the virtual space. It is a space that looses its homogeneity, that is, the principle of metric ratio, the natural laws that connect its parts. It is a space of virtual conjunction.[100] As one can observe, the *espace quelconque* embodies a radical change in our understanding of cinematographic narrative space; it represents the character of continuous dynamics through the absence of coordinates in the space. It is an image without coordinates, without borders,

96 | See Bonitzer P. 1982, especially, *Qu'est-ce qu'un plan?*

97 | Note that Bonitzer analyses the research of these "pure surfaces" as a need of the modern film, especially as a need derived from the video technology that creates such spaces. Bonitzer P. 1982, p. 37.

98 | Even if Deleuze's idea about *espace quelconque* is independent from the continuity of the space theorized by Balázs, it could be important to remember Balázs' idea about the separation between the object and the space highlighted in the continuity of the narrative space. See Balázs B. 2001, especially *Die Kontinuität des Raums*, p. 60.

99 | See Deleuze G. 1985, especially, *Au-delà de l'image-mouvement.*

100 | See Deleuze G. 1983, especially *L'image-affection: Qualités, puissances, espaces.*

thus it represents a system in becoming that can be analyzed through concepts from topology. In consequence, it set free the cinematic narrative from its Euclidean connotations.[101]

|Prop. XI, XII| On the grounds of this view, Greimas's influences on film analysis, and consequently, linguistic ones, were overcome. In fact, as mentioned above, Greimas points out in his *Sémantique structurale* that the minimal structure of every signification derives from the presence of two terms in relation to each other. As we have seen, the Kuleshov effect at that time represented scientific proof of Greimas's statement. However, if we analyse the close-up not as a synecdoche but as an abstraction of spatio-temporal coordinates, the Kuleshov effect no longer represents a phenomenon generated by the mere association between a close-up of a face without any clear expression and an object, rather it derives from a complex spatial organization that sets in motion a system of emotions.[102] As we can see, in the spatial organization of film, the creation of meaning is articulated in these two groups of connections. The first ones are represented by the *real connections*, which correspond to the coordination of space-time exerted by the concrete organization of space. It is developed, according to Deleuze, in the field of the *image-action*, in the mid shot. The second is represented by the *virtual conjunctions*, or *image-affection*, which derive from the spatial construction of the close-up.[103] The emotional links described by Deleuze through the composition of the close-up show virtual conjunctions that, in turn, create a complex entity in narrative space. He describes the process of the creation of these emotional links by using an interesting allegory referring to the proprieties of liquids. The composition of the complex entity, according to Deleuze, can be equated to the melting, boiling, condensation and coagulation of liquid substances.[104] This entity is complex because it assembles a huge quantity of singularities each in continuous change. The state of becoming is due to its 'liquid nature' that allows grouping and dividing sub-sets into the inner space of the shot. Hence the composition of a close-up is a special inner spatial arrangement, which is distinctive of an *image-affection*, and exerts a strong influence in the succession of shots.

|*Fig. 3.22*|

|Prop. IX, XVII| In this long take from Bresson's *Pickpocket* (1959), (Fig. 3.22) it is possible to see how the director created a fragmentary space in which its 'pieces' are

---

101 | See Frahm L. 2010.
102 | Deleuze G. 1983, p. 155.
103 | Deleuze G. 1983, p. 146.
104 | Deleuze G. 1983, p. 146.

linked by the shot of the hands of the thieves. According to Deleuze, Bresson creates a Riemannian space. This scene shows how the hands of the thieves undergo a transformation. They are no longer objects in the image, they become space that impose a direction establishing links in the fractionary space. Objects, namely the hands of thieves, represent dimensions or particular directions in the sub-sets, which create the space.[105] The space developed by Bresson in this scene links and makes homogeneous the fractional space.[106]

The composition of this kind of space finds its conceptual source in Leibniz's thinking. In fact, Leibniz formulated a theory that states that the world is composed of assembled series. These sets or series 'appear' to humans only in small parts and in disorder. As a consequence, for Leibniz, the world represents chaos, because chaos means an infinite series of choices. Following this framework, Deleuze argues that a 'flat' image, for example a close-up without depth of field, represents a multidimensional geometry. Thus, the *image-mouvement* only represents the first dimension in space. In other words, it represents the first step of the complex geometric set in becoming. At the same time, it is possible to posit that it represents its *Initiator Element*. On the semiotic plane, the *image-mouvement* represents the matter, a non-linguistic but semiotic matter, which constitutes the first dimension of semiotics. The objects in the frame establish inner links between the different dimensions. These connections determine the disappearance of the object because they replace it with the inner relations. Hence, Deleuze argues that the famous sentence by Godard "ce n'est pas du sang, c'est du rouge" was not only a pictorial formula but also a formula distinctive of cinema that establishes a system of infinite links replacing the image itself.[107] Further, Deleuze's theories on film narrative space are similar to the ideas in Grassmann's *Die Ausdehnungslehre von 1844*, which proposes that geometry should no longer be considered as a mere study of physics or space perception but as the study of independent structures or complex sets (see *Toward Fractality.*) It is therefore possible to observe some analogies between the concept of continuous form proposed by Grassmann and that of the set in perpetual becoming in film narrative proposed by Deleuze.

|Prop. XI, X| The phenomenon of the replacement of the object by the inner relations in the frame enables a radical change of the analysis of film narrative.[108] The analo-

---

105 | Deleuze G. 1985, p. 22.

106 | See Deleuze G. 1985.

107 | Deleuze G. 1985, p. 35.

108 | It is possible to find some analogies between this phenomenon of cinematographic narrative and Foucault's analysis on the substitution of the expanse by the location. In his words, "Cet espace de localisation s'est ouvert avec Galilée, car le vrai scandale de l'ouvre de Galilée, ce n'est pas tellement d'avoir découvert, d'avoir redécouvert plutôt que la terre tournait autour du soleil, mais d'avoir constitué un espace infini, et infiniment ouvert; de telle sorte que le lieu du Moyen Age s'y trouvait en quelque sorte dissout, le lieu d'une chose n'était plus qu'un point dans son mouvement, tout comme le repos d'une chose n'était que son mouvement indéfiniment ralenti. Autrement dit,

gies between Grassmann's and Deleuze's theories on multidimensional space allow a new knowledge of spatial construction; allows an analysis based on the concepts of the topology. In this construction, the physics, or objects as matter, and the space of perception start to be understood as a complex set in which the becoming or generation (*Erzeugen*), the position of the single spaces in the complex set (*Setzen*), and the links established between them (*Verknüpfen*) are the fundamental factors of this kind of spatial composition. In both conceptions of space the object becomes a dimension. In more detail, Grassmann's work represents the first research on multidimensional geometry and one of the most important steps to the recognition of non-Euclidean geometries, mainly to topology.[109] Similarly, the space organization proposed by Deleuze is also a multidimensional space in which the infinite links create a 'structure' that cannot be represented either with a structural model or a genetic axis. His idea of spatial organization does not accept a structure that over-encodes or creates a hierarchical axis. In other words, it does not represent a structure in arborescence. An arborescence structure usually presents a hierarchical system where the links between the objects are subjected to a hierarchical chain and in which the object receives information only from a superior object in a direct line.[110] Deleuze theorizes a centerless system in which the communication is not hierarchical and many different signs are able to communicate. He also theorizes a space where the single object becomes a dimension or a direction.[111] As briefly mentioned above, his theory finds its practical demonstration in the scene by Bresson examined above (fig. 3.22).

|Prop. XXV| The transformation of the object into space imposes another way to examine the impression of reality. In this system, the correspondence of the object with its representation is based on movement. If we abstract the object from the continuity of movement, there will no longer be a distinction between the image and the object represented. In this transformation, Deleuze highlights an important change in the narrative spatial composition. The construction of such fractionary spaces and the use of the jump-cut (*faux-raccord*) therefore represent the first important step of the shift from the *image-mouvement* to the *image-temps*. According to Deleuze, modern cinema creates a new spatial construction in which the space is fractalized. In this space, actions, perceptions and spaces are not linked in the same way. Thus, the editing and the layered space of the single frame acquire extreme importance in modern cinema. In fact, the strict relation between the single frame and the editing in the *image-movement* loses its dominance in the construction of this fractal narra-

---

à partir de Galilée, à partir du XVIIᵉ siècle, l'étendue se substitue à la localisation. De nos jours, l'emplacement se substitue à l'étendue qui elle-même remplaçait la localisation. L'emplacement est défini par les relations de voisinage entre points ou éléments; formellement, on peut les décrire comme des séries, des arbres, des treillis." (Foucault M. 1984, p. 46.)

109 | See Lewis C.A. 1975.

110 | Deleuze G. – Guattari F. 1980, p. 25.

111 | Deleuze G. – Guattari F. 1980, p. 31.

tive. In modern cinema, the single shot starts to show its own role in editing by using complex constructions and depth of field. In Bonitzer's words, the editing changes its axis, and it does not answer the question of how the images are linked to each other but what the images show in their internal composition.[112] Through this new way of analyzing the cinematographic image, images become virtual and actual at the same time. As Deleuze says, cinema does not present images; it puts a world around images. Its spatial organization is based on a kind of enclosed structure that aims at creating bigger links, from single layered images up to the sphere of feelings, dreams and time. Indeed, cinematographic images establish a specular phenomenon between virtual image and actual image.[113] This phenomenon was highlighted by Bergson in *Matière et Mémoire* in the chapter devoted to memory:

"En d'autre termes enfin, les centres où naissent les sensations élémentaires peuvent être actionnés, en quelque sorte, de deux côtés différentes, par devant et par derrière. Par devant ils reçoivent les impressions des organes des sens et par conséquent d'un *objet réel* ; par derrière ils subissent, d'intermédiaire en intermédiaire, l'influence d'un *objet virtuel*. Les centres d'images, s'ils existent, ne peuvent être que les organes symétriques des organes des sens par rapport à ces centres sensoriels."[114]

The same phenomenon is used by Deleuze in order to show the bifacial character of the cinematographic image, an image which is both actual and virtual. Its character presents a recursive phenomenon of reflection; in other words, it is an *image-mirror*:

"C'est comme si une image miroir, une photo, une carte postale s'animaient, prenaient de l'indépendance et passaient dans l'actuel, quitte à ce que l'image actuelle revienne dans le miroir, reprenne place dans la carte postale ou la photo, suivant un double mouvement de libération et de capture."[115]

The relationship between the actual and virtual image, following Deleuze's logic, exert a phenomenon of 'expansion' that creates links between different scales and different spheres. By means of the succession of links generated by the virtualization of the image, Deleuze can theorize a new kind of film narrative that is a set of many 'presents'; as a simultaneity of a past-present, a present-present and a future-present. In this kind of organization, the narrative act is understood as the creation of an *image-temps*, which substitutes for the *image-movement* by distributing different presents to the

---

112 | See Bonitzer P. 1982.
113 | Deleuze equated the virtual image with Bergson's concept of *souvenir pur*, thus the virtual image does not represent a conscious state or a psychological state. This kind of image, according to Deleuze, exists outside the conscious. Deleuze G. 1985, p. 107.
114 | Bergson H. 1896, p. 145.
115 | Deleuze G. 1985, p. 93.

characters in the diegesis and by looking to construct a plausible combination,[116] e.g. *L'année dernière à Marienbad* (1961).[117]

The differences between the spatial construction of *image-mouvement* and *image-temps* – or modern cinema – start to be clear. The first radical change is highlighted in the new status of the Whole in modern cinema. In classical cinema the Whole was confounded with an indirect representation of time testifying to a continuous changing of time – thus, the important role played by the *hors-champ*, which reflects an exterior and a modifiable world. Conversely, in modern cinema the narrative space is not constructed by means of the attraction or association of images in order to create an indirect representation of time but through the discontinuity of the space, exemplified by the jump-cut, which started to create an important narrative notion that Deleuze called *interstice between the images*, which can be seen as inflection points in the image. The clearest example of this phenomenon is represented by Godard's oeuvre. In fact, Godard does not aim at creating an association between images, rather he chooses a further image that forms an interstice between the two images. In this case, the narrative act no longer represents an operation of association but an operation of differentiation. The Whole starts to be a conjunction, which constitutes the objects. The interaction between images in this new spatial analysis creates a kind of borderline that does not belong to any image.[118] However, it is also possible that the layered space of the frame composes a space where different layers of presents coexist. Thus, the depth of field acquires a new role: it explores a region of past, a continuum.[119]

As mentioned above, the depth of field realized by Wells allows the creation of a continuum that is developed in time. In other words, we can say that it creates a region in time. The many links created by means of the depth of field allows a special interaction between the multiplicity of planes in the image. They also make possible the coexistence of many different present-times in the image. Every single plane develops an independent time in the complex multiplicity. Thus, this structure, highlighted in the single shot, is also reflected in the totality of the film where many different times, or "ages," coexist.

---

116 | Deleuze G. 1985, p. 133.

117 | It is interesting to note how Deleuze uses forms to describe the narrative created by Resnais and Robbe-Grillet. Deleuze describes Resnais' way of composing the narrative space as the use of layers or regions *"nappes ou régions du passé"* and Robbe-Grillet's way as the use of points of the present time. By analyzing these different ways to create the narrative space, Deleuze proposed a study of some analogies between the mathematics and the construction of the narrative space in film. In fact, he highlights a relation between Resnais and Prigogine and between Godard and René Thom. Note that both scientists were important exponents of chaos theory. Deleuze G. 1985, p. 137.

118 | See Deleuze G. 1985, esp. *La pensée et le cinéma*.

119 | Deleuze G. 1985, p. 140.

|*Fig. 3.23*|

Deleuze, by recognizing this spatial organization, was able to highlight a complex narrative space where the coexistence of layers or continuums might express different times contemporaneously. He likened the study of this space to mathematics, especially to *Baker's Transformation* and *Baker's Map*,[120] (Fig. 3.23) which can give an idea of how film narrative space can be analyzed in topological terms. Deleuze highlights this special narrative by analyzing the narrative composition of *L'année dernière à Marienbad*.

There, the two characters, A and X, compose a spatial relationship in time. According to Deleuze, the personage X is placed on a layer that is close to A, while A is in a layer from another "age" and it is placed far away from X's time.[121] The fragmentation of the space is reflected in the composition of different times spread throughout the layers. Consequently, Deleuze posited that the need for topology arose, because fragmentation and topology are inseparable. Analyzing Resnais's works, Deleuze concludes that Resnais creates a superposition of maps, which defines a set of transformations from layer to layer.[122] This space also shows a fragmentation of the objects.

The development of the cinematographic image allowed Deleuze to highlight two kinds of images, which can be opposite: Organic Image and Crystalline Image.[123] The latter generates a fragmentation of the narrative in the audiovisual field and creates a non-Euclidean order. The opposition between these two kinds of images is analyzed by Deleuze in the narrative actions of description, in the relationship between the real and the imagination, and in the narrative and the relationship between time and truth. The first opposition, in the description, resides in the fact that the organic image presupposes the independence of the object. In other words, the place described is showed as independent from the description realized by the camera; it generates a preexisting reality. On the contrary, the crystalline image, in describing the object, creates it, but at the same time, replaces it. The description itself constitutes the object, a decomposed and multiplied object.[124]

---

120 | *Baker's Map* is a chaotic map used in the study of dynamic systems theory. It is known as Baker's Map because it simulates the operation that bakers apply to dough after kneading, namely cutting it in half, stacking the two halves on each other, and then pressing them together.

121 | See Deleuze G. 1985.

122 | Deleuze G. 1985, p. 160.

123 | The analysis of these differences is developed by Deleuze G. 1985, in the chapter *Les puissances du faux*.

124 | See, for example, frontal transparencies used by Hans-Jürgen Syberberg and *An Actor's Revenge* (1963) by Kon Ichikawa, especially the scene when the fog fades. The

The second opposition deals with the relationship between real and imaginary. The organic image, through the continuity of space, – a continuity created by means of the fluidity or sequentially generated by the invisible cut and the cause effect laws developed in its narrative Euclidean spatial organization – produce a homogeneous space. It develops the real, that is, the relations between the objects are localizable, the sets are actual and logical.[125] In these images the unreal, for example the dreams and the imaginary, is created by means of opposition, namely by the creation of some discontinuity that is able to generate an image that is actual in the mind of the spectator. On the other hand, the crystalline system articulates real and unreal as well as actual and virtual where it is not possible to make out their identity.[126] Concerning narrative, an organic system is opposed to the crystalline one because the first one organizes schemes that make the actor react to specific situations or they act in order to reveal the situations. This system becomes complex because of the use of ellipsis and flashbacks. Deleuze compares this space to a group of dynamics as theorized by Kurt Lewin in his studies on organizational development and process management. In the organic system theorized by Deleuze, the narrative act is based on the definition of a field of oppositions, tensions, distribution of aims, obstacles, means etc... Its abstract form corresponds to an Euclidean space because the tensions in this space are solved by means of economic laws, that is, the maxima and minima laws. For example, the most appropriated way: the minimum of effort in order to get the maximum of effect. As Deleuze posits:

"Cette économie de la narration apparaît donc aussi bien dans la figure concrète de l'image-action et de l'espace hodologique, dans la figure abstraite de l'image-mouvement et de l'espace euclidien. Les mouvements et les actions peuvent présenter beaucoup d'anomalies apparentes, ruptures, insertions, superpositions, décompositions, ils n'obéissent pas moins à des lois qui renvoient à la distribution des *centres de forces* dans l'espace."[127]

On the contrary, the crystalline narrative establishes another kind of situation where the actors are 'conscious.' They do not react to the situation, 'they can see the situation.' Thus the connections described through the narrative of the organic system disappear and the law of tensions – or the solution of problems – no longer organizes space. This is a space without a well-defined dimension. Thus, Deleuze describes the modern image as 'the kingdom of incommensurables,'[128] in which the divisions of shots take their own identity, namely, the cut is no longer seen as a part of the image

same phenomenon is also highlighted in the tendency of Neo-Realism and La Nouvelle Vague to shoot in exterior in order to extract the description and give it a creative role.

125 | See Kappelhoff H. 2005.

126 | A good example of this process is represented by Mankiewicz's films.

127 | Deleuze G. 1985, p. 167.

128 | Deleuze G. 1985, p. 362.

but denotes a specific territory in the space. If the concrete space does not represent a group of dynamics, its abstraction no longer represents an Euclidean space. In fact, as mentioned above, the laws of minimum and maximum disappear. Thus, Deleuze compares the crystalline narrative to non-Euclidean geometries. For example, Bresson creates a Riemannian Space as well as *Neo-Realism* and *La Nouvelle Vague*. The narrative space developed by Robbe-Grillet is understood as a Quantum Space and Resnais's narrative as Topologic Space. The main feature of these spaces is that they create relations that are not localizable.[129]

The fourth point analyzed by Deleuze is the change of narrative that the crystalline image makes possible through the use of the *fake*. According to Deleuze, with the crystalline image, narrative ceases to be truthful. It plays with the power of the fake to displace the truth, because the crystalline system sets in motion the simultaneity of 'incompatible presents.' While the organic system imposes legitimate (= chronological) connections in the narrative space, the crystalline system changes continuously the connections modifying the whole narrative, from which derive disconnected spaces and non-chronological (*déchronologisés*) moments. While the organic system create a truth form, which is unified and makes possible the identification between character and beholder, the crystalline system sets in motion the power of the fake, which is inseparable from a multiplicity.[130]

The difference between these two kinds of images is also highlighted by the assimilation of sound technology into the cinematographic art. At first sight, the introduction of sound seems to confirm the role played by the *hors-champ*. The sound does not create or provide evidence of the existence of the *hors-champ*. To use Deleuze's words, it just populates the *hors-champ*. Noises and voices could be placed exterior to the frame testifying the perpetually changing nature of the Whole as perpetual change. Sound gave to cinematographic spatial construction a new kind of continuity that can be clearly perceived during a spatial ellipsis. In fact, the dimension of sound articulates the space during a spatial ellipsis. However, the change of spatial organization was able to be seen not only in the sequence of images. Sound technology also creates a change in the inner composition of the frame. Some analyses noted a diminishing of the use of depth of field.[131] This kind of flatness of the image, which seemed to appear after the introduction of sound, can be due to the introduction of a new dimension represented by the sound.

During the silent era, the allusions to sound allowed the director to show a covered space through, according to Deleuze, an 'unheard word.' For instance, this is the case of the noises of machines (Fig. 3.24) in *Metropolis* (1927). However, it was the covered space that allowed the beholder to reconstruct (= to understand) the silent act.

---

129 | Deleuze G. 1985, p. 169.

130 | It is interesting to note that Grassmann theorized the first multidimensional geometry in order to apply this research to the fabrication of crystals.

131 | Deleuze G. 1985, p. 302. This analysis is based on Comolli J.-L. 1972, n° 230-231.

|*Fig. 3.24*|

With the appearance of sound in narrative space, it is the heard voice that is spread through the visual space.[132] Thus, the gamut of sound, represented by the heard word, noises, sounds and music, made it possible to deal with another dimension.

Every element of the gamut of sound plays a different role in narrative space. The interaction between sound and space can be analyzed in three different ways. As pointed out by Deleuze, a) noises are aimed at isolating objects from other objects. b) The sounds mark relationships in the space and they are also in relation one each other and c) phonation divides these relationships.[133]

The work of Deleuze on cinema marked the end of a big discussion that occupied not only philosophers and linguists, but also directors, over decades. His works allowed us to analyze film narrative as a complex spatial construction and to put an end to the central question concerning the status of cinema, and in particular its possible identification with a language. The narrative space developed by the cinematographic camera started to be understood as an intelligible matter from which language constructs objects, unities and signifying operations.[134] According to Deleuze, this narrative space constitutes pre-linguistic images derived from movements and processes of thought as well as pre-signifying signs. These latter, in turn, derive from points of view on movements and processes. According to Deleuze, this narrative space: "constitue toute une « psychomécanique », l'automate spirituel, ou l'énonçable d'une langue, qui possède sa logique propre."[135]

Thanks to Deleuze's consideration of informatics, the process of narrative spatial construction applied by cinematographic technology became clearer. It lost its linguistic connotations and started to be seen and analyzed by means of topological or geometrical terms. Certainly, the technical improvements modified the spatial construction of film narrative and changed the way the beholder interacts with the image, as

---

132 | See Deleuze G. 1985, especially *Les composantes de l'image.*

133 | Deleuze G. 1985, pp. 304-305. Note that Deleuze does not consider the development of sound as an essential step in the evolution of film narrative. In fact, of more relevance in his work is the passage from *image-mouvement* to *image-temps.* Certainly, they represent the way to construct narrative spaces in different periods. Narrative space being already a multidimensional space, sound represented a new dimension in this complex space.

134 | Deleuze G. 1985, p. 342.

135 | Deleuze G. 1985, p. 342.

well as the organization of the inner data, thus producing many different kinds of semiotic chains and different philosophical questions. Deleuze's analysis allows the conception of the narrative space as a multidimensional geometry, to which technical improvements add new dimensions or new objects and new ways of interaction for the objects in the narrative space. In fact, for Deleuze the digital image represents a new kind of object in a multidimensional space. In more detail, the new images elaborated through digital technology do not present any exteriority or *hors-champ*. The fundamental change enabled by these new digital objects in the film narrative space is that they generate a perpetual reorganization which allows the birth of a new image from any point of the image. Thus, Deleuze highlights new directions in the organization of narrative space. For example, he suggests that the digital image creates an omnidirectional space that continuously varies its angles and coordinates.[136] This new image transforms the screen into an information table, a surface where data are inscribed. The information in this space replaces nature, characters, objects and words.[137]

---

136 | See, also, Couchot E. 1988.
137 | Deleuze G. 1985, pp. 347-348.

3.3 IDEAL ELEMENTS IN NARRATIVE SPACE

|Prop. XIX| In *Cinéma 2. L'image temps* Deleuze formulated the theory that recognizes film narrative space as a multidimensional space able to organize new dimensions. It is possible to assume that the arrival of new dimensions in audiovisual narrative is due to some technological developments. Although Deleuze proposed a historical film analysis focused on the synchronic classification of cinematic images and signs,[1] which implies an in-depth study on the changes determined by technological improvements, he did not realize an in-depth-analysis of video and digital images. Anyway, he had already posited that television allowed the interstice between sound and visuals, as well as the irrational cut. In addition, Deleuze predicted somewhat to a degree the impact that the electronic image – video technology and television – and the digital one could have on cinema.[2] Indeed, when *Cinéma 2. L'image-temps* was published, it was difficult to forecast the radical change that digital technology could bring about in the organization of the audio-visual narrative space.[3] However, Deleuze granted a new nature to the image by pointing out that the absence of exteriority (of *hors-champ*) is the most important characteristic of the electronic image. This conclusion was clearly influenced by Bonitzer's analysis. According to Bonitzer, video technology leads to a metamorphosis of the nature of the image; he defined the electronic image as a *'pure surface.'* In addition, he suggested that in the video space, due to the 'lack of depth,' the *mise-en-scène* could be linked with the *mise en page* (page layout).[4] Bonitzer also stated that through video technology the image is released from perspective ("l'image est libéré de la perspective").[5] Hence, the spatial organization derived from video technology does not correspond to the same layered composition theorized by both Deleuze and Bonitzer for the analog image.[6] According to Bonitzer, the image elaborated by means of video technology is an image that 'can be infinitely inlaid' (*incrustable à l'infinit*):

---

1 | See Fahle O. 1999, p. 115.

2 | Note that the birth of audio-visual is not represented by the technical possibility to include sound in the image. As posited by Deleuze, the audiovisual was born when the sound acquired, in spatial terms, its place in the multidimensional space. This phenomenon was achieved by means of video technology. According to Spielmann, video technology allowed a new kind of 'audiovisuality' of the medium: "Unter der Audiovisualiät eines Mediums soll nicht ein bloß additives Verfahren (Ton plus Bild) verstanden werden, sondern vielmehr die Möglichkeit einer intramedialen Transformation zwischen beiden Ausdrucksformen." (Spielmann Y. 2005, p. 17).

3 | The research on the interaction between the electronic image and the digital function of the algorithmic image was possible from the end of the 70s, and this possibility started to be popular some ten years later. See Spielmann Y. 2005.

4 | See, in general, Bonitzer P. 1982.

5 | Bonitzer P. 1982, p. 41.

6 | Bonitzer P. 1982, p. 40.

"Tous les trous sont toujours bouchés par ce qui vient affleurer en surface, il n'y a pas de trou puisqu'il n'y a que des incrustations, des fleurs qui viennent éclore à la place des yeux, un nez qui émerge à même la bouche, un lapin dans le pavillon de l'oreille et le tout en musique, muzak."[7]

From a technical point of view, the video image creates another kind of continuum. The points that are spread in the images in a temporal succession compose video lines invisible to the viewer. The temporal succession implies that the variation of points, which are never visible at the same time, is constituted in time and less in space: it is an interval.[8] Hence, the development of an image video is based on the intervals between the points. The very elementary condition of reproducing an image by means of video technology is that the intervals, the variation of points, are allowed. Consequently, the electronic image imposes an inner change, a variation of its minimal components (the points), which are only punctual in character; they represent a momentary entity in continuous becoming.

As mentioned in the first part of this work, and highlighted by Engell, the point is just a metaphor for something that is not possible to represent, a metaphor for the non-extensibility.

"Im Punkt findet eine Metaphorisierung des Raums durch Zeit und der Zeit durch Raum zugleich statt. In dieser metaphorischen Funktion gibt eine Rede vom Fernsehbild als Punkt-Bild einen Sinn. Nicht der Bildpunkt selbst, sondern seine Dimensionslosigkeit bestimmt daher das elektronische Bild. Der Punkt ist nicht „etwas", das mit „anderem" verknüpft werden könnte, sondern er ist die raumlose Metapher der Verknüpfung des „etwas" mit dem „anderen" selbst."[9]

Video technology broke the spatial organization of the image down to its minimal components. Subsequently, this phenomenon led to the birth of a new geometry, the transformation of narrative space. As noted above (see *Toward Fractality*), Karl G.C. von Staudt tried to prove Grassmann's theories through the creation of elements of a new nature, a nature that refuses the Euclidean definition stating that points have no parts. In so doing, von Staudt designed points having internal structures. The same phenomenon can be perceived in the space of the video image as well. This transformation allowed images to be contained in the most basic element of the image. Afterward, the process started by video technology was perfected by digital technology, in which the point could have an internal structure. As remarked by Deleuze, in a digital image, a new image can derive or be contained in any point of the image. We could therefore apply to audiovisual narrative the same phenomenon highlighted by Shapiro regarding non-Euclidean geometries. Shapiro posited that:

---

7 | Bonitzer P. 1982, p. 42.
8 | See Engell L. 1999.
9 | Engell L. 1999, p. 471.

"we are accustomed, even today, to think of a line as a locus of points. However one can just as well think of a point as a locus of lines."[10]

With regard to digital images, it could be possible to state that: **we are accustomed, even today, to think of an image as a locus of points or grains. However, one can just as well think of a point as a locus of images.**

|**Prop. XVII**| The video image is not defined by a spatial notion imposing the relationship frame – *hors-cadre,* but is defined by the temporality of its intervals and the way of its reproduction, that is, by its inner dynamics.[11] Further, the dimension of the video image is not able to contain elements like geometrical figures understood as objects. This dimension contains, in Engell's words, *Nicht-einfach-vorhanden-bleiben-können* elements (elements that just cannot continue to exist).[12] In other words, this dimension contains a continuum, a set of transformations. The perpetual becoming of this space develops both a virtual image and an actual image that are indivisible. As stated by Engell, the perceived image is never present because it is composed of two coalescent images that create a unity that presents both an actual and a virtual image. The actualization of an image in the unity also means the virtualization of the former one.[13] The actuality is assured by the continuity of the image due to its *present time,* which is in fact a *changing present* or a present that goes by. For this reason, Engell points out that television is time that becomes image. Further, video image can also create a flux of signals in the inner mechanism of the machine, and through this phenomenon it is possible to identify the process that radically modifies the way of representing nature through optic media. The electronic system of the camera allows not only a *re*-presentation, seen as an act of remembering an absent object by means of the image. In fact, the translation elaborated by means of the analog photographic medium establishes a direct relation between the framed object and its representation organized on the film surface. In other words, the objects of 'our reality' are directly translated into the Euclidean dimension of the analog photographic medium. Conversely, video technology, in order to translate the object of 'our reality,' exerts an electrical translation of the optical input. In fact, the video camera represents a new instrument of translation (Cathode Ray Tube) included into a classical instrument (the camera obscura). Hence, it is possible to assume that the video camera realizes a translation from a translation to a non-dimensional space, or to a space in pure becoming. Thus, while the photographic image is defined as a **representation**, the elec-

---

10 | Shapiro S. 1997, p. 148.

11 | Engell L. 1999, p. 470.

12 | Engell L. 1999, p. 470. It is important to note that Engell's analysis highlights an opposition to McLuhan's theory, which stated that the interval between points in the image is only spatial.

13 | See Engell L. 1999.

tronic image is connoted as a **presentation**.[14] This phenomenon has been described by Y. Spielmann as follows:

"Hybridisierung muß als Horizont technisch-ästhetischer Veränderung bei der Diskussion elektronischer Präsentationsformen berücksichtigt werden, weil die audiovisuellen Medien Video und Fernsehen nicht in gleicher Weise wie andere optische Medien das Reale, etwas, das der physikalischen Realität angehört und als Lichtspur aufgezeichnet wird, >repräsentieren<. Die elektronischen Medien sind insofern reflexiv und nichtrepräsentativ zu nennen, als das Video- wie das Audiosignal aus der Zirkulation elektrischer Impulse in der Geräten hervorgehen kann und keine externe Input erfordert."[15]

|Prop. XVIII| Video technology represents a hybrid technology. It realizes a translation of optical signals into electrical signals that could subsequently be translated into a binary code. Further, video technology can present both objects translated by visual media and abstract mathematical formulae. The nature of the electronic image allows us to highlight some analogies between the space developed by video technology and some Proto-Fractals such as the *Sierpinski Carpet*, a fractal plane that does not have an area because of its infinite holes. Like the video image, the *Sierpinski Carpet* also represents a pure surface without depth. As described above (see Chapter *Fractus, Fracta, Fractum*), the *Sierpinski Carpet* is able to contain all possible one-dimensional (in the topological dimension) objects. In addition, the *Sierpinski Carpet*, due to its nature of becoming and its capacity to include infinite series of objects, can be considered as an open structure, as a *Super Object*.

|*Fig. 3.25*|

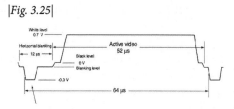

Just as in the *Sierpinski Carpet*, where objects can be 'hidden' in its super structure and the object does not appear "exactly as it appears independently, but rather as one of its topological equivalent mutants,"[16] the electronic image, as a pure surface, encases in a continuous form, as a super object, the infinity of the forms compressed into an electrical pulse of one volt, where all colors and tones are compressed between the black (= 0 volts) and white (= 0.7 volts).[17]

---

14 | See Couchot E. 1989.

15 | Spielmann Y. 2005, pp. 55-56.

16 | Peitgen H.O. – Jürgens H. – Saupe D. 1992, p. 112.

17 | Remember that the negative part is placed from 0 to -0.3 volts and it is dedicated to the signal of synchronization.

The nature of the electronic image as described above makes the space developed by video technology a **space without space**. Further, video image also represents a 'bridge' between the analog image and the digital one.[18] It does not represent a pure, symbolic 'space of data without *topos*' as that represented by the digital image, nor a localizable phenomenon as that represented by the analog image.[19] Similarly, one can argue that Proto-Fractal objects represent a bridge between Euclidean geometry and non-Euclidean geometries, and, in particular, fractal geometry.

Proto-fractal objects represent a visual proof of the existence of topological spaces and fractional dimensions. They are the first step to the development of fractal geometry, which shares some aesthetical components with the audiovisual space generated by means of the digital medium.[20] Like fractal geometry, video technology, and subsequently digital technology, allows a new spatial organization of narrative spaces as well as a new composition of the object or phenomenon that is presented.

Since its beginnings, the phenomenon of non-connectivity or self-reflection developed by video technology drew the attention of philosophers and artists.[21] In fact, the circulation of electrical pulses allows one to deal with both the exterior information, like optical or acoustical inputs, and the generation of a flow of electrical pulses without the need for any exterior input. Baudrillard identified this property with the original function of video technology. He highlighted that the only function of this technology consists in the creation of an image that could be static and refractory:

"Einer Refraktion, die nichts mehr vom Bild, von einer Szene oder von der Kraft der Repräsentation hat, die nicht im geringsten dazu dient, zu spielen oder sich vorzustellen, sonder die immer nur – sei es einer Gruppe, einer Aktion, einem Ereignis oder einem Vergnügen – dazu dienen wird, *an sich selbst angeschaltet (connected) zu sein.*"[22]

Through video technology, the electronic image started a process of virtualization of the image, in which the object represented becomes 'potential' and drives its own process. Electronic images lose the materiality imposed by the analog medium, that is, the photochemical process that imposed – film, glass, paper, etc. – a surface. However, let us consider that the process of dematerialization of the image is not only due to the absence of a material surface, but also to the composition of the image itself. A video image is incoherent due to its composition in fields and in half-images. Contrary to analog images, which develop a coherent vertical movement and a fixed and well-defined relationship between the projector and the screen, video images are composed

---

18 | See Spielmann Y. 2005.

19 | See Couchot E. 1993.

20 | Note that fractal geometry has been developed by means of computers, the same digital instrument that has organized, for the last twenty years, the audiovisual narrative space.

21 | See Spielmann Y. 2005, p. 57.

22 | Baudrillard J. 1989, p. 119.

of vertical and horizontal signals that place the image in a temporal process of building and rebuilding synchronic images in the screen and in the camera.[23]

The relationship between monitor and video camera enables the interaction by means of series of inputs and outputs in a closed circuit. Further, in the analog image, the film, as a material surface, imposes both the duration and the direction of the movement of each frame. This rigidity, imposed by the materiality of the film, disappeared with the advent of video technology, which generates a flowage (*Fließbewegung*) of the signal.[24] Certainly, the possibility of creating images through an electrical signal, that is to say, in the absence of an exterior input or optical information, was perceived as the most interesting phenomenon produced by video technology. This possibility enabled the realization that video technology was not only a tool of translation of natural objects but also a powerful tool able to provide a new dimension where complex phenomena and new objects could be created and analyzed.

During the early 70s, the space generated by video technology, the pure surface theorized above, allowed the development of new electrical objects that manifested some topological characteristics, in particular the possibility to deform objects through electrical processes. One of the most studied phenomena of the dimension created by means of video technology was the phenomenon of reflection and speculation generated by the repetition of the electrical signal.[25] The video feedback phenomenon represents a good example to understanding some spatial and temporal dynamics. The self-visual information presented on the monitor generates not only a self-similar infinite object but also presents the creation of an object placed on the dimension of the pure surface. The self-similar infinite object derived by the video feedback is in fact the result of the recursive operation generated by the system established by the interaction between camera and monitor. Indeed, monitor and camera do not establish a pure optical communication based on the reflection of a self-image but a sort of communication where the electrical pulse is repeated. In the case of video feedback, video being a technology that translates an optical signal into electrical pulses, the phenomenon does not drive the natural specular experience but a closed circuit of electrical information that is repeated in intensity and frequency.

If two mirrors are placed face to face in an empty space and there is nothing between them, the result, as claimed by Flusser quoting Wittgenstein, is the infinity of nothingness (*Unendlichkeit des Nichts*).[26] In the case Video feedback the enclosed cir-

---

23 | See Cubitt S. 1991.

24 | Spielmann Y. 2005, p. 83.

25 | It is important to quote Eco's words about the specular image. He argues that a specular image cannot be considered an icon but a 'double.' In his words, "Ingenuamente si potrebbe dire che lo specchio mi fornisce una "icona" dell'oggetto, se si definisce l'icona come una immagine che ha tutte le proprietà dell'oggetto rappresentato. Ma l'esperienza catottrica mi dice che (se pure esistono segni detti "icone" dotati di tali proprietà) l'icona assoluta catottrica non è una icona ma un doppio." (Eco U. 1985, p. 18.)

26 | Flusser V. 2008, p. 183.

cuit of electrical pulses generates an electrical representation and places the repetition of the same pulse on the temporal continuity of video technology. In other words, the video feedback is the incrustation on the pure surface of a model or pattern of pulses that is placed in the temporality of the video dimension, the intensity and frequency of which is repeated and constant. Being unable to reflect, video technology can become a mirror by means of the repetition and inversion of the image. By inverting the image, video technology creates the apparent mirror effect. Consequently, the video-feedback phenomenon cannot be analyzed as a simple reflection or specular reflection. Therefore, Flusser highlights the difference between the feedback and the mirror reflection through the blindness of the mirror:

"Was Sie im Monitor sehen, ist nicht Ihr eigener Blick, sondern der Blick der Kamera, des Kameramannes. Es ist ein Spiegel, der Ansicht eines anderen auf uns spiegelt."[27]

Consequently, the apparent specular phenomenon of video feedback creates, through the recursive pattern or the repetition of the same frequency and intensity in the enclosed circuit, a surface that recalls not only the two dimensional *Sierpinski Carpet*, but also other proto-fractal objects such as the *Menger Sponge* (see *Fractus, Fracta, Fractum*).

Steina Vasulka investigated the possibilities offered by video space to create specular phenomena in her work *Orbital Obsession* (1977). In this film, (Fig. 3.26) Vasulka explores the potentialities of recursive formulas in order to generate specular phenomena and structures placed in *abyme*. In order to do this, the image is not only superimposed but also altered by the "simultaneous 'record' and 'play' [of] the effects as they occur."[28] Vasulka generated specular phenomena by combining video feedback structures, mixing many image sources (by means of a Video Sequencer and a Multikeyer that allows up to six video sources to be layered in a single video output[29]) and re-assigning coordinates to the image in the plane location.

|Fig. 3.26|

The possibilities to create complex objects in video space were investigated particularly during the Seventies. The research into that dimension was not only focused on

---

27 | Flusser V. 2008, p. 183.
28 | See Spielmann Y. 2004.
29 | See Schier J. 1992.

the possibility to generate special spaces, like that of video feedback, but also on the development of new objects that could be placed in the new space offered by video technology. The new nature of the objects in that dimension was explored in depth by subjecting objects, generated through electrical pulses, to transformations exerted by means of variations of frequency and tension. Certainly, these attempts to manipulate and create images through electronic signals, without images generated by the camera, represented a need to analyze the properties of video not as a heir of photography and film, but as a new medium that translates and creates new spaces, new dimensions and new phenomena.

Video technology allowed to model and sculpt the pure electronic structure of the line that composes the video-image. By using a Scan Processor, in their *Study No. 25* (1975), the Vasulkas created new objects modeling the inner video signal. In this case, (Fig. 3.27) the object is not a translation of a natural object through the use of an optical signal, it is an object generated by the machine itself. The creation of these new elements can be represented through what has been described by Flusser as the emersion (*Emportauchen*) from the zero dimensionality of the space to the dimension of the image that can create the illusion of a three dimensional element.[30] Even if every electronic and digital image follows this passage, in the new elements created by Vasulkas the phenomenon is more evident because it is the direct emersion of the minimal component of the image to the plane.

|*Fig. 3.27*|

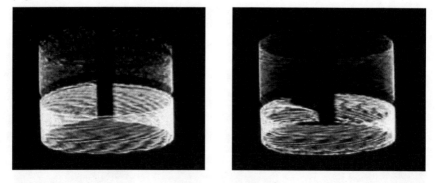

The inner signals of video lines started to show their potentialities to be modeled and be placed into a space in which they can acquire shape and volume. An important phenomenon analyzed in that work was the diffraction of the 525 lines (NTSC) that generated a three dimensional object, a cylinder (Fig. 3.27). The flowage character of the signal was propitious for subjecting not only objects translated through optical information but also objects generated by the electrical signal under complex transformations of size and shape.

---

30 | See Flusser V. 1996, especially *Konkretisieren*.

Vasulkas' works cross an important period of adaptation and preparation for the rise of digital technology in audiovisual narrative. They prepared and developed the space for digital narrative through video's hybrid nature.[31] Their works focused on the development of a 'lexicon' for describing digital space. They based their work on the belief that "circuits contain the language,"[32] certainly a geometrical language.

Vasulkas' first conclusion about video technology was that video was a mean of establishing a new system of codes. However, already during their first works, the Vasulkas realized that, due to the capacity of video to generate images and its own structures, this technology represents indeed a "system of languages that proposes a new set of codes."[33] As they posited, they looked "to change the image in new points of view."[34] Their aim was clearly defined by Steina Vasulka when she argued, "the challenge for me was that of creating a space which had nothing to do with the stereotypes and the idiosyncrasy of human vision."[35] This new idea was certainly animated by the possibility offered by video technology, which was perceived not only as an instrument of translation of natural objects but also as an instrument that generates images. Due to this new possibility offered by video technology, the medium started to be understood as both creator and translator and consequently, it proposed another relationship between man and machine.

The first part of this text analyzed the necessity, generated by technology, to create spaces into which natural objects and phenomena could be translated so that they can be observed and analyzed from another point of view. All visual media generate a new way to represent nature as well as a new way to analyze it. However, video technology, being not only a technology that translates natural objects into a plane in which mankind could analyze them with a high degree of objectivity but also a medium that creates objects, started to propose another relationship between humans and technology, in other words, between humans and machines.[36] That phenomenon can be understood in Woody Vasulka's words when he states:

"There is a human vision and that of machine. Why is that human beings must always try to impose their vision of the world? Who says that these two eyes and this sort of vision are the right ones?"[37]

---

31 | Hatanaka M. – Koizumi K. – Sekiguchi M. 1998, p. 10.

32 | Hatanaka M. – Koizumi K. – Sekiguchi M. 1998, p. 11.

33 | Riley R. 1996a, p. 11.

34 | Gazzano M.M. 1995, p. 15.

35 | Gazzano M.M. 1995, p. 16.

36 | It is interesting to quote Steina Vasulka's words concerning her first vision of a video feedback: "Each time we believed that we were stealing fire from the gods." (Gazzano M.M. 1995, p. 20.) On this subject see also Couchot E. 2007.

37 | Gazzano M.M. 1995, p. 17.

The former need for objectivity was radically changed by the technical possibility of creating video images. Video technology did not generate the same notion of objectivity that the former visual media did. Further, video technology, through its capacity to create electronic images, generates another argument for the machine's consciousness as well as another human understanding of the notion of objectivity in the reproduction of natural objects and phenomena.[38] Certainly, those important changes generated a sort of subjectivism that was extended to the machine, which in the case of video technology was expressed through images created by the machine itself.[39] The analogy with the process that developed non-Euclidean geometries became stronger once mankind understood video technology as an instrument that creates new realities and presents some complex phenomena, and not as an instrument that allows us to discover reality. Like the process that developed non-Euclidean geometries, which eliminated the idea that there is only one geometry to represent the world, video technology created new worlds, new objects and dimensions, like Steina Vasulka claims:

"I understand the need to hold on to the last remaining reality, which is that of our vision, the one which television cameras bring to our houses or offer to our experience, but, on the other hand if we could, if we knew how to renounce every reality, or better, renounce all the present representations of reality and we could manage to base ourselves upon only that which interests us or concerns our needs, our desires, we may discover that it is precisely our desires which are the right idea of the world."[40]

or:

"For the first time we could see images which were not of this world. Which came from somewhere else."[41]

Video technology represented a change to the interpretation of media as a prosthesis of human senses. In fact, the technical possibility to create both images in closed circuits and images generated by electrical pulses give another status to machines. The capacity of the machine to 'bring images which came from somewhere else' exteriorized that mechanism of representation from human control. It was not longer the mechanical reproduction that Benjamin noted during the photographic era (See *Photographic Technology: A Translation Tool of Nature's Shadows* and *Photographic Technology: A Nature's Pencil*). Indeed, the mechanical reproduction started to become a video production, which, with the arrival of digital technology, became digital producibility (*producibilità*).[42] This process was already noted by the Vasulkas who were aware of the intervention of the machine in the production of images: "for *Artifacts* I mean that the machine contributes to the creative process as too many elements

---

38 | See Youngblood G. 1970.
39 | See Spielmann Y. 2005.
40 | Gazzano M.M. 1995, p. 16.
41 | Gazzano M.M. 1995, p. 20.
42 | See Caronia A. – Livraghi E. – Pezzano S. 2006.

depend on it."[43] Woody Vasulka also states: "I have to share the creative process with the machine."[44]

|Fig. 3.28|

The new objects (Vasulka's hand in *Artifacts*, Fig. 3.28) presented in this performance where transformed by the machine – the Digital Image Articulator (DIA), which modified the algorithms of the image transposing visual elements into mathematical components – in real time. Thanks to DIA, the beholder could see the process of the image's construction. Thus, Vasulkas' interest in machines changed.

Video technology was no longer perceived by the Vasulkas as a simple prosthesis of the human body but as an own entity equipped with an own creative capacity, almost a consciousness.[45] This new understanding of video technology pushed them to investigate how machines react and interact with each other without human intervention.[46] Certainly, the research developed by the Vasulkas caused a break with cinematographic conventions, for example, some camera movements, the framing, and the codes of editing.[47] However, their research was mostly focused on the 'irruption' of new objects generated by video technology, and also on the narrative made potentially possible by the video space as well as by the new objects. These interests were applied to the research on the technical possibility of seeing sound on the geometrical plane.

Musicality, as a mathematical model, generated an important interest in the translation of sounds into electrical signals. Video technology allows one to create images through sounds or a dimension where sounds could be images. It seems that the interest in musicality of some artists and researchers in the field of video was based on the

---

43 | Gazzano M.M. 1995, p. 20.

44 | Sturken M. 1996a, p. 28.

45 | Contrary to Vertov's ideas of the consciousness of the machine, which had the ability to discover objects present in nature as well as the ability to impose on humans a particular rhythm (see Vertov D. 2011), Vasulka's ideas about the consciousness of the machine were based on the machine's capacity to create objects and new relations between the objects translated to the video space.

46 | Sturken M. 1995, p. 36.

47 | For example, Vasulka's *Evolution* (1970) in which the author highlighted as an essential distinction between video and cinematographic image the different positioning of the frame. In fact, cinematographic image is developed vertically as opposed to video image that is developed horizontally. Vasulka argued that the horizontal framing allowed by video technology could be a means to release the video frame from its cinematographic conventions. See Sturken M. 1995, p. 21.

mathematical character of music. The translations of sounds into images represented an easy way to understand the video dimension and, of course, digital spaces. It is possible to see that the influence of music on the research of video spaces underwent a bifurcation. From one side, the vibrations of some instruments represented an easy way to create electronic images, movements and effects. This is the case of Vasulka's *Violin Power* (1978), in which the musical instrument becomes an image-generating tool that creates abstract visual transpositions of vibrations.[48] The same phenomenon can be seen in *Voice Windows* (1986), in which Joan La Barbara's voice modifies the image by creating new windows in the image. On the other side, some musical compositions could be translated into image as an ensemble. That is to say, the flexibility of the video-image allows the organization of the visual space in order to represent a musical construction, not only basing the spatial composition and its dynamic on the rhythm of the music but also by creating forms and applying transformations to specific objects. In other words, the music could shape the whole image as well as the single objects in the image. A clear example of this phenomenon was given some years later by Rybczynski's *Orchestra* (1990). In *Orchestra*, Rybczynski organized the space following the pattern imposed by the music; a phenomenon highlighted by Flusser as *Musikalisierung des Visuellen*. In *Orchestra* the visual information follows an abstract principle of organization that is governed by the musical composition. In the first part of this film the space is seen as an infinite space due to the perception of the sequence as an endless long shot. The characters are placed in a recursive space in which the camera 'dances', following the characters, organizing a kind of circular choreography. Further, the accompaniment is clearly translated into the continuous form of the image in which the space where the actions are realized is not well defined. The infinity of the space is achieved by the recursive superposition of different planes.

|*Fig. 3.29*|

The phenomenon of the musicality of the image becomes clearer in the second part of the film, in which the music is Chopin's *Piano Sonata n.2 Marche funèbre: lento*. Apparently, the scene is a long take in a lateral track shot. I say apparently because the continuity is given by the video space in which many different planes are superposed in succession. The scene starts with a fixed mid shot in which each chord that composes the melody is played by a different character. The fixed shot composes in fact a unique space in which the characters are superposed and coexist contemporaneously

---

48 | See Sturken M. 1995.

(Fig. 3.29). Each chord determines the appearance of each new character in the visual field.

As the track shot starts, the sounds, played on the piano with the left hand, are performed by boys. They play the arpeggi of the harmony. The girls represent the right hand, the solo. The recursivity and the self-similarity play a fundamental role in the creation of continuity in this track shot. The same character can be present in the visual field twice in order to continue with the sequence, to follow the movement of the camera (Fig. 3.30). The characters repeat their movements following the music but at opposite sides of the visual composition. In this part, the track shot is also a superposition of different spaces perfectly correlated. Consequently, the viewer perceives this movement as continuous.

|*Fig. 3.30*|

The phenomenon of musicalization of the image became stronger during the nineties.[49] Thanks to the technological improvements of video and digital images, the flexibility of the image and the capacity to manipulate it allowed one to represent in a better way the sound elements in the image. This is the case of some of Gondry's music videos, where the tendency to translate a musical element into an image was always present. Consider for example, Gondry's worldwide famous music video *Around the World* by Daft Punk made in 1997, despite the fact that in this video, the representation of musical elements was based on a choreography performed by dancers. It is with the music video *Star Guitar* (Chemical Brothers, 2002) that Gondry explored the potentialities of digital technology to represent sound elements in space. This video is composed as a long take, or a continuous shot, filmed from a train window. It was realized with DV footage from a train traveling from Nîmes to Valence, in France. Gondry shoots the journey ten different times. In this video, each single object in the image corresponds to a beat.

---

49 | It is interesting to note that during the euphoric moment of the popularization of non-Euclidean geometries, there were some analyses on the 'translation' of sounds into geometric forms. One example is Lord Kelvin's research published in Paris in 1893 entitled *Conférences scientifiques et allocutions*. In this volume, Lord Kelvin attempted to 'reduce' sound through graphical representations. For example, he attempted to represent the sound of a whole orchestra with a curve.

As noted above, in Rybczynski's *Orchestra* the translation of some musical elements into images was especially focused on the representation of the accompaniment. Video technology at that time did not allow him to create a perfect correspondence between the solo and the image. Although Rybczynski attempted it in the second part of the film (Chopin's *Piano Sonata n.2 Marche funèbre: lento*), the correlation between sound and image was not perfect. Conversely, Gondry focused on the representation of single beats and thanks to the precision enabled by digital technology, Gondry succeeded in representing musical elements by objects in the image.

The development from video to digital technology highlighted above through the examples of Rybczynski and Gondry is also present in Vasulkas' works and shows completely the hybrid character of video technology. Certainly, their works span the period from the beginning of video technology to the contemporary digital narrative. As mentioned above, the aesthetical component of Vasulkas' works is based on technical improvements. Further, beginning with their early works, they tried to establish a special interaction with the machine in which the machine itself played an important role in the creative process.

The first Vasulkas' period is defined by the Scan Rutt/Etra, developed by Steve Rutt and Bill Etra.[50] Through the Scan Rutt/Etra, Woody Vasulka attempted to separate the lens-bound from the visual code in order to develop a different idea of spatial composition. Surprisingly, in order to do so, he applied the same method used by Mandelbrot in the development of fractal geometry. In fact, Woody Vasulka and Mandelbrot started the development (independently but at the same time) of a new spatial representation by analyzing objects and phenomena at different scales. The improvements of technology allowed them to compose an image then analyze it at different scales. Like the 'deepening' on the image applied by Mandelbrot in his first studies (on the communications interference and the economical curves of cotton production), the Scan used by Vasulka also exerted a 'deepening,' a zoom-in, in the electronic composition of the image. Woody Vasulka was fascinated by the Rutt/Etra because he could apply "the inevitable descent into the analysis of smaller and smaller time sequences." This deepening phenomenon, according to Lucinda Furlon, represents the "first step toward discovering a new code."[51] More than a code, one can say that it represents another geometry that allows both a dimension where irregular phenomena and irregular shapes can be presented, and where new flexible objects (*Bildobjekten*) can be placed, observed and used in a new narrative space. In fact, Vasulkas' images do not represent a kind of sign or content; they represent a kind

---

50 | Woody Vasulka acquired the Scan in 1974 and used it to simplify the electronic image down to its scans lines, rendering a topographic effect to the imagery. "The Rutt/Etra reduces the image to its electronic waveform (the basic element of the video signal) forming a kind of skeletal image; the light density of the image is spatialized (the bright areas of the image are raised, the dark areas lowered) and rendered three-dimensional." (Sturken M. 1995, p. 30.)

51 | Furlong L. 1983, p. 15.

of object, new objects, electronic *Gegenstände*.[52] Indeed, the images produced by the electronic signal were images able to give important support to the *wahrnehmung-stheoretische Ansatz* proposed by Wiesing and based on Husserl theories. Certainly, a linguistic approach to the analysis of these images could just create confusion. Taking the image as an object, an object of perception, because it is something that one can see, it is possible to understand that the notion of code, in the analysis of Vasulkas' images, moves the experience away. That is to say, when one understands the image as a signifier or as a carrier (content), one cannot relate the appreciation of an image to the pure act of seeing (or, following Husserl, as a pure relation between *Bildobject-Bildsubject*) but with something that one can only read. Thus, as claimed by Wiesing, the meaning of a sign imposes a notion of rule. Hence, concludes Wiesing, according to Husserl, a pictorial representation is not a "Form von symbolisiertem Sinn, sondern eine Form artifizieller Präsenz."[53] The same kind of understanding of the image was proposed by Couchot through both the intelligibility of the image and its temporality, this latter understood as the coordination or *resonance* between the *imageur*, who creates the image, and the *regardeur*, at the moment of seeing the image. According to Couchot, the intelligibility of the image depends on this effect of *resonance*, because through it, the *imageur* and the *regardeur* can share the actuality of the image. In Couchot's words, they can share the "présent fondateur à partir duquel s'organise le temps propre à chaque espèce d'image."[54] According to Couchot, this kind of 'agreement' between the *imageur* and the *regardeur*, which establishes the temporality in order to generate the intelligibility of the image, does not imply a symbolic system, coding or lecture. It sets in movement a cognitive process that guides the meaning. For Couchot, the meaning of the image, more than a phenomenon deriving from codes and from an action of lecture, is a presence that creates a link with the *imageur* or emitter through the temporal dimension.

This kind of analysis is pertinent to the analysis of Vasulkas' images. Vasulkas' images are mostly created by the machine and represent *pure artificial presences* because they do not attempt to **represent** natural objects – i.e. does not exert a translation of a natural object onto another dimension – but to **present** a new object. Thus, Vasulkas' images highlight the indeterminacy of the image theorized by Didi-Huberman. According to Didi-Huberman, the human process of analyzing images is placed in two constant phenomena. The first is based on some cultural notions derived from artistic canons, social conventions and philosophical theories; the second is represented by the pure contact with the image as a simple piece of reality.[55] Thus, Vasulkas' images place the viewer in a pure moment of indeterminacy, lived as a non-zone. It is impos-

---

52 | See Wiesing L. 2005, especially *Die Hauptströmungen der gegenwärtigen Philoso-phie des Bildes*.

53 | Wiesing L. 2005, p. 31.

54 | Couchot E. 2007, p. 10.

55 | See Didi-Huberman G. 1990, especially *L'image comme déchirure et la mort du Dieu incarné*.

sible to tilt the balance in favor of artistic canons because these images were totally new; they were the 'first words' of the machine, neither to the side of the objective translation of a piece of nature. These images belonged to the universe of circuits, volts and frequencies. Thus, Vasulkas' images can be considered image-objects generated by a deep and mysterious relationship between humans and machines.

When McLuhan stated that the electrical medium was a sort of exteriorization to the world of the neuronal system – "whereas all previous technology (save speech, itself) had, in effect, extended some parts of our bodies, electricity may be said to have outered the central nervous system itself, including the brain."[56] – his theory was based on the framework that posits that media are prostheses of human senses, extensions of our body.[57]

"In a culture like ours, long accustomed to splitting and dividing all things as a means of control, it is sometimes a bit of a shock to be reminded that, in operational and practical fact, the medium is the message. This is merely to say that the personal and social consequences of any medium – that is, of any extension of ourselves – result from the new scale that is introduced into our affairs by each extension of ourselves, or by any new technology."[58]

As one can note, McLuhan's appreciation of the electrical medium was above all based on the dissolution of spatial and temporal notions, or the disappearance of space and time generated by the rapidity made possible by electric information. Specifically, the

---

56 | McLuhan M. 2003, p. 332.

57 | It is possible to compare the externalization of the human consciousness theorized by McLuhan with Flusser's ideas on automation. Indeed, Flusser, in the first stage of his analysis, posits that machines cannot be anthropomorphized because they obey human orders. However, he also affirms that machines will emancipate themselves. The emancipation of machines from human control could be understood as the process described by McLuhan as the outsourcing of the human consciousness, a process that in Flusser's ideas would be progressive and would depend on the machines' self development, in other words, in how machines 'learn' and how they develop the capacity for making decisions, and - why not - how they develop feelings. The emancipation of the machines can be recognized in the limitations that the machines impose on humans. Flusser uses as example the digital photographic camera, through which it is possible to see that the limits on the creativity of the photographer are imposed by the machine – "der Fotograf kann nur wollen, was der Apparat kann" – and the simulation of human performances that this machine developed, for example, auto-focus, choice of sensitivity of the sensor, etc. See, Flusser V. 1996. In addition, Flusser's ideas on automatism and McLuhan's recall the concept of expanded cinema theorized during the early seventies by Youngblood G. In fact, through the concept of expanded cinema Youngblood theorized the expansion of consciousness. See Youngblood G. 1970.

58 | McLuhan M. 2003, p. 19.

rapidity and the possibility to bind the many unities creating a single field was the phenomenon that allowed him to theorize the exteriorization of the human nervous system.[59]

"Above all, however, it is the speed of electric involvement that creates the integral whole of both private and public awareness. We live today in the Age of Information and of Communications because electric media instantly and constantly create a total field of interacting events in which all men participate. Now, the world of public interaction has the same inclusive scope of integral interplay that has hitherto characterized only our private nervous systems. That is because electricity is organic in character and confirms the organic social bond by its technological use in telegraph and telephone, radio, and other forms. The simultaneity of electric communication, also characteristic of our nervous system, makes each of us present and accessible to every other person in the world."[60]

Is it not legitimate to think that the exteriorization of the nervous system theorized by McLuhan also implies the exteriorization of some components of the sensory system or even of some mechanisms of the unconscious human mind? If it is so, a new kind of relationship between humans and machines as well as between humans and nature could be established and in my opinion, Vasulkas' images could represent a first analysis of this new relationship.

The phenomenon of externalization was already explained with the outsourcing of sight by means of the camera obscura. However, when the externalization established almost a neuronal system in the ambience, from which McLuhan derived his interest in the first telegraph cable that was laid across the Atlantic (1858), the possibility of modifying nature changes as well as the capacities of the machines. Machines go beyond the simple extension of human senses. More than a extension of human senses, the machine, through electrical technology, acquired an autonomy that generated what McLuhan considered an integral and decentralist phenomenon. Further, according to McLuhan, from the machines' autonomy derives an interesting phenomenon of the codification of the environment.[61]

---

59 | It is interesting to remember that the chapter dedicated to the telegraph in McLuhan's *Understanding Media* is entitled: *Telegraph: The Social Hormone.* This heading shows clearly his point of view of media as prolongation of the human body, and also how media follow, in this sense, organic processes, how they simulate the function of the human body.

60 | McLuhan M. 2003, p. 333.

61 | The phenomenon of automation analyzed by McLuhan was strongly focused on the means of production. He claims that automation was perceived by society as the phenomenon that makes it obvious that information represents a commodity. Certainly, this analysis was affected by the radical change of the means of production at that time. Through both concepts of automatism and codification of nature, codification under-

"By putting our physical bodies inside our extended nervous systems, by means of electric media, we set up a dynamic by which all previous technologies that are mere extensions of hands and feet and teeth and bodily heat-controls – all such extensions of our bodies, including cities – will be translated into information systems. (...) An external consensus or conscience is now as necessary as private consciousness."[62]

The phenomenon of externalization of the consciousness theorized by McLuhan was accompanied by a mysterious phenomenon created by the codification, or digitalization, of the environment as well as the praxis. It consisted of the means of storing and moving information becoming "less and less visual and mechanical, while increasingly integral and organic."[63]

Video camera is able to transform, translate, treat, decompose, modify and generate an optical input. In addition, digital technology exerts a translation of that electrical pulse by codifying it into binary code, which totally alienates the human component from that process. The binary translation executed by the camera is done, in a first stage, for the neuronal system externalized on earth e.g. a signal, internet, satellite TV etc., and in a second stage, for the human component that is totally dependent on the instrument of translation, like the personal computer or the simple screen. The digital camera, as well as the video camera, generates images for the machines, then translates them for humans.[64] This phenomenon was described by Flusser as follows:

"Die technischen Bilder sind Ausdruck des Versuchs, die Punktelemente um uns herum und in unserem Bewusstsein auf Oberflächen zu raffen, um die zwischen ihnen klaffenden Intervalle zu stopfen; des Versuchs, Elemente wie Photonen oder Elektronen einerseits und Informationsbits andererseits in Bilder zu setzen. So etwas können weder die Hände noch die Augen, noch die Finger leisten. Denn die Elemente sind weder faßbar, noch sind die sichtbar oder greifbar. Deshalb müssen Apparate erfunden werden, die für uns das Unfassbare fassen, das Unsichtbare imaginieren, das Unbegreifliche konzipieren können. Und diese Apparate müssen, um von uns kontrolliert werden zu können,

---

stood as the possibility to translate everything into information, into an electrical pulse and later into a binary code, allowed him to theorize another economic model based on information. (It is important to remember that Marcuse published *One-Dimensional Man* in the same year as *Understanding Media*.) However, the automation allowed him to see that the electronic medium has as a goal the molding of the collective consciousness, especially through advertisement. Note that McLuhan posited that the electric medium not only pre-establishes every single desire but also that "advertisement will have liquidate itself by its own success." (McLuhan M. 2003, p. 306.)

62 | McLuhan M. 2003, p. 86.

63 | McLuhan M. 2003, p. 188.

64 | This phenomenon can also be analyzed through Kittler's thoughts about digital image, seen as an autonomous technical image, it is to say, an image that alienates the human component. See Kittler F.A. 2001.

mit Tasten versehen sein. Die Apparate sind Voraussetzung für die Erzeugung der technischen Bilder."[65]

The process analyzed in the chapter dedicated to the creation of truth through technology (*Veritas Filia Temporis*) goes further. In that chapter, the process that gave supremacy to technology was dealt with. As proposed in that chapter, technology acquired its supremacy because from being an indispensable means to satisfy human needs, it became the only human need. Improved technology meant improved human capacity to manipulate the environment and generate a stronger feeling of objectivity in the analysis of nature. On the one hand, the machine started to modify nature; on the other, it was the only means to analyze it. The machine, in communicating with itself, codified nature to the point of totally alienating the human component from both direct action on nature and direct analysis of natural phenomena. This corresponds with the complete impossibility to represent the world without the mediation of the machine, and seems to determine a change in the concept of praxis as theorized by Marx.[66]

First the electric technology and then the digital started to mediate the relationship between object and subject, codifying nature as well as praxis, and this became evident not only in the production of value but also in the representation of nature and society. The preference for the representation over the real thing (see the chapter *Perspective: The Geometry of Sight*) ceases. Not only is there no longer this kind of preference but the possibility of choice is also gone. There is simply a total impossibility to discern the real object from its representation. The object presented can be non-existent in nature; the machine can create it. Even the translation of the object performed by the machine represents a mere creation of the machine, a codification of an existing object that can only be interpreted by machines. This phenomenon definitely accentuated the indeterminacy of the image, which was already perceived in the painting when the photographic technology apparently sets the representation free from the psychological component that looked for objectivity (see *Photographic Technology: A Nature's Pencil*). More than a change of the psychological component in the pictorial representation, it is possible to propose that it was the manifestation of a breakdown of the fixed relationship between object-subject, exerted by the electric medium.

The constant transformation of the world realized through technology places mankind before the impossibility to represent the world as a clear and fixed entity. The indeterminacy, expressed in chaos theory, allowed the representation of the world by means of the indeterminacy of the image. Thus, the indeterminacy of the image

---

65 | Flusser V. 1996, p. 21.

66 | Let us briefly remember that Marx intended praxis as the essence of mankind. It represents the means establishing the relationship man-nature that was manifested in the production of value, or work.

became an important narrative tool.[67] This narrative tool has already been described by McLuhan as the tactile character of electricity that established in the entire world of arts the iconic qualities of touch and sense interplay.[68] According to McLuhan, Impressionism found its extreme form in the *pointillisme* of Seurat, which is close to the technique of sending pictures by telegraph.[69] Further, McLuhan, in his analysis, already allowed for the perceiving of a phenomenon of fractalization. In fact, by analyzing Berenson's words, "the painter can accomplish his task only by giving tactile values to retinal impressions," McLuhan states: "such a program involves the endowing of each plastic form with a kind of nervous system of its own. The electric form of pervasive impression is profoundly tactile and organic, endowing each object with a kind of unified sensibility, as a cave painting had done."[70] Through the figure of the nervous system and the tactile values given to the retinal impression, McLuhan theorized a *mosaic* that generates another kind of spatial organization in which the heterogeneous factors of the single unity create a new unity.[71] That is to say the many points on the screen, like the points in Seurat's paintings, represent a *complexus* formed by many single unities that are linked to each other, e.g. by chromatic laws. Of course, this new structure is derived from the new interaction imposed by the electric medium between object and subject.[72] A new relationship that accentuates the presence of machines, their tactile nature as mediated elements, and their consciousness as

---

67 | See the analysis of some post-impressionist painters, like Cézanne, proposed by Boehm, in which the author develops a theory of the image based on both the indeterminacy (*Unbestimmtheit*) of the image and the potentiality (*Potentialität*) that it acquires through the indeterminacy. Boehm G. 2007.

68 | McLuhan M. 2003, p. 334.

69 | McLuhan M. 2003, p. 334.

70 | McLuhan M. 2003, p. 334.

71 | Flusser also highlights this phenomenon of mosaics generated by technical images. He does not consider the space created by the technical image as a flat representation but as "*Punktelementen zusammengesetzte Mosaiken.*" Flusser V. 1996, p. 10.

72 | Flusser analyzes this phenomenon as the break with the linearity imposed by the linear text ca. four thousand years ago. According to Flusser this new conception of the space, or the way to represent it, is definitively exerted by digital technology. In his words, "Im Kern des Universums wollen die Partikel den Leitfäden nicht mehr gehorchen (zum Beispiel den Kausalketten), und sie beginnen zu schwirren. Und im Kern des Bewußtseins sind wir daran, die kalkulierbare Körnstruktur unseres Denkens, Fühlens und Wollens (zum Beispiel den Propositionskalkül, die Entscheidungstheorie und das Kalkulieren des Handelns in Aktome) herauszuschälen. Das heißt: Die Linearität zerfällt ,spontan' und nicht, weil wir uns entschlossen hätten, die Leitfäden zu verwerfen." (Flusser V. 1996, p. 20.)

intermediate entities that generate, through the fractalization of space, what Flusser calls 'the end of history.'[73]

"Die Erzeuger der technischen Bilder, die Einbildner (Fotografen, Kameraleute, Video-filmer) stehen am Ende der Geschichte sensu stricto. Und in Zukunft werden alle Menschen Einbilder sein: Sie werden alle über Tasten verfügen, die ihnen erlauben werden, gemeinsam mit allen anderen Bilder auf Computerschirmen zu synthetisieren. Sie werden alle am Ende der Geschichte sensu stricto stehen. Die Welt, in die sie gestellt sind, kann nicht mehr gezählt und erzählt werden: sie sind in Punktelemente (in Photonen, Quanten, elektromagnetische Elemente) zerfallen. Sie ist unfaßbar, unvorstellbar, unbegreiflich geworden. Ein kalkulierbarer Haufen. Und ihr eigenes Bewusstsein, ihre Gedanken, Wünsche und Werte sind in Punktelemente (in Informationsbits) zerfallen."[74]

|Prop. XI, XXVI| The constant transformation of the object, evidenced by electric technology, drew Deleuze's interest and brought him to the study of anamorphism. The constant transformation or codification undergone by the object transforms the object into a *objectil* and the subject into a *superject*, that is to say into a point of view on a transformation, in a point of view on a Site (see *Self-Similarity: Fold Into Fold*). In fact, the anamorphic technique converts the subject into a witness to a transformation of the object. The same phenomenon is manifest in the relationship object-subject established since the appearance of electric technology. The object is constantly modified and codified by the machine and the machine also mediates the relationship between object and subject. As one can see, the subject is a witness to a transformation, to a transformation whose state is in constant becoming. Further, the transformation of the object (*Bildobjekt*) in the field of electronic or digital images establishes two well defined semiotic levels. The first semiotic level, which is closer to the concept of representation proper to analog systems of reproduction, presents correlational image-objects with natural objects, image-objects that are representations of natural objects. The second semiotic level cannot be interpreted as a representation but as a model, a potential sign that presents what it should or could be to the beholder.[75] Of course, every digital image is indeed a model, and the semiotic level where it is placed depends on its similarity with the object in nature.

It is not an accident that video artists like Vasulka and scientists like Mandelbrot looked for direct contact with the images and schemas that can only be created by the

---

73 | According to Lyotard this phenomenon is a fundamental character of the prostmodern. Borrowing Lyotard, "On peut donc en tirer la prévision que tout ce qui dans la savoir constitué n'est pas ainsi traduisible sera délaissé, et que l'orientation des recherches nouvelles se subordonnera à la condition de traduisibilité des résultats éventuels en langage de machine." (Lyotard J.-F. 1979, p. 13.)

74 | Flusser V. 1996, p. 37.

75 | See Flusser V. 1996.

autonomy of the machine. These images represent a first approach to the consciousness of machines and to the new nature of the world.

This is the case of some of Vasulka's images that were entirely generated by electrical pulses of video machines, (Fig. 3.32) and of Mandelbrot's *Julia Set* (Fig. 3.31), where he used the computer to calculate and print an image of a function of chaotic nature.[76]

|*Fig. 3.31*| |*Fig. 3.32*|

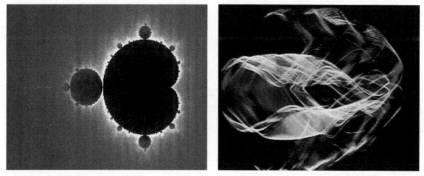

|**Prop. XXII**| The images-objects (*Bildobjekten*), perceived as artificial presences, generated one of the most important changes of the narrative dimension, especially of editing. In fact, the dimension of video imposes a change in the way of assembling images, and a new aesthetic of editing derives from this change. The first aesthetical innovation is that in the narrative space of video, there is no clear division of images, but transitions. As noted by Engell, there is a continuously multiple exposure.[77] In turn, the awareness of the new nature of the image generates another way to conceive the narrative space. Woody Vasulka conceived the narrative space as a single flexible object, like an object placed on a topological dimension. His detachment from some cinematographic conventions is due to the idea that the image is no longer developed in a sequence of images on a time-line, but rather becomes a 'yielding object' that can be modeled.[78] See, for instance, Vasulka's films *The Commission* (1983) and *Art of Memory* (1987). In these films, Vasulka avoids the cut editing by means of the creation

---

76 | The *Julia Set* (named after the mathematician Gaston Julia) is a set defined by a function that consist of values of small perturbations that can cause radical changes in the sequence of the iterated function. Thus, it is considered a chaotic set.

77 | See Engell 1999, especially *Die Berührung und der Schnitt*.

78 | Note that digital technology enabled a non-linear editing in which the sequence of images during editing loses its linearity. In fact, in analog and video editing the images must be accessed sequentially. On the contrary, through non-linear editing one can access any video frame without following the sequence of the image. That is to say, without the use of a shutter, one can modify the duration, replace frames, etc.

of a dimension containing flexible objects that are linked to each other. In these films, the passage from object to object starts in the inner construction of the image.[79] In *Art of Memory* he attempts to bind the video object to the non-existence of the frame (*cadrage*). In this film the image is conceived as a three dimensional object that is flexible. In other words, by means of transformations of the object, a diegetic time is developed. This phenomenon of the flexibility of the object made Woody Vasulka more and more interested in the precision of the digital manipulation of the image. Thus, from the Rutt/Etra, which manipulates the image through the regulation of the changes of voltages, Vasulka started to look for a digital manipulation of the image, an image that could be manipulated due to its composition in pixels. Thus, as mentioned above, he started the research on the electronic image through DIA.

During the 70s, some researchers attempted to understand the nature of the new space generated by video technology as well as the elements that could be contained in it. The fractality of the video image was studied by many authors who found out new proprieties of these elements. One of the most important characteristics of this new image was the new nature acquired by the points in the image. Before the invention of video technology, the point in the image was a simple component of the image without parts; it was the smallest unity of the image. Points or grains were the product of the film stock, of the material surface. The more sensitive the surface of the film was, the bigger was the surface of the sensitive grain. The dimensions of the grains determined the sensitometry of the surface.[80]

|*Fig. 3.33*| |*Fig. 3.34*|

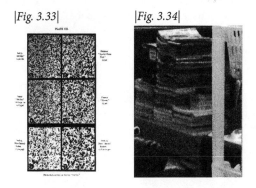

The granularity of the image is due to the presence of small particles of metallic silver that have been exposed sufficiently to photons. The size of the grains determines the speed of the film (Fig. 3.33). In the absence of a sensitive material surface, in the video

---

79 | Of course, we are not talking about morphing. That is a phenomenon that came later, once the digital technology started to be better accepted in the construction of audiovisual narrative spaces.

80 | The sensitometry was classified under various numerical scales, for example ISO (International Organization for Standardization), ASA (American Standards Association) or DIN (Deutsches Institut für Normung) or DNA (Deutscher Normenausschuß).

image as well as in the digital, the grain simply disappears. The 'grain' that is present in some video or digital images is produced by variations of brightness or color information in the sensor, and it is known as image noise (Fig. 3.34). In digital cameras, the image noise is due to a leakage current in the sensor. Thus, the elementary composition of the image changed down to its most essential components. Some artists started to analyze the smallest particle of the image in order to find its potentiality in the new narrative space. This is the case for the Vasulkas, mentioned above. In particular, they broke down the electronic image into its smallest parts in order to place them into the video space, a kind of *ideal element* that creates three-dimensional shapes.

Another interesting attempt to study the point in this new space is *Kwadrat* (1972) by Rybczynski. In this video, Rybczynski expressed the nature of the point in the digital image by using an analog camera. He deconstructed the image into a series of smaller squares in continuous movement. In *Kwadrat*, Rybczynski determined, in the space of the image, a new notion of scale. By deconstructing the image into its most elementary components, Rybczynski composed a choreography of black and white pixels in motion, which, at another scale, corresponds to human figures dancing from color to color. From the 2:00 minute mark of the film, the human figures, due to the change of scale, start to disappear; they are deconstructed again into many points in continuous movement, but this time, in pixels that manifest many colors (Fig. 3.35).

It is interesting to quote Rybczynski's observations about this film:

"It was a mix of photography and animation and it took up my whole vacation – sixteen hours a day. I analyzed, through a film camera, a loop of thirty-six squarish black-and-white photographs representing a human being moving in a circle. What was the logic of my analysis? I decided to photograph the loop on film and repeat it 36 times. During every new repetition I divided the film window, which I made in the shape of a square, so that in every circle there was an increasing number of subdivisions; today I would say different resolutions. I put a white square of paper in the subdivisions where in the photograph there was a part of a figure; where there was not, I put a black square. I had to rearrange the white and black squares at least a hundred thousand times. On the lens I put a color filter, and then rotated it – but I don't want to bore you. What is most important about this is that not being aware of computer imaging – it was 1970, in Poland – I manufactured my own 'digital' processing on film. Strange that I needed 26 years of work – including my work during all my next 25 vacations – to come back to *A Square* with full awareness and understanding of why."[81]

The deconstruction of the image through the change of scale highlighted the narrative potentialities of the point, its capacity to contain images and to become image. As mentioned above, according to Deleuze, the digital image allows an image-object to be contained in a point that is part of another image-object.

---

81 | Rybczynski Z. 2007, p. 139.

|Fig. 3.35|

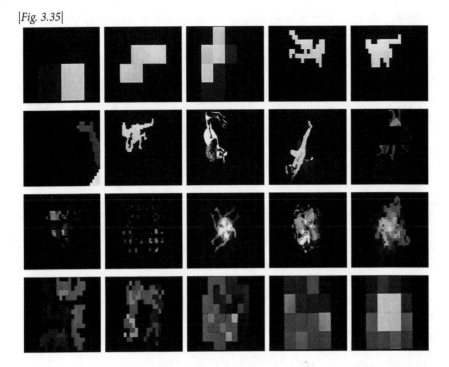

The pure surface or the information table, as Deleuze described the space of the electronic image, was realized by recognizing the point in the image as a picture cell[82] or a picture element, which is characterized by its coordinates on the surface, the coordinates on a infinite surface.

|**Prop. XIV**| Through digital images,[83] it is possible to understand the tendency that has governed, for almost three decades, our relationship with nature. If we modify our interpretation of nature, the codifying phenomenon highlighted by McLuhan completely changes. McLuhan's theory about the codification of nature has certainly been influenced by the linearity imposed by writing technique. Technology was understood by McLuhan as an extension of our body, thus the codification of nature could only be developed in function of human cognition. A kind of anthropocentrism dominated his theories, even if human needs were not the reasons for the improvement of technology. Within this framework, nature must be codified in order to be 'read' by human intellect. In other words, the process of the continuous transformation of nature through technology produced a readable *text*, which represented an *in*-formation

---

82 | The term was coined by Lillestrand in 1972. See Lillestrand L.R. 1972.

83 | Let us remember that digital images elaborate elements based on topological concepts, like the transformation of objects, and the coordinates system that enables the recursive space in which the point contained in an image can be a link to an external image or can itself contain an entire image.

of nature understandable by mankind. From the codification of nature derived a sign that was deciphered by humans. Thus, the world meant something to mankind.[84] Subsequently, with the fractalization of space[85] – enabled by fractal geometry in the field of geometry, by video and digital technology in the field of narrative space – nature started to be codified through pixels, information bits in which the coordinates of the single unity and its relationship with the totality become the essence of the codification; becomes the creation of an inteligible space. Certainly, the textual character of the former codification was lost. According to Flusser, the structure of nature as derived by its fractal form was deprived of meaning: "Gleichgültig, ob es sich um Fotos, um Filme, um Videos oder Computerbilder handelt, sie haben die gleiche Bedeutung: dem Absurden einen Sinn zu geben."[86] At this point, mankind is submerged in pure information that must be conceptualized. In addition, the conceptualization of everything imposed on mankind a relationship with a kind of *metaobject* or reproductions without prototype. They can be described as communicative artifacts, which, even though they exist in the communicative relationship between humans and also between man and nature, are not reproductions of existing things.[87] Baudrillard called these *metaobjects* 'simulacres'.

The relationship man-nature mediated by reproductions without prototype generates a special phenomenon that dissolves the world as a point of reference; "la substance référentielle se fait plus rare."[88] Thus, the concept of 'high definition' became a fundamental concept in order to attribute meaning to *metaobjects*; it allows the conceptualizing of the world. When Baudrillard highlights this concept as the 'key word' of our mediatic context, he summarizes the essence of the new codification of nature as follows:

"La plus haute définition du medium correspond à la plus base définition du message – la plus haute définition de l'information correspond à la plus base définition de l'événement – la plus haute définition du sexe (le porno) correspond à la plus base définition du désir – la plus haute définition du langage (dans le codage numérique) correspond à la plus basse définition du sens – la plus haute définition de l'autre (dans l'interaction immédiate) correspond à la plus basse définition de l'altérité et de l'échéance, etc."[89]

|Prop. VII| According to Baudrillard, an image is no longer an image, it is just the 'emanation' of the digital code that generates it, an emanation in the fractalized and

---

84 | Flusser V. 1996, p. 51.

85 | It is interesting to note that this geometric phenomenon recalls also the quatum theory. According to David Böhm, in a quantum level all matter is interconected. See Böhm D. – Hiley B.J. 1993.

86 | Flusser V. 1996, p. 52.

87 | See Duarte G. 2011.

88 | Baudrillard J. 1995, p. 51.

89 | Baudrillard J. 1995, p. 51.

infinite space.[90] Thus, the pixels in the image, supposed to be the smallest components of a set, develop a topologic knowledge in which their essence becomes their position. They no longer represent a space but a direction, a vector that guides a concept.[91] Consequently, the new nature of the point in the image generates another kind of fractalization; it made possible another kind of cartography of the narrative space.

Through Vasulkas' works the tendency to consider the image as a single and flexible object that could be modeled or transformed in order to develop a diegetic time has been highlighted. At that point, the narrative act in the audiovisual space was no longer organized following the conceptual framework that understood it as a succession of images. The image, due to its temporal nature (its state of continuous becoming), starts to be understood as an *ideal element*, an image-object placed in a kind of topological dimension that through its transformations, develops a diegesis. The position of the single pixel became an important factor in modeling the object, and in organizing it and its transformations. It is therefore possible to understand Rybczynski's interest in both the single point and the coordinates system generated by video space. After his work *Kwadrat* (1972), made on an analog medium, he analyzed the potentialities of the point to establish a system of positions on the topologic space. In his work *New Book* (*Nowa Ksiazka*), made in 1975, Rybczynski explored the potentialities of the new conception of the image as a single element that allows inner transformations. Further, the new nature of the point in this film was highlighted by means of the structure of the film narrative.

|*Fig. 3.36*|

As demonstrated by the above sequence, the frame contains nine different images corresponding to nine different and correlated spaces (Fig. 3.36). In this film, the fractalization of the image represents a powerful narrative instrument. Through it, the beholder can perceive both the new inner structure of the point and the new nature of the image that no longer corresponds to a sequence of images but to a single flexible

---

90 | Borrowing from Baudrillard: "L'image de haute définition. Rien à voir avec la représentation, encore moins avec l'illusion esthétique. Toute l'illusion générique de l'image est anéantie par la perfection technique." (Baudrillard J. 1995, p. 51.)

91 | As noted by Cubitt, "A vector is any quantity that has magnitude and direction. Computer imaging uses vectors to define shapes by describing their geometry rather than allocating an address and color value to every pixel." He adds further that "[t]he vector takes us one step further: from being to becoming, from the inertial division of subject, object, and world to the mobile relationships between them." (Cubitt S. 2004, pp. 70-71.)

object placed in a kind of topological space. The correlated coordinates of each single unity in the image generate a fractalized space that becomes harmonious through the assembling of different perspectives. *New Book* certainly proposed a new spatial organization of the narrative space. The unity, in the image, derives directly from the position of each sub-set, from its relationship with the whole and the generation that each single unity develops through the inner movements and the relations with the whole set. Further, in this fractalized narrative space, diegetic time becomes the factor that harmonizes the different planes of the image. The nine different shots composing the total image-object are long takes correlated in time by means of the characters, which are able to move from space to space, harmonizing the totality. The characters represent vectors that homogenize the fractal space reported on the whole screen. In this film they are "the principle of transformation, the quality of changing what we expect from moment to moment."[92] By means of their passage through the different unities, the characters reorganize the space of the image. Hence, nine different long takes of nine different shots become a single diegetic unity that is understood as a single long take, a single shot. The space organized through the vectors recalls in this sense some Riemannian concepts of topology.[93] In the spaces organized by Rybczynski, the characters accomplish the function of the Riemannian 'laces' that coordinate the different spaces of the *complexus*, harmonizing both the diegetic time and the space.

|Prop. XVII| One year after *Nowa Ksiazka*, Rybczynski explores again, in *Oh, I Can't Stop! (Oj! Nie Moge Sie Zatrzymaci!)* (1976), the narrative role of the inner movements of objects and characters seen as vectors or directions in the image. The film also represents a fractalized space in which the many planes are correlated by inner movements that move across the many single unities of the *complexus*. In addition, in *Oh, I Can't Stop!*, Rybczynski exposes the well-defined different planes that compose a single object, which are correlated by the movements of objects and characters ('laces'). In this film, Rybczynski creates a kind of linearity of space (=of the *complexus*), in which the different planes are clearly independent spatiotemporal unities that, placed in the fractal space organized by the director, become interdependent unities without losing their singular nature. Each plane presented in the set shows specific spatiotemporal notions through the different speed of the inner vectors. As one can see, the same vector (a person or an object in movement) undergoes evident variations of speed in the different spaces correlated by the track shot. This phenomenon allows us to understand that each different plane proposed in the series has an independent nature that affects the speed of each 'lace' while crossing many planes. For example, some cars appear in a determined plane and the speed of their movement changes considerably from plane to plane; it can be faster or slower. The independence of each

---

92 | Cubitt S. 2004, p. 72.

93 | As mentioned in the first part of this text, Riemann extended some notions of geometry, in particular metric notions like length, area and volume. In his research he also theorized broken surfaces unified by 'laces' or 'passages lines.' See Dieudonné J. 1994, p. 37.

plane can be recognized if one analyzes this film frame by frame. In fact, through this kind of analysis, on can see that each frame corresponds to an independent space that can present motionless vectors, that is, vectors that do not move to other planes, as well as vectors that can be present in many different spaces.

In the pictures below, I analyze sixty-nine seconds of the film corresponding to the time code from 00:06:28 to 00:06:41. In these sixty-nine seconds (=1656 frames) there are 1656 different spaces that become a harmonious unity thanks to the vectors that correlate every single space.

|*Fig. 3.37*|

In the images above, one can see how the translation of a natural space, achieved by the camera (the film was made with a 35mm camera), alters the single images: they become independent images, independent spaces (Fig. 3.37). Through this sequence, Deleuze's theory on the long take becomes clear. As highlighted by Deleuze, the viewer perceives the sequence as a long take composed by many single layers. In the first image above, one can see a man walking on the street and a truck coming in the direction of the viewer. The second image is the successive image in the sequence, the frame that comes after the first image here explained. In that space, the truck does not follow a fluid movement; suddenly it hides the character, a vector that in the next frame of the sequence appears on the street. Then, the truck disappears in three frames. What was represented, in a classical or Euclidean space, as a covered distance by a body in movement, becomes a fractalized space in which a vector, in this case the truck, crosses three frames uniting them as a 'lace.'

|*Fig. 3.38*|

In this second sequence, it is possible to see a mid shot composed of two people on the left side of the frame and a truck in the background. In the successive frame, there is no longer the person dressed in blue; in his place another vector accompanies the other person. This person is a fix vector that is present in all five photograms we are dealing with, while the person dressed in blue only occupies one frame in the whole sequence. The truck occupies two frames (two spaces) then disappears, followed by another truck that also occupied two frames. As one can see, some vectors occupy only a couple of spaces but their movement assures the homogenization of the space, which is perceived by the viewer as a fluid movement. The fluid movement perceived by the viewer in this fractalized space is assured by the correlation of different planes achieved through the movement of vectors, that is, by the inner movements in the image.

The irregularity of the movement of each vector in the plane allows us to affirm that every plane shows its heterogeneous character through a specific speed that is always different in each space of the sequence. That is to say, the same object changes speed and direction according to the space that it occupies at a specific time in the sequence. It is possible to observe this in the series of images presented above (Fig. 3.39). In the first frame, there is only one vector, a truck that appears in the foreground of the image. In the four frames that follow, the same vector apparently covers a determined distance. But the distance covered by the vector in the first two frames is shorter than the distance covered in the last three frames. Through this movement, we see both the independence of each frame (each frame is a unique space) and how the vectors modify their speed in each space when crossing many frames. In addition, by means of this new nature of space, Rybczynski highlighted the cinematographic illusion of movement.

|Prop. XVI| As mentioned in the chapter dedicated to the development of cinematographic technology (See *A New Space Which Accepts Movement*), especially through Bergson's analysis of cinematographic mechanisms, the human mistake in studying movement resides in the way an action is analyzed. Movement, which cannot be divided into a series of fixed moments, has been long analyzed using spatial notions. Consequently, time was also erroneously considered a homogenous and divisible entity because it was also analyzed using spatial notions. As mentioned in that chapter, cinematographic technique re-creates the concept of movement by using a series of single 'fixed-image objects,' called '*coupes immobiles*,' placed in succession. Hence, Bergson argues that a cinematographic camera is a geometrical device par excellence, as its mode of visual perception simulates "human intelligence" and is highly similar to human perception. Let us also remind ourselves of the relevant importance of Zeno's paradoxes in Bergson's theories. As mentioned previously, Zeno's paradoxes were created to support Parmenides of Elea's thoughts on motionlessness (ἀτρεμής), a concept developed in his unique, surviving (in a fragmentary form) work, *On Nature*. In this work, he deals with the concept of reality (in his words "*what-is*"), where

reality was described as one, where change is impossible and entities are unchanging. Consequently, reality was theorized as an eternal entity (*aletheia*) that is static and immutable. Parmenides' aim was to place reality only in the *logos* and not in perception because, according to him, perception (*Doxa* - δόξα: a Greek world that describes common beliefs or popular opinions) is misleading. Bergson tried to separate the analysis of time and movement from perception, and brought them to *logos*. Indeed, he developed an analysis of time free from spatial notions and from human perception that sees a movement as a body that covers a distance. Thus, he saw in the cinematographic camera a perfect simulator of human perception because it breaks up movement in fixed moments correlated to precise spatial notions. Further, he describes the cinematographic camera as a perfect geometrical device. However, it is an Euclidean geometrical device that perfectly simulates human perception, as Euclidean geometry allows. Through *Oh, I Can't Stop!* it is possible to develop another conception of movement. As noted above, the notion of movement in this film was generated by the correlation of different spaces, which was made possible by the inner vectors represented by characters or moving objects. Through this film, Rybczynski criticizes the notion of movement derived through Euclidean spatial organization particularly the movement created through the cinematographic camera. In the space of his film, movement does not represent an action that is strictly perceived through a covered distance: the movement is an indivisible action. Thus, the vectors' movement is totally independent from the notion of covered distance, in fact, they are independent from the space.

|*Fig. 3.40*|

If we consider the series of images presented above, (fig. 3.40) in five frames there is a group of static vectors occupying five different spaces. In the first frame, there are three vectors on the right side of the image. In the next frame, there are four vectors, in the next, five, and in the next, three. These static vectors provide both spatial coordinates and coordinates in time. In the fractal space proposed by Rybczynski, the viewer mentally re-builds the fluidity of the movement. Giving a reference point in space, the static vectors generate the feeling of the fluid movement of the camera. In addition, their sudden disappearance in the sequence generates a new perception of time, in which time is totally separate from the succession of images that represents the space. In fact, the sudden disappearance of some static vectors highlights the indivisibility of the action as well as of time. In the space of *Oh, I Can't Stop!* the vectors seem to regulate the speed of the succession of frames. In fact, the perceived speed of the succession of frames is proportional to the quantity of vectors contained in each frame. In other words, the vectors' direction and quantity modify the perceived speed of the images in the sequence. In spaces with many vectors in movement, the succession of frames perceived is faster than the succession of spaces with static vectors or with few vectors. This phenomenon is clear in the change of speed of what the viewer perceives as a track shot. In the first few minutes of the film, the succession of frames perceived by the viewer is slow. There are no vectors in the space, no characters, no moving objects. Conversely, in the last part of the film, in a city street, many vectors are in movement, and thus the succession of perceived frames is faster. *Oh, I Can't Stop!* is a survey on the fractalized space of the sequence, a space in which the new nature of the point allows it to homogenize heterogeneous spaces and to correlate them by means of inner movements. Since the point acquired an inner structure, a whole sequence of frames could be understood as a sequence of heterogeneous subsets manifesting different inner structures that are correlated by the relationship between moving objects in the plane. It is possible to compare the sequence developed by Rybczynski to proto-fractal objects, mainly to the *Cantor Set*. In fact, if one analyzes a classical track shot or a long take, there is a succession of frames that corresponds to a unique space in which time and space are perceived by the viewer as a single unity that can be divided.

|*Fig. 3.41*|

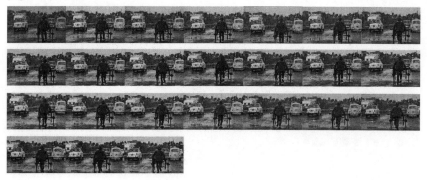

The series of frames presented above (Fig. 3.41) corresponds to one second of a track shot of Fellini's *Roma* (1972). The movement is divided into 24 frames per second in order to simulate the human perception of movement. In fact, the frame rate responds to a physiological need. The visual cortex perceives one image for about one-fifteenth of a second; consequently, if another image is perceived during that period, the visual cortex perceives it as a continuity.[94] It is possible to understand the series of frames as a straight line generated by the cinematographic camera and in particular as a straight line composed by many frames (= points in the straight line).

---

94 | See Brownlow K. 1980.

|*Fig. 3.42*|

Conversely, in the sequence corresponding to one second of Rybczynski's *Oh, I Can't Stop!* (1976), (Fig. 3.42) the reproduction of movement does not create an *ordino* based on natural human perception. In the series of images (24 frames, one second of an apparent track shot), the movement, even though it is understood by the viewer as a kind of continuity (as a track shot), presents a fractalized space in which continuity derives from the movements of vectors. It is possible to affirm that the notion of movement generated in this fractalized space is not the result of a purely physiological process but of a logical reasoning that generates a kind of continuity in the discontinuity of the fractalized space. Movement in *Oh, I Can't Stop!* derives more from *logos* than from *Doxa*.

|*Fig. 3.43*|

The analogies between Mandelbrot's studies on communication signals and Rybczynski's track shot in *Oh, I Can't Stop!* become clear. Both applied a kind of deepening analysis (a zoom) on a continuous form. Fractalizing a sequence, a duration, both highlighted the heterogeneous factors of the unities that compose the whole set in order to recognize a new harmony. This harmony takes into account the relationship between different scales, different spaces that compose the whole unity. As mentioned above, Mandelbrot used the *Cantor Set* (Fig. 3.43) as a pattern in his research on communication signals. In the *Cantor Set*, the principal straight line from which every point derives is, in the study undertaken by Mandelbrot, the specific time of a signal that presents many interferences. In a classic track shot, e.g. in Fellini's track shot shown above, (Fig. 3.41) the straight line represents a take from which every frame in the sequence derives. The point in the straight line corresponds to a frame in the sequence, a sequence of frames (24 frames per second) that respond to the physiological need to generate the feeling of continuity. In the track shot analyzed above (24 frames of a sequence of Rybczynski's *Oh, I Can't Stop!* shot in 35mm, fig. 3.42), the sequence of frames is fractalized, recalling the structure of the *Cantor Set*. The series of frames, the straight line, represents a set from which derives another series of frames that forms a subset, which enables a one-to-one correspondence between the two sets. The whole movement of the take, i.e. the 'real' movement translated by the camera, is contained in the sub-sets that are presented in the long take of *Oh, I Can't Stop!* analyzed above. Thus, this film highlights the new structure of the audiovisual narrative space using a new scale of the sequence of frames that demonstrated, through a one-to-one correspondence, that the whole can be in the part. Further, this new structure enables a new topological space in which many sets can coexist because, as noted above, the image is no longer understood as a sequence of frames. It starts to be a single flexible image-object that undergoes transformations.

|Prop. XIII| This new structure of the image cannot be perceived as a *mise en abyme*. There is not a superposition of two different spaces, it is not one space contained in another. This new structure allows inlaying in the pure surface of many heterogeneous image-objects that become part of a homogenous fractal object. The analysis of Rybczynski is clear. He started, with *Kwadrat* (1972), to analyze the pure composition of the image. Through this work he conceptualized the point in the image. What represented a simple optical result of a chemical process became an informative entity in a topologic space. Three years later, with *New Book*, he explored the potentialities of this system as well as the new topologic qualities. The spatial organization of *New Book* makes allusion to the potentiality to organize new spaces, in which an entire image can be contained in a single point, as well as to the role of vectors in creating a continuum in the space. One year later, in *Oh, I Can't Stop!*, he analyzes not only the narrative potentiality of a fractalized sequence of frames but also the role played by the inner movement of the image (vectors) from which the coordination of the many different spaces derives. These three works allowed him to develop a new space in which many different spatiotemporal coordinates are presented at the same time. His research on this phenomenon goes further with *Tango* (1980). In this work (awarded with an Oscar), Rybczynski organized a fractal object in which the space is well defined but time is completely distorted.

|Prop. XXV| In *Tango*, (Fig. 3.44) the fractality of the space is organized through the detachment of the vector from its natural place. Each vector belongs to another place, that is, the narrative space is shaped as a unique space in which many different times coexist. This space is perceived as a superposition of many different movements belonging to different places. The relativism of the vectors' movement generates a special phenomenon for the viewer. In fact, in *Tango* the vectors' movement is perceived as the juxtaposition of many different spatiotemporal factors in the same space. In this special space, where many vectors coexist, recursivity is generated and becomes an

important narrative tool. The repetition of the vectors' actions in the film highlights both the coexistence of many different times in the same space and the homogeneity of the *complexus* in which the individual heterogeneous factors of each component are not lost. Further, in the space of *Tango*, the spectator experiences only one present time in its strictest sense. In other words, the virtuality and actuality of the images are also distorted because time is no longer perceived as a sequence, as the linear succession of past, present and future, consequently, the succession theorized in the classic narrative is totally replaced.[95]

|*Fig. 3.44*|

On the one hand, the viewer of this film does not perceive the succession due to the juxtaposition of different spaces with their own time. On the other hand, the coexistence of different times in the spaces and its recursivity completely eliminate the possibility to place the *complexus* in a specific coordinate of time thus, to project it to the Whole. Consequently, every space that makes up the *complexus* has its own time. However, their interaction with the other spaces and their recursivity place the single unities in the *complexus* in a timeless space. Thus, there is the inexistence of sequence,

---

95 | As noted by Fahle "Im Bewegungsbild ist die Zeit noch der Bewegung untergeordnet, die Aktion bestimmt die zeitliche Ordnung. Der Modus der Sukzession ist also eine untergeordnete Zeitform. Im modernen Film setzt sich dann aber ein direktes Bild der Zeit frei, Aktionen treten gleichsam hinter die zeitlichen Aspekte des Bildes zurück. Damit findet auch das filmische Bild eine neue Bestimmung, werden doch jetzt erst Möglichkeiten der Zeitgestaltung sichtbar, die zunächst verdeckt waren. Wesentlich ist dabei die Aufhebung der zuvor strikten Trennung der modalzeitlichen Ebenen. Vergangenheit, Gegenwart und Zukunft sind nicht mehr in gleicher Weise voneinander differenzierbar wie zuvor, sondern gehen ineinander über, verschachteln sich oder koexistieren in einer filmischen Einstellung." (Fahle O. 2007, p. 125.)

of succession, that enables one to discern the actual image and its virtual one. If one analyzes the narrative act in the audiovisual space as a spatial organization derived from the interaction between objects in *absentia* and objects in *presentia* – interface and database – with *Tango* it is possible to see that the well-defined boundaries between these two different spaces are starting to be blurred.

|*Fig. 3.45*|

It is possible to see fractional dimensions between the two well-defined spaces of database and interface. Thus, *Tango* can be seen as a kind of palimpsest.[96] In *Tango,* there is a space that recalls another space or dimension, a space that is used as a bridge bringing the viewer to another text. The composition of the narrative space of *Tango* places thirty-six different vectors and twenty-three different spaces on the same surface.[97] However, as noted above, editing started to be understood as the creation of objects of a topological nature that allowed transformations. Thus, it is possible to understand *Tango* as a flexible image-object in which recursivity is able to correlate different spaces using their inner vectors. In fact, all through the film, the vectors repeat their movements in a loop. This complex spatial organization also highlights the nature of the narrative spaces generated through video technology. According to Deleuze, the *hors-cadre* disappears when objects are placed on the pure surface of video. In fact, the hypertextual character developed by Rybczynski's film erases completely the *hors-cadre* through the coexistence of different spaces in the plane. Through the disappearance of the well-defined borderline between objects in *absentia* and objects in *presentia*, the *hors-cadre* starts to be explicit in the image in *presentia*.[98] This phenomenon is highlighted by Rybczynski through the recursivity of the single spaces in the *complexus*. When the vector is out of our visual camp, its presence in the object in *presentia* is already explicit through its recursive movement. The viewer knows that the 'invisible' object is there. In addition, the viewer knows precisely its movement, its direction, its relationship with the different vectors, its speed and its narrative role in the plane. Consequently, the fractal space generated in this film does not allow a classic structure in which every image has its own *hors-cadre*; this is due to the contemporaneity of the different spaces and the timeless nature of the *complexus*. Further, the fractal nature of the space also drastically changes the nature of the objects, characters or vectors present in the plane.

---

96 | From Greek παλιν *palin,* which means 'again,' and ψαω *psao,* which means 'scrape.' This practice was common among Romans, who wrote on wax-coated tablets that were usually reused after being smoothed. Indeed, This practice adds a new dimension to text; it creates a kind of hypertext. See Genette G. 1982.

97 | See Kermabon J. 1990.

98 | See Noake R. 1988.

The research on video technology was also focused on the development of new objects placed in this particular space, the pure surface. In this space, objects acquired more flexibility, a property of some objects placed in a topological space. Rybczynski developed a fractal space in which he organized a narrative. Further, as mentioned in the last examples, he analyzed the new nature of objects placed in that special space. However, some technical limitations prevented him from fractalizing the single object in the video space. Certainly, the attempt to create a topological object in the audiovisual narrative space is clear in *New Book* (1975). As Rybczynski himself says talking about his film *The Fourth Dimension* (1988): "I got the idea for this film at the time of *Nowa Ksiazka*, but I did not have the chance to translate it into images early on."[99] In *The Fourth Dimension*, Rybczynski completely accomplished the creation of a topological object. In fact, in this film, a natural object, an Euclidean representation of an existing object (e.g. a human figure, a door, etc.) is placed in the video space and acquires a new nature, a topological quality.

The process followed by Rybczynski is almost the same as that of Vasulka in *Study n° 25*. Both manipulate the most basic components of the image. However, Vasulka creates a geometrical object by changing the frequency of the single video line, while Rybczynski manipulates every single video line that composed an image derived by the optical process of the camera. In other words, Rybczynski highlighted the change of dimension executed by video technology dealing with an image derived from the classic process of image reproduction; he manipulates its electrical composition. The creation of this film was based on the comprehension of the image as a decomposable entity containing many single elements, in this case, video lines. Rybczynski describes his method as follows:

"I shot the actors in their set with all the movements, then in the printing phase I visualized the image in 480 lines and reproduced the images delaying, for example, each frame by one line. Thus, the last line ended up being 480 images later in respect to the higher one, so that when the head of a character is rotated, his feet are still in their original position."[100]

Rybczynski composes a fractal space like in *Tango*, but in *The Fourth Dimension* he highlights the flexibility of the object in that space in which the object is no longer a representation nor a presentation; it is an organization of a system in which its minimal components can be isolated.[101]

---

99 | See Kermabon J. 1990.

100 | See Kermabon J. 1990.

101 | It is interesting to note that Virilio posits that Rybczynski's method in this film can be compared to the way in which a geologist approaches and analyzes each single stratum: "The horizontal lines are to him what the layers of sedimentation are to a geologist." See Virilio P. 1989.

|*Fig. 3.46*|

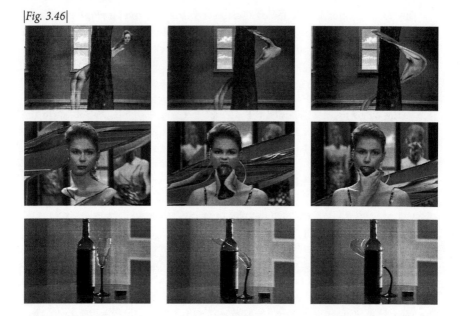

The Fourth Dimension (1988) represents a system in which the correlation of different times of a single object weaves a topological object. Further, this film illustrates not only the nature of the object placed in the video space but also shows a new structure of audiovisual narrative, namely a structure that shares some characteristics with the rhizome theorized by Deleuze. Rybczynski, especially in this film, realized that the space of video does not correspond to a structure defined by points but rather by lines – vanishing points – as a dimension or stratification that composes a narrative space in becoming.[102]

---

102 | See Fragier J.-P. 1989, p. 62.

3.4 A New Relationship Between Paradigma and Syntagma

The screen, as theorized by Deleuze, became a table of information, a surface on which the image as representation disappears. Data are inscribed on this table. Thus, information replaces nature.[1] Consequently, digital images no longer represent a window – a concept inherited from perspective (see *Perspective: The Geometry of Sight*) – and the viewer does not deal with the perceptible, but with the legible.[2] In fact, as already noted, the line and the point changed their nature in the image. Borrowing from Deleuze:

"la ligne et le point se libèrent de la figure, en même temps que la vie se libère des axes de la représentation organique : la puissance est passée dans une vie non-organique, qui tantôt trace directement sur la pellicule une arabesque continue d'où elle va tirer des images par *points-coupures*, tantôt va engendrer l'image en faisant clignoter le point sur le vide d'une pellicule obscure."[3]

|Prop. I| As postulated by Ascott, the single frame is no longer produced though the photographic technology but through the post-photographic technology, a technology that "captures images ('seen' images from still, video, and other cameras), constructs images ('unseen' data from remote sensors and data banks), and generates images (from raw numbers); it treats them, stores them, associates them, distributes them, and transmits them into a media flow that is – in very serious sense – unending and ubiquitous."[4] The post-photographic technology allowed the development of new *ideal elements* in the audiovisual narrative, modifying completely the relationship between paradigm and syntagma.

Ascott noted how, through digital technology, the process of the transformation of the image passes into the hands of the viewer as much as to the artist.[5] This *apertura* of the image, its flexibility in the process of generation, transformation and sharing, transported some aesthetical components of the infinitely layered space of data.[6] In

---

1 | Deleuze G. 1985, p. 347.
2 | See Marks L.U. 2010.
3 | Deleuze G. 1985, p. 280.
4 | Ascott R. 2003, p. 248.
5 | Ascott R. 2003, p. 248.
6 | Bolter J.D. also found this phenomenon in the electronic text. He posits that the architecture or structure of the text is realized in time as the reader reads. However, Bolter also argues that this phenomenon was already present in text in the manuscript and print. He posits that "[w]hat we have traditionally called the structure of the text is the relationship between the linear experience of reading and the network of allusions among elements that are separated in the physical space of the book." (Bolter J.D. 1991, p. 159). Certainly, through digital technology, the text, as well as the image, can be directly transformed, for example, by hypertextual links. The network of allusions becomes

other words, the open structure of the post-photographic image is reflected in the organization of the narrative space in the audiovisual field.

|Prop. VII| Since the appearance of digital technology, the computer has offered a new way for taking part in the creative organization of signs. It started to organize our writing with new techniques; we started to create a new space.[7] In fact, the narrative act started to be understood more as a topographic action than as a hierarchical organization of events, images or thoughts. The phenomenon described by Bolter as topographic writing, in contrast to topical writing – where topographic writing is not "the writing of a place, but rather a writing with places"[8] – was not a phenomenon exclusive to writing technology. In the audiovisual field, due to the multilayered nature of the image, the narrative act progressively becomes a cartographic act. In addition, the narrative started to be strongly influenced by concepts coming from the development of geometries – of course narrative, as a pure spatial organization, could also just be analyzed through geometrical notions – and digital technology brought to the audiovisual field many concepts of fractal geometry. In fact, the personal computer, being the instrument that made fractal geometry possible (see *Fractus, Fracta, Fractum*), transmits a fractal *ordino* to audiovisual narrative. As already pointed out, machines influenced the narrative spatial organization. In addition, machines developed a kind of consciousness, a kind of autonomy in the creative process. I highlighted this phenomenon through both Vertov's relationship with the cinematographic camera and Vasulka's relationship with the video camera. It is legitimate to propose that the influence, or 'consciousness', of the computer expresses itself through the fractal *ordino* of the narrative.

|Prop. VIII| In the chapter *Visualizing Multidimensional Spaces,* I noted that cinematography, due to the inheritance of the camera obscura, was in such a sense enclosed in a Euclidean space. Deleuze demonstrated that cinematographic narrative developed some narrative spaces that had a non-Euclidean form. With the introduction of digital technology to audiovisual narratives some effects and image constructions that recalled topologic spaces and Proto-Fractal spaces emerged – for example, the already analyzed works by Rybczynski. Some films, music videos and advertisements started to show, or to mimic, fractal forms. For example, in some of Gondry's music videos, and in a sense in all his works, some fractal concepts and some fractal forms are clearly present. Consider, for instance, the music video *Let Forever Be* (1999) realized by Gondry for The Chemical Brothers.

This video concentrated into its narrative gamut a number of fractal forms. In the series of images bellow, (Fig. 3.47) we can see that the narrative space is composed entirely by means of a phenomenon of self-similarity. From a single unity, a clock,

---

a real net of information concretely connected to one another. We will deal with this phenomenon in the next chapter.

7 | See Bolter J.D. 1991.

8 | Bolter J.D. 1991, p. 25.

Gondry creates, through a recursive effect from which derives the self-similar compositions, temporal and spatial ellipses.

|*Fig. 3.47*|

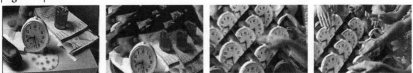

In some scenes, like in the example bellow, from a single object or character, an identical one is derived. The multiplication of this object generates a series of 'copies.'

|*Fig. 3.48*|

It is interesting to note that this video is composed in two well-defined spaces. The first one, perceived as the natural (or Euclidean) space of the character, was realized in the character's room and in the mall. The second one, where the fractalization of the character, the recursivity of actions and the self-similar phenomena happen, was clearly realized in a studio. In the second space, the foreground is always black. The passages from one space to another are always made through the multiplication of the character or by a change of scale of the space (Fig. 3.49).

|*Fig. 3.49*|

|*Fig. 3.50*|

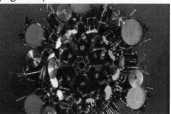

In this last image, (Fig. 3.50) one can observe that the phenomenon of self-similarity and the deformation of the objects accomplished in the second space clearly recall some fractal forms. Another interesting example of fractal aesthetics by Gondry is the music video *Come into My World* (2001) realized for Kylie Minogue.

In both examples recursivity represents an important narrative factor. Fractal forms required recursivity to construct an endless space as well as to manifest the multi-dimensionality of the narrative space (See *Ideal Elements in Narrative Space*). The popularization of fractal geometry generated a particular curiosity of the arts to represent infinity through recursivity. Thus, recursivity became a present phenomenon in the last phase of video technology and the first phase of digital technology in audiovisual field. Rybczynski was not alienated to this phenomenon and, as noted in the last chapter, he attempted to create infinite spaces in his film *The Orchestra* (1990). According to him, both recursivity and self-similarity are highly present in nature; thus he represents nature through both phenomena.[9] In fact, in the last part of *The Orchestra*, known as *Stairway to Lenin*, Rybczynski composes an infinite space based on the *ostinato* of Ravel's *Bolero*. In another work, a music video he developed for the Pet Shop Boys – *Opportunities (Let's Make Lots of Money)* (1986) (Fig. 3.51) – Rybczynski clearly uses recursivity in order to create an infinite space showing a multidimensional nature.

|*Fig. 3.51*|

Recursivity and self-similarity play an important aesthetic role highlighting the infinity of the narrative space. Both phenomena, highly present in the aesthetics of the audiovisual field during the Eighties and Nineties, represented a clear allusion to fractal geometry and infinite spaces.

Now I would like to draw attention to the creation of those multidimensional spaces composed by the correlations of different unities. It is through this phenomenon that the influence of fractal geometry modifies the relationship between paradigm and syntagma.

|Prop. X| As noted above, recursivity represented a narrative tool able to highlight the multidimensional narrative space of the audiovisual narrative. In the previous examples, and especially in Rybczynski's works, recursivity enabled the correlation of many dimensions in the image. These dimensions showed a new kind of compositing (see *Ideal Elements in Narrative Space*). From the camera obscura to the digital image there has been a repeated human will to fractalize the world and to put its pieces together later on in order to construct a new space. This phenomenon was analyzed in-depth using the Panoramas (see *The Panorama: An Example of 'Gigantomanie des Mediums'*). With the photographic technology, and especially cinematographic technology, this phenomenon changed. This was because of the juxtaposition between the mobilized gaze – brought by new technologies in transport, urban planning and

---

9 | See *Invideo*, Milan 2008, interview with Rybczynski.

architecture developed during the beginning of the nineteenth century – and the virtual gaze brought by photography.[10] The immobility of the viewer in front of a projected picture imposed a new kind of compositing in which the fractalized space was represented in the single plane of the image – the screen. Thus, Méliès introduced into the cinematographic narrative the use of depicted foregrounds, a method already used in photography.[11] This synthesis of a coherent space, improved during the 30s with the rear-screen, gave cinematography a greater capacity to create fake-realities.[12]

In his analysis of compositing, Manovich highlights a kind of editing that applies a sort of incrustation of an image to the image, which corresponds to the development of a new dimension in narrative space. The montage within a shot showed the human will to generate multidimensional spaces and, through the development of video technology, this practice became more and more common. In fact, the electronic keying was already the basis of TV news in the 1970s, – for instance, the journalists in the studio presenting the news while images are screening in foreground.

In 1987, Rybczynski worked with this technique in *Steps* (1987), in which the incrustation of video images was done on a space developed through analog film. The plot of this film is based on a virtual journey through Eisenstein's legendary *Battleship Potemkin* (1925): a group of American tourists 'travel' inside Eisenstein's film. As noted by Manovich, in *Steps,* "Rybczynski connects three generations of fake-reality technologies: analog, electronic, and digital."[13]

Another interesting example of video compositing noted by Manovich is Godard's *Histoire(s) du cinéma* (1989-), in which the unity of the narrative space is generated by mixing a number of video images in a multidimensional space (Fig. 3.52). This is understood by the viewer as a single shot composed of many different planes.

|*Fig. 3.52*|

---

10 | See Friedberg A. 1994.

11 | See Sadoul G. 1949.

12 | Manovich L. 2001, p. 147.

13 | Manovich L. 2001, p. 150.

As noted in the last chapter, through video technology, the image started to be understood as a 'yielding object' that can be modeled. This is the case for some of Vasulka's works noted in the same chapter. Indeed, the creation of *ideal elements* in the narrative dimension of the audiovisual field completely transformed the relationship between paradigm and syntagma, and this transformation is clear in spaces built through video compositing as well through digital compositing.

Digital compositing differs from video compositing in its unlimited number of image layers. Further, the different layers accept spaces from any other media. That is to say, the narrative space accepts in a single shot filmed figures, images created with 3-D computer graphics, analog footages, old engravings, etc., – for example, in Spielberg's *Jurassic Park* (1993). This new possibility offered by digital compositing seems to fulfill the desire of painters, mainly Cubist such as Picasso and Braque, to represent the *fourth dimension* (see *Visualizing Multidimensional Spaces*). Further, this new possibility offered by digital technology allows the audiovisual narrative to acquire a real capacity to be free from Euclidean impositions. Thanks to digital technology, the camera loses its strong inheritance and limitations from the camera obscura. Now, we can say that we are in front of a different medium, a medium free from Euclidean rules – that is, a fractal medium. The fractalization of the narrative space can be perceived in the necessity to privileges montage within a shot generated by digital technology. As noted by Manovich, in many interfaces programs for computer-based editing and digital compositing, "(...)the horizontal dimension representing time, while the vertical dimension represents the spatial order of the different image layers making up each image. A moving image sequence appears as a number of blocks staggered vertically, with each block standing for a particular image layer."[14] In addition, programs for compositing, such as Combustion or After Effects, add a third dimension, in which "individual elements making up a moving image can freely move, rotate, and change proportions over time."[15]

|Prop. XXVII| In 1962 Umberto Eco published *Opera aperta. Forma e indeterminazione nelle poetiche contemporanee*. It is important to remember that at the time the influence of formalists on film studies was very present. In that work, Eco dealt with the televised space and its influence on the development of the plot in contemporary narratives. By analyzing the aesthetics of television, he highlighted the exclusive capacity of television to transmit events in real time: live TV. The first aspect that took his interest was the editing in live TV. As he noted, the director mixes at least three different cameras simultaneously with the event. Thus, Eco affirms that through the editing in live TV the viewer watches an interpretation of the event. The *choice* in this case completely changes with regard to the cinematographic *choice* in the editing phase. The *choice* in live TV is, according to him, "una composizione, una narrazione, l'unificazione discorsiva di immagini isolate analiticamente nel contesto di una più vasta

---

14 | Manovich L. 2001, pp. 155-156.
15 | Manovich L. 2001, p. 156.

serie di avvenimenti compresenti ed intersecantisi."[16] This *impromptu* represents an important narrative tool that enable the weaving of the narrative space. Eco identified those recursive forms in some jazz elements like the *riff*. Indeed, the recursive form of the *riff* allows the creation of an organic composition full of improvisation.[17]

As noted by Eco, quoting Aristotle's *Ars Poetica*, the choice of some actions of a whole event creates a narrative unity.[18] In the field of live TV, the aim changes because the director is obliged to institute immediately both a coherence and a unity within the chaos of events.[19] The Leibnizian understanding of chaos is clearly highlighted, chaos as a synonym of the infinite of choices.[20] In live TV, the director is obliged to isolate single facts from the whole event that is happening; thus, live TV establishes a new relationship between the stylistic device (*artificio*) and the spontaneity (*spontaneità*).[21] To borrow from Eco:

"La crescita della sua narrazione appare così per metà effetto d'arte e per l'altra metà opera di natura; il suo prodotto sarà una strana interazione di spontaneità ed artificio, dove l'artificio definisce e sceglie la spontaneità ma la spontaneità guida l'artificio, nel suo concepimento e nel suo compimento."[22]

As a consequence, Eco highlights the inclination of the contemporary narrative toward the dissolution of plot (*dissoluzione dell'intreccio*), where the plot is understood as the position of unambiguous links among the events that turn out essential to the final *denouement*.[23] As remarked by Eco, contemporary narratives express what he calls 'unessential' or 'stupid facts,' – for example, the facts that occurs to Leopold Bloom or to some characters of Robbe-Grillet. However, those unessential facts are essential in the diegesis; they represent a development of the plot and it is precisely in the presence of those apparently unessential facts that Eco sees the *apertura* of the contemporary narrative. The *apertura*, in those literary works, is the possibility to be understood in many different ways, the possibility to recognize a chaotic world. In

---

16 | Eco U. 2006⁷, p. 189.

17 | It is interesting to note that Deleuze and Guattari recognize the *ritornello* as an important function to organize the exterior space; the chaotic space. See Deleuze G. – Guattari F. 1980, especially *1837 – De la riournelle*.

18 | See Aristotle, *The Poetics*. (Translation: Fyfe H.W. 1965.)

19 | See Eco U. 2006⁷, p. 194.

20 | The individuation and reproduction of experiences means for Aristotle poetry.

21 | It is also important to note that according to Eco, live TV shares some properties with the specular image produced by a mirror. He states that "L'immagine televisiva, dal punto di vista pragmatico, partecipa dei vantaggi della immagine speculare, e degli svantaggi delle altre impronte foto e cinematografiche." (Eco U. 1985, p. 36.) Where the advantage is basically the absolute rapport to the referent.

22 | Eco U. 2006⁷, p. 197.

23 | Eco U. 2006⁷, p. 199.

Eco's words, "nel rifiuto dell'intreccio si attua il riconoscimento del fatto che il mondo è un nodo di possibilità e che l'opera d'arte deve riprodurre questa fisionomia."[24]

In the cinematographic art, this phenomenon also started to be present. Eco noted this phenomenon in some films by Antonioni, mainly in *L'avventura* (1960) and *La notte* (1961). Concerning these films, Eco wondered if a viewer alienated to the practice of live TV could accept a narrative like that of Antonioni's in which the viewer can find scenes that manifest a kind of primary narrative material that generates the illusion of seeing a natural succession of events. In these films by Antonioni there are moments in which the plot is completely undone, moments in which nothing happens.[25] Hence, Eco compares the narrative of *L'avventura* to the narrative construction of live TV. He posits that in *L'avventura*, the viewer could ask himself if some scenes were made by a live TV practice, that is to say, if the images were 'broadcasted in real-time.' Further, he states that in some of Antonioni's scenes as well as in live TV, there is an attempt to represent the multidimensionality of life without the use of prefixed links.[26] And, we can add, this multidimensionality is represented in a fractal narrative space. The simulation of the prefixed links of real life in the non-contemporaneous editing imposes a special analysis of casualness. That is to say, while the editing in live TV deals with a *casual casualness* component, Antonioni's *L'avventura* deals with a *wanted casualness*.[27] Thus, both do not attempt to create a plot in the classical meaning because both directors attempt to communicate a kind of indeterminacy. In Eco's words:

"Il racconto, come intreccio, non esiste proprio perché nel regista c'è la *calcolata volontà* di comunicare un senso di sospensione e di indeterminazione, una frustrazione degli istinti 'romanzeschi' affinché questi si introduca fattivamente al centro della finzione (che è già vita filtrata) per orientarsi attraverso una serie di giudizi intellettuali e morali. L'apertura presuppone insomma la lunga e accurata organizzazione di un *campo di possibilità*."[28]

The essence of the new narrative, derived from the influence of live TV and analyzed by Eco, is its difference from the traditional plot generated within an Aristotelian logic, in which the world is represented under prefixed laws, logic and functional ways that are deterministic and represent a determined world. In the new narrative, the fundamental difference from the Aristotelian way of organizing the plot is the dissociation of the classic links through which the world was represented and life was told. Certainly, in the period in which Eco wrote these thoughts, the materiality imposed by the film stock and its linearity allowed only a phenomenological analysis. Accord-

---

24 | Eco U. 2006[7], pp. 199-200.
25 | Eco U. 2005[8], p. 319.
26 | Eco U. 2006[7], p. 201.
27 | Eco U. 2006[7], p. 201.
28 | Eco U. 2006[7], p. 202.

ing to Eco, this fragmentation of the plot, manifested in the dissolution of dramatic knots, required a phenomenological change that could liberate the viewer from the millenary attitude of "how it ends."[29] However, with the development of video technology and then digital technology, Eco highlighted the dissolution of the plot or the presence in *syntagma* of some spaces. It is to say, actions and objects usually placed in *paradigma*, became a truly externalization of *paradigma*. To follow a more adequate terminology, there was a real externalization of database, through which database and interface became a single, heterogeneous, multidimensional space.

The already analyzed video compositing technique represents an example in terms of the spatial composition of the image. For instance, *Steps* represents in this way the collision between database and interface, which made the database an externalized entity. A remarkable example of the phenomenon described above is Peter Greenaway's works, especially *The Pillow Book* (1996). In this film, the database is externalized. It becomes highly present in the diegesis. The externalization of the database in this film proposes a new understanding of narrative. What Eco formulated three decades earlier, taking as an example Antonioni's *L'avventura*, in Greenaway's case was no longer a simple dissolution of the plot. The action of choice in order to construct the unity of the plot following Aristotelian theories radically changed. The fractal narrative space allows the presentation of a new unity in the *complexus*, a unity of heterogeneous factors.

The dissolution of the plot allowed the understanding of the narrative act in the audiovisual field as the creation of a multidimensional space and the development of a non-Euclidean space, as theorized by Deleuze. However, one can theorize that the digital space is a concrete fractal space in which dimensions and half dimensions between the original two well-defined spaces of database and interface are developed. The narrative act, through the externalization of the database could be seen as the creation of an infinite space in which many different scales find their harmony. The coexistence of these different scales could be identified in the hypermediacy enabled by digital technology.

As noted above, Greenaway gave another function to video compositing. He used this technological possibility to construct a fractal narrative, making allusion to a navigable database. In *The Pillow Book*, the director composed a narrative space working on its minimal components. He also highlights the fractalization of the images by avoiding what Manovich considers a mistake of compositing, that is, to match different spaces in perspective, scale and lighting.[30]

In the images bellow, (Fig. 3.53) we can see how Greenaway creates sets of individual shots in order to externalize the architecture of the database. In this film, the diegetic time is always vague. By externalizing the inner space of the narrative, the viewer interprets some sub-frames as future or past actions of the diegesis. Thus,

---

29 | Eco U. 2006[7], p. 204.
30 | Manovich L. 2001, p. 5.

the fractalization of the narrative act accomplished in *The Pillow Book* is seen in the manifestation of its structural narrative process.

|*Fig. 3.53*|

In this film, one can see the fractal structure adopted by digital media and the World Wide Web. The very narrative structure of this film seems to be composed by a number of separate objects stored independently. Manovich calls this fractal nature of digital media 'modularity.' One might say that the digital logic developed in the audiovisual narrative, and highlighted in the externalization of the database, expresses this phenomenon of modulation. In the case of *The Pillow Book*, this is shown through the sets, subsets, Chinese characters and texts contained in a single shot. Certainly, the fractalization of the medium into a HTML structure is complete. In fact, it consists, borrowing from Manovich, "of a number of separated objects – GIF and JPEG images, media clips, Virtual Reality Modeling Language (VRML) scenes, Shockwave and Flash movies – which are all stored independently, locally, and/or on a network. In short, a new media object consist of independent parts, each of which consist of smaller independent parts, and so on, down to the level of the smallest 'atoms' – pixels, 3-D points, or text characters."[31] As we can see, Greenaway brings editing closer to programming and allows us to see that fractal geometry, as an episteme, imposes a new kind of structuring narrative spaces where the narrative act must be understood as the creation, or programming, of a fractal space – an infinite, navigable space.

|**Prop. XXIII**| The creation of this fractal narrative space started to be familiar to the larger public through the hyperlinking developed by digital media. Since the improvement of some multimedia frameworks like QuickTime 3, the fractalization of the narrative space has become even more evident for the viewer due to the technical possibility of embedding hyperlinks in the multidimensional space of the image.[32] By comparing QT movies with Cornell boxes, Sobchack defines the spaces created by hyperlinking as dynamic, contingent and associative. According to Sobchack, QT movies and Cornell boxes "refuse mundane space-time, drawing us into enclosed and nested poetic worlds far more miniature, layered, and vertically deep than we usually find in cinema."[33] The geometry developed by this kind of hypertextual space gen-

---

31 | Manovich L. 2001, p. 31.

32 | See Manovich L. 2001, p. 157.

33 | Sobchack V. 1999, p. 29.

erates associative dynamics, which are more contingent than determined. Sobchack claims, dealing with the mechanism established by memory boxes, that "[i]ts search engines driven to the past by a present moment of desire (not utility), this is the eccentric, extensible, yet localized logic of the *hyperlink* that radically transforms the phenomenology of the file cabinet and its database."[34] Sobchack also notes how this new architecture of the audiovisual space makes explicit the database.[35]

The database externalizes its single elements through the ambiguity of associational links. This fragmentation of the narrative space produces a fractal space in becoming in which the whole architecture takes into account the single unities of the *complexus* in the different scales. Consider how Sobchack describes this fractal structure, recalling Leibniz's concepts:

"with the QT memory box and its hyperlinking logic, there is the hierarchical logic of the computer "desktop" upon which it is opened. That is, the larger frame of the vitrine or desktop allows the smaller frame of the memory box an intensified condensation and concentration of its visible contents into an *aesthetic totality:* a poetically meaningful and contained microcosm nested within the dispersed and different order and meaning of the macrocosm that surrounds them."[36]

|*Fig. 3.54*|

The externalization of database recalls the appearance of the ancient *Wunderkammern*, where the viewer values personal sensibilities and desires over logic and the chaotic clutter of the arrangement of objects did not represent a problem for the viewer. Sobchack analyzed the 'totalizing impulse' developed by the *Wunderkammern* as "a celebration of mastery, order, and structural homology: that is, comprehension of the 'universe in all its richness and variety' is represented mimetically in a single chamber complacently 'nested' within the larger frameworks of both the master's residence and God's 'master plan."[37] As we can see, those spaces present some self-similar phenomena, stimulating a non-hierarchical perceptual act. Thus, the externalization of the database in the audiovisual narrative space, like the *Wunderkammern*, generates a fragmentary space in which the heterogeneous character of the single unity is harmonized through

---

34 | Sobchack V. 1999, p. 31.
35 | Sobchack V. 1999, p. 31.
36 | Sobchack V. 1999, p. 32.
37 | Sobchack V. 1999, p. 32.

the correlations between different scales. Further, every single heterogeneous unity that generates and homogenized *complexus,* without losing their singular character, is infinitely extendable in meaning.

Through QT hyperlinking, one can theorize an overcoming of the systems theorized by Leibniz, or the folded structures by Deleuze. These spaces show fractal characteristics. In fact, one is not dealing with a 'relatively enclosed' structure contained in another one, rather with a constellation of externalized objects that, by means of infinite links, weave infinite, heterogeneous unities without losing their heterogeneous nature. Thus, digital narrative spaces generate the need for integrating the database and the interface. Antonio Caronia gives an interesting example of this in his analysis of the concept of post-symbolic communication proposed by Jaron Lanier in 1989. Caronia highlights within digital narratives a phenomenon of externalization of cognitive elements, which produces another cognitive level as well as a new communicative level. According to Caronia:

"la logica di questo nuovo livello influenza tanto l'organizzazione interna dei dati (il *database*) quanto la loro presentazione e la loro comunicazione alla componente umana (l'interfaccia), e rivela possibilità espressive in entrambi gli ambiti."[38]

Certainly, digital technology imposed a new organization of data, which not only takes into account the classification, order and navigability of data presented to humans through the interface, but also the order in the former inner data: the organization of the database.[39] This phenomenon re-elaborates the order of information as well as the way of stocking it. Consequently, it affects the production of knowledge.[40]

We are in front of the thousand-year-old human will of converging (in a single location),[41] the totality of human knowledge. This desire aims, on the one hand, at the development of a space in which all possible natural objects and artifacts can be stored, and on the other, at the creation of a space in which knowledge can be preserved and produced. The first place is represented by Samuel Quiccheberg's plan for organizing objects, which is considered the first museological treatise and represents the *Wunderkammern* mentioned above. The second one can be illustrated through Giulio Camillo's *Memory Theater,* in which the viewer is placed in a parceled space composed by cabinets containing text and objects.[42] These two different kinds of classification have accompanied us over centuries. On the one hand, humankind

---

38 | Caronia A. 2006, p. 127.

39 | See Vesna V. 2007.

40 | Note that Morin associates knowledge with organization, differing from the concept of information, which is a simple computation. See Morin E. 2005, p. 145.

41 | On the need to gather, archive and preserve knowledge and on the improvement of our ability to do so thanks to computer technology, see, among others Zinna A. 2004, especially, pp. 155-257. With references therein.

42 | Vesna V. 2007, p. 29.

organized visual memories that were drastically influenced by the architecture of the museum. On the other, humankind developed systems of classification of intellectual content, like the Library of Alexandria, or the organization and classification of the content of a work like Jean D'Alembert and Denis Diderot's *Encyclopédie*.

Visual media and narrative were not extraneous to this human will. In the chapter *Mise en Abyme, blazon into blazon*, I noted how armory developed some techniques to make coats that were able to contain an infinity of information, through which history could be stored and interpreted, developing in this way a kind of encyclopedism as well as a narrative. Also, I analyzed the phenomenon of encyclopedism in the chapter dedicated to Panoramas and Moving Panoramas. As already noted, some Panoramas attempted to contain huge quantities of information, linearly organized in order to be presented to the viewer as a travel in time. This phenomenon is also present in cinematography – for instance, Leger's ideas of the 'monster film' or Vertov's *Man With a Movie Camera* (1929). If we consider Manovich's analysis of Vertov's film, one can see that many films attempted to develop a kind of encyclopedism. Further, this film, as one can note in the quote from Manovich below, constructed not only an encyclopedic logic but also, through a phenomenon of *mise en abyme*, constructed a special narrative space. Borrowing from Manovich:

"The overall structure of the film is quite complex, and on the first glance has little to do with a database. Just as new media objects contain a hierarchy of levels (interface – content: operating system – application; web page – HTML code; high-level programming language – assembly language – machine language), Vertov's film consists of at least three levels. One level is the story of a cameraman filming material for the film. The second level is the shots of an audience watching the finished film in a movie theater. The third level is this film, which consist of footage recorded in Moscow, Kiev and Riga and is arranged according to a progression of one day: waking up – work – leisure activities. If this third level is a text, the other two can be thought of as its meta-text. Vertov goes back and forth between the three levels, shifting between the text and its meta-texts: between the production of the film, its reception, and the film itself. But if we focus on the film within the film (i.e., the level of the text) and disregard the special effects used to create many shots, we discover almost a linear printout, so to speak, of a database: a number of shots showing machines, followed by a number of shots showing work activities, followed by different shots leisure, and so on. The paradigm is projected onto syntagm. The result is a banal, mechanical catalog of subjects which one can expect to find in the city of the 1920s: running trams, city beach, movie theaters, factories..."[43]

However, digital technology erased the division between the storage of objects and the storage of information. Traditional spaces of storing information, or cultural memory – that is, libraries and museums – collapsed with the development of digital technology. This phenomenon not only affected the storage of information (in which

---

43 | Manovich L. 2001, pp. 210-211.

the former objects are comprehended because of its codification in bits) but also the narrative. As noted by Manovich,

"Many new media objects do not tell stories; they don't have a beginning or end; in fact, they don't have any development, thematically, formally, or otherwise, that would orga-nize their elements into a sequence. Instead, they are collections of individual items, where every item has the same significance as any other."[44]

The fractalization of narrative became stronger as many intermediate dimensions started to be recognized between paradigm and syntagma. The viewer sees the com-plex structure of the database as a simple mass of items through which he/she can perform different operations, e.g. view and search. In this multimedia space, the line between objects in *absentia* and objects in *presentia* disappears. What in some films like *The Pillow Book* was an allusion to the navigability of a fractal narrative space, in a CD-ROM becomes a reality. If we take, for instance, a CD-ROM in which the user finds a digital projection of an archeological site, a tour inside the human body, or a virtual museum, the enjoyment is completely free from linearity. In other words, the narrative loses its strict linear way to be enjoyed and starts to be, in Manovich words, "just one method among others of accessing data"[45] – a geodesy of the database.

At this point, we could conclude that the narrative act in the present day multime-dia context is an articulation between the spatial disposition of digital objects in the narrative space and the method of navigation, the method of accessing the data. With the important particularity that objects disposed in the space, in the space in becom-ing, are always in *presentia*. Due to both the many visible links and the possibility for the viewer to directly interact and modify the narrative structure of the space as well as the simple lecture of the message, the externalization of the database becomes evident. This last point brings us to the notion of algorithm, which is more evident in video games, as noted by Manovich.[46]

"An algorithm is the key to the game experience in a different sense as well. As the player proceeds through the game, he or she gradually discovers the rules that operate in the universe constructed by this game. The player learns its hidden logic – in short, its algorithm. Therefore, when a game play departs from following an algorithm, the player is still engaged with an algorithm, although in another way; the player is discovering the algorithm of the game itself. I mean this both metaphorically and literally. For instance, in a first-person shooter, such as "Quake," the player may eventually notice that under such-and-such condition the enemies will appear from the left – that is, the player will literally reconstruct a part of the algorithm responsible for the game play."[47]

---

44 | Manovich L. 2007, p. 39.

45 | Manovich L. 2007, p. 40.

46 | In general, see Manovich L. 2007.

47 | Manovich L. 2007, p. 42.

Let us consider data as initiator and algorithm as generator of a fractal object. In fact, a computer program by reading data and executing an algorithm generates a recursive system that allows the generation of new data.[48] Hence, the algorithm, in the case of video games but also in the case of other interactive media, becomes a kind of plot, a path in the narrative space. Further, in such a recursive system, the creator deals with the collection of data and the programming of its lecture in order to generate more data – in order to establish a system for processing data. This process of generating data, which recalls the creation of a fractal object, brought, as noted by Manovich, a 'new cultural algorithm,' which is summarized by him as follows: "reality->media->data->data-base."[49] This new cultural algorithm totally modifies the former taxonomic sight that accompanied mankind over centuries. On the one hand, the capacity to store information becomes endless. On the other hand, the fractal space, enabled by the digital medium, places data in an infinite, heterogeneous *complexus* in which all the information objects are linked and both the open nature of the fractal space and the infinite links that bind every single heterogeneous object in the *complexus* develop a space in continuous becoming able to generate new data – in other words, a database that is continuously generating. Although Manovich considers database and narrative as natural enemies, the framework developed in this text bring us to understand the narrative status of the database as a natural *iter* due to the fractalization of the narrative space. Certainly, classic narrative creates a "cause-and-effect trajectory of seemingly unordered items (events)"[50] while database represents the world as a list of items, but items that are organized following Mandelbrot's logic of harmony between different scales. Thus, the externalization of the database develops a fractal order, which is highly narrative and which narrative structure corresponds to the non-Euclidean space developed since the inception of modern cinema. This fractal order of the narrative can also be seen in some websites in which the narrative derives from a path crossing many different scales. This can be expressed through the presence of many different media converging into the digital medium (e.g. harmony between text, images, music and moving pictures) or between a viewer's creation of semiotic chains (e.g. YouTube's video suggestion).

|Prop. IV| The fractal logic of the narrative in the audiovisual field is manifested as the shaping of the infinite amount of information present in the database. As noted by Manovich, the digital medium brought the concept of interface – within other media, the work and the database were the same – allowing the separation of the content of the work and the interface and thus making possible the creation of different interfaces for the same database. This phenomenon can also be seen in every video editing program (Final Cut, Premier and so forth) in which the editing process is based on the creation of the database from which the editor establishes links between elements,

---

48 | In narrative, the algorithm can be understood as the reconstruction of the logic that the writer used to create the events.

49 | Manovich L. 2007, p. 44.

50 | Manovich L. 2007, p. 44.

thus producing a topologic space. In this space, he/she designs a "trajectory leading from one element to another."[51] The database can be changed by adding new elements from different media, and from the same database many interfaces can derive, that is, many different trajectories can derive from it. Certainly, this phenomenon accentuates the externalization of the database. It makes explicit the fractalization of the audiovisual narrative. One can also see a kind of mechanization of the narrative due to the fractalization of the narrative space. As noted above, the most important part of the narrative is focused on the recollection of information, i.e. in the generating of the database. Thus, the structure of the narrative developed by the author start to be simplified by "plug-ins," which mechanize the narrative, giving predominant importance to the quantity of information stored in the database. It is important to note that these "plug-ins" respond to transformations of the geometric forms, which are systematized manipulations of mathematical functions. Its first appearance, as noted by Manovich can be found in the films of John Whitney Sr., e.g. *Permutations* (1967)[52] (Fig. 3.55).

|*Fig. 3.55*|

When audiovisual narrative is focused on the creation of a database, an infinite multidimensional set of information, then the narrative act consists of spatializing the database. As noted by Manovich, the narrative act consists of distributing and correlating elements in the space[53] – to be more precise, in the fractal space. This new character of the audiovisual narrative places us in front of a phenomenon that was for a long time thought to be intrinsic and exclusive to writing. The hypertextuality of the audiovisual space, which recalls in some way the transformation undergone by the written text through the use of digital word processors, such as Microsoft Word.

---

51 | Manovich L. 2007, p. 49.
52 | Manovich L. 2007, p. 53.
53 | Manovich L. 2007, p. 55.

3.5 HYPERTEXT: A DIGITAL EPISTEME

In his work, *Writing Space,* published in 1991, David J. Bolter highlights the hypertextual character of the written text. In the section devoted to hypertext,[1] he focuses his attention on the role played by association. In any text, he posits, "one word echoes another; one sentence of paragraph recalls others earlier in the text and looks forward to still others."[2] The act of writing is understood as the creation of a network of 'verbal elements' in which the development of a hierarchy plays a fundamental role by structuring the spatial order of the text as well as the order of the ideas. For instance, in the modern book, the table of contents defines the hierarchy. However, whereas the hierarchy established by the table of contents represents an arborescent structure, the index establishes a network. It reflects in this sense a database. Borrowing Bolter's words:

"In one sense the index defines other books that could be constructed from the materials at hand, other themes that the author could have formed into an analytical narrative, and so invites the reader to read the book in alternative ways."[3]

|Prop. X| We can see that the hypertextual link manifests a thousand-year-old idea to gather, file and preserve knowledge, which could only be fully realized through digital technology. Through the electric technologies and then digital technologies, the former encyclopedism changes due to the possibility of the reader to create links and store them, making the text a space in continuous change, a space in becoming. Hence digital technology transforms the database in an embracing entity in which mankind is completely submerged. As noted by Lyotard, the database becomes the 'nature.'[4]

But before mankind could submerge in this info-sphere, it was necessary to overcome the arborescent structure of the text and to develop a real network.

The first attempt to do so is represented by Vannevar Bush's *Memex,* an engine able to store knowledge in a simulation of the human mind. Vannevar's aim was to create a real network based on the capacity of association of the human mind.

"The real heart of the matter of selection, however, goes deeper than a lag in the adoption of mechanisms by libraries, or a lack of development of devices for their use. Our ineptitude in getting at the record is largely caused by the artificiality of systems of index-

---

1 | The term *Hypertext* was coined by Theodor H. Nelson in the 60s. By it, he meant non-sequential writing, or, "as popularly conceived, this is a series of text chunks connected by links which offer the reader different pathways." See literary Machines 0/2.

2 | Bolter J. D. 1991, p. 22.

3 | Bolter J. D. 1991, p. 22.

4 | "L'encyclopédie de demain, ce sont les banques de données. Elles excèdent la capacité de chaque utilisateur. Elle sont la « nature » pour l'homme postmoderne." (Lyotard J.-F. 1979, pp. 84-85.)

ing. When data of any sort are placed in storage, they are filed alphabetically or numerically, and information is found (when it is) by tracing it down from subclass to subclass. It can be in only one place, unless duplicates are used; one has to have rules as to which path will locate it, and the rules are cumbersome. Having found one item, moreover, one has to emerge from the system and re-enter on a new path. The human mind does not work that way. It operates by association. With one item in its grasp, it snaps instantly to the next that is suggested by the association of thoughts, in accordance with some intricate web of trails carried by the cells of the brain."[5]

Memex was a device "in which an individual stores all his books, records, and communications, and which is mechanized so that it may be consulted with exceeding speed and flexibility. It is an enlarged intimate supplement to his memory."[6]
|Prop. VII| The hypertextual network, being an entity in continuous becoming, can be extended indefinitely. The network can create a web of topics (recalling the etymology of the word *topos* τόπος, Greek 'place') without following any hierarchy.[7] Indeed, in a digital hypertext there is no hierarchy but the design of a space. As remarked by Bolter, "we have a writing that is not topical: we might also call it 'topographic.'[8] Thus, electronic writing represents a visual description whose many links and quality of space in becoming required an analysis in spatial terms. As a diagrammatic space, the hypertext realized through electronic writing develops a network from which derives a kind of diegetic time.

We are dealing with nonlinear texts that recall some fractal characteristics as well as topologic properties. The nonlinearity of the text[9] represents a work "that does not present its scriptons[10] in one fixed sequence, whether temporal or spatial."[11] Consequently, a non linear text develops a different kind of dynamic in which, following Aarseth, "the contents of scriptons may change while the number of textons remains fixed (*intratextonic* dynamics), or the number of textons may vary as well (*textonic* dynamics)."[12] Thus, a nonlinear text develops many semiotic chains; it creates a 'gal-

---

5 | Bush V. 1945.

6 | Bush V. 1945.

7 | It is interesting to note that Deleuze-Guattari developed their *Mille plateaux* as a hypertext, or a book composed of communicating plateaus, and they compared the intercommunicability of those plateaus to a brain. Further, in this sense, the structure of their book reflects their concept of Rhizome developed in the same volume. See Deleuze G. – Guattari F. 1980.

8 | Bolter J.D. 1991, p. 25.

9 | As noted by Aarseth, this concept derives from the mathematical branch of topology.

10 | The term scripton is defined by Aarseth as "an unbroken sequence of one or more *textons* as they are projected by the text." (Aarseth E.J. 1994, p. 61). *Texton* denotes a basic element of textuality.

11 | Aarseth E.J. 1994, p. 61.

12 | Aarseth E.J. 1994, p. 61.

axy of signifiers and not a structure of signifieds' through the infinite ways and possibilities of linking topics. This phenomenon was described by Barthes as follows:

"Interpréter un texte, ce n'est pas lui donner un sens (plus ou moins fondé, plus ou moins libre), c'est au contraire apprécier de quel pluriel il est fait. Posons d'abord l'image d'un pluriel triomphant, que ne vient appauvrir aucune contrainte de représentation (d'imitation). Dans ce texte idéal, les réseaux sont multiples et jouent entre eux, sans qu'aucun puisse coiffer les autres ; ce texte est une galaxie de signifiants, non une structure de signifiés ; il n'a pas de commencement ; il est réversible ; on y accède par plusieurs entrées dont aucune ne peut être à coup sûr déclarée principale ; les codes qu'il mobilise se profilent *à perte de vue*, ils sont indécidables (le sens n'y est jamais soumis à un principe de décision, sinon par coup de dés) ; de ce texte absolument pluriel, les systèmes de sens peuvent s'emparer, mais leur nombre n'est jamais clos, ayant pour mesure l'infini du langage."[13]

This possibility responds to the human necessity of embracing huge amounts of information. As noted by Bush, the existent quantity of information surpasses the human capacity of embracing it in its totality. Thus, through the *memex* – or Nelson's hypertext – mankind finds a fundamental tool that enables us to locate information, generate information and follow different conceptual sets in the same database. However, the non-existence of enclosed systems in narrative goes further through digital technology.[14] The development of fractionary dimensions between objects in *presentia* and objects in *absentia* externalizes the database. What in the writing text was an allusion – a metaobject – through digital linking became a presence in the interface, a fractal object. This last phenomenon completely changed the organization of narrative spaces. As noted above, the externalization of database theorized by Eco shows another way to see narrative. Eco noted how Aristotle's thoughts about narrative started to be overcome in contemporary narrative. Through digital technology – mainly the hypertextuality offered by this technology – the basis of Aristotle's concepts on the definition of plot radically changes. For instance, just think about the definition that Aristotle gives to plot, in which the plot "must not therefore begin and end at random(...)"[15] The text no longer represents a definite magnitude that spans from a beginning to an end. It creates a non-linear text.[16] From my point of view, the *horror*

---

13 | Barthes R. 1970, pp. 11-12.

14 | One can see that Bergson's theories of the non-existence of closed systems were also applied in texts, for example, see Foucault M. 1969, especially *Les régularités discursives*, pp. 29-54.

15 | Aristotle, *The Poetics*, 1450b (Translation: Fyfe H.W. 1965.)

16 | It is interesting to note that one of the characteristics of the Rhizome described by Deleuze-Guattari is that each plateau can be read starting anywhere and it can also link to any other part. See Deleuze G. - Guattari F. 1980.

vacui plays a fundamental role in the structure of the classical plot.[17] If we consider that Aristotle theorized the necessary sequence of events as fundamental or essential in the construction of plot,[18] then we could assume that the non-narrative moments of contemporary narrative, exemplified in cinema by Antonioni's *L'avventura*, represent the *fear of an empty space*. In Aristotle's words, it represents 'the worst.'[19]

|**Prop. XI**| The *horror vacui* in narrative is the absence of linearity in the development of the plot and it was avoided by both the linearity of the narrative imposed by the medium and by the linearity of the narrative structure. If we assume that the development of a narrative space acquires some topologic qualities, we start to create the narrative space through different ways of linking subjects or objects. Assuming that every text, sentence or object can be linked to any other is to assume the nonexistence of vacuum. Consequently, contrary to the printed book, which determines a beginning in the series of pages – which does not necessarily mean that the reader follows this prefixed order[20] – the electronic text, through the spatial character and the infinite ways of linking, makes vacuum impossible.

The spatialization of the digital hypertext can also be observed in the way digital hypertext solved the problem of the non-linearity of plot, in other words, the absence of a well-defined beginning and end. As noted by Landow, digital hypertext 'solved' the problem of the beginning and end in the text by "offering the reader a lexia labeled something like 'start here' that combines functions of title page, introduction, and opening paragraph."[21] Thus, following Landow, the 'sequence of events' described by Aristotle, in our digital context, starts to become "a quality of the individual reader's experience within a single lexia and his or her experience following a path, even if that path curves back on itself or heads in strange directions."[22]

On the one hand, the digital medium, and in particular its immateriality, displaces the sequentiality of the page-turning chain. On the other hand, the narrative structure has to face the multidimensional character – a multidimensionality that also accepts images and sounds – as well as the nature in becoming, represented by its capacity to generate infinite links and to accept infinite quantities of information. Borrowing Coover's words, the "hypertextual story space is now multidimensional and theoretically infinite, with an equally infinite set of possible network linkages,

---

17 | Another interesting figure used by Murria is the labyrinth, see Murria J.H. 1997. The author also develops an interesting in-depth analysis of non-linear narratives from the electronic medium.

18 | See Aristotle, *The Poetics* (Translation: Fyfe H.W. 1965.)

19 | See Aristotle, *The Poetics* 1451b. (Translation: Fyfe H.W. 1965.)

20 | Some novels also present different ways to read; that is to say, they present different narrative structures, for instance, Cortazar's *Rayuela*, in which the reader is invited to chose one of the two lecture sequences proposed by the author. See, Cortázar J. 2008.

21 | Landow G.P. 2006, p. 227.

22 | Landow G.P. 2006, p. 221.

either programmed, fixed or variable, or random, or both."[23] In addition, the openness of the text allows the reader (or viewer) to introduce new elements, which can be sounds, images, links or texts, thus converting the text into a multidimensional entity in becoming.[24] Hence, the state of becoming of the written text blurs the boundaries between reader and writer.[25]

|Prop. XII, XXVII| The so-called *hyperfiction* represents an interesting example of a narrative structure in becoming. Consider for instance *Hotel*, developed at the Brown University, a narrative structure recalling the universality of the *Sierpinski Carpet*.[26] In this narrative, the reader could add a new room to the fiction, even change the narrative structure and delete the former structure created by other readers. Another interesting example is the program *Storyspace* in which the authors provide to the reader some paths and menus.

The structure in becoming not only dissolves the linearity established by the beginning and the end of the plot but also, as remarked by Eco, by dealing with the contemporary narrative in the audiovisual field, undoes the narrative knots that tie the classical narrative structure theorized by Aristotle. That is to say, the characters as well as the plot no longer respond to equilibrate the 'disequilibrium' – in other words, to accomplish the character's aims, or to follow the laws of cause and effect.[27] This is a phenomenon that Deleuze identified in the cinematography of modern cinema and compared to the development of non-Euclidean geometries. Following the theoretic framework developed in the present work, we can consider that classical narrative reflects Euclidean geometry. A classical narrative cannot accept irregular phenomena, chaos or non-linear vectors. It is 'afraid' of non-linearity and 'non-narrative' times. For the classical narrative, chaos is synonymous with disorder; it does not represent an infinite set of possibilities. One can also posit that the traditional development of the plot, like Euclidean geometry (see *Fractus, Fracta, Fractum*), distances nature of our representation of it. It idealizes in such a sense what nature really is and creates a kind of parallel world. Borrowing from Landow:

"we experience the narrative as removed from our physical world, and therefore as we enter the narrative world, we imaginatively and experientially leave our own to the extent to which we immerse ourselves in the story; when we return to our physically and emo-

---

23 | Quoted by Landow G.P. 2006, p. 221.

24 | For an in-depth analysis of linearity and its relationship with technology, see Großklaus G. 2003.

25 | See Barthes R. 1970.

26 | Peitgen H.O. – Jürgens H. – Saupe D. 1992, pp. 112-121.

27 | It is important to remember that the plot (or syuzhet) is a system. In Brodwell's words, "The syuzhet is a system because it arranges components – the story events and states of affairs – according to specific principles." Also, "Syuzhet' names the architectonic of the film's presentation of the fabula." (Bordwell D. 1985, p. 50.)

tionally existing world, we may bring the emotions, attitudes, and ideas of the story back with us and thus experience our everyday world in a somewhat different way."[28]

However, when one conceives narrative as a spatial organization, one starts in some way to recognize the irregularity of nature and the irregularity of life. This is the case for Jeremy Hight's *34 North 118 West,* in which the narrative structure is the city. In this project, a map of the city represents the narrative structure, which in turn, gives access to the many narratives placed in the city. The viewer uses a G.P.S. unit, which enters his or her real position into the database (the city and the narratives therein). In addition, at precise places, numerous "hot spots" allow the viewer to listen to recorded, fictional narratives.[29] While walking the city, the viewer is confronted with different sounds from different places and times. According to Landow, Hight's project changes the cause and effect laws through the assumption of the city as a narrative structure:

"One of Hight's most interesting points is that a 'fictional narrative is an agitated space.' Ever since Aristotle, students of narrative have understood that it involves disequilibrium and disturbance, for the antagonist, whether person, place, or thing that blocks the main character, in essence creates the story. With no obstacle there is no story. Instead of simply emphasizing the process – and hence the temporal, sequential aspect of narrative – Hight also conceives it in more spatial terms. A story, for him, is a storyworld; or perhaps one might say that narrative requires a world within which to take place. Furthermore, he points out that a 'city is also an agitated space' that exist as 'data and sub-text to be read in the context of ethnography, history, semiotics, architectural patterns and forms, physical form and rhythm, juxtaposition, city planning, land usage shifts and other ways of interpretation and analysis. The city patterns can be equated to the patterns within literature: repetition, sub-text shift, metaphor, cumulative resonances, emergence of layers, decay and growth."[30]

This example, which physically places the viewer into the database, develops a narrative fundamentally based on the distribution of narrative objects in the space. Thus, as one can see, it makes the city – that is, the narrative space of the database – a "rich palimpsest of human meanings and experiences."[31] Further, in this way, the narrative, seen as a pure spatial organization, a navigable database, brings narrative closer to the experience our everyday world.

From this discussion emerges the problem of the differences between hypertext and hypermedia. Hypertext enables us to link words, sentences, images, sounds and geographic locations developed by satellite images. For this reason, Landow notes that

---

28 | Landow G.P. 2006, p. 247.
29 | Landow G.P. 2006, p. 247.
30 | Landow G.P. 2006, p. 248.
31 | Landow G.P. 2006, p. 249.

in the network generated by digital hypertext the terms hypermedia and hypertext can be used interchangeably.[32] However, if we consider that the hypertextuality in a written text derives from the visual character and the multidimensionality of the text enabled by digital technology, then the phenomenon of hypertextuality described above would differ from the hypertextuality theorized in printed text, as in Barthes' theory. Contrary to digital hypertextuality or, to follow strictly the theory here exposed, the fractality of the narrative space, the hypertextuality theorized by Barthes remains an application of the non-existence of completely enclosed systems. The hypertextuality of a printed text can be just an allusion, due to the materiality of the medium.[33] If so, it is important to create a different terminology.

As noted above, the term hypertext, coined in the 60s by Nelson, basically designates non-sequential writing that offers to the reader different pathways. But we also noted that this kind of experience could be offered to the reader by a printed book (see, for instance, Cortázar's *Rayuela*[34]). Another interesting aspect noted by Nelson is the connectivity of text. Certainly, this characteristic of hypertext highlighted by Nelson derived from his project of electronic text and it is not materially possible in a printed book. We also noted that digital technology radically changes the connectivity of the text. Further, it strongly combines hypermedia to hypertext to the point of confusing the two terms. In fact, a digital hypertext naturally tries to create a multidimensional space in which different media are combined. Images, sounds and sentences are combined in a digital hypertext due to the visual character that the written text acquires in the digital field. According to Genette, hypertextuality is "toute relation unissant un texte B (que j'appellerai *hypertext*) à un texte antérieur A (que j'appellerai, bien sûr, *hypotexte*) sur lequel il se greffe d'une manière qui n'est pas celle du commentaire."[35] He continues by positing that:

"J'appelle donc hypertexte tout texte dérivé d'un texte antérieur par transformation simple (nous dirons désormais *transformation* tout court) ou par transformation indirecte : nous dirons *imitation*."[36]

Genette also notes that a hypertext can be a note in the text as well as *transtextualités* between different genres. In other words, a hypertext can be considered: a) the relationship between texts; and b) the conceptual relationships, citations, mimetic, and

---

32 | Landow G.P. 2006, p. 3.

33 | This characteristic of the text is also highlighted by Kristeva and designated as text productivity (*Productivité*). According to Kristeva, the text is a "permutation de textes, une intertextualité: dans l'espace d'un texte plusieurs énoncés, pris à d'autres textes, se croisent et se neutralisent." (Kristeva J. 1969, p. 52.)

34 | For an in-depth analysis of non-linear text and *Ergodic* literature, see Aarseth E.J. 1997.

35 | Genette G. 1982, p. 13.

36 | Genette G. 1982, p. 16.

so on. Without doubt, many conceptual links derive from all the texts in the world. Every text influences another. He defines that as *'l'aspect universel de la litterarité,'* which means, in his words, that:

"il n'est pas d'œuvre littéraire qui, à quelque degré et selon les lectures, n'en évoque quelque autre et, en ce sens, toutes les œuvres sont hypertextuelles. Mais, comme les égaux d'Orwell, certaines le sont plus (ou plus manifestement, massivement explicitement) que d'autres : *Virgile travesti*, disons, plus que les *Confessions* de Rousseau. Moins l'hypertextualité d'une œuvre est massive et déclarée, plus son analyse dépend d'un jugement constitutif, voire d'une décision interprétative du lecteur : je puis décider que les *Confessions* de Rousseau sont un remake actualisé de celles de saint Augustin, et que leur titre en est l'indice contractuel – après quoi les confirmations de détail ne manqueront pas, simple affaire d'ingéniosité critique. Je puis également traquer dans n'importe quelle œuvre les échos partiels, localisés et fugitives de n'importe quelle autre, antérieur ou postérieur."[37]

Due to the breadth of the concept and in order to narrow its meaning, Genette limited the term hypertext to its primary meaning: i.e., a text B that derives from a text A. As one can see, there is the necessity to draw a difference between the concept of hypertext, which recalls Nelson's term and the hypertext discussed in formalistic studies from, for example, Levy-Strauss, Barthes, and also Genette's ideas and a concept of hypertext that recognizes the multidimensionality of the narrative space made possible by digital technology. As noted above, Landow overcame this terminological problem by avoiding the distinction between hypertext and hypermedia and by understanding the hypertext as an episteme, an episteme of postmodernism.[38] Indeed, the concept of hypertextuality, developed during the twentieth century, is the product of cultural, scientific and artistic changes that occurred at the end of nineteenth century, and these changes are designated as postmodern.[39] An important characteristic of postmodernism is that, through the construction of narrative, it "raffine notre sensibilité aux différences et renforce notre capacité de supporter l'incommensurable."[40] According to Lyotard, the narrative form represents the formation of knowledge (*savoir*), where the knowledge consists of not only denotational statements but it also includes:

---

37 | Genette G. 1982, pp. 18-19.

38 | It is interesting to quote at this point Foucault's words about the challenges of his period. In fact he describes his *époque* as *l'époque de l'espace.* Foucault posits that: "Nous sommes à un moment où le monde s'éprouve, je crois, moins comme une grande vie qui se développerait à travers le temps, que comme un réseau qui relie des points et qui entrecroise son écheveau." (Foucault M. 1984. p. 46.)

39 | Lyotard J.-F. 1979, p. 7.

40 | Lyotard J.-F. 1979, p. 9.

"les idées de savoir-faire, de savoir-vivre, de savoir-écouter, etc. Il s'agit alors d'une compétence qui excède la détermination et l'application du seul critère de la vérité, et qui s'étend à celles des critères d'efficience (qualification technique), de justice et/ou de bonheur (sagesse éthique), de beauté sonore, chromatique (sensibilité auditive, visuelle), etc."[41]

|Prop. IV| Thus, the narrative, according to Lyotard, creates the social ties by sharing and developing a set of pragmatic rules.[42] Posmodernism recognizes the creation of new narratives – narratives that generate and support scientific knowledge – new rules and new ways of articulating languages as a fundamental aim of the development of scientific research. The postmodern thought recognizes determinism[43] as the central problem of the production of knowledge, and proposes a change of paradigm in which the concept of system changes. The idea of a stable system in which the relation between input and output are computable as a matter of principle disappears, as well as the idea that one knows all the variables of every phenomenon (see *Some Words About Chaos*).[44] This change of system is exemplified by the change of the scientific aim. That is to say, under the deterministic logic, *to discover* is synonymous to determining a perfect order for a complex phenomenon. Borrowing from Morin, "un Ordre parfait légiférant une machine perpétuelle (le cosmos) elle-même faite des micro-éléments (les atomes) diversement assemblés en objets et systèmes."[45]

The recognition of chaotic phenomena generated interest in the many fields in which the irregularity appears. As noted in the first part of this text, the scientific

---

41 | Lyotard J.-F. 1979, p. 36.

42 | Lyotard J.-F. 1979, p. 40.

43 | Determinism is defined by Lyotard as follows: "Le déterminisme est l'hypothèse sur laquelle repose la légitimation par la performativité : celle-ci se définissant par un rapport input/output, il faut supposer que le système dans lequel on fait entrer l'input est à l'état stable ; il obéit à une « trajectoire » régulière dont on peut établir la fonction continue et dérivable qui permettra d'anticiper convenablement l'output." (Lyotard J.-F. 1979, p. 88.)

44 | Mandelbrot expressed the same problem as follows: "Afin de suggérer quels objets doivent être considérés comme fractals, commençons donc par nous souvenir que, dans son effort pour décrire le monde, la science procède par des séries d'images ou modèles de plus en plus « réalistes ». Les plus simples sont des continus parfaitement homogènes, tels un fil ou un cosmos de densité uniforme, ou un fluide de température, densité, pression et vitesse également uniformes. La physique a pu triompher en identifiant de nombreux domaines où de telles images sont extrêmement utiles, en particulier comme points de départ de divers termes correctif. Mais dans d'autres domaines la réalité se révèle être si irrégulier, que le modèle continu parfaitement homogène déçoit, et qu'il ne peut même pas servir comme première approximation." (Mandelbrot B. 1995, pp. 6-7.)

45 | Morin E. 2005, p. 19.

world started to study the limits of precision, the conflicts and the paradoxes. And, according to Lyotard, all these studies characterize the postmodern. He also affirms that through this interest the postmodern science:

"change le sens du mot savoir, et elle dit comment ce changement peut avoir lieu. Elle produit non pas du connu, mais de l'inconnu. Et elle suggère un modèle de légitimation qui n'est nullement celui de la meilleure performance, mais celui de la différence comprise comme paralogie."[46]

Thus, the change of *savoir* generates a change in the notion of system, in which it is possible to conceive the *unitas multiplex*; that is, "la conjonction de l'un et du multiple."[47]

Scientific thought influences, through the new notion of system, the organization of narrative spaces. In the present work, I noted how science, by improving the instruments of analysis, shapes the ways of structuring narrative. Throughout this text, I dealt with the transformation of nature by mankind. I analyzed the machine – and the mechanization of processes – as a fundamental element linking this eternal relationship. Thus, I proposed technique and technology as a translation tool that mediates the relationship between object and subject. My interest in geometry in the first part of this text was focused on its capacity to translate natural objects and phenomena. In this respect, perspective represented an interesting 'bridge' linking the scientific translation of nature (the geometry) to the field of pictorial representations – thus, artistic expression. We noted how the mechanization of this technique allowed the creation of a device (the camera obscura) that simulates the same mechanism. We also analyzed how the machine started to create a different relationship with nature in which mankind became alienated. We analyzed it through the Marxist concept of praxis, through which it is possible to understand how technology acquired supremacy thanks to a complex articulation of phenomena, which can be summarized in three steps:

- technology as a means to resolve human needs;
- technology as a primary aim of science in order to improve science; and
- technology as the only means to develop knowledge, and thus only means to analyze nature.

In these three steps, one can see that technology starts not only to represent a means but also an aim. I think that this process generated a complex phenomenon of codification of nature by the machine, a phenomenon that placed mankind into a state of total dependence on the machine. This phenomenon was highlighted in this text by

---

46 | Lyotard J.-F. 1979, p. 97.
47 | Morin E. 2005, p. 19. Morin also differentiates the complex thought from determinism by arguing that determinism or, in his words, '*la pensée simplifiante*', unifies by deleting the diversity, or juxtaposes without conceiving the unity.

the fundamental role played by the computer. In the long process analyzed throughout this text, every visual medium analyzed faced the irregularity of nature and, in it, found its limits. As noted in all the cases studied above, every visual medium generated the feeling of reaching the 'perfect objectivity' in representing natural objects and phenomena. However, even though the interest in irregularity and chaotic movements was always present – for instance, Marey's studies on chaotic movements through photography – neither technology nor philosophy could understand and accept Chaos. Digital technology, by creating a higher codification of natural phenomena, as well as by allowing for the development of fractal geometry, represents to mankind a fundamental instrument to deal with those phenomena and shapes that do not respond to the deterministic thoughts that had accompanied mankind over centuries. As analyzed above, every technological improvement introduced a new concept of system, a new way to structure the environment, a new way to organize the knowledge and, thus, a new way of expressing ideas, a new way of telling events, a new way of representing the world – in other words, it affected our cognitive processes.

If we assume (being McLuhan's disciple) that every medium, and thus every technological improvement, has its own message, which is recognized in the transformation that it exerts on social relationships, on the human relationship with nature, we have to assume that the hypertext in our digital context responds to a different need and allows different performances than the hypertextual phenomenon analyzed by Barthes and Genette. It is then also possible to understand Landow's ideas of hypertext as an episteme – thus a concept that also embrace hypermedia – or as an hybrid, or a bridge between the hypertext proposed by Barthes and the phenomenon we deal with in our everyday life in the World Wide Web.

|Prop. VII| It is important to remember that the word hypertext was coined in a context highly influenced by electric media. It is possible to assume, following a McLuhan's logic, that the hypertext derived directly from the influence that electric media exerted on the organization of knowledge. Hence, one can assume that digital technology remediate in this field the hypertextual character of the printed text. However, the problem emerges when we use the term hypertext to describe not only the ways of storing and organizing information as an encyclopedia – e.g. Wikipedia – but also to describe the practice of giving an hypertextual form to the development of plot, as well as to describe the development of plot by means of many different media. Of course, if we consider that the term hypertext refers to the episteme that guides the articulation of verbal and non-verbal information, we can accept this statement. However, if we follow the development of this way of organizing narrative spaces as well as the ways of storing and linking, we would see that at a given moment, the written text starts to follow the same process that we analyzed in the last chapters regarding the audiovisual narrative and what we called the fractalization of the narrative space. Hence, one can consider the term hypertext as relative to the field of writing – to the printed book. When this form of composing a written text acquires clear spatial notions and develops a multidimensional space in which one can deal with different media (e.g. images, video, sounds, text) we consider this phenomenon, generated by

digital technology, a fractal text, and its organization aimed at developing a plot, as fractal narrative. Fractal narrative is consequently a narrative that finds its best accomplished form in the Web. And the improvements on the Web, for instance the *Web 2.0*,[48] improved fractal narrative. With the development of the web, the primary aim of which was to develop a hypertext, the written text started to be seen as a visual and multidimensional space that is navigable. This transformation was an answer to the confusion that readers had to face while navigating large networks.[49] In fact, during the Nineties, some systems started to address the problem by developing maps of the structure of the hypertext networks, like the *NoteCards* developed at Xerox Parc by Randall Trig, Thomas Moran and Frank Halasz. As remarked by Shipman, those hypertext maps dislodged the user's main interaction with the hypertext from a document viewer to a network map.[50] He also noted some interesting changes derived from the move from a document-centered hypertext system to map-based hypertext system. In his words:

"relations between nodes could be expressed in more than one way. Maps showed interconnectedness explicitly, usually in the form of a direct graph. But also node proximity came into play; relationships among different nodes or documents could be indicated simply on the basis of their relative location."[51]

From that moment onwards, hypertext acquired a stronger spatial character; it started to design a strictly fractal narrative space. In fact, a new term arose to define the new nature of some hypertexts favoring spatial indications in the structure. These systems that developed a new method of interacting with information were called Spatial Hypertext Systems. Consider for instance VKB (Visual Knowledge Builder) or VIKI, a system that "dispensed with visible link structure and made spatial manipulation and grouping the central action provided to the user. Working in the background, an algorithmic spatial parser highlighted incipient groupings."[52] The spatial character of theses systems provided easy access to the structure of the network. The benefits of Spatial Hypertext were summarized by Shipman as follows:

"(1) It takes advantage of people's considerable visual recognition and intelligence; (2) it facilitates constructive ambiguity; (3) it supports emerging problem-solving strategies; and (4) it reduces overhead in communicating with others."[53]

---

48 | For a more in-depth discussion on this topic, see O'Reilly T. 2005.

49 | See Conklin J. 1987.

50 | See Shipman III, F.M. 1999.

51 | See Shipman III, F.M. 1999. It is possible to note in this quotation an interesting analogy with the words of Grassmann about the continuous form analyzed above (see *Toward Fractality*).

52 | Kolb D. 2009.

53 | Shipman, III F.M. 1999.

This system transforms the text in an area of recognition in which the reader traces paths through linking. Thus, the spatial hypertext provides incentives for the expansion of the network. The reader starts to create and to expand the hypertext through linking, recalling the art of geodesy. Further, this cartographic system generates the disappearance of links, or the explicit relationships between nodes, by developing an abstract way of structuring information.[54] In addition, the phenomenon generated by these practices decentralized the text. In other words, the reader in this geodesic-reading-act continually shifts the center of the research.[55] The center, at this point, changes; it no longer represents a being, but a function adequate to the reader, recalling a concept of topologic spaces and fractal geometry. Thus, since VIKI, the goal was to connect those systems to the Web in order to totally de-centralize the text.[56]

The spatial hypertext responds to the need to chart infinity. Further, the spatial relations performed by these systems suggest internal connections, likenesses and separations that generate meanings.[57] In this spatial continuous form, the items are not characterized by their position in the *complexus,* but by the articulation of its bonding (*Verknüpfen*), generation (*Erzeugen*) and positioning (*Setzen*). Due to its continuous form, the space acquires a multidimensional character in which movement, location and generation of items can be recognized. Kolb compares the spatial character of the hypertext to Leibniz's concept of space derived from the recognition of monads (see *Self-Similarity: Fold Into Fold*). He affirms that:

"Leibniz's relational space has become quite familiar to us. It behaves like a pure node-and-link hypertext. It is the spatiality of web pages relating to one another. The spatiality of the web is created by the prior relations between the items that fill it. The web's link structure is not located **in** any other space. There is no prior space locating web pages externally; their relations are created by their links. They generate a spatiality of near and far, with perspectives from a given node toward other nodes."[58]

However, the fractal narrative took its first step in the audiovisual field. Like the phenomenon of the externalization of the database analyzed above, the video image, thanks to satellite and cable transmissions, generated the feeling of possessing an endless space in constant becoming. This phenomenon was understood by Cubbit as the incessant flow of TV broadcasting, where the VCR played a fundamental role. It is possible to consider that the incessant flow of images in TV represents an infinite

---

54 | It is interesting to see that Landow compares the hypertext to Borges's *Aleph* because "from the vantage point each provides one can see everything else." (Landow G.P. 2006, pp. 57.) Or in Borges's words "el lugar donde están, sin confundirse, todos los lugares del orbe, vistos desde todos los ángulos." (Borges J.L. 1997⁹, p. 188.)

55 | See Landow G.P. 2006, p. 56.

56 | See Shipman III. F.M. – Furuta R. – Marshall C.C. 1997.

57 | See Kolb D. 2009.

58 | Kolb D. 2009.

database in a state of continuous becoming, and that the VCR represents a kind of device that brings those images into *presentia*. The VCR develops a kind of interface through the editing that one can accomplish though it. Cubitt affirms that "[t]he domestic video cassette recorder (VCR) is itself a kind of production device, as it can be for seizing moments from TV's incessant flow, compiling, crash editing."[59] Further, according to Cubitt, the organization of the infinite space – or database – through the VCR required a kind of alphabetization of the viewer, a new kind of capacity of the citizen to organize a narrative and an infinite space.[60] He argues:

"[t]hese complex modes of storytelling in video – spatial orientation, time orientation, knowing who to believe and who to disbelieve – demands equally complex work on the part of the viewers..."[61]

Certainly, the viewer started to develop a new way of articulating narrative in the fractal narrative space, and this practice became clearer with the development of digital technology, mainly with the development of the Web. Thus, if we assume that the development of the Web as database generates a space in continuous becoming, it could be possible to compare this continuum to a fractal space. Database as initiator and interface – understood as the design of links between the objects – as a generator are able to develop an infinite fractal narrative space. Further, editing, seen as the choice of narrative spaces to be placed in *presentia*, changed under the influence of technological improvements. We noted how digital technology, by externalizing the database, developed a new kind of narrative space. The same phenomenon is noted in literature as *ergotic* – a Greek term from physics coined by Aarseth, deriving from *ergon* 'work' and *hodos* 'path' – and after the use of digital technology in the audiovisual field, it could also be discerned in audiovisual narrative – for instance, in some audiovisual narratives that allow the viewer to choose a narrative direction at key points in the story. This branch of digital filmmaking is usually called *hypertext cinema*.[62] Landow recognizes another branch of digital filmmaking in which, contrary to *hypertext cinema*, "the filmmaker or a computer program decides the order in which the audience views the segments."[63] He terms this kind of filmmaking *randomized* or *multiple cinema*. An interesting example of this is represented by Ian Flitman's *Hackey Girl* (2003), a "video-wall diary describing the artist's journey from Hackney London, where there are significant immigrant populations of Turkish extraction, to

---

59 | Cubitt S. 1991, p. 4.

60 | It is interesting to note that the VCR had an immense popular success because it enables personalizing the broadcasting. In fact, it represents a first step to the end of the hegemony of the hertzian broadcast. See Stiegler B. 2009.

61 | Cubitt S, 1991, p.6.

62 | See Landow G.P. 2006, especially *Digitizing the Movies: Interactive versus Multiplied Cinema*.

63 | Landow G.P. 2006, p. 255.

Istanbul in Turkey where he decided to live. It is a love story documenting the artistic involvement with Hackney Girl's eponymous heroine, Yasemin Güvenç, a Turkish actress, who went back to Istanbul to work."[64] This film presents at the beginning a black screen with a collage of sub-sets in which only one contains a video. The viewer encounters more than a hundred sections 'edited by the computer'; that is to say, every screening shows a different order of the plot construction. It can start either with the young woman leaving London for Istanbul or with the couple's life in London. Another example, which presents another level of *ergodic* audiovisual narrative, is Bonilla's *Limbo*, the second part of *A Space of Time*.[65] *Limbo* is based on QuickTime VR (or QTVR – *QuickTime Virtual Reality*) technology that allows the author to create panoramic images, or nodes, in which single objects can be linked together creating a 360° navigable space. The author defined *Limbo* as "una narrativa interactiva en la que los usuarios deben de navegar en un ambiente virtual para extraer de él las escenas que componen la historia."[66] *Limbo* presents two versions: in the first, a statistical algorithm organizes the order of the scenes, and in the second, the order is determined by the navigation pattern of the user. In this space, the viewer, by moving the mouse, navigates inside an old building.

Another interesting phenomenon is the transformation of the narrative space in formats still using linear film stock. As we will see in the next chapter, film narratives have also shown new ways of articulating the plot, ways clearly influenced by the fractality developed within digital technology, especially the web.

---

64 | From the website www.blipstation.com in which one can find a lower resolution version of the film.

65 | *A Space of Time* is presented by Bonilla as follows: "A Space of Time is not a story, it is a space that contains one. David, the main narrator, is a homeless person who has found shelter in a century-old abandoned building. Once settled he starts suffering temporal lobe epileptic attacks and having visual and auditory hallucinations. Reality then becomes a mix between his past, the building's past and their common present. As he explores and inhabits the aged structure he comes to believe that it contains fragments of time, and that these fragments narrate instances of the people who have entered it. Through a series of interviews, David cleverly intertwines his life and the stories he believes are held inside 'the container". From hypergraphia.wikispaces.com

66 | Bonilla D. 2006.

3.6 TOWARD A STRICT FRACTAL NARRATIVE

|Prop. IV| In the last chapters we dealt with the fragmentation of the audiovisual narrative space. Deleuze's works on cinema not only represented the overcoming of formalist theories in film analysis, his research also allowed an understanding of film narrative as a pure spatial organization, or even more, as a narrative that in its modern form develops non-Euclidean spatial organizations. The process of the development of non-Euclidean narrative spaces seems to have its basis in the *apertura* of the narrative space. In other words, in the destruction of the plot centered on the character as well as in the "action as the attempt to achieve a goal."[1] The form theorized by Deleuze as S-A-S is undone in the fractality of narrative space, generating the dissolution of the 'coherent' and 'logic' development of the plot.

Dealing with this transformation of the narrative space, Fahle takes as an important example Welles' *Citizen Kane* (1941), which embodies a new instrument of understanding film narrative space. In this film, one can observe that the character no longer represents the center of the action – the phenomenon that sets the mechanisms of cause and effect in the narrative structure[2] – and the film starts to acquire a kind of self-awareness. Borrowing from Fahle:

"Kane bleibt der Fluchtpunkt der verschiedenen Sichtweisen, entzieht sich aber der Klärung letztlich. In dieser Auffächerung der Erzählperspektiven kündigt sich der moderne Film an, der ab Ende der 1950er Jahre neue ästhetische Maßstäbe für das Verständnis des Films etablieren wird, ihn epistemisch neu begreift, indem er nicht mehr vor allem über Erzählmechanismen, sondern über divergierende Bildschichten verstanden werden soll. Das Bild steht nicht mehr nur in Funktion der Narration, sondern reflektiert seinen eigenen Status, seine eigene Herstellungsweise."[3]

Thus, the cinematic narrative space since the Fifties started to be organized, due to its non-Euclidean character, no longer as an arrangement of forms but as an arrangement of relations (*Beziehungsgefüge*).[4] It would be possible to argue that the decentralizing of the subject in the narrative – the decentralizing of the character that generates the rupture of the cause and effect laws in the narrative – highlights the non-Euclidean organization of the narrative space in which the lack of the center as a being and the nature of the image as a self-reflexive entity dislodge the system of representation. The cinematic image is no longer a representation of the object nor an image-object. The image governed by the fractal *Ordnung* develops, through self-reflection, a web of infinite links in which the image establishes links between itself and objects, between perception and imagination, and between representation, presentation and interpre-

---

1 | Brodwell D. 1985, p. 157.
2 | See Brodwell D. 1985, especially Part Three, *Historical Modes of Narration*.
3 | Fahle O. 2005, pp. 14-15.
4 | See Engell L. 2003.

tation.[5] According to Fahle, through this phenomenon of reflection (*Reflexionsphä-nomen*), the film not only develops a relationship to itself[6] ("ein Verhältnis zu sich selbst"), he also posits that the film becomes reflexive.[7] But also the narrative spaces, especially since the Sixties, started to acquire a multidimensional form in which the plurality of narrative perspectives are fragmented and cohabit with each other in a form of contemporaneity (*Gleichzeitigkeit*) and incongruity (*Unvereinbarkeit*). Thus, Fahle posits that:

"[d]ie Hauptfunktion des Films ist nicht mehr die Repräsentation der (erzählerisch geformten) Außenwelt, sondern die Erforschung der optischen und akustischen Räume, also der medialen Räume, die der Film, vermittelt durch die Protagonisten, selbst eröffnet."[8]

At that point, Fahle's analysis is focused on the connection between this form of cinematographic narrative space and the postmodern in order to display the main features of the modern. By understanding the postmodern as a concept of pluralization, Fahle creates an interesting link between the postmodern theory – and the transformation of the narrative forms that it implies – and the phenomenon of pluralization in the cinematographic field.[9] By arguing that "[i]n der Postmoderne verschwinden nun diese Meta-Erzahlungen zugunsten von Sprachspielen, die nicht mehr als *letzte Sinndomänen begriffen werden können, sondern eher als Sinnknotenpunkte* oder –schnittstellen, in denen sich verschiedene, heterogene Äußerungsformen treffen,"[10] he questions the influence of postmodern thought on cinematic narrative. This de-

---

5 | Engell L. 2003, p. 12.

6 | It is important to remember the phenomenon of the refraction of the video image highlighted by Baudrillard, which was quoted in the chapter *Ideal Elements in the Narrative Space*. Conversely to the phenomenon analyzed by Fahle, Baudrillard focuses on the nature of the video image and its capacity to connect, through a self-reflexive phenomenon, different elements in its state of continuous becoming. However, both theories propose the alienation of the cinematic image from the representation of natural objects, or the outside reality. On the one hand, Baudrillard arrives at this conclusion through the mere nature of the video image; on the other hand, Fahle analyzes narrative construction of analog film, which presents the same phenomenon. As one can see, the phenomenon is contextualized in two different technological contexts.

7 | Fahle O. 2005, p. 15.

8 | Fahle O. 2005, p. 16.

9 | In the introduction of *La condition postmoderne* Lyotard summarizes this phenomenon as follows: "La fonction narrative perd ses foncteurs, le grand héros, les grands périls, les grands périples et le grand but. Elle se disperse en nuages d'éléments narratifs, mais aussi dénotatifs, prescriptifs, descriptifs, etc, chacun véhiculant avec soi des valences pragmatiques *sui generis*." (Lyotard J.-F. 1979, pp. 7-8.)

10 | Fahle O. 2005, p. 17. Emphasis added.

velopment of a complex organization of narrative spaces progressively influenced the narrative in the cinematographic field. In fact, new textual forms embodying postmodern thought started to be present in cinematography. Different genres and different narrative forms started to converge and to be represented in the narrative space and started to acquire the form of a *complexus*, a web of heterogeneous constituents.[11] In more detail, the so-called modern and postmodern cinema display a special phenomenon of the combination of different styles and narrative forms that can be understood as the recognition of a non-Euclidean narrative space, a space that becomes a *complexus* – thus a fractal space. As shown by Fahle:

"Erzählung, Stile, Ikonographien eröffnen immer eine Meta-Ebene, da sie nicht nur den vorhandenen Film, sondern auch viele andere filmische und mediale Schichten gleichzeitig in das visuelle Geschehen einbringen."[12]

The transformation of the narrative space, its fractalization, is a process that finds its first steps in the modern film. As noted in the chapter *A geodesy of film Narrative,* this process is analogous to the development of non-Euclidean geometries. Fahle, who analyzes this process as the development of modern film, postmodern film and *Zweiten Moderne,* posits that the phenomenon of the self-referentiality of the image plays an important role in the new way of articulating the narrative space. In the postmodern, images express themselves. They are no longer a representation of something coming from the outside world. Borrowing from Fahle:

"Bilder sind dann nicht mehr Zeichen, um eine Bedeutung zu transportieren, sondern sie sind Zeichen ihrer eigenen Zeichenhaftigkeit, nicht mehr nur Oberflächen, die auf anderes verweisen, sondern Oberflächen, die Aussagen über Oberflächen treffen."[13]

This statement recalls the phenomenon of specularity analyzed in the chapter *Ideal Elements in Narrative Space.* As demonstrated in that chapter, Eco affirms that the mirror – and thus the specular images – does not produce an icon but an absolute copy (*doppio assoluto*). Further, Eco adds "l'immagine speculare non è un doppio dell'oggetto, è un doppio del campo stimolante cui si potrebbe accedere se si guardasse l'oggetto in luogo della sua immagine riflessa."[14] Thus, the phenomenon of the self-reflection of the cinematic image and the cinematic narrative analyzed by Fahle questions the specularity of the narrative. In this case, the specularity of the narrative allows us to suggest that cinematographic narrative is composed by surfaces (*Oberflächen*), which, as noted by Fahle, testify, or reflect, other surfaces, other spaces. In addition, the same phenomenon of reflection spatializes the narrative through the

---

11 | See Morin E. 2005.
12 | Fahle O. 2005, p. 19.
13 | Fahle O. 2005, p. 20.
14 | Eco U. 1985, p. 18.

surfaces. Like the *Sierpinski Carpet*, the image represents a surface that is a non-place, a surface that is not a surface. Foucault, who compares the images reflected with utopia, posit:

"le miroir, après tout, c'est une utopie, puisque c'est un lieu sans lieu. Dans le miroir je me vois là où je ne suis pas, dans un espace irréel qui s'ouvre virtuellement derrière la surface, je suis là-bas, là où je ne suis pas, une sorte d'ombre qui me donne à moi-même ma propre visibilité, qui me permet de me regarder là où je suis absent: utopie du miroir."[15]

The reflexivity of the image develops a kind of 'hereafter', a *Vorstellungsraum* that accentuates the indeterminacy of the image.[16] It also develops fractionary dimensions between the interface and the database, which, when dealing with a material medium, e.g. the film stock, acquire a hypertextual quality.[17]

|Prop. XIII| The cinematographic image, since the inception of modern cinema, has become a reflecting entity that is part of a web of heterogeneous factors or, better, a part of a fractal object. It is important to note that, free from their linguistic connotations, these reflections can be understood as spaces in the *complexus*. They are plateaus. Thus, it is no longer possible to understand this phenomenon of reflection as a simple *mise an abyme* in which the story contains another story. This was the case of Truffaut's *La nuit américaine* (1973) and Fellini's *8½* (1963), already analyzed in the chapter *Mise en Abyme: Blazon into Blazon*. As noted in that chapter, Fellini's *8½* places the oeuvre into the oeuvre, generating a *'simple' reflection*. This means that the image's reflectivity is not infinite, but places the film into the film. Unlike the *'simple' reflection'*, we are now dealing with reflecting images that generate an infinite web of heterogeneous components; we are dealing with proper *reflections until infinity*. It is possible to identify this reflexive character of the images in the mechanism of 'quotations' or 'footnotes' introduced in some films during the 90s. Consider, for instance, Altman's *The Player* (1992). As noted by Fahle, this mechanism of quotations shows how the images are placed in the constellation of the film, in the archives of styles. The image is able to express meta-films. It is an interface of the whole database of filmic

---

15 | Foucault M. 1984, p. 47.

16 | It is interesting at this point to quote Bachelard on the dialectic of inside – outside: "L'en-deçà et l'au-delà répétent sourdement la dialectique du dedans et du dehors: tout se dessine, même l'infini." (Bachelard G. 1964, p. 192.)

17 | It is interesting to quote Schuster's words about the concept of *Vorstellungsraum*: "Der Begriff Vorstellungsraum bezeichnet hier mehr als die mentalen Arbeit, sondern allgemein den Anteil des Betrachters, mithin dessen Aktivität im Zuge der Wahrnehmung: sein Denken, Erinnern, Vorstellen, Mutmaßen ebenso wie Emotionen und die körperliche Beteiligung." (Schuster M. 2000, pp. 130-131.)

images.[18] Thus, the system of filmic presentation becomes a point of view on a database, a point of view on *a site* that is in constant becoming.

"Sie sind Bilder des Wandels und seine Agenten zugleich. Sie sind Bilder, die zeigen, wie etwas anders wird und die etwas verändern, während und indem sie selbst sich wandeln. Ihr Augenmerk gilt dem entscheidenden Prozess, in dem etwas zu etwas anderem umgebildet wird, das es zuvor nicht war."[19]

|**Prop. VI**| Such a film construction is defined by a kind of *initiator*, which may be a collection of images from a meta-film or from a database, and a *generator*, which is the film-interface composed by a number of connected-reflected images. Consider the analogy with the construction of the *Koch Snowflake* (see the chapter *Fractus, Fracta, Fractum*). Like in a *Koch Snowflake*, the *initiator* and the *generator* determine the structure in becoming and organize the set. In the creation of such a set, the reflection becomes indispensable. As noted by Deleuze, the way in which the *Koch Snowflake* is developed needs a reflecting phenomenon analogous to the self-similarity expounded by Leibniz. Hence, Deleuze defines the act of rounding exerted on the angles of the *Koch Snowflake* as a baroque act. As in the case of a fractal object, the self-similarity means self-creation, self-development to infinity. Indeed, it establishes a recursive system, a system of reflections. The *Koch Snowflake*, like the modern film, is self-developed. Both of them build themselves, define themselves and reflect themselves.[20] This reflecting nature of the entities (images) composing the set established by the *initiator* and *generator* or, in the case of the modern film, by the film and meta-film or by the database and the interface, makes this system a system in continuous becoming. Thus, as noted above, the film loses its fixed laws of cause and effect or, in Engell's words:

"Das zweit, weitergehende Merkmal aber ist, dass moderne Filme auf Veränderung, auf Umformung des Gegebenen und Bestehenden ausgerichtet sind und sich dabei auch selbst auf Veränderung gründen. Sie gehen nicht feststehenden Erzählstrukturen, Bildgrammatiken und Figurenklischees aus, außer, um sie wenigstens in bestimmten Zügen in Frage zu stellen und zu deformieren, und sie vermeiden nach Möglichkeit auch, ihrerseits feste und berechenbare Schemata auszubilden."[21]

---

18 | Fahle O. 2005, p. 105.
19 | Engell L. 2003, p. 8.
20 | In Engell's words: "Das erste Merkmal ist, dass sie ein Bild ihrer selbst entwickeln. Moderne Filme bilden sich, betrachten sich, definieren sich, reflektieren sich." (Engell L. 2003, p. 9.)
21 | Engell L. 2003, p. 10.

|**Prop. V**| Since the advent of modern film, the essence of the image started to be its inflection, its fold.[22] Through the inflection, the image acquires its reflexive nature, its capacity to set a system of reflections in which it becomes infinite. As noted above, quoting Fahle, the image, as surface, reflects other surfaces. However, this reflexive nature allows us to theorize that the cinematic image, due to its inflection that makes the image a reflecting entity, is no longer a surface. Like in the Koch's curve, which is more than a line and less than a surface, the cinematic image crosses an infinite number of angular points (reflections of other images' reflections) and at no point admits a tangent (the state of becoming does not stop at any point). Thus, being in everlasting movement, in change through the reflections, the image organizes a structure having a fractal dimension. Like in the straight line, where it is possible to mark two points A and B and where in between these two points it is always possible to mark a point C (an inflection point), in the cinematic image, a meta-image marks an inflection point in-between images. Thus, the inflection points generate a dynamic effect in a recursive form.

|*Fig. 3.56*|

|*Fig. 3.57*|

The image, due to its reflecting nature, is no longer an image-object nor a representation of an object, nor an image in a series of images, but a point of view on a site. Thus, in this new structure of the narrative, movement cannot be understood as a vector

---

22 | It is interesting to note the analogy between the cinematographic image in modern cinema and the line of the impressionists, in particular the line as conceived by Matisse. Merleau-Ponty posits that the line drawn of the pictorial composition by Matisse is figurative – it is no longer an imitation of nature. Borrowing from Merleau-Ponty, "La ligne n'est plus, comme en géométrie classique, l'apparition d'un être sur le vide du fond; elle est, comme dans les geometries modernes, restriction, segregation, modulation d'un spatialité préalable." (Merleau-Ponty M. 1964, p. 77.)

or direction; neither can the sequence of images be seen as a linear sequence frame by frame.[23] The inflection of the image develops a kind of whirligig movement that creates infinite structures and establishes symmetries between the scales, like in the *Koch Snowflake*. Further, as noted by Deleuze, the inflection point does not establish a system of coordinates:

"elle n'est ni en haut ni en bas, ni a droite ni a gauche, ni régression ni progression. Elle correspond à ce que Leibniz appelle un « signe ambigu ». Elle est en apesanteur ; même les vecteurs de concavité n'ont rien à voir encore avec un vecteur de gravité, puisque les centres de courbure qu'ils déterminent oscillent autour d'elle."[24]

According to Deleuze, following Klee's thoughts, the inflection found its representation in "a non-dimensional point" or "between dimensions."[25]

Through the works of Jonas Mekas, it is possible to understand the relationship between database and interface as a relationship based on the inflection of the image. In fact, in his works, the database, following a kind of digital logic in which the database acquires the principal importance in the narrative, is paced by a series of inflected points. In *presentia*, the viewer finds a series of images clearly perceived as inflected images of a vast database. In fact, Mekas creates a large database by shooting events in his life. Then he organizes a fractal narrative space by putting together all these films. The editing, based on inflected images that manifest different speeds of projection, different photographic ambiences, intertitles, music and also his voice, creates a fractal space in which the viewer sees a series of sequences of images that do not follow a logical order. Thus, the viewer sees this narrative as a space composed by fractionary dimensions in between the database and the interface. One cannot see a well-defined narrative space nor a structured interface. However, Mekas' films become highly narrative due to the extension of his database and the use of his voice as a guide in the journey through it.[26] Mekas' films represent an interesting attempt to make the database an expressive entity, a narrative space in *presentia*.

Another interesting example, which is more current, is the technique of datamoshing. Datamoshing, or compression artifact, is a distortion of the image, audio or video, generated by an application of data compression that causes a diminishing of quality. These data errors, during the late 90s, started to be intentionally produced by some artists[27] – for example, Takeshi Murata and Nicolas Provost. Provost, not only employs the datamoshing as an aesthetic effect, but also demonstrates the narrative

---

23 | As noted in the chapter *Ideal Elements in Narrative Space*, the image video accomplished this change by means of technological improvements that transformed the images in a pure surface.

24 | Deleuze G. 1988, pp. 20-21.

25 | Deleuze G. 1988, p. 21.

26 | For an in-depth analysis of Mekas' works, see James D.E. 1992.

27 | The datamoshing technique was analyzed as Glitch art.

potentialities of the 'absence' of data in the narrative space.[28] In addition, his works have as their database important films from the history of cinema. For example, his work *Long Live the New Flesh* (2010) (Fig. 3.58) uses as its database films like *The Shining* by Stanley Kubrick, *American Psycho* by Mary Harron, *Alien* by Ridley Scott and of course some of Cronenberg's films.

|*Fig. 3.58*|

Provost's works propose the database as a fractal space in which the images are completely fractalized and whose pieces are strictly correlated in the *complexus* formed by the whole database of filmic images. The images, in this film, clearly show their reflecting nature and their ability to weave a strict fractal space through their capacity to be inflected. Further, the narrative space he developed is based on the fractal dimensions in between the database and the interface.

The symmetries developed by the inflected image also display some self-similar characteristics. As noted in the chapter *Self-Similarity: Fold Into Fold*, an object is self-similar if the whole can be divided into 'parts,' each of which preserves its similitude with the whole. In that chapter, I analyzed the reflecting nature of the image as well as how the inflection generates a recursive system of reflections. It is possible to theorize a self-similar phenomenon of the cinematic image due to its reflective nature. When the Whole in the film is discussed, we deal with the vast concept of the database, which, as we have seen, is composed by infinite reflections between the reflecting-surfaces. If we take a sequence – as noted above with the example of Eisenstein's *Battleship Potemkin*, the scene of the Odessa's stairs – we can see that the inflection point – in that case *The Untouchables* (1987) (Fig. 3.56, 3.57) – projects us to the Whole, to the database that composes the filmic universe. Thus, we are dealing with a phenomenon of self-similarity understood as symmetry across the scales, a pattern inside the pattern, a fold that follows a fold.[29] However, the phenomenon of self-similarity here presented does not correspond to the phenomenon of *Strict Self-Similarity* but rather to the phenomenon of *Self-Similarity at a Point* (see *Self-Similarity: Fold into Fold*). In fact, in this case, the inflected image can be multiplied to infinity. We can go deeper

---

28 | It is interesting to compare this digital distortion to the *Defekte* as analyzed by Thomas Weber. Further, in this oeuvre by Provost, one find the convergence of two interesting phenomena analyzed by Weber, the first already highlighted (*Defekte*) and the Deformationen of bodies. About this subject, see Weber T. 2008, especially *Kapitel 2, Medialität als Dysfunktion. Analogien zu Medientheorien*, pp. 65-112.

29 | See Gleick J. 1987.

and deeper into the database and we can mark more and more inflection points. Further, like every self-similar system, it implies recursivity and becomes, the images being reflecting entities, a system that accepts the formula n+x. In other words, the image accepts an inflection point everywhere.

This nature of the image places us again in front of the concept of the vector as explained in the chapter *Ideal Elements in Narrative Space*. The image, since the advent of the modern film, has progressively become a vector due to its self-referentiality and its inflection points, through which it redefines movement as a function of the relations in the *complexus*.[30] For instance, see how the cinematographic narrative progressively started to accept a shift of shots, e.g. from a panoramic to a close-up. This narrative possibility, which nowadays is very common, shows a structure in which movement derives from the spatial relations in the *complexus*. Further, through these changes of shots, the narrative decentralizes the protagonist, placing him or her in the position of an observer of the continuous construction of the surrounding world.

We have already noted how the jump-cut developed within the *Nouvelle Vague* started to create interesting inflection points in the cinematographic narrative. Deleuze noted how the jump-cut was perceived as a 'fault' of movement, as a disturbance of associations that shows the direct action of the Whole on the unities of the set.[31] Through this analysis of the jump-cut, he highlighted the nature of continuous becoming of cinematographic database, but a different kind of becoming regarding the classic film.[32] In fact, while classic cinema developed continuous becoming by means of association – that is to say, through an image reflected into its image in *absentia* – with the jump-cut the image exerts a phenomenon of differentiation.[33] When Deleuze states: "[u]ne image étant donnée, il s'agit de choisir une autre image qui induira un interstice *entre* les deux"[34] he highlights through the interstice between images the inflection point from which a break in the succession is exerted. If the linearity of images is analyzed as a curve, the jump-cut marks the inflection point and, as we know, there can be in infinite number of inflection points in a curve. Thus, the series of images is a curve on which one cannot trace a tangent. Borrowing from Deleuze:

"En d'autres termes, c'est l'interstice qui est premier par rapport à l'association, ou c'est la différence irréductible qui permet d'échelonner les ressemblances. La fissure est devenue première, et s'élargit à ce titre. Il ne s'agit plus de suivre une chaîne d'images,

---

30 | See Cubitt S. 2004, p. 72.

31 | Deleuze G. 1985, p. 233.

32 | Thanks to the acceptance of the jump-cut as a tool able to develop a new narrative spatial organization, the 180° rule is no longer indispensable in establishing a diegetic space. Cubitt S. 2004, p. 224.

33 | It is important to remember that Deleuze also understood the jump-cut as a phenomenon that isolates the image from the world. Thus, it starts the phenomenon of reflexibity noted above.

34 | Deleuze G. 1985, p. 234.

même par-dessus des vides, mais de sortir de la chaîne ou de l'association. Le film cesse d'être « des images à la chaîne...une chaîne ininterrompue d'images, esclaves les unes des autres », et dont nous sommes l'esclave (« *Ici et ailleurs* »). C'est la méthode du ENTRE, « entre deux images », qui conjure tout cinéma de l'Un. C'est la méthode du ET, « ceci et puis cela », qui conjure tout cinéma de l'Etre = est. Entre deux actions, entre deux affections, entre deux perceptions, entre deux images visuelles, entre deux images sonores, entre le sonore et le visuel : faire voir l'indiscernable, c'est-à-dire la frontière (« *Six fois deux* »). Le tout subit une mutation, parce qu'il a cessé d'être l'Un-Etre, pour devenir le « et » constitutif des choses, l'entre-deux constitutif des images."[35]

The jump-cut embodies an inflection point in the filmic image giving more relief to the space than to time. As noted by Cubitt, "Movement here is sculptural, architectural, or geographical rather than temporal, and space itself is malleable."[36] The infinite inflection points in the image generate indeed the movement, a movement based on the many shifts generated by the fractal structure of the images, which at this moment, as noted above, does not represent a sequence in the meaning of a series of images, but a fractal space in which many different scales – *plateaus* – coexist and interact.

The awareness of the fractal character developed by the cinematographic image since the dawn of modern film – the period when the narrative started to develop non-Euclidean spatial organizations – implies a phenomenon of multiplication of viewpoints analogous to that developed by Cubist painters (see *Visualizing Multidimensional Spaces*).

During the nineties, some mainstream films developed interesting inflections in the narrative structure by multiplying the viewpoints in a scene. This phenomenon, which recalls the multiplication of viewpoints discussed above in some classic films like *Battleship Potemkin* (in the scene in the kitchen), presents a different particularity. The jump-cut (understood as the recognition of an inflection point in the image) allowed, if we analyze the series of images as a straight line in which *initiator* and *generator* develop a set in becoming, the construction of a new curve in which no tangent can be traced. Both the freedom given by the inflected image, embodied by the jump-cut, and the decentralization of the character allowed the creation of independent spaces that interact independently to the 'logic' construction of the diegesis. In other words, spaces that develop a different continuity or that create a flexible space composed by the interaction of different scales. See for instance Robert Rodriguez's *Desperado* (1995) as analyzed by Cubitt.[37] In his analysis, Cubitt shows how in some sequences of the film – sequences composed of many shots that do not always respect the 180° rule, e.g. a sequence of 2 minutes and 3 seconds composed of 47 shots – the director, through both the interruption of the 'natural' sequence of

---

35 | Deleuze G. 1985, pp. 234-235.

36 | Cubitt S. 2004, p. 224.

37 | See Cubitt S. 2004, especially *Neobaroque Film*.

shots and the establishment of a mobility of space, creates a narrative space in which the action can be developed at the same time in the "objective reality of omniscient narration" as well as in the "subjective and therefore potentially illusory space of the protagonist's consciousness."[38] This phenomenon of the multiplication of viewpoints also found expression in the multiplication of the cameras in the space. Consider, for instance, the well-known case of Lars von Trier's *Dancer in the Dark* (2000), in which the director constructed the narrative space using, in some scenes, more than one hundred cameras, following, in a sense, the logic of live TV. By using this method, von Trier composes a fractalized space in which the jump-cut becomes a natural tool of the spatial composition, and the movement is created though it. See, for instance, the scene where Björk interprets *I've Seen it All*. In this scene, the viewer can see how the action is dislodged by means of the passage from point of view to point of view in a non coherent spatial organization, or, in other words, in a spatial organization that does not respect the former rules of the cinematographic narrative, such as the 180° rule. In this scene, the action is developed strictly by the change of planes and not by the characters' actions, thus highlighting the topologic nature of the narrative space. In fact, the image, through the intensive changing of points of view (the duration of the scene is 4 minutes and 40 seconds and it is composed of 127 different shots), attains the self-development theorized above. In the image below, one can see how the editing monitor for this scene was composed.

|*Fig. 3.59*|

During the editing von Trier coordinated many points of view coming from the different cameras positioned around the scene and then constructed the scene on the inflection points allowed by each camera. In this scene, the viewer is not dealing with the phenomenon of *wanted casualness* discussed in the last chapter. There is neither the presence of non-narrative times, like those noted in Eco's analysis of *L'avventura*, nor the multiplication of viewpoints determined by the Cubist influence on cinematographic narrative, as in the *Potemkin* scene analyzed earlier. Here, there is a kind of 'spectacularization of the narrative.' This narrative space keeps the viewer waiting "for the moment in which the various unraveled lines are knitted into a satisfying coherence."[39] The viewer is dealing with a fractalization of the narrative space generated by the inflected line, by the inflected image. Thus, the movement is perceived by means of the state of continuous becoming of the geometrical space, in which the images are not perceived as a mul-

38 | Cubitt S. 2004, p. 227.
39 | Cubitt S. 2004, p. 239.

tiple image composed by many parts but as an infinity of folds folded in many differ-ent inflections. This phenomenon generates a special universe of images that recalls the compressed universe described by Leibniz. As Deleuze noted, Leibniz theorized a kind of force that compresses the universe and sets the matter in a curvilinear move-ment. Further, Leibniz described this curvilinear universe as a universe governed by three important notions: the fluidity of matter, the elasticity of corps, and the 'spring' as mechanism. The flexible corps theorized by Leibniz are formed by coherent parts, which form the fold and always keep a kind of cohesion.[40] As in the *Koch Snowflake*, von Trier's scene does not allow a static view, that is, a succession 'point by point' that follows the 'natural' movement of matter in an Euclidean space. Fold by fold, the image composed by von Trier fades the outlines and, in this continuous becoming generated by the inflections, the movement is generated.

Another interesting oeuvre able to add complexity to the narrative space is the *The Matrix* trilogy from the Wachowski Brothers: *The Matrix* (1999) – *The Matrix Re-loaded* (2003) – *The Matrix Revolutions* (2003). For instance, in *The Matrix Reloaded* we can see a scene that evidences the complexity acquired by the cinematic image. I refer to the pursuit scene in which the Twins (Neil and Adrian Rayment) chase the Keymaker (Randall Duk Kim), Morpheus (Laurence Fishburne) and Trinity (Carrie-Anne Moss) on a highway. This scene, also composed by many points of view that sometimes do not respect the 180° rule, shows the interesting phenomenon of har-mony between different planes. When Trinity takes the motorcycle and rides down the highway the wrong way, the scene appears to be composed of different dimensions coexisting in the same plane. There is a long take in which Trinity avoids the oncom-ing cars and the camera goes through the cars and trucks.

|*Fig. 3.60*|

In the three images above (Fig. 3.60), one can see how the camera seems to go through the truck. The last image is an image of the wheels of the truck, an image that is seen by the viewer as if the camera follows Trinity and the Keymaker in between the wheels of the truck. In this image, the truck, as a hologram, loses its 'materiality' in the space. The narrative space of *The Matrix* is highly ambiguous. The geography of the diegesis in this film is radically unclear.[41]

---

40 | Deleuze G. 1988, p. 9.
41 | Cubitt S. 2004, p. 230.

The fractal space of this film is also evident in the different spaces that compose a single shot. For instance, in many scenes it is possible to see that different objects, present in the same plane, respond to different spatial laws. The shot is composed of many spaces in which different objects react to different 'physical laws.' For example, in the pursuit scene analyzed above, it is possible to see moving objects (vehicles or characters) that move at different speeds, in other words, as if different parts of the image follow different physical laws. Throughout the film, the elasticity of corps is also shown through the interchangeability of the characters.[42] For instance, the Twins are in a permanent phase transition between deposition and sublimation depending on their interaction with different objects present in the space as well as on their passage from plane to plane. For instance, they go through solid objects such as walls by means of sublimation.

|*Fig. 3.61*|

Not only the characters embody this characteristic of the matter in the narrative space. In fact, some objects, like buildings, are highly flexible. For instance, in the scene in which Trinity is piloting the helicopter after saving Morpheus, the helicopter crashes into a building that undergoes a wave effect due to the impact (Fig. 3.62).

|*Fig. 3.62*|

Another interesting example of the complexity of the space in this film is the well-known *Bullet-Time Effect*, which became the distinguishing mark of the film.

The *Bullet-Time Effect* shows a new composition of the fractal space. In the images bellow, (Fig. 3.63) the feeling of movement is generated by the articulation of the shift of axis of the different shots and by the articulation of the different speeds of the objects present in the image.

---

42 | This phenomenon is analyzed by Weber as deformation of bodies. See Weber T. 2008.

Fig. 3.63

As noted by John Gaeta, visual effects supervisor for this scene, this effect is "a stylistic way of showing that you are in a constructed reality and that time and space are not the same as...you know, us today, living our lives."[43] The viewer of *The Matrix* lives the experience of a non-Euclidean space, a space that constructs its sequence by means of fractal concepts, such as symmetry between the scales (different planes in which corps that coexist in the same plane react to different laws of physics), self-similarity (copies of the same character that interact in the same plane) and auto generation (an image that generates through digital technology an infinite number of images).

The *Bullet-Time Effect* is a perfect example of the self-generation of the image. As in the *Cantor Set*, from a line one can derive an infinity of lines that contain the principle one. The image in *The Matrix* acquires the same property by applying digital interpolation. This method is in fact the conversion of a sampled digital signal by means of an upsampling process or by increasing the sample rate of the image's signal.[44] Indeed, by upsampling a sequence one creates new sequences by means of replicas of the original signal's spectrum. This process restores the original spectrum by increasing the resolution of the image.[45] The image is indeed the basis of non-existing footage; that is to say, from an image one creates sub-images that are theoretically present in between images. In Gaeta's words, "not every frame that a camera captures is the only frame that will be seen."[46]

|Prop. XIX| The many planes that compose the images are fractalized, but they are still part of the *complexus*. In this complex spatial structure, composed by many different planes coexisting in an apparent surface, the point of view of the viewer can be anywhere at any distance from the object without respecting 'natural laws.' It can also be on any plane that composes that apparent surface as well as on different corps at the

---

43 | See *The Matrix Making of.*

44 | For an in-depth analysis, see Crochiere R.E. – Rabiner L.R. 1983.

45 | It is important to note that this method was enabled by fractal geometry.

46 | See *The Matrix Making Of.*

same time – corps that respond to different points of gravity, different states of matter, and each one respecting the nature of its own plane at its own scale.

In *The Matrix* we see a similar phenomenon to that highlighted in the scene from *Dancer in the Dark*: the multiplication of cameras. However, in *The Matrix*, this multiplication, as noted above, responds to the need to compose a fractal image in which different planes with their own physical laws coexist. Consequently, while we can compare the spaces of *Dancer in the Dark* or *Desperado* to a *Koch Snowflake*, we cannot do the same with *The Matrix*. Due to the inflection point described above, the space of *The Matrix* differs from this fractal figure. We posited above that the surface of *The Matrix* was not a real surface and we called it an 'apparent surface.' As noted by Schuster, "Der Nullpunkt räumlicher Konstruktion ist in *Matrix* als ein weißer, reiner >Licht-Raum< gegeben, ohne topologische Angaben oder Geometrische Koordinaten, objektlos, bar jeder Orientierungsachsen und –punkte."[47] In fact, the many planes that compose the image, the different objects coexisting on the same plane, and the different speeds, states of matter and so on, allow us to theorize that the plane in this image does not exist. However, when we are in front of this image we perceive a well defined perimeter. This phenomenon of the nonexistence of a well defined or tangible surface can be compared to Gardies' theory of the invisible space, in which he highlights:

"Ainsi, d'une certaine manière, dans le récit filmique, bien que toujours présent, l'espace est invisible; le monde diégétique est habité par cette population singulière que sont les lieux (à quoi il conviendrait d'ajouter, pour être plus complet, ces «êtres» singuliers que sont aussi les paysages, forme spectaculaire et d'apparat sous laquelle se laisse deviner las possible présence de l'espace). En ce sens, l'analyse de l'espace d'un récit ne saurait se réduire, comme il advient trop souvent, à l'analyse additionnelle des lieux. Tout au plus ces derniers représentent (ou renvoient à), sur la base de quelques traits pertinents, leur espace d'appartenance: la chaleur humide de la bambouseraie «appartient» à l'espace latinoaméricain; le château de Xanadu et la petite maison de l'enfance sont deux composantes de l'espace de Kane, placé, lui, sous le signe de l'appropriation."[48]

|Prop. XVIII| Like the *Sierpinski Carpet* or the *Menger Sponge*, the image in *The Matrix* does not have an area because of the many different planes that compose the image as well as the high quantity of images generated by digital interpolation. It is possible to understand this kind of image as a *Super Object*, an object of universal character in which not only photographic representations are juxtaposed, but also objects created by digital 3D, inflections of the minimal unity – like images generated by digital interpolation – etc. Like in the *Sierpinski Carpet*, what is in front of our eyes is not actually there. Somehow, there are digital 3D objects, characters, surfaces and several forms that we cannot conceive in our physical space, and that the camera is

47 | Schuster M. 2000, p. 137.
48 | Gardies A. 1993, p. 86.

technically unable to capture, but our intellect is able to project them and to make them real through the creation of a fractal space in which different natures and irregular phenomena coexist.

The world created by the fractal image, expounded with respect to *The Matrix,* is a world created by different unities that coexist in the same plane. These unities are also able to project themselves onto the entire narrative structure. We observed how some characters – e.g. the Twins and their nature of being in a continuous phase transition of deposition and sublimation – lie in the nature of the space in which they act. For instance, the topologic character of the shapes (as in the scene of the helicopter crashing against the building).

I would like to draw attention now to a self-referential phenomenon developed in some narrative structures. This phenomenon creates a narrative space that can be understood as fractal due to the creation of patterns that manifest some self-similar characteristics. Consider for instance Harold Ramis' *Groundhog Day* (1993), which is constructed by using the self-similar phenomenon of the pattern covered by Phil Connors (Bill Murray). The recurrent narrative starts at six o'clock on the morning of February 2 when the clock-radio starts to play *I got you, Babe* by Sonny & Cher. This film is an excellent example of the decentralization of the character. In fact, the protagonist is forced to learn to live in a recursive pattern, in a recursive world. No matter what he does – even if he kills himself – the pattern starts again, and again, and again at six o'clock with the song *I got you, Babe.* Due to the decentralization of the character and the recurrent pattern composing the narrative space, it is possible to conclude that the character is submerged in a fractal space that manifests a phenomenon of self-affinity (see *Self-Similarity: Fold Into Fold*). Consequently, the self-affinity phenomenon reveals the pattern, or the algorithm, as stated by Cubitt:

"Locking into a pattern at its conclusion, the database narrative reveals its gestalt. The task of the protagonist is to realize themselves as elements of an infinitely repeatable, enclosed horizon of rule-governed patterning. The neobaroque hero inhabits his environment with utter omniscience like *Desperado's* Mariachi, like Brandon Lee's character in *The Crow.* The diegesis is a knowledge base, its secrets resources to be picked up and used, like the energy and weapons in computer shoot-'em-ups."[49]

This new characteristic of the narrative space – its fractality – also allows the creation of different narrative patterns in the same film. Some films present an organization of narrative spaces that completely breaks up the linearity of the plot by presenting new arrangements using the different scales, or narratives planes, that compose the structure. Consider for instance the self-similar (*self-similarity at a point*) structure of *Memento* (2000) in which the inflection point brings the viewer to the same space in a former diegetic time. In this film, the flashbacks create a structure in *mise en abyme,* which is also represented by the character's photos, through which the viewer

---

49 | Cubitt S. 2004, p. 240.

identifies the person at different stages of the diegesis. Further, one can see recursive phenomena that serves as a reference points in the complex spatial narrative, e.g. the repetition of some scenes that provide the viewer with spatial information. Other narrative structures, like *Pulp Fiction* (1994), exert a fractalization by breaking up into pieces the 'natural' development of events and placing them in a different order, thereby exerting an act of inflection in the narrative structure.

It is interesting to note that these non-Euclidean narratives were also used to present chaotic phenomena. This is the case for *Run Lola Run* (1998) by Tom Tykwer in which the narrative structure is composed of three well defined patterns, each one similar to the well know Butterfly Effect used to explain the theory of chaos to the large public[50] (see *Some Words About Chaos*, especially the *Lorenz Attractor*). In this film, we deal with a self-similar (*Self-affinity*) phenomenon. In fact, the director applies the same pattern three times and the decentralized protagonist can only react to the pre-established pattern showing that a small change in the original data completely changes the final effect. It modifies completely the dynamics of the set.

These fractal narrative structures generated an interesting logic analogous to the logic developed by the hypertextuality analyzed in the last chapter. As already noted, hypertextuality is a recurrent human will that answers to the nonexistence of completely enclosed systems. From a theoretical point of view, hypertextuality is manifested in every text, even in printed books. However, as noted in the previous chapter, the term was coined within a technological context that attempted to develop an electric book able to make real the links between different texts. It is legitimate to think that the fractalization of the audiovisual narrative space, highlighted by Deleuze through the analysis of non-Euclidean spaces in cinematographic narrative, also generated the will to make the narrative space in films an open space – a truly open space. Certainly, the film stock represented a limitation, just as the printed book represented a limitation for the development of a real hypertext. However, we can assume that the process of fractalization of the film narrative – represented by the awareness of fractionary dimensions between the database and the interface, by the development of topologic spaces in the narrative, or by the comprehension of the narrative space as a space derived by links between objects – acquired, with digital technology, the technical possibility to develop a real web. And this possibility influenced the cinematographic narrative developed in film within the digital context.

If the printed book started to manifest some hypertext characteristics, which were fully developed in digital text, the cinematographic narrative also started to show some fractal characteristics in its attempts at developing a completely open narrative, a real web, a real fractal object. This phenomenon was clearly evidenced by Quart's concept of hyperlinking cinema. Indeed, she noted a clear tendency towards fractal narrative structures in feature films during the late nineties and the turn of the twenty-first century. This fractal characteristics of the narrative were analyzed by Quarts as hyperlinking cinema, a practice that is found in the narrative structures of films

---

50 | See Wolfram S. 2002.

like *Magnolia* (1999), *TimeCode* (2000), *Crash* (2004) and *Happy Endings* (2005).[51] It is very interesting that Quarts recognizes in these films the influence of the development of the World Wide Web. By calling these films 'post-web' films, she allows us to see how some fractal characteristics of these narratives derive from a kind of web-logic, which I call fractal. In fact, in this text we assume that fractal geometry, being a geometry developed by the digital medium, influences the narrative space – especially the narrative spaces built through the digital medium – not only on the aesthetical level. Further, we assume fractal geometry to be an episteme that governs the representation of our environment and society.

Earlier in this text we noted how the hypertext was developed in order to imitate our mental process. According to Quart, hyperlinking cinema responds to the same need. She posits that the information in these films, the way they are structured in the narrative space, "reflects our mental processing." In addition, the fractal space developed by *Happy Endings*, through its hyperlinking possibilities, allows the construction of a narrative web in which the many links between different diegetic times respond to a necessity of the viewer. Borrowing from Quart, "*Happy Endings* anticipates what viewers want to know about a given moment and fills them in before they even realize what they wanted."[52]

The fractalization of the audiovisual narrative through the development of fractionary dimensions between database and interface started to respond to the need that Quart analyzes as the anticipation of what 'the viewers want to know.' However, this fractalization of the narrative – the externalization of the database – finds a limit in the single image. Thus, one starts to see the split image as a common narrative tool.[53] See, for instance, the already mentioned *Timecode* or *Conversations with Other Women* (2005). Through these last examples one can see that the digital context developed in this way a new need in the cinematographic image. In fact, in Greenaway's *The Pillow Book* we noted that through the compositing the database was externalized, developing a diegetic time in which supposed future actions were actual. In *Happy Endings*, for example, the compositing creates and at the same time responds to the need for a more complex plot. That is to say, the compositing in the so called hyperlinking cinema – the split image – represents a solution to the complexity of the plot, a kind of Butterfly Effect plot in which different situations, apparently non-connected stories, meet.

---

51 | See Quart A. 2005.

52 | See Quart A. 2005.

53 | It is interesting to note that the split image had already been attempted in cinematography before the development of digital technology. For instance, Abel Gance's attempt for his film Napoleon (1927) or Stanley Donen's Indiscreet (1958), among others. However, in these cases, the plot of the film was not based on the division of the image. It responded more to an aesthetical component, which was the case for Gance's film, or to avoid censorship, as in Donen's case.

It is interesting to note that the complexity of these plots started to encourage the use of the split image and footnotes.[54] Thus, one can suppose that the narrative possibilities offered by the phenomenon of hyperlinking uses special constructions like the split image to provide for a complex plot and, at the same time, creates the need for more complex plots. It brings the spatial organization of film narrative closer to the strict fractal space of the web. By means of the inflection of the image, 'footnotes' and multitasking, the fractal narrative in film (that is, film using film stock) acquired the possibility to develop a fractal space in which the whole plot is composed by many different stories that coexist in the same structure. The tendency was clear in the first decade of the twenty-first century. See, for instance, Alejandro González Iñárritu's *Amores Perros* (2000), *21 Grams* (2003) and *Babel* (2006). We can also take as examples Stephen Gaghan's *Syriana* (2005) and Clint Eastwood's *Hereafter* (2010), among others.

One can theorize that these complex narrative structures are the result of a clear influence of digital technology and in particular, the web – that is, the interlinked hypertext. Certainly, these films attempt to acquire the form of a hypertext fiction. However, the film stock, due to its materiality, represents the impossibility to develop a strictly fractal narrative space. This, in my opinion, has become a social need.

---

54 | See Quart A. 2005.

4 Fractal Narrative

> Cosa resta della democrazia quando vien meno l'indipendenza dei processi di formazione del pensiero? Al di là delle definizioni politologiche, o giuridiche, il concetto di democrazia presuppone la libera attività della mente umana. Quando si verificano le condizioni di una modellazione macchinica della mente umana, ogni discorso sulla democrazia è ridotto a vaniloquio puramente formalistico. E l'evoluzione attuale dell'Infosfera sembra prefigurare prospettive di preformazione della mente umana.[1]

4.1 MEDIA-ACTIVISM: THE CREATION OF FRACTAL SPACES

|Prop. XVII| The analysis conducted throughout this text allowed us to highlight an epistemological change in the modern science that enabled the understanding of space as a mental thing – as a mental place – illustrated through the visual media that 'govern' the cultural production in a determined context. We also noted that the image, on a material surface such a film stock, creates tangible limits. As already noted, the off-screen was seen as the witness of the existence of a bigger structure that 'contained' the actual image. But, in the digital context, the immateriality of the image – the absence of film stock – develops a kind of producibility of the image. That is to say, the limits of the image disappear; they disappear in their formal *Gestaltung* and they start to respond to the will of the viewer. As already noted in this text, the transformation of the center in a functional entity implied the disappearance of the limits of the image. This phenomenon became stronger in a digital image. The digital image develops a new kind of 'Panorama' by shifting the point of view of the viewer and placing it into the whole database. We can consider that the viewer is dealing, in the digital context, with a database-panorama.[2] This phenomenon becomes evident in video games. Dealing with this phenomenon, Schuster posits that:

---

1 | Berardi F. 2006, p. 6.

2 | See Schuster M. 2000.

"[d]er Wandel ist radikal: Wir begegnen nicht mehr Bild-Räumen, sondern Raum-Bilder, und anstelle der Beziehung vom Bildraum zu Bildfläche beim Einzel- und Bewegungsbild ist diejenige von Raum-Bilder zu einer Nutzeroberfläche getreten (und zuweilen sind Nutzeroberfläche, Bildschirm über das Interface-Touch-Screen kurzgeschlossen)."[3]

The theory conducted throughout this text posits that thanks to digital technology a new geometry became possible and, like every geometry, it responds to and generates a social need. Both geometry and technology encourage and shape social dynamics. Consider for instance the influence of geometry on architecture and how architecture shapes social relationships. Think about how technology transforms the organization of the urban space by changing distances. Think also about the means of production and how both geometry and technology influence them. At the beginning of this text, we already meditated upon the introduction of geometry as an instrument to respond to a social need. The ancient Egyptian rulers, in wanting to rationally organize land production, wanted at the same time to exert a form of social control over their subjects (see *Geodesy, or the First Translations of Nature*). Geometry and technology shape the social space. More specifically, they shape the social, public and private spaces, the spaces of participation, of control, of oppression, but also the spaces of freedom. Through both geometry and technology, we shape the space where society lives its frictions, its conflicts and the solutions to them.[4]

Visual media, and especially mass media technologies, were in this text analyzed as apparatuses developed by means of the convergence of geometry and technology. Every visual medium studied in this text was first analyzed as a scientific instrument before it entered into the social sphere where they became instruments that influence the organization of narrative spaces. The introduction of both the digital medium and fractal geometry into society is very recent; thus, it is very difficult at the moment to clearly highlight how the convergence of this new technology and fractal geometry shape our social space. However, as already analyzed, it is possible to see how fractal geometry, through the introduction of digital technology into the organization of narrative spaces in the audiovisual field, influences narrative. Certainly, this way of organizing narrative spaces influences social dynamics.

Following this framework, if we go back to the end of the last millennium – 1999 to be precise – we can see an interesting convergence between new technologies and fractal narratives that possibly illustrates for us a new social vector generating a new social structure. In fact, in that year, through the so-called hyperlinking cinema, cinematography was trying to illustrate what audiovisual narrative could be in the coming years through the improvement of the Internet. Also, at that same moment, the Internet was starting to develop the *Web 2.0*. It was developing the technical means to realize links in the video image. In other words, it was developing the means to make real the hypertextuality of the audiovisual narrative space. But the most im-

---

3 | Schuster M. 2000, p. 151.
4 | See Virilio P. 1977.

portant factor of the development of the fractal narrative arrived when people started to be aware of one common need, when people started to focus on one aim. And this aim was embodied by the term 'Media Activism,' which emerged during the protests against the corporations in Seattle in 1999.

Media-activism means a radical change of the axis and the vectors that guide mass media communication,[5] that is to say, a change in the social structure created and maintained by mass media corporations in which one voice informs everybody (Fig. 4.1).[6] Media-activism proposed a true fractalization of this classical and authoritarian structure by giving more people the possibility to inform other people (Fig. 4.2). If one defines the classical structure of mass media communication as one-dimensional, because in it 'one point informs many points,' media-activism proposes an opposite structure, a fractal structure in which many points can inform many others.

|*Fig. 4.1*| |*Fig. 4.2*|

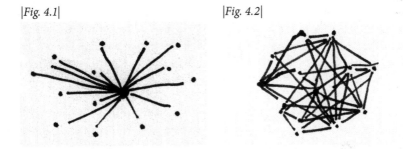

In other words, media-activism proposed the development of a social model that finds its illustration in the fractalization of the narrative, a narrative space in which heterogeneous factors coexist and interact on the same fractal surface. It proposed, in Berardi's words, "la presa di parola da parte di una massa sempre più ampia di produttori semiotici."[7]

Media-activism was in fact the semantization of the socio-political struggle originating in the sixties and seventies. As noted by Berardi, this struggle found its beginnings in the *free speech movement* started at Berkeley in 1964, or in the well-know attempt of *Radio Alice* in Italy in 1976,[8] which was very influenced by the technological improvements of that period. Certainly, many philosophical precedents accompanied this new social struggle, for example, McLuhan's theories, Marcuse's *One Dimensional Man*, and Horkeimer and Adorno's works, among others. In my opinion,

---

5 | For an interesting analysis of this process of change of vectors in communication and art, see Lévy P. 1997, especially chapter 6, *L'art et l'architecture du cyberspace. Esthétique de l'intelligence collective.*

6 | It is important to remember the etymology of the verb to *inform*, which derives from the Latin verb *informare*, in the sense of giving form to the mind.

7 | Berardi F. 2006, p. 3.

8 | See Berardi F. – Guarneri E. 2007.

these theories represent a concept, in the sense in which this term was employed by Deleuze and Guattari. In their theoretical construction a concept is made up of many components, of a multiplicity of elements. However, it was still a concept, it designed a possible world in the abstraction of thought, and implied that technology extends the social control exerted by a dominant class, namely the bourgeoisie. The concept is similar to that described by Deleuze and Guattari as follows:

"nous considérons un champ d'expérience pris comme monde réel non plus par rapport à un moi, mais par rapport à un simple « il y a... ». Il y a, à tel moment, un monde calme et reposant. Surgit soudain un visage effrayé qui regarde quelque chose hors champ. Autrui n'apparaît ici ni comme un sujet ni comme un objet, mais ce qui est très différent, comme un monde possible, comme la possibilité d'un monde effrayant. Ce monde possible n'est pas réel, ou ne l'est pas encore, et pourtant n'en existe pas moins : c'est un exprimé qui n'existe que dans son expression, le visage ou un équivalent de visage. Autrui, c'est d'abord cette existence d'un monde possible. Et ce monde possible a aussi une réalité propre en lui-même, en tant que possible : il suffit que l'exprimant parle et dise « j'ai peur » pour donner une réalité au possible en tant que tel (même si ses paroles sont mensongères)."[9]

Following the passage quoted above, a concept is not a representation of an existing reality – it structures the social interaction, the imaginary, sometimes it designs a possible world, or a world just arround the corner.[10] Further, a concept also shows some characteristics of fractal objects. For example, it is possible to identify some symmetry between different scales, different components coexisting in the same plan.

"Dans un concept, il y a le plus souvent des morceaux ou des composantes venus d'autres concepts, qui répondaient à d'autres problèmes et supposaient d'autres plans. C'est forcé parce que chaque concept opère un nouveau découpage, prend de nouveaux contours, doit être réactivé ou retaillé."[11]

A concept is also a web of heterogeneous factors that enter into relationships to each other. Thus, a concept, even if finite, generates a kind of self-development through relationships and links with the totality of the elements in the set.

"Mais d'autre part un concept a un devenir qui concerne cette fois son rapport avec des concepts situés sur le même plan. Ici, les concepts se raccordent les uns avec les autres, se recoupent les uns les autres, coordonnent leurs contours, composent leurs

---

9 | Deleuze G. – Guattari F. 1991, pp. 22-23.
10 | See Berardi F. 1995, p. 6.
11 | Deleuze G. – Guattari F. 1991, p. 23.

problèmes respectives, appartiennent à la même philosophie, même s'ils ont des histoires différentes."[12]

The self-development of the concept is generated by its capacity to bifurcate and trace links to the other concepts.

"En effet, tout concept, ayant un nombre fini de composantes, bifurquera sur d'autres concepts, autrement composés, mais qui constituent d'autres régions du même plan, qui répondent à des problèmes connectables, participent d'une co-création."[13]

Media-activism could be considered a concept placed at the intersection between many planes concerning the production of capital, mass media structures, new technologies, and the way these shape society and the production of the imaginary. The literature on each of the components composing this junction of infinite concepts is very extensive. However, I would like to draw attention to one special phenomenon progressively developed by capitalism since the Second World War: the development and application of electronic technologies in order to hinder the political pressure exerted by the proletariat.[14]

As noted by Berardi, the structure of modern society, its complete economical, judicial and psychological structure, is grounded in the condition of the exchange of life (time) for the means of support. Thus, when the development of electric technologies started to make unnecessary the exchange of the amount of life-time for the material production, industrialized societies started to face a paradox.[15] The time necessary for the material production decreased, but the right to existence was (is) still attached to the same amount of time spent in the production of value.[16] Borrowing from Berardi:

"Succede che il pregiudizio salariale costringe le potenzialità dell'intelligenza entro una gabbia economica, giuridica, psicologica, che le inceppa, le spreca o lo perverte."[17]

Consequently, in the industrialized countries, unemployment increased, generating the offshoring of the centers of material production to less-developed countries where the workers were paid less and where the labor unions had less power and, in some cases, their agents were threatened with death. Through offshoring, capitalism concentrates the knowledge capital – that is, a production of value focused on the

---

12 | Deleuze G. – Guattari F. 1991, p. 24.

13 | Deleuze G. – Guattari F. 1991, p. 24.

14 | See Marcuse H. 1964.

15 | Berardi F. 1995, p. 25.

16 | Himanen analyzed how the cognitive production disarticulates the capital formula in which time is Money. See Himanen P. 2001.

17 | Berardi F. 1995, p. 25.

scientific research that finds its stock exchange, or its arena, in the 'war of patents'[18]– in the industrialized countries, generating a network in which, as noted by Berardi, research, expressiveness and communication become functions of the production.[19] This creates the kingdom of infoproduction. For these reasons, during the nineties, a new cartography of social classes was drawn. The flow of capital started to focus on non-material production (the infoproduction) making the former struggle between bourgeoisie and proletariat meaningless. In my view, that does not mean, as many theories posit, that in the industrialized countries there are no longer social classes. It is just that the former bourgeoisie, the class that accumulated the richness, the plus value produced by the proletariat and the means of production, can no longer be well defined or no longer responds to the former class structure. There is not a well-defined division between the bourgeoisie and the producing class because in the infoproduction era the labor power is a mental work and the product is the human mind. Consequently, production and enterprise became one, and they gave to creativity an exchange value (*Tauschwert*). As a result, one started to identify a new social class, defined by McKenzie Wark as a Hacker Class.

"We are the hackers of abstraction. We produce new concepts, new perceptions, new sensations, hacked out or raw data. Whatever code we hack, be it programming language, poetic language, math or music, curves or colorings, we are the abstracters of new worlds. Whether we come to represent ourselves as researchers or authors, artist or biologist, chemists or musicians, philosophers or programmers, each of these subjectivities is but a fragment of a class still becoming, bit by bit, aware of itself as such."[20]

The Hacker Class is gradually becoming aware of being a class. Media-activism can be interpreted as a manifestation of this awareness. On the one hand, the Capital, which is not only the accumulation of goods and resources, but also a form of production, started to develop a new form of production based on cognitive work; on the other hand, the Hacker Class, the class that generates the plus value through cognitive work, 'monopolized' the technological skills. In fact, this class is constantly developing the Web to respond to a self-natural need, the need to share information. The Hacker Class focuses on social needs and responds to them by developing new technologies through its monopoly of technology. The development of technologies became its richness, the development of accessible technologies its strategy, the reification of knowledge and information its limit.

It can be seen that the Capital sets in motion a vicious circle in which the first source of richness is the improvement of technologies and cognitive work as well as the accessibility to technologies and to information. The Capital encouraged a form of production in which, in the name of comfort and pure consumerism, the priority of

---

18 | See also on this subject Heidegger M. 1977.
19 | Berardi F. 1995, p. 28.
20 | Wark M. 2004, § 001.

production was given to digital technologies and accessibility to information. However, through the production of and accessibility to these technologies, the consumers were not acquiring a material object, but rather objects able to process, share and generate more information. Consequently, the consumers were acquiring the means of production, dislodging the vector established by the industrial revolution: the consecration of the bourgeoisie as owners of the means of production. This establishes a vicious circle generating a short circuit in the whole system. The Capital encourages the accessibility to and the research into digital technologies, and these new technologies, in the hands of people, become a gun pointed at the Capital itself. In fact, the possibility to share and create information offered by the digital technologies provides the Hacker Class, the productive class, with the flexibility formerly held only by the bourgeoisie. The Hacker Class acquires the adaptability of the bourgeoisie, its capacity to reify everything and to place the means of production in the hands of a reduced number of people. Information being the basis of the production of capital – specifically, the accessibility to technologies – the productive class acquires the means of production. Thus, when the Capital sets in motion a form of production concentrated on the improvement of and accessibility to digital technologies and information, the result was the contradiction we have been living since the late nineties. Consider for instance the Capital needed to improve the international network in order to reify more ideas through patents. But, at the same time, this network is the worst enemy of the Capital. Think, for example, about the development of the P2P computer network, and Napster in 1999.[21] The citizens see this process as a contradiction because they perceive that the only way of improving the production is the development of the network as well as the free exchange of ideas and the free circulation of knowledge. But the political and some economic powers, even if they seem to encourage this system, do not accept this improvement because it represents a big loss of profit. However, I would like to draw attention to the change of mass media structures produced by the development of the Hacker Class, a process that is closely correlated to the development of the cognitive production noted above.

During the seventies two important phenomena occurred at the same time. The first is the privatization of mass media in Europe and the growth of cable television around the world and the second is the development of free radios.

The first phenomenon can be summarized in the change that occurred in the United States in 1974 when the jurisprudence started to be favorable to the development of cable TV and satellite TV broadcasting.[22] At the same time (from 1975 onwards), in

---

21 | For an analysis of the network as a model of production in the e-economy, see Castells M. 2001.

22 | See Barbier F. – Bertho Lavenir C. 1996, especially *La televisión, un média fascinant?* See also Winston B. 1998, especially PART IV *The intricate web of trails, this grand system.*

Europe, the multiplication of private broadcast TVs occurred.[23] These processes came to an end in the eighties when the landscape of media communications on the Old Continent completely changed. In 1989, the primetime of the broadcasting program was occupied in England not only by the former BBC1 and BBC2, but also by the private ITV, Chanel 4 and SKY1; in the Federal Republic of Germany, the public ARD 1, ZDF and ARD 3 shared the slot with the private RTL-Plus and SAT; in France, the new private broadcast Canal +, La Cinq and M6 arrived to accompany the public TF1, A2 and FR3.[24] In Italy, things were very different. In fact, the privatization of TV was a sort of wild process that enabled one great enterprise, owned by Silvio Berlusconi, to own the monopoly of the private stations. Thus, the public RAI 1, RAI 2, and RAI 3, was joined by Berlusconi's Canale 5, Rete 4 and Italia Uno. Perhaps it was precisely this special context in Italy, which imposed a kind of media-authoritarianism, that encouraged the second phenomenon noted above, namely the creation of free radios. The centralized model established by TV all around the world was even more oppressive in Italy. As noted by Berardi, the instruments that could be employed to break the control of this model were represented by the converging use of radio and telephone. In fact, the telephone represents a centerless medium in the communication process.[25] Borrowing from Berardi:

"La mia esperienza radiofonica a metà degli anni Settanta si era spontaneamente focalizzata intorno all'idea che il telefono è un modello acentrico, proliferante, e può opporsi al modello della comunicazione centrica dominante. (...) La diretta telefonica, come la usavano le radio libere in quelli anni, fu un'anticipazione del modello reticolare. Perciò l'esplosione di Internet all'inizio degli anni Novanta non mi colse impreparato."[26]

Combining radio and telephone meant placing the voice of a single citizen in the continuous flow of information. The radio listener could make his/her voice heard by thousands of people thanks to the telephone, and this caused a radical change in the consumerism model of the cultural industries. One started to break the continuous flow of information by developing a new model of communication. Thanks to technological improvements, this innovation led to video servers like YouTube, which "offer access to stocks of traces called data and metadata, and no longer to the flow of programs that constitute radio and television channels."[27] Gradually, the free radios, adopting a kind of information based on the convergence of the telephone and radio,

---

23 | It is important to note that in England one started the process of privatization in 1954 through an authorization given by the government to some local stations financed by advertising. The ITV (Independent Television) has been allowed to broadcast since 1954. However, the public BBC still occupied the largest part of the broadcasting.

24 | Barbier F. – Bertho Lavenir C. 1996, p. 248.

25 | Berardi F. 2006, p. 3.

26 | Berardi F. 2006, p. 3.

27 | Stiegler B. 2009, p. 52.

became an instrument of independent information. They became a vector of cultural and political auto-organization and were looked upon suspiciously by the established political and economic powers during the seventies.[28]

The privatization of mass media, the introduction of cable TV and free radios can be considered as the beginnings of the fractalization of the social order introduced by TV. This fractalization completely modified society. Consider, for instance, what Wolton says about the social role played by traditional Television:

"qu'elle soit publique ou privée, l'intérêt de la télévision généraliste est d'établir un lien constant avec la question centrale de l'identité nationale. Plus l'offre de la télévision est généraliste, en prise avec les multiples composantes de la société, plus la télévision joue son rôle de communication nationale, si important à un moment d'ouverture des frontières. La télévision est le principal miroir de la société ; il est essentiel, pour la cohésion sociale, que les composantes sociales et culturelles de la société puissent se retrouver et se repérer dans le principal média."[29]

The social tie established by TV as the principal medium was assured by the apparent pluralism of media. In such a system, the contradictions, inaccuracies and lies of the media generate the indifference of the people, overcome by the sheer quantity of information.[30] The pluralism of TV as an instrument of social control can be compared to the phenomenon of the cultural industrialization described by Horkheimer and Adorno as follows:

"Emphatische Differenzierungen wie die von A- und B- Filmen oder von Geschichten in Magazinen verschiedener Preislagen gehen nicht sowohl aus der Sache hervor, als daß sie der Klassifikation, Organisation und Erfassung der Konsumenten dienen. Für alle ist etwas vorgesehen, damit keiner ausweichen kann, die Unterschiede werden eingeschliffen und propagiert. Die Belieferung des Publikums mit einer Hierarchie von Serienqualitäten dient nur der um so lückenloseren Quantifizierung. Jeder soll sich gleichsam spontan seinem vorweg durch Indizien bestimmten „Level" gemäß verhalten und nach der Kategorie des Massenprodukts greifen, die für seinen Typ fabriziert ist. Die Konsumenten werden als statisches Material auf der Landkarte der Forschungsstellen, die von denen der Propaganda nicht mehr zu unterscheiden sind, in Einkommensgruppen, in rote, grüne und blaue Felder, aufgeteilt."[31]

Let us now go back to the phenomenon we mentioned above – the media-activism – which arose from a number of social movements born in the sixties.

---

28 | This was the case for the Italian free radio *Radio Alice*. The station started in 1976 and was closed by police on March 12, 1997. See Berardi F. – Guarneri E. 2007.

29 | Wolton D. 2000, p. 70.

30 | See Marcuse H. 1964.

31 | Horkheimer M. – Adorno T.W. 1947, p. 146.

|*Fig. 4.3*|

HALTE
A L' INTOXICATION

At the beginning, the target of these social movements was not clearly outlined. Its first manifestations and actions were focused on socio-cultural politics, thus on the process through which the collective intelligence had been developed. Consider, for example, the social movements of 1968, when students and workers started to fight together. Students all around the world rose up against a system that strictly bound up the production of knowledge with the capitalistic production. They fought for the independence of knowledge from the Capital, the industry and the war. The workers in the factories and the students in the universities shared the same goal; to change the process of work and to reduce the time of labor by means of the technologization of production.

In the class struggles of the sixties and seventies, the independence of knowledge from the economic powers meant a kind of auto-organization of knowledge. This notwithstanding, even though riots were not directed against the mass media and the control they exerted over society, during the social movements of 1968, especially in France, the students criticized some aspects of the mass media structure (Fig. 4.03). Above all, they criticized the expedients and the lies that mass media used in order to maintain the established political and economic class.

During the sixties and seventies, a radical change in the social manipulation exerted by mass media occurred. On the one hand, the Vietnam War demonstrated to the American public, and to the world, a systematic use of censorship by the political powers. On the other hand, mass media started to exert a deeper social control not only based on lies or the censorship of information.

The Vietnam War represents a good observation point for the understanding of a number of new phenomena. At the beginning, between 1965 and 1968, the American TV stations adopted a well-defined propagandistic position encouraging the American heroism against the 'communist aggression.'[32] The old myths, used during the Second World War, were adapted to the new political scenario. The professionalism of the American soldiers and their power were constantly screened on television.[33] This position however, could not be maintained for long. Therefore, a second phase, between 1968 and 1973, started. The mass media could no longer continue with this kind of propaganda due to the large number of American victims in Vietnam. This

---

32 | The Vietnam War also showed that anticommunism as a mechanism of social control was well established. See Chomsky N. – Herman E.S. 1988.
33 | See Hallin D. 1989.

number could no longer be kept secret and the victims could no longer be anonymous. Progressively, the information coming from the front changed. Subsequently, when the looming defeat became clear, mass media started to show the real conditions of the young Americans on the front and the atrocity of war, thus generating in the public opinion a real refusal of the American intervention in Vietnam.

After the Vietnam War the political and military powers learned their lesson and the behavior of the media regarding military conflicts started to follow one of the following schemas. The first schema is that of a 'clean war.'

'Clean war' is characterized by the 'absence' of civilian or innocent victims. When a 'surgical strike' unfortunately kills some innocents, the term 'collateral damage' is there to erase the cruelty of war – to 'clean the war.' The 'clean war' is also characterized by the politico-military control over the mass media. As we know, there is no possibility of war without victims and destruction. Thus, the 'clean war' sometimes becomes almost an 'inexistent war.' An example would be the war of Malvinas between Argentina and England, and the conflict in Panama, which had a very limited echo in the mass media. They are almost inexistent conflicts. To obtain these results, that is, to erase the war, necessitates a strict control over the information coming from the front. The armies undertook this task. In the last twenty years, we started becoming familiar with the journalist wearing the military uniform of the US Army, informing us from the front on television, especially in the conflicts in the Middle East.

The second schema, and the more interesting one for our analysis, is the spectacularization of war, best exemplified by the Gulf War or 'Operation Desert Storm.' Live TV, which makes this conflict a spectacle, characterizes this second schema of manipulation. The live information develops a kind of 'unreal' space in which the image becomes meaningless because it is unable to report the event.[34] The immediacy of live TV creates a paradox, described by Virilio as *le paradoxe logique*. In his words:

"Le paradoxe logique, c'est finalement celui de cette image en temps réel qui domine la chose représentée, ce temps qui l'emporte désormais sur l'espace réel. Cette virtualité qui domine l'actualité, bouleversant la notion même de réalité. D'où cette crise des représentations publiques traditionnelles (graphiques, photographiques, cinématographiques) au profit d'une présentation, d'une présence paradoxale, télé-présence à distance de l'objet ou de l'être qui supplée son existence même, ici et maintenant. C'est cela, finalement, « la haute définition », la haute résolution, non plus tant de l'image (photographique ou télévisuel) que de la réalité elle même."[35]

The new way of social manipulation developed after the Vietnam War generated a social response that, as already noted, found in the technological improvements a means to fractalize the mass media structure. However, it is important to note that the social struggle that generated the fractalization of the mass media structure was

---

34 | Baudrillard J. 1991, p. 22.
35 | Virilio P. 1994, p. 135.

not only focused on the fight against the lies of the mass media. This creative-punk movement was developing new flows of production and communication completely opposed to the hierarchy established during the industrial revolution. In other words, the aim was not to uncover the lies of the political and economic powers, but to create a new way of communication. Consequently, movements like *Radio Alice* were creating a new social imaginary.

The independence and auto-organization of knowledge proposed in 1968, thanks to the fractalization of the arborescent structure of mass media, became in the late seventies the establishing of a new flow of production and information. Subsequently in the nineties, this new flow of information and production started to be reified and invaded by a new face of the Capital – its actual globalized face – which attempted to reify knowledge through the privatization of public universities in Europe, through the economic dictatorship by means of the war of patents, and the jurisprudence that allowed a kind of war against the so-called 'counterfeiting' and 'hacking,' which was extended to every single product, from pharmaceutical to cultural products.[36] The independent structures of cognitive production developed during the eighties started to become victims of this new state of the Capital that found in the dissolution of the Soviet empire a legitimation for privatizing and reifying every form of production of knowledge. But this time the struggle started in a different social context in which the accessibility to technology, and especially digital technology, by the citizens was greater. In fact, in the nineties, the economic production was already largely supported by the cognitive work based on the network. Consequently, media-activism found a fertile context to make its voice heard.

The process of the formation of the Hacker Class expounded above allows us to understand production as a technological instrument that determines the order of signs. Thus one can assume, following the framework developed first by Benjamin and then by McLuhan, that technology should not be analyzed as "productive power" (*Produktivkraft*), as limited by the Marxist analysis, but as a medium. That is to say, as a force producing meaning.[37] In Baudrillard's words:

"La révolution structurale de la valeur anéantit les bases de la « Révolution ». La perte des référentiels affecte mortellement d'abord les référentiels révolutionnaires, qui ne trouvent plus dans aucune substance sociale de production, dans aucune vérité de la force de travail la certitude d'un renversement. Car le travail n'est plus une force, il est devenu signe parmi les signes. Il se produit et se consomme comme le reste. Il s'échange avec le non-travail, le loisir, selon une équivalence totale, il est commutable avec tous les autres secteurs de la vie quotidienne. Ni plus ni moins « aliéné », il n'est plus le lieu d'une « praxis » historique singulière engendrant des rapports sociaux singuliers. Il n'est plus, comme la plupart des pratiques, qu'un ensemble d'opérations signalétiques. Il

---

36 | Consider, for instance, the ACTA (Anti-Counterfeiting Trade Agreement).
37 | "(...) comme forme et principe de toute une nouvelle génération du sens." (Baudrillard J. 1976, p. 86.)

entre dans le design général de la vie, c'est-à-dire dans l'encadrement par les signes. Il n'est même plus cette souffrance, cette prostitution historique qui jouait comme promesse inverse d'une émancipation finale (ou, comme chez Lyotard, comme espace de la jouissance ouvrière, accomplissement de désir acharné dans l'abjection de la valeur et la règle du capital). Plus rien de tout cela n'est vrai. La forme signe s'est emparée du travail pour le vider de toute signification historique ou libidinale et l'absorber dans le processus de sa propre reproduction : c'est l'opération du signe que de se redoubler en lui-même, derrière l'allusion vide à ce qu'il désigne."[38]

From this discussion emerges the question of the role played by the medium used by media on the social organization. In the last chapter, we analyzed how technology, by means of different carriers, can allow for different ways to organize the narrative space. Further, technology progressively dematerialized the medium. If we assume that technology guides the way mankind articulates thoughts and, consequently, the way mankind organizes social structures, we would agree with Benjamin's theory, which posits that technology guides the sensorial perception and human cognitive activity. In Benjamin's words:

"Innerhalb großer geschichtlicher Zeiträume verändert sich mit der gesamten Daseinsweise der menschlichen Kollektiva auch die Art und Weise ihrer Sinneswahrnehmung. Die Art und Weise, in der die menschliche Sinneswahrnehmung sich organisiert – das Medium, in dem sie erfolgt – ist nicht nur natürlich sondern auch geschichtlich bedingt. Die Zeit der Völkerwanderung, in der die spätrömische Kunstindustrie und die Wiener Genesis entstanden, hatte nicht nur eine andere Kunst als die Antike sondern auch eine andere Wahrnehmung."[39]

The phenomenon noted by Benjamin when dealing with the reproducibility made possible by technology requires an analysis of technological determinism, which I would like to focus in the notion of media carrier.

Technology was understood as a living organism able to develop itself. In other words, one supposed that the process of technological development was autonomous.

"L'analyse des techniques montre que dans le temps elles se comportent à la manière des espèces vivantes, jouissant d'une force d'évolution qui semble leur être propre et tendre à les faire échapper à l'emprise de l'homme."[40]

This idea produced a reductionistic thought that condensed the complex phenomenon of the relationship between technology and society into two statements. The first is that society does not have an influence over technology and its development.

---

38 | Baudrillard J. 1976, pp. 23-24.

39 | Benjamin W. 2002c (1939), p. 356.

40 | Leroi-Gourhan A. 1964-1965, p. 206.

The second posits that social dynamics are completely at the mercy of technological developments.

We started the analysis of this problem in the chapter *Veritas Filia Temporis* using the myth of Prometheus, following a Marxist logic and assuming that the supremacy of technology completely modified the relationship between mankind and nature. In the analysis of the development of technology and its influences on the way we articulate narrative spaces – and thus social dynamics – one can see that the evolution of media technologies has gone unnoticed. As noted by Debray, "[...] l'évolution passe inaperçue et ne s'annonce pas comme telle."[41] Thus, we assumed that the appearance of new media in society is not noticed due to the constant process of remediation of the media. In addition, we noted that every visual medium we analyzed had been developed in the scientific field, with scientific aims, and only subsequently became a popular instrument able to influence the organization of narrative spaces. As noted by Bolter-Grusin:

"[A] medium is that which remediates. It is that which appropriates the techniques, forms, and social significance of other media and attempts to rival or refashion them in the name of the real. A medium in our culture can never operate in isolation, because it must enter into relationships of respect and rivalry with other media."[42]

Think, for instance, about the influence that TV had on cinematographic narrative, about how television built its own way of organizing narrative spaces using cinematography, and how it generated new social dynamics using moving images. Consider, for instance, how television represented a new shared social reality and how broadcast scheduling conditioned the timetable of every citizen, making every single citizen a consumer in his or her leisure time. Indeed, by bringing moving images into the living-room of every house, society started to be organized through different dynamics, the dynamics of the spectacle, which is not just a set of images but a social relation. Borrowing from Debord, "[l]e spectacle n'est pas un ensemble d'images, mais un rapport social entre personnes, médiatisé par des images."[43]

However, digital technology represents a radical change that can influence the role played by the old forms of media. In particular, it is the dematerialization of the medium characterizing this technology that represents a radical change. It affects the construction of the narrative space by allowing non-linearity,[44] and influences the other media because digital technology, through the dematerialization of the carrier, enables the establishment of a universal network in which only data can circulate. In addition, the dematerialization enables to contain other media. Consider, for in-

---

41 | Debray R. 1991, p. 202.

42 | Bolter J.D. – Grusin R. 2000, p. 65.

43 | Debord G. 1967, *titre 4*.

44 | Consider, for instance, that in the field of audiovisual media this technology allows a non-linear editing.

stance, the fact that every image, sound, word and 3D object can be translated into bits.

"Elle traduit [la dématérialisation] et accompagne logiquement le mouvement général de désincarnation qui, par révolutions industrielles successives, abouti à l'agriculture sans terre (hors sol), à la langue sans mots (les bits), aux voitures en matières plastiques (sans métallurgie), aux guerres sans combats. Et, dans notre domaine, aux bibliothèques sans livres, modèle idéal futuriste où le document physique ne sera plus directement manié, mais consulté à distance, sur un écran, sous la forme d'un sosie numérisé."[45]

As noted by Debray, there is a progressive phenomenon of the 'lightening' of the medium, starting with the inscriptions on stone and clay in Mesopotamia, then the papyrus in Egypt and, passing through classical antiquity, arriving at parchment, paper and finally, electrons and photons.[46] This path towards immateriality, and especially the diffusion of digital technology, progressively allowed access to information to a larger part of society. This new situation modified in turn some social dynamics from which new economic and political interests, new social vectors, derived. As noted by McKenzie Wark, in every socio-historical context there is a vectorialist class that is surpassed by a new technology. We can, for example, point to the fact that the clergy, in some countries, lost its power due to the new possibilities offered by the printing technique and the translation and vulgarization of the Bible. The same phenomenon is attested in other fields. Consider, for instance, the loss of influence and power the clergy underwent in Italy when the fascist government realized that mass media, especially the cinematographic production, was an instrument of social control in the hands of the Catholic Church. This characteristic of cinematography was best described by Mussolini when he said, after the construction – ordered by him – of the cinematographic studios in Rome, 'il cinema è l'arma più forte' (cinema is the strongest weapon). Thus, fascist dictatorship started to control the cinematographic production.[47] One can also recall that the spread of machine-based manufacturing (the Industrial Revolution) consolidated the social power of the bourgeoisie. An interesting example of this, as suggested by Marx and Smith, is the theoretical link that was hypothesized between Whitney's invention of cotton gin and the reinvigora-

---

45 | Debray R. 1991, p. 209.

46 | Printing is also an interesting example of the phenomenon of lightening and immateriality. As noted by Debray, since its development there has been no major change in this technology. Then the linotype machine was developed, a machine that allowed the printing of five thousand characters per hour. In 1950 this technology was improved with Phototypesetting, which used a film negative image of the characters. This method became obsolete when digital technology was developed. In fact, the digitalization allowed the processing of millions of signs per hour.

47 | See Argentieri M. 1979 and 1998.

tion of the slavery system and the outbreak of the Civil War in the United States.[48] The same could be said about digital technology, that by shaping a particular kind of society that bases its production of value on information and communication, digital technology itself brought about the formation of the Hacker Class. However, the technological deterministic thought places these complex phenomena into the oversimplified structure of popular narrative, which shapes them in a linear way. For example, Whitney's invention incentivizes slavery and gives shape to a social movement that, in turn, generates a civil war. In addition, the popular perception of these linear tales coincides with the perception and understanding of new technological devices as *creationes ex nihilo*. Sometimes accounts of technological developments are composed in such a way to show the devices as a *deus ex machina* that came 'to liberate the oppressed people.' Consider, for example, the popular understanding of Gutenberg's invention that seemed to have been suddenly created by the genius of a German blacksmith. This view generates the idea that technology is an independent entity, "a virtually autonomous agent of change."[49]

Leroi-Gurhan's deterministic theory, in which technology is seen as a kind of 'biological organism,' found its legitimation in these linear narratives. However, as exemplified by non-deterministic science and fractal geometry, our social landscape is composed of irregular shapes and chaotic phenomena and a fixed law cannot determine social dynamics. This concept makes our task even more complicated.

As noted in the previous chapters, a technological development generates new thoughts about conceptual and social structures. For example, one cannot know for sure if Leibniz's theory of monads could have been possible without the invention of the microscope. What we know is that van Leeuwenhoek's invention influenced Leibniz's thoughts (see *Self-Similarity: Fold Into Fold*). The same can be said about Bergson's philosophy and its relationship with the cinematographic machine.

We noted in the first part of this text that technology represents a means, but at some point it starts becoming an aim. However, every technological improvement is developed in a complex social, economic, cultural and political context and even though technology becomes an 'aim' it is still closely connected to this context. Therefore, to develop an accurate investigation of determinism in connection with media-activism, one should consider if technology brings with it the social need to transform the hierarchy imposed by the mass media. This is certainly a legitimate question, especially considering what we said above about free radios, in which the technological improvement of radio transistors and the possibility to bring together telephone and radio played a fundamental role. But, in turn, we should also consider if the social needs – in our case, the media-activism – influenced these technological improvements. This is also a valid question because we have experienced the fact that social movements reconfigure old media and develop new ones.

---

48 | Smith M.R. – Marx L. 1996 (1994), p. x.

49 | Smith M.R. – Marx L. 1996 (1994), p. xi.

The close relationship between society and technology can be interpreted in two divergent ways. The first posits that technology, independently from other factors, generates social needs. For example, in the case of the free radios, communication is seen as a non-hierarchical network thanks to the improvement of the transistor and the technical possibility of converging radio and telephone. The opposite conclusion maintains that social efforts generate new technologies in order to solve a social problem. According to this viewpoint, the social movements all around the world during the sixties found a solution in the change of the axis of communication imposed by mass media and thus in the convergence of the transistor and the telephone. These two opposing assertions open a causality dilemma, a sort of chicken or egg dilemma. This dilemma results from a linear way of thinking imbued with a sort of *faux évolutionnisme* in which technological improvements are considered as an autonomous sequence that deletes social diversity. In other words, it develops a framework that determines the reaction that society will have when facing a new technology. Lévi-Strauss describes *faux évolutionnisme* as follows:

"Très exactement, il s'agit d'une tentative pour supprimer la diversité des cultures tout en feignant de la reconnaître pleinement. Car, si l'on traite les différents états où se trouvent les sociétés humaines, tant anciennes que lointaines, comme des stades ou des étapes d'un développement unique qui, partant du même point, doit les faire converger ver le même but, on voit bien que la diversité n'est plus qu'apparente."[50]

The analogy becomes clear when we analyze with the notion of progress, a notion that has accompanied us since the early Modern Age. As noted in the first part of this text, the classical idea of the contemplation of nature and the passivity of mankind with regard to nature was modified during the early Modern Age. Especially, for Bacon, this passivity meant the impossibility to set up an operationalism that could improve the human life conditions. Thus, the passivity was seen as an obstacle to progress:

"Human knowledge and human power meet in one; for where the cause is not known the effect cannot be produced. Nature to be commanded must be obeyed; and that which in contemplation is a cause is in operation as the rule."[51]

After Bacon's contribution, inventions and technological developments came to be understood in a different way; they started to displace God from the first philosophical and scientific plan. It is precisely in Bacon's *Nuovum Organum* that the philosopher accepts the epistemological imperfection of the human being, an imperfection that could be remedied by technology as prosthesis. The *Nuovum Organum* represents a new instrument – the prosthesis – that assures progress.[52] Thus, the notion of prog-

---

50 | Lévi-Strauss C. 1987, p. 23.

51 | Bacon F. 1960 (1620), Book I, § 3.

52 | See Duarte G. 2011.

ress is strictly correlated with technological improvements. Progress, understood as a linear series of technological improvements, influenced the comprehension of social development as a linear suite completely governed by science as embodied by technology. From the relationship between science and technology, in which science depends on technological improvements, and at the same time technology, as the only means to assure progress, depends on scientific developments, emerges a paradox. Indeed, in this framework, technology does not respond to social needs, but to needs imposed by the technology itself, which are developed and solved within the scientific field.

Assuming that cultural progress is a coalition between cultures in which every culture shares its developments, one accepts that the exchange of ideas between very different cultures is the basis of cultural progress. Consequently, the farther apart these cultures are, the richer the exchange between them becomes. In other words, the exchange between completely heterogeneous cultures means progress. But from this process of exchange that assures cultural progress emerges a phenomenon of the homogenization of participating cultures. Thus, the notion of progress, embodied by technical developments generated two tendencies. According to Lévi-Strauss, the first tendency consists of the assimilation of a given culture by another. In this framework, a given culture adopts and adapts the technological developments of another one to its own needs. This first tendency modifies the *status quo* of the assimilating culture by changing the established vectorialist class. The second tendency, and the more painful and disgraceful in our modern history, was the imposition on another culture of a technique thus, a structure, considered the best one. In other words, one imposes the cultural coalition. According to Lévi-Strauss, the first tendency can be illustrated by capitalism and the second by imperialism and colonialism.[53] However, both cases respond to the same will: to expand the cultural coalition. Both cases generate the same phenomenon, the homogenization of different cultures. Consequently, one finds again a paradox: the homogenization of different cultures is contrary to the aim that encourages the coalition of cultures. As noted above, only through the coalition of very different cultures can progress be established. Thus, by eliminating diversity, one destroys progress. Borrowing from Lévi-Strauss:

"Quoi qu'il en soit, il est difficile de se représenter autrement que comme contradictoire un processus que l'on peut résumer de la façon suivante : pour progresser, il faut que les hommes collaborent ; et au cours de cette collaboration, ils voient graduellement s'identifier les rapports dont la diversité initiale était précisément ce qui rendait leur collaboration féconde et nécessaire.

---

53 | It is interesting to note that by analyzing colonialism as an imposition of the coalition of cultures one can understand that the colonial expansion during the nineteenth century allowed Europe to develop their industry. Thus, following Bataille's logic, one can also analyze this colonialist period as the focusing of the excess energy from the industrial expansion.

Mais même si cette contradiction est insoluble, le devoir sacré de l'humanité es d'en conserver les deux termes également présents à l'esprit, de ne jamais perdre de vue l'un au profit exclusif de l'autre ; de se garder, sans doute, d'un particularisme aveugle qui tendrai à réserver le privilège de l'humanité à une race, une culture ou une société ; mais aussi de ne jamais oublier qu'aucune fraction de l'humanité ne dispose de formules applicables à l'ensemble, et qu'une humanité confondue dans un genre de vie unique est inconcevable, parce que ce serait une humanité ossifié."[54]

Mankind understood technology as the generator of social change. In turn, technology was understood as the only way to attain progress. Consequently, progress was embodied by technology. This phenomenon generated the understanding of progress as a linear succession, guided by technological improvements, and completely ignored the difference between cultures and societies. The fact of seeing progress as a linear succession creates the idea that some cultures were 'more advanced' than others; it generates a *faux évolutionnisme*. Further, as linear succession of events, generated by technology, it creates the erroneous idea that every culture could react in the same way to the assimilation of a new technology, and even worse, one assumed that if the same technology does not generate the same impact on a different culture it was due to the culture having a different 'level of civilization' or a 'cultural backwardness.'

Technological determinism responds to the same linear logic applied to a complex social phenomenon. The dialectic generated by the understanding of history as a series of changes determined by technology generated the idea that society is completely governed by technology and deprived of any free will. Further, following this linear thought, came to understand the future as a space already modeled by new technological changes.[55] However, this deterministic view manifests two version of technological determinism. Borrowing from M. R. Smith, we can say that there is "a 'soft view,' which holds that technological change drives social change but at the same time responds discriminatingly to social pressures, and a 'hard view,' which perceives technological developments as an autonomous force, completely independent of social constraints."[56]

One cannot reject the fact that there exists a kind of sequence of technological developments, which derives from our historical sense. For example, the steam-mill

---

54 | Lévi-Strauss C. 1987, p. 83.

55 | It is interesting to quote M. L. Smith's words about technological determinism. "About technological determinism we could also argue that the issue is not really technological at all but rather a curious cultural and political fetishism whereby artifacts stand in for technology, and technology in turn signifies national progress. Perhaps, in industrialized societies, technologies are visible primarily by means of the trapping with which each culture dresses them. To understand technology as lived experience, we need to acquire a comparative view of how different cultures perceive, define, and meet technological changes and opportunities." (Smith M.L. 1996 (1994), p. 39.)

56 | Smith M.R. 1996 (1994), p. 2.

could not exist before the hand-mill, and the development of nuclear power could not precede electricity.[57] One can also assume that technological changes represent a new productive force that modifies production. Accordingly, technology brings new social relations; it brings a new vectorialist class. What in my opinion is impossible to affirm is that technology, as a self-developed entity, guides society; that would be to say that, borrowing from Winston, "it is the movement of the leaves on the trees which creates the wind."[58] Certainly, society is constantly modified by technology, but the impact of technology on society cannot be determined prior to its diffusion. Further, what is called 'the impact of a new technology on society' is actually a long process in which the technology is also constantly reconfigured according to the social needs. Consider, for instance, the change of the structure of mass media, especially of television, which occurred in Italy during the seventies, and the convergence of radio and telephone developed in Bologna during the same period. By following this framework, one can assume that technological developments are not derived from a kind of autonomous force of technology. Even assuming that technology no longer represent a means to solve human needs, it still represents an aim, and one can see that the social context determines the type of push towards the development of certain kinds of technologies. In Heilbroner's words:

"[...] the direction of technological advance is partially the result of social policy. For example, the system of interchangeable parts, first introduced into France and then independently to England, failed to take root in either country for lack of government interest or market stimulus. Its success in America is attributable mainly to government support and to its appeal in a society without guild traditions and with high labor costs."[59]

Consider also some American postwar projects like ARPANET, a project of the Defense Department's Advanced Research Project Agency, which represented the foundation of the World Wide Web until the nineties. Indeed, ARPANET was developed to respond to the needs of the Government, the industry and the universities.[60] Consequently, we can assume, as posited by Hughes, who gave to the concept of a technological system a broader meaning that:

"[t]echnological systems contain messy, complex, problem-solving components. They are both socially constructed and society shaping. Among the components in technological systems are physical artifacts, such as the turbogenerators, transformers, and transmission lines in electric-light and power systems. Technological systems also include organizations such as manufacturing firms, utility companies, and investment banks, and they incorporate components usually labeled scientific, such as books, articles and

57 | See Heilbroner R.L. 1996[3] (1994), p. 55.

58 | Winston B. 2009, p. 2.

59 | Heilbroner R.L. 1996[3] (1994), p. 63.

60 | For more information about this Project, see Hughes T.P. 1998.

university teaching and research programs. Legislative artifacts such as regulatory laws can also be part of technological systems. Because they are socially constructed and adapted in order to function in systems, natural resources, such as coal mines, also qualify as system artifacts."[61]

Technological improvements are the results of complex social dynamism.[62] By bringing this phenomenon to media technologies, it would be possible to understand media, as proposed by Stauff, following Foucault's thoughts on governmentality,[63] as "technologies of government." It is to say, "as procedures that allow for strategic accesses to modes of conduct of individuals and population, but only insofar as they recognize and account for the 'nature' of these subject areas. This means that media are likewise formed by 'problematizing' social and cultural practices, in their turn conversely allowing for the manipulation of these practices."[64]

As noted in the chapter *The Panorama: An Example of 'Gigantomanie des Mediums,'* visual media are technologies that establish a specific kind of relationship between object and subject. Thus, they are able to dislodge the natural relationship between the observer and the observed. Further, thanks to their status as 'objective translators', visual media are highly efficient for social control. Society constantly forgets that the media are not simple information carriers but also, and above all, creators of information. And in our social context, they are in the hands of a vectorialist class. In other words, even though media are seen as simple and neutral carriers and accumulators of information, they are actually elaborators of information in the ser-

---

61 | Hughes T.P. 1987, p. 51.

62 | About the relationship between technology and society, see Hörl E. 2011.

63 | Governmentality as defined by Foucault is the "ensemble of reflections, strategies and technologies that are aimed at control and the processing of a subject area. There are two mainly aspects that differentiate the model of governmentality historically and theoretically from other forms of control, governance or regulation. For one, the subject area (to be regulated) is not considered as a preexisting or 'natural' one, not as a given 'problem' that demands a 'solution,' but as a problematization that has to be located on the same level with the methods and goal-definitions of the regulation. Those methods producing knowledge about specific operations and situations, the technologies permitting access to specific operations and situations, and the subject area with its specific 'interior' rules constitute each other reciprocally. Secondly, governmentality is characterized by a certain mode of using power that Foucault defines with the term government. In contrast to a regime that simply subordinates, governing aims at considering the peculiarities of each subject area and making them productive. Thus, the necessity arises to gather knowledge about the governed subject. In place of the general normative rules the question emerges how to adequately guide behaviors." (Stauff M. 2010, pp. 264-265.)

64 | Stauff M. 2010, p. 263.

vice of a dominant class.[65] Further, as noted by Berardi, information is not knowledge but rather semiotic difference; it is not comprehension, but rather the 'registration' of inputs,[66] and it is the acknowledgment of that that determined the birth of media-activism. In fact, the self-organization of the mass media represented the primary aim of media-activist; they found in this self-organization the dislodgement of the structure imposed by media companies. Doing so, media-activism directly attacked the established truth imposed by both the political and economic powers.

Technological developments allowed for the creation of a real network in which not only the knowledge, on which the production is based, could freely circulate, but also media-activists used this network to develop interesting narrative spaces in which a new 'social reality' was shared, a shared social reality that constantly diverges from the established reality maintained by the political and economic powers. The media-activists' aim was to create fractal spaces of communication in which what people experienced could be shared. In other words, they sought spaces with fractal structures that enable the convergence of many subjectivities while keeping the heterogeneity of the individual views.[67] Certainly, media-activism, in 1999, found in the Internet the most adequate fractal space to share information.

At first glance, the Internet was understood as the technology that will liberate the Mediascape, and, as Berardi observed, as "l'inizio di una rivoluzione destinata a rompere il dominio economico e politico sul sistema dei media."[68] This first thought about the Internet was clearly influenced by a deterministic thought because it believed that the fractal structure allowed by the Internet implied or determined a precise social use of it. Certainly, this fractal structure, which at the end of the last millennium was very present in many social fields, made possible a new way of communicating. But, being a technology of communication, the Internet was a dispositive

---

65 | See, De Kerckhove D. 1991.

66 | See, Berardi F. 1995.

67 | It is interesting to note that Hughes theorized that the interaction between the components of a technological system influence the way society interacts with it. Borrowing from Hughes, "Since components of a technological system interact, their characteristics derive from the system. For example, the management structure of an electric-light and power utility, as suggested by its organizational chart, depends on the character of the functioning hardware, or artifacts, in the system. In turn, management in a technological system often chooses technical components that support the structure, or organizational form, of management. More specifically, the management structure reflects the particular economic mix of power plants in the system, and the layout of the power plants mix is analogous to the management structure. The structure of a firm's technical system also interacts with its business strategy. These analogous structures and strategies make up the technological system and contribute to its style." (Hughes T.P. 1987, p. 52.)

68 | Berardi F. 2006, p. 6.

and not an automatism.[69] However, by developing and improving the decentralization of communication, media-activism proposed, in 1999, a new model of communication based on the creation of fractal spaces. Consider, for instance, the phenomenon of decentralization illustrated by the BBS (Bulletin Board System), the site Warez, the IRC (Internet Relay Chat), or Napster, as well as by the improved P2P system such as Kazaa and eMule.

Thanks to the development of Napster, P2P systems started to become popular and widely diffused in 1999. These last systems were focused on the free exchange of information, mainly music, as was the case for Napster. However, the technological possibility of share information freely also allowed the creation of spaces for discussion, like the already mentioned IRC, and even more of spaces of communication that, following the P2P model, proposed a non-hierarchical structure of communication; they allowed a fractal space. Consider, for instance, Indymedia, which was born on November 30, 1999, to inform people about the demonstrations in Seattle during the WTO summit. "Don't hate the media, become the media" is the slogan of the Independent Media Center: Indymedia. This slogan exemplifies the aim of Indymedia of developing a strictly fractal space in which everybody can freely participate in the social communicative process; a space in which no hierarchy exists and in which there is no homogenizing phenomenon. In this communicational space everybody can participate in the social debate, in the information. Further, it is a space free from any economic interest and economic power due to the absence of advertising and its independence from the laws of the free market. Consequently, it is a medium that does not need 'soft news' because it does not need to respond to the advertising rules. Additionally, due to its independence, it is an informational space that is not a victim of *l'effet paravent*,[70] because it does not need to respond to political pressures nor to the ratings race.

The P2P model started, at the end of the last millennium, to design a communicative fractal space without a center. Following the phenomenon expounded in the chapter *Hypertext: A Digital Episteme*, the social communicative activity developed on Indymedia modified the center of the structure of communication as well as the center of the narrative space. This was due to the presence of many communicative sources embodied by the citizens participating in the information. While the classical

---

69 | See, Berardi F. 2006.

70 | *L'effet paravent* (holding screen effect) is an information strategy analyzed by Ramonet largely used by political powers and by mass media. *L'effet paravent* consists of hiding an event in the incessant flow of information, by replacing it with other information. Information hides information. For example, in 1989, while the mass media were focused on the Romanian revolution, the USA took advantage of this 'distraction' to invade Panama. The same strategy was used in 1998 by Clinton, who attempted to guide the media attention to artificial military problems in the Gulf region and by bombing Sudan and Afghanistan in order to distract the public attention from the Lewinsky scandal. See Ramonet I. 2001, p. 52.

mass media established a hierarchical model that could be represented by a tree structure, the alternative mass media, like Indymedia, which follow the network developed
by the P2P system, could be illustrated by a fractal object deprived of any hierarchy,
a new kind of 'forest.'

|*Fig. 4.4*|

In the field of cinematography one can also find some interesting attempts to create
fractal spaces in which the participation of citizens is allowed. Consider, for example,
La Commune (Paris 1871) by Peter Watkins, which was also realized in 1999. Even
though the film was made for the big screen, Watkins developed in *La Commune* a
narrative in which the characters, through the use of simulations developed by the
director, directly participate in the creation of the plot.[71] Even though the materiality
imposed by the film stock did not allow him to create a truly open narrative space,
in my opinion Watkins made an important attempt to open up the cinematographic
narrative by following the narrative logic developed in that period by the new structures that emerged from the media-activist experience.

Media-activism gave birth to a different way of sharing information, a new way of
communicating. Starting in 1999, many independent and open spaces of information
started to appear all around the world. Think, for example, of Wikipedia, founded in
2001, or the controversial Wikileaks. These open spaces are seen by the political and
economic powers as potential dangers to the maintenance of the *status quo*. They not
only represent spaces to denounce, that is, spaces of free speech that cannot be easily
controlled, but also spaces to attack the hierarchy established by classical media.[72]

---

71 | For more detail on this subject, see Duarte G. 2009.

72 | It is interesting to note the cases of censorship suffered by Peter Watkins through-
out his entire carrier. The most widely-known case of censorship suffered by this important British director was in 1965 when the BBC, supported by the British government,
banned his film *The War Game*. Watkins, talking about the censorship applied to *The
War Game* describes it as follows: "I was creating reality. I was creating a form which was
false. That was only seen as a problem by the BBC because in *The War Game* I was trick-

Consider, for example, the 2004 FBI operation against Indymedia[73] in which Linux was also a victim, and, more recently, the attacks against Wikileaks.

Since 1999, it has been possible to highlight two tendencies of the remediation exerted by digital media over traditional media. On the one hand, one can see the already analyzed attempts at creating open spaces. These attempts follow in the footsteps of the free radios. In fact, they are digital media that ground their existence in their openness, in the freedom of information, in the file sharing, and in the mobility of the user. On the other hand, one can see an economic and political will to adapt the logic of the old media to the digital medium. That is to say, the will to continue with the social structure derived from traditional mass media by applying their dynamics to the digital medium. These cases are primarily based on the hypermediacy allowed by the digital medium and are clearly exemplified by online newspapers in which the communicative structure remains the same as the printed newspapers. In these cases, we can only find videos, audios, texts, and sometimes, spaces for the comments of the readers. Another interesting example is the online encyclopedias, which are developed under a hypertextual form and also present a hypermedia characteristic. However, it is important to note that some encyclopedias are not open spaces like Wikipedia.

Our society is still debating about the great opposition between these two different tendencies. Some people think that open spaces like Indymedia are very dangerous. Some of them argue that these spaces are not objective, and this assertion may represent proof of the fact that a large part of society believes in the objectivity of traditional mass media. However, if we outline the question in these terms, namely if we focus the debate exclusively on the understanding and role of important concepts like

---

ing the audience. There was such a thing for the BBC as real objectivity; and then there was my subjectivity, and they wanted to try and make a separation. Obviously it was a problem for the BBC. I think that's why the film was banned. Because I was challenging the foundation of the BBC and television, which is that what we are doing is being objective. Which we were all taught as young television makers: You must not be subjective; if you are subjective, you must leave television and work in another field. We were told that." (Duarte G. *Conversations With Peter Watkins*, in preparation) From these words one can see that the motive behind banning this film was not its content but the new narrative – the attack on mass media hierarchy that it represented – that Watkins was developing in the mid-sixties.

73 | In October 2004 the FBI order to be turned over two of the servers, located in the UK, that hosted Indymedia. Governmental attacks on Indymedia affected local Indymedia sites in Ambazonia, Uruguay, Andorra, Poland, Western Massachusetts, Nice, Nantes, Lilles, Marseille, Euskal Herria, Liege, East and West Vlaanderen, Antwerp, Belgrade, Portugal, Prague, Galizia, Italy, Brazil, UK, part of the Germany site and the global Indymedia Radio site. See Sydney Morning Herald, 2004-10-08.

censorship, classified information, free information and participative democracy,[74] we lose the opportunity to develop a truly fractal narrative, which, in my opinion, could best represent and give voice to the irregularity of our societies.

|Prop. XVII| We noted above that the Internet exerts a process of remediation of the older media. Through the example of Indymedia, which marks the beginning of media-activism, we noted the tendency to fractalize the mass media spaces by giving voice to a greater number of people, thus changing the communicative model imposed by traditional mass media. In other words, Indymedia is more than an independent space of communication; it represents an attempt to transform the hierarchy imposed by traditional mass media, and consequently, the way people inform and are informed. But we also noted that this remediation was also present as the 'hypermediation' of the traditional newspapers, encyclopedias and even television broadcasting. However, if we take the example of Indymedia, we have to consider that this free medium, during its thirteen years of existence, was unable to translate the fractality of its inner structure into a narrative form. Certainly, on the Indymedia website many different dimensions coexist: many links to free radios, articles and videos. In summary, one can find there a hypermedia space. But even though this site develops a hypertextual form, which is a fractal space (see *Hypertext: A Digital Episteme*), in my opinion, this hypertextual form can go further, can be even more fractal, can be even more narrative.

The free media that exist today are limited by a lack of narrative. They have not yet developed a new way to compose fractal narrative spaces. And, as we already noted, those spaces have been in our social imaginary since the end of the Second World War, when the cinematographic narrative started to develop non-Euclidean narrative spaces, but were limited by the materiality of the medium. Now, the medium no longer represents a limit to the development of strictly fractal narrative spaces. To explain this better, I would like to draw attention to the interesting experience of YouTube, created in 2005, in which one can see that the audiovisual hypertext, which is already a fractal form, can reach a higher level of fractality by creating infinite links just by following the paths of the users.

As noted in the chapter *Hypertext: A Digital Episteme*, the fractalization of the hegemony of the Hertzian broadcast, and the fractalization of the model of cultural industries began with the invention of the VCR.[75] Nowadays, this process of fractalization can be summarized with a slogan with which we are very familiar: "Broadcast Yourself." Through YouTube's slogan, as noted by Stiegler, one can see an "industrial revolution taking place in the domain of what one should no longer call the cultural industries, but rather the cultural technologies."[76] In fact, YouTube represents a new medium that remediates the immediacy and hypermediacy of the television of the

---

74 | For an in-depth analysis of the relationship between democracy and new media, see De Kerckhove D. - Tursi A. 2006.

75 | See Stiegler B. 2009.

76 | Stiegler B. 2009, p. 41.

nineties. Further, as noted by Grusin, YouTube offers mobility to the user, a new way of participating in the media process. Borrowing from Grusin:

"As at the end of the 20th century, there is still of course a rhetoric of newness surrounding our culture's embrace of the latest social-networking platforms like YouTube, MySpace, Facebook and Twitter – particularly in the mainstream media. This newness participates in the "info-media-capitalist" need to sell more technical media devices by making them faster, more powerful, more interactive and more immediate. But in our current era of wireless social networking the emphasis is not on radical new forms of mediation but on seamless connectivity, ubiquity, mobility and affectivity. YouTube provides perhaps the paradigmatic instance of this new media formation, insofar as its popularity is less a result of having provided users with new and better forms of media than of making available more mediation events, more easily shared and distributed through e-mail, texting, social networks, blogs or news sites."[77]

The progressive fractalization of the narrative space that started after the Second World War, and analyzed in this text through a parallel between non-Euclidean geometries and the ways of organizing the narrative space in film and the audiovisual field, was projected onto society and accomplished by means of digital technology. It is possible to understand Grusin's words as the projection of fractal narratives allowed by digital technologies onto the social dynamics, which expresses more the fractality by the possibility of sharing information and participate to media process – by the ubiquity and connectivity offered by digital technology – than by the development of new ways of building narrative spaces. In other words, fractal spaces like YouTube are socially perceived as cultural spaces of participation but not as fractal narrative spaces. The problem, in my opinion, is not the 'professionalism' or 'amateurism' of the videos broadcasted on YouTube. Theses qualifications only apply to this new narrative space the same idea of hierarchy employed in traditional mass media.[78] It would be more appropriate to place the problem in the middle of a narrative theory that takes into account the capacity of this medium to fractalize the narrative by means of the fractal nature of digital images that allow the linking of every image in the database. In other words, it would be more appropriate to analyze YouTube and other video servers as fractal narrative spaces in which there is no longer a chain of action and reaction, nor a temporal succession that can be determined as a linear vector or trajectory. That is to say, it could be more appropriate to analyze these spaces as a nonlinear narrative, a fractal space developed through tags, tag clouds, linking, users' comments, users suggestions, keywords, and so on. As noted by Elsaesser, "YouTube is a user-generated-content site with a high degree of automation,"[79] and this is due to the role played by the machine, which generates the access points on which the user

---

77 | Grusin R. 2009, p. 65.
78 | See Müller E. 2009.
79 | Elsaesser T. 2009, p. 181.

depends. However, the machine does not only develop the narrative. By navigating through the site, the user creates algorithms and tag clouds provided with an internal logic that generally escape to the user who follows it.[80] Borrowing from Elsaesser:

"the structured contingency is on the one hand, strongly informed and shaped by mathematics, via the site's programming architecture and design, based on its search and sort algorithms. On the other hand, the chaos of human creativity, eccentricity and self-importance prevails."[81]

It is precisely this chaotic characteristic of the narrative developed in spaces like YouTube that, in my opinion, represents the richest narrative instrument that could allow us to build a fractal narrative. In fact, from this chaotic quality of the fractal narrative space derives an interesting phenomenon of self-reflexivity and a chaotic chain reaction that is highly narrative and highly informative. Certainly, these phenomena can also develop, as is the case today, narrative spaces in which banality prevails. As noted by Elsaesser:

"On the one hand, a site like YouTube is inherently addictive, as one video drags one along to another and another and another. Yet after an hour or so, one realizes how precariously balanced and delicately poised one is, between the joy of discovering the unexpected, the marvelous and occasionally even the miraculous, and the rapid descent into an equally palpable anxiety, starting into the void of an unimaginable number of videos, with their proliferation of images, their banality or obscenity in sounds and commentary. Right next to the euphoria and the epiphany, then, is the heat-death of meaning, the ennui of repetition and of endless distraction: in short, the relentless progress of entropy begins to suck out and drain away all life. 'Epiphany' and 'entropy,' one might say, is what defines the enunciative position or 'subject effect' of YouTube, encapsulated in the recursiveness of its own tagline 'broadcast yourself,' which, being circular, accurately describes its specific 'mode of address' as an infinite loop. YouTube's scripted spaces or picaresque narratives are held together not by a coherent diegesis nor a coherent subject-position, but by a perpetual oscillation between the 'fullness' of reference and recognition and the 'emptiness' of repetition and redundancy, the singularity of an encounter and the plurality of the uncountable in which the singular occurs."[82]

In my opinion, spaces like YouTube lose their narrative potential because they are seen as simple, infinite databases with the additional function that it suggests related videos in the interface. However, YouTube does not only consist of video files, but also tags, hyperlinks, user comments, etc. Further, YouTube adds statistical information

---

80 | See Elsaesser T. 2009.

81 | Elsaesser T. 2009, p. 181.

82 | Elsaesser T. 2009, pp. 183-184.

derived from the number of views and recursive links, among other things.[83] Borrowing from Kessler and Shäfer,

"Since moving-image files are not machine-readable – meaning that the program cannot identify the semantic content of this kind of file – information management relies on metadata that names, describes or categorizes whatever there is to be seen. This is an essentially hybrid constellation, since users provide semantic input, which the machine then processes algorithmically, producing different types of clustering with a corresponding organization of video files and metadata. Ultimately, this technological infrastructure can be seen as a specific affordance enabling new forms of media practice. In a way, thus, understanding YouTube means describing it in terms of a 'hybrid interaction' where humans and machines – users and information management systems – are inextricably linked."[84]

The understanding of video servers like YouTube as simple databases creates what Elsaesser describes as an 'infinite loop' in which meaning disappears. However, if one starts to lose the strong connotation of audiovisual narrative as a strict interaction between objects in *absentia* and objects in *presentia*, and starts to see those spaces as fractal narrative spaces in which, in between the database and the interface, there is an intermediary dimension, a fractal dimension created by linking, one starts to discover that the referential expanse offered by YouTube is a narrative tool that is highly communicative. Further, if one accepts the non-linearity of the plot as a natural quality of digital narrative spaces, the self-reflexivity and recursiveness can then be understood as the possibility to develop an infinite and open space, because they develop a system x+n that accepts new elements. Therefore, they develop a system in becoming and a fractal narrative space that allows a kind of convergence of different points of views on the same event. Thus, the recursivity derived by tags might be understood as a semantic convergence of different interpretations of one event. One can posit that the recursiveness generated by the user's tagging in YouTube develops a king of anaphora, which derives from a semantic convergence of many different users, and, as an anaphora, it reinforce an assertion.

As one can note, we are dealing with the phenomenon highlighted by Manovich in his fundamental *The Language of New Media* when he analyzes the Graphical User Interface as a mirror that reflects human activities.[85] Certainly, this reflection of human activities to the Internet – for instance, the algorithms generated by the users, which constitute the organization of the narrative space in YouTube – are instruments of control generally used by companies to discover, or better know, a potential customer. But, through this mirror effect, one can also note that we are transforming the narrative act into an almost unconscious organization of data in a fractal space. That

83 | See Kessler F. – Schäfer M.T. 2009.
84 | Kessler F. – Schäfer M.T. 2009, p. 279.
85 | See Manovich L. 2001.

is to say, we are accomplishing what Vannevar Bush attempted with his MEMEX. As noted in the chapter *Hypertext: A Digital Episteme*, Bush's aim was to simulate the human mind, which, according to him, operates by association of thoughts when storing and organizing data.[86] However, the conscious and unconscious links that users embed in video servers are not only a way of storing information, but also a way of building and organizing a non-linear narrative, that is, a fractal narrative. In my opinion, this narrative act is still unconscious due to the understanding of video servers as databases. Of course, we are also unconsciously improving the interaction of mankind–machine with respect to the construction of fractal narrative spaces and in the future, the viewer will better understand the interaction with those fractal spaces as well as employing tags, links, and all the instruments at their disposal to develop non-linear plots in those fractal narrative spaces.

As noted by Mark Surman, executive director of the Mozilla Foundation in a lecture at Transmediale 2011 in Berlin, we are entering into a moment of the reinvention of the Web, of new media. According to him, the behavior of society toward these spaces is changing and some people are starting to use new media following another logic. It is interesting to note that Surman posits that the period of 'disruption' – that is to say, the first 15 years of the Internet – when it was seen by the big industries as an enemy is over, because people started to see the Internet as a free space. Even some important companies started no longer to see it as an enemy but as an important instrument of control as well as an extension of its economic power by means of the establishment of a monopoly. Certainly, it represents a big danger for the possibilities of freedom and progress that the Internet is offering us. But, according to Surman, we are precisely at the time to take decisions about the future of the open space that the Internet represents.

From this discussion emerges the concept of freedom in the field of the Internet, and Surman proposes an interesting concept composed of four important points, or four freedoms.

He called the first one **use**, and according to him, it is the freedom of using the web and the possibility of seeing inside it: the way it works, its coding and programming. Then comes the second freedom, which is the freedom of **study**. This means the freedom of seeing inside of the programming code in order to **remix** it, which is the third freedom. And the last freedom is the freedom to **share** this information. These freedoms are at the moment inherent in the Internet. For example, the programming code of every website is visible. As noted by Surman, that is the basis of freedom, the possibility to see how the website works.

From this analysis, Surman develops an interesting concept of choice, linking it to cinematography. His concept of choice is basically the way people generate vectors to remediate the older media. In fact, Surman gave as example the development of photographic technology and the choice it incorporates, that is, the framing. Then, he compared the choice in photography to the larger choice allowed by the Lumière

---

86 | See Bush V. 1945.

Brothers' invention, in which the movement imposes another way of framing (of creating a space), another form of choice. Then comes the editing, the montage, which perfectly captures the concept of the choice, a choice that give an important social role to the cinematographic medium, the choice of how to organize the narrative space in order to allow this medium to tell stories, the choice of placing planes into a sequence to create emotions. Thus, inventing the montage was a choice. It was the idea of one man, which was followed and transformed by many others and from which derives infinite ways of creating narrative spaces, of telling stories, of informing people. Today, this choice is changing. As noted above, we are establishing a new relationship with the machine through which we are developing a strictly fractal narrative space. In order to better explain the change to today's choice, Surman shows how the Internet community is developing new and easy ways to enable the construction of what we defined in this text as fractal narrative.

Surman's example was the development of HTML5, a markup language that is an improvement on the former versions and is easily readable by humans as well as by computers. Especially, through HTML5, the presence of video in the Internet changed; thanks to HTML5 video is connected to the web in a way it was not. With HTML5, video is no longer contained in the web. In fact, Video was television on the web. HTML5 makes video a part of the web. Thus, one makes possible a way of manipulating, editing and linking videos on the web. In other words, one is creating a solid path towards fractal narratives. Consider, for instance, the project *Popcorn Maker* by Mozilla. A project focused on the development of an easy way to organize fractal narratives using the whole web as a database with the particularity that the database is the interface and vice versa.

As noted above, HTML5 makes video part of the Internet, it is no longer contained in it as a different entity. Thus, *Popcorn Maker*, even though it can be seen by the users as a classical interface, a program for video editing, it is actually a means to displace the center through the infinite database. As opposed to traditional programs for video editing in which one creates a database and then places the different elements from the database into a sequence, with instruments like *Popcorn Maker*, one uses the whole database – the World Wide Web – because one displaces the 'interface' through it, creating a radical change of perspective.

Through these last examples, it is possible to conclude that the lack of narrative in the attempts of media-activism represents a real limit to this interesting social movement. When I say lack of narrative, I mean the lack of acknowledgment that narrative, in our technological context, means to build and think the narrative space as a fractal space. The technological context in which we live today allows us to compose a strictly fractal narrative space and, as noted above, many attempts have aimed to develop it. However, as in the case of the Hacker Class, who are unaware of their status as a class, media-activists are also unaware of the social impact that a strictly fractal narrative could have on society. In my opinion, this social movement is focusing on the accessibility of information, forgetting the development of fractal narrative spaces.

Taking into account the framework developed throughout this text, can one better define the fractal narrative? Could it be possible to develop a kind of axiomatic system that does not pretend to regulate or to govern fractal narrative, but that can allow us to better understand the fractal characteristics of the narrative spaces that are being constructed today following the media-activist logic?

Let's take the risk.

4.2 FRACTALIS NARRATIO ORDINE GEOMETRICO DEMONSTRATA

This last part of the text, inspired by Spinoza's *Ethica Ordine Geometrico Demonstrata*, is an attempt to demonstrate in a rigorous form what we analyzed throughout this text. In fact, as you will see in this last part, I propose a series of definitions and axioms.

This last part represents in the organic unity of the theory expressed in this text the solid basis of the whole text. As you may seen, (for the readers who followed a linear lecture through the text) sometimes there were links to propositions developed in this last segment. The links are additional aids to further understand the framework that made possible the development of the proposition that will be explained.

Fractalis Narratio Ordine Geometrico Demonstrata is an attempt to introduce a new way to analyze the image and the narrative we are dealing with in our digital context. It does not pretend to be an instrument that guides or determines the organization of fractal narrative spaces. It is an instrument that helps to define the nature of the digital image as well as an instrument to highlight its potential.

Definitions

I - By an image that is self-developed, I mean an image of which the essence involves the arrangement of a web of infinite links.

II - An image is called infinite when it is not limited by the materiality of the medium and when its nature allows it to establish a recursive self-developed system, from which derives a state of continuous becoming.

Explanation: In analog film, the viewer can develop a series of 'quotations' and similarities to other films, to other images, but these are allusions limited by the materiality of the film stock, whose nature is unable to be self-developed. Conversely, digital images, due to their immateriality, are able to establish recursive and self-developed systems.

III - By fractal image I mean a self-developed multidimensional space (hypermediacy) that can be a representation of an existing object as well as an algorithmic image. It is a space that presents different levels of narrative due to its self-developed characteristic, to its capacity to present existing objects and to its state of becoming. The fractality of the image can be actual – i.e. an image forming a web through links – or potential – i.e. through quotations and resemblance to other images. A fractal image (actual), is an image that is neither an interface nor a database, but a momentary center in the database (the Whole) in which the Whole is reflected and which reflects the Whole in its totality.

IV - By fruition I mean which the intellect perceives as constituting the essence of the fractal image. Fruition allows the viewer to guide the state of becoming of the Whole by both modifying the paths of reading and by adding new images. The modifications exerted by the viewer can be conscious – e.g. when the viewer creates links – or unconscious – when the machine, using statistics, generates suggestions or vectors. Consequently, fruition represents a narrative act.

Explanation: Contrary to classical narrative, which understands narrative as a linear order of cause and effect, fractal narrative is the organization of spatial paths – which are not distributed following a system of arborescence – through the totality of the Whole.

V - By narrative I mean the organization of an expressive space by means of vectors that displace the point of view through the Whole. These vectors are seen as paths of reading by the viewer. A path of lecture responds to a displacement of the point of view through the Whole, which is in continuous becoming.

VI – By self-similarity I mean either a reflecting characteristic of the image, from which can derive a phenomenon of *self-similarity at a point, self affinity* or *strict self affinity*, or any aesthetic or conceptual phenomenon that allows the creation of a recursive system.

VII – By inflection point I mean a split in the sequence of images. It can be 'closed,' which is to say, there does not derive from it an intersection of links but represents a rupture in the natural sequence of perceived time (e.g. jump cut), or it can be 'open,' that is, a point in the sequence at which many different sequences coexist in the fractionary dimension in between the database and the interface. The inflection point also exerts an effect of self-similarity from which derives the absolute infinite nature of the narrative space.

Explanation: I say absolute infinite, not infinite through allusions, because for a narrative that generates infinity through allusions, its infinity can be denied by the inexistence of effective inflection points and by the impossibility of openness generated by the material medium, whereas a narrative that is absolutely infinite is self-developed and involves no closure.

VIII – By the Whole I mean the universal database. This can be actual, e.g. the World Wide Web, or potential, e.g. the allusions to other images (analog metadata), the system of quotation, or the hyperlinking cinema. Every image is a part of the Whole, and fractal images are a reflection of the Whole in its totality. In other words, the whole is in the part.

IX – The space called open is a space that allows a recursive system that does not imply the repetition of the same path, image, text or sound, but recursivity is understood as a system X+n in which a new element at any level of its structure can be added. Every fractal image is an open space.

X – By initiator I mean the image or reflecting surface on the set seen as producer of a 'succession' of links and vectors, which are understood as the generator or point of inflection. The initiator is the primary element, which allows a point of inflection, or generator. In a fractal narrative, initiator and generator are apparent states that determine the structure in becoming. Initiator and generator are conceptual elements in fractal narrative spaces where the existence of the one implies the existence of the other.

Axioms

I – Everything that exist in the Whole exist either in itself or in something else.

II – That which is fractal is infinite.

III – In a given fractal image an infinity of reflections converge on the fractal plane of the image in which cause and effect laws and linear sequences do not necessarily apply.

IV – A new fractal image in the Whole has an unpredictable effect.

V –The semiotic chains created or followed by the viewers respond to his/her own perception or expression, and they can be understood or not understood by the users.

VI – Each initiator must allow generators as many viewers use it as a momentary center in the whole.

VII – A fractal image establishes a one-to-one correspondence to the Whole where the Whole (the database) is in the part (the fractal image).

Propositions

Proposition I

Every image present in the Internet is by nature a fractal image.

Proof: This is clear from Def. III, IX and Ax. II.

Proposition II

Every image is a reflection of the Whole while a fractal image is the Whole reflected.

Proof: This is evident from Def. III, VIII and Ax. III, VII. A fractal image not only reflects images of the universal database through allusions, but are also self-developed reflecting entities able to connect to and connected to every single object present in the Internet. Consequently, they reflect the Whole in its totality.

Proposition III

Between a fractal image and the Whole there is a bijection.

Proof: This is clear from Def. VIII and Ax. VII.

Corollary: It follows that both, if understood as separated sets, have the same magnitude, i.e. the same quantity of elements.

Proposition IV

Every fractal image is *Initiator* and *Generator* of a set of causes and effects, which is reflected upon any surface of the Whole and does not imply linearity.

Proof: A new fractal image in the Whole has an unpredictable effect (Ax. IV). In fact, every initiator allows an infinite number of generators (Def. I, III). Therefore, being a reflecting entity of the totality (Ax. I, III), a fractal image is strictly connected to the Whole, the state of continuous becoming of which generates sets of causes and effects that are not linear and that are reflected in some part in the Whole, even if they are not visible to the viewer.

Proposition V

Every fractal image is *initiator* of a fractal narrative space.

Proof: As the fractal image is self-developed, (Def. I) and also infinite (Ax. II), its nature allows and encourages fruition, which implies the organization of a fractal space (Def. IV). Thus, a single fractal image means an infinite number of possible vectors (Def. X; Ax. VI), which organize a narrative fractal space (Def. V, VII).

Corollary I: Therefore, due to the nature of the fractal image, the fractal narrative is clearly not the linear organization of a sequence of images in the database (Def. III). In fact, the fractal image reflects the Whole in its totality and allows displacing the point of view of the viewer through it.

Corollary II: It follows that every single fractal image, being self-developed (Def. I) and also infinite (Ax. II) implies a temporal dimension, even if it is perceived by the viewer as a fixed image. In fact, the fractal image is a reflecting entity of the Whole, and it is an inflection point in it. Thus, the possibility to create links, or the allusion to links that the viewer can understand, give to the fixed image a temporal dimension, perceived by the viewer as the passage (potential or actual) from the image to another through the infinity of links that the image itself enables.

Note: The development of a fractal narrative space, intrinsic in the nature of the single fractal image, can be a conscious act as well as an unconscious one (Def. IV).

Proposition VI
The Whole is an indivisible and infinite entity in a state of becoming.

Proof: The infinite nature of the single fractal image (Ax. II) reflects the infinite nature of the Whole. Being also an open space, (Def. IX) the Whole is in continuous becoming (in *devenir*) and its equivalent is movement and not space; thus it is indivisible.

Proposition VII
The fractal narrative is the cartography of infinity.

Proof: This is clear from (Def. IV) and from the recursive quality of the Whole as attested in the last proposition (Prop. VI).

Another proof: The narrative is the organization of a space by means of vectors that displaces the point of view though the Whole (Def. V), which is infinite. Consequently, the fruition – that is, a conscious or unconscious narrative act – creates paths of lecture through infinite images that reflect an infinite space (Def. IV, VII). The fractal narrative is a narrative that is absolutely infinite (Ax. II), that is, a narrative consisting of many links, each of which expresses a center in function of the viewer and from which many links can be followed or freely created (Def. VI, X; Ax II, III). Thus, the fruition that the fractal image implies brings in its nature the understanding of the fractal image as well as the infinite links that it allows as paths, which the viewer follows or creates. Consequently, it generates the understanding of the narrative act as a cartography of the infiniteness of the Whole, which is reflected in the single image (Ax. V, VI).

Another Proof: The nature of fractal images is multidimensional (by Def. III) and they are also entities reflecting the Whole (Ax. I, III). Through their self-developing characteristic they imply fruition (Def. I, IV). Consequently, the fruition and the nature of the images encourage the creation of links that mark paths in the infiniteness of the Whole (Def. IV; Ax. V).

PROPOSITION VIII
Every fractal image represents a recursive system.

Proof: As a fractal image is infinite (by Def. III; Ax. II) and self-developed (Def. I), its state is in continuous becoming. Therefore, a fractal image is considered an open space that always allows new links, new relations with other spaces, and the addition of a new image (Def. VI, IX).

Corollary: Hence it follows that a fractal image is neither followed nor preceded by another image in a sequence (by Def. IV; Ax. III). In fact, a fractal image is a momentary center in a centerless system, converging with the ideas of Epicurus and Democritus, which posit that in an infinite world the existence of a center is impossible.

PROPOSITION IX
Fractal narrative means the establishment of a recursive system.

Proof: The single images that compose a narrative space are infinite (by Ax. II) and they are inflection points in the Whole (Def. VII; Ax. VI). Thus, the fractal narrative is understood as an interaction between an initiator and a generator, which makes the image an inflection point in the Whole (Ax. VI). If the Whole is an infinite, indivisible entity that is in a state of becoming (by Prop. VI), one can assume that its nature of continuous becoming – from which derives its infiniteness – allows always new images, new links, whose establishment represents the narrative act in the fractal space (Def. IV, IX). Consequently, it is the establishment of a recursive system in continuous becoming.

Corollary: What follows is a clear difference from the way narrative was previously understood. The fractal image, by changing the interaction between the space in *absentia* and the space in *presentia*, dislodges the linearity that characterized the narrative organization in the past. Consequently, the fractal image develops, through the nature of continuous becoming of the Whole, a recursive system, which reflects the infiniteness of the Whole itself.

PROPOSITION X
The recursivity of the fractal narrative is a continuous form with spatial notions.

Proof: The fractal image is a reflecting entity in which the Whole is reflected and which reflects the Whole (by Def. VI; Ax. I, III). If every image that composes the narrative is self-developed (by. Def. I) and is present in the Whole (by Def. I, V), then the interactions of the individual images that organize and define the narrative space would be determined by their positioning in the infiniteness of the Whole, by their bound or reflections in other images that compose the determined narrative space (Def. IV; Ax. V) and by their generation (Def. I, X; Ax. VI). Consequently, the continuous form developed by this recursive system is a form from which one can derive topologic notions in which the fractal image that is in contact with the human component can be understood as a momentary center in this centerless system.

PROPOSITION XI
The existence of the fractal image belongs to its functionality in the Whole.

Proof: If a single fractal image is a momentary center, a point of view on a site in becoming (by Def. III), in a infinite and centerless system in which the image is determined by its position, links, proximities to other images and by the generation that it develops (by Prop. X), then the fractal image is more a passage to other images than an entity defined by itself. It is determined by the reflections of the Whole and the vectors that it generates (Def. I, IV; Ax. I).

Corollary: Hence, the continuum embodied by the Whole makes every fractal image a temporal modulation. Consequently, the fractal image, as a momentary center existing in function of the viewer (by. Def. III), follows a group of transformations perceived by the user as a passage from one image to another (by Def. X; Ax. V). Thus, the viewer becomes a point of view on a dynamic everlasting process (Ax. VI) that can be guided by the viewer itself (by Def. IV). As one can see, in this dynamic spatial organization the center does not refer to a point of view; it is the point of view that refers to a center.

PROPOSITION XII
To be viewer of a fractal narrative means to exert an act of order.

Proof: The viewer gives form to the event, to the object (by Def. IV). Thus, a fractal image represents a metamorphosis (by Def. I, II) while the viewer, through fruition, exerts an anamorphosis (by Def. IV, V). In fact, the Whole represents a constant passage from form to form (metamorphosis), while the fruition is an act of taking form from the *in*form (anamorphosis) through the viewer's way of navigating as well as by means of the creation of paths.

PROPOSITION XIII
The very nature of a fractal image does not allow a *mise en abyme*.

Proof: In a fractal space nothing can be contained. In fact, space is generated through the relationships between the images (Def. I, VIII; Ax. III); it is not a holder of objects.

Note I: If one understands *mise an abyme* as the action of placing the image in the center of a bigger image that contains it, one can see that this action is refutable in our field of fractals for two fundamental reasons. The first is that the fractal nature of the image does not allow the definition of a center (Def. IX; Ax. II); the center is a functional entity, not a coordinate in a determined space. The second reason is that the essence of the image is determined by its self-developed quality (Def. I, II) and by its quality of transparency, it cannot contain something inside it; it can only reflect, link and guide to other images.

Note II: The understanding of *mise en abyme* as the oeuvre into the oeuvre is generated by the reflecting nature of the fractal image, which creates a specular phenomenon, which in turn sets infinite links (by Def. VI, VII, X; Ax. III), and through the inflection point, which creates series of similarities (Def. III). Thus, as a reflecting entity, it cannot contain an oeuvre in itself; it just creates a recursive system based on a specular phenomenon.

PROPOSITION XIV
A fractal image is a Panorama of the Whole.

Proof: Being self-developed (by Def. I) and an inflection point in the Whole (Ax. VI), the fractal image enables the viewer to embrace the Whole in its totality through the fractality of the space of the single image (by Def. VIII).

Corollary: Hence, one can posit that a fractal image develops a phenomenon of *allschau* in our digital environment (by Ax. I, VII) in which the database became nature. Consequently, man's relationship with nature is completely dependent on the *traduisibilité* into a binary code by the machine. Further, the phenomenon of *allshau*, sometimes understood as God's vision, encourages some reflections about the conception of God. If one understands God as the only entity in the universe who is able to embrace with its vision the Totality, one can assume that a fractal image gives God's point of view to the beholder in our technological context.

Note: In our digital context, the idea of the objective translation of nature through visual media has been completely lost due to the possibility to create the represented object, and its 'representation' does not imply its existence in the world (by Def. III). However, the externalization of the process of sight, which started with the geometrical analysis of this natural function and was accomplished through the development of the camera obscura, achieves its highest form with the fractal image. On the one hand, technology codifies nature, making it a translatable entity; on the other hand, mankind is completely alienated from this translation due to the dependence on the machine.

Proposition XV

The fractal image, as an inflection point on the Whole, generates in the beholder the idea of both an actual and potential infinity.

Proof: As an open space, the fractal image (by Def. I, IX; Ax. VI) establishes a recursive system perceived by the beholder as potentially infinite. In turn, the Whole is also seen as potentially infinite because it allows the recursive operation of adding new elements (Def. VIII). The perception of the Whole as actual infinity is generated by the nature of the Whole, which corresponds to the totality of existing objects in an infinite space (Def. VIII; Ax. III).

Corollary: It follows that the perception of the Whole as actual infinity derives from the erroneous understanding of the Whole as a material entity, as a space-holder of elements (by Prop. XIII). As we know, the fractal image is infinite due to its immateriality (by Def. II; Ax. II) as well as to its reflecting nature, which develops a recursive system, and thus a potential infinity.

Proposition XVI

The fractal image deals more with *logos* than with *doxa*.

Proof: If the very nature of the image involves the arrangement of a web of infinite links (by Def. I), and its presence encourages the development of a narrative by means of links or reflections (Def. III, IV; Ax. VI), one can assume that the representation of nature or society would imply *logos* to create vectors in an infinite space. In other words, the event is not only reported and placed into an interface, it is developed through links (by Def. III; Ax. V). Consequently, 'reality' is not offered as an entity that one can perceive, it is an entity in continuous becoming that is being continuously constructed through reflections. Thus, dealing with a fractal image, one does not have a relationship of object-subject, one has to appeal to the *logos* to establish a relationship between a point of view and an infinite space in continuous becoming.

Other proof: The self-development of the fractal image (by. Def. I) and its existence in the Whole (Ax. I) makes perception an act that implies the *logos* to embrace the potentialities of the fractal image. As a surface without area (Prop. XIX), a fractal image reflects infinite images and links the single image to the Whole (by Def. VI; Ax. III). Thus, being an infinite and an open space (Def. IX; Ax. II), the fractal image becomes a navigable space that requires reasoning. Further, to navigate a fractal image means to displace the point of view on the Whole (Ax. VI) as well as to create a series of paths, which are governed by a kind of logic that is sometimes not perceived by the viewer due to the participation of the machine (by Ax. V). Consequently, the perception of a single fractal image means the interaction with an entire system that appeals to the logical function of linking as well as a logical following of paths.

Proposition XVII

The notion of movement in a fractal narrative space is derived from its multidimensional nature and not by *coupes immobiles* placed in sequence.

Proof: Being an image whose essence involves the arrangement of a web of infinite links (Def. I) and whose fractality determines a multidimensional space constructed by an infinite number of links between images (Def. III; Ax. III), the fractal image does not allow a simple sequence of *coupes immobiles* from which one derives the notion of movement. Instead it develops, in its multidimensionality, different links and vectors (Ax. VI), which determines and generates movement. Consequently, the very nature of a single fractal image, in which the viewer finds and embeds links, develops a particular notion of movement that derives from the spatial-continuous form established by the image (Prop. X).

Proposition XVIII

The fractal image is a *Universal Object*.

Proof: This is clear from Def. IX and Ax. II.

Proposition XIX

If a fractal image is analyzed as a surface, it must be understood as a surface without area.

Proof: If one considers the fractal image as a surface, then it is a surface on which an infinity of reflections converge (Ax. II, III). Thus, being a *Universal Object* (by Prop. XVIII) that accepts an infinite quantity of information, it is a surface whose area is infinite.

Note: This fractality allows the consideration of the fractal image as a reflecting entity, which is a more suitable term due to the implication of materiality contained in the word 'surface.' Further, as surfaces without area, these images can be exemplified by some proto-fractal objects like the *Sierpinski carpet*.

Proposition XX

In the fractal image, *concinnitas* is an action upon different scales.

Proof: Being a self-developed multidimensional space (by Def. III), the fractal image, as an infinite reflecting entity (Def. VI; Ax. II), cannot follow a traditional extension of a rational organization of form. In fact, as a self-developed image, its form takes into account the development of links through an infinite space (Def. I). Thus, the principle of *concinnitas* in a fractal form must derive from an act of harmonization between the many scales developed in the multidimensional and infinite space of the image.

Corollary: It follows that *concinnitas* can be achieved by means of a specular phenomenon, which is immanent in the fractal image (Ax. III), and it is exemplified by self-similarity (by def VI). In fact, self-similarity makes the development of vectors coincide with the changes of scale.

PROPOSITION XXI

A fractal image is perceived as an immediate past as well as a determination of the future.

Proof: Being an entity whose essence involves the arrangement of a web of infinite links (by Def. I) and one that is in constant becoming, the fractal image's presence, or momentary reflection, determines a displacement of the center that is constantly displaced by the nature of the image itself (by Def. X; Ax. VI). Consequently, a fractal image is always actual as well as are the reflections or links that it manifests. Thus, one can posit that the state of continuous becoming of the fractal image makes the perceived time a indivisible and infinite entity, in which the viewer found as actual as well as immediate past the momentary center (the fractal image). In fact, the perceived image implies a link to another image (Def. I, X; Ax. VI), which is seen by the viewer as the determination of the future immediate. As initiator and generator, the actual image is an immediate past and the determination of the future in the diegesis.

PROPOSITION XXII

The organization of a fractal narrative space establishes a kind of homeomorphism between the single fractal image and the Whole.

Proof: Due to the one-to-one correspondence established between the single fractal image and the Whole (Ax. I, VII), the organization of the narrative space, which responds to links between objects in this centerless system (by Def. I, VIII), is the modulation of the same space (the Whole, which is reflected in its totality in the single fractal image) through a system of similarities (Def. VIII). Consequently, to organize a fractal narrative space means to give form, by displacing the center, to the Whole, which is reflected in its totality in the fractal image (Def. IV).

Corollary: It follows that the fractal image and the Whole are homeomorphic (Ax. I, III). Thus, the fractal narrative can be understood as the organization of the inner structure of the image, which is infinite. By displacing the center through linking, the viewer gives form to a flexible object and creates the narrative space in which the Whole is reflected in its totality.

PROPOSITION XXIII

A fractal image can be considered a *materia informis* that takes shape through the mental process (*logos*) of the viewer.

Proof: As a multidimensional space (Def. III), the fractal structure of the image appeals to the logic of the viewer to organize and guide the semiotic chains derived from the infinity of the Whole (Def. IV, V). Consequently, a single fractal image, as a reflection of the Whole in its totality (Ax. I, III), is a *materia informis*, which offers infinite possibilities to the viewer who, using *logos*, gives it a form. (by Prop. XII).

PROPOSITION XXIV
The first analysis of fractal images in the audiovisual theory is the concept of *espace quelconque* (Any-Space-Whatever).

Proof: The *espace quelconque*, as an image free from imaginary connections with the space, exemplifies a fractal space in which the objects lose their individuality and create through links an unlimited space. It embodies the virtual space that loses the principles of metric ratio; it is a space of virtual conjunction. Thus, the *espace quelconque* highlights the character of continuous dynamics through the loss of coordinates, which characterizes the fractal image. (Def. III; Ax. I, V). Further, the *espace quelconque* clearly exemplifies a topologic space – a non-Euclidean space – which shares some characteristics with the fractal image.

PROPOSITION XXV
The fractal image represents the coexistence of infinite layers – or continuums – that can express different times contemporaneously.

Proof: The multidimensionality of the fractal image (by Def. III) develops a fractal space that allows the coexistence of many different times through the infinite layers that compose the single image. Being a reflecting entity in which the Whole in its totality is reflected (Def. VIII; Ax. I, III), the multidimensionality of the fractal image allows the reflection of the infiniteness of the Whole, which is in constant becoming. Thus, it enables the coexistence of many continuums contemporaneously.

Another Proof: The fractal dimensions that the fractal image establishes between the former, well-defined spaces, paradigma and syntagma (by Ax. I, III), makes many continuums – present in both the Whole as an entity in becoming and in the fractal image as momentary points of view on the Whole – coexist contemporaneously in the fractality of the image.

PROPOSITION XXVI
The fractal image represents a model, a potential sign.

Proof: Being self-developed, the essence of the fractal image involves the arrangement of a web of infinite links (Def. I). Further, as a reflecting entity in which the Whole is reflected in its totality (Ax. I, III), the fractal image is more than a representation of an existing object; it is a model, a potential sign that presents what it should or could be to the beholder. It is a model developed in time and space (Prop. XVII), which generates a chaotic narrative space understood as an infinity of possibilities to be interpreted, read or guided.

Corollary: From this status of the fractal image, that is to say, a model developed in time and space, emerges the difficulty to discern the difference between the fractal narrative and fractal image. In fact, a single image as a model developed in time (through the infinity of links that it allows, by Ax. III) can be seen as a narrative space, a fractal narrative space that expresses a temporal dimension. Certainly, the disappearance of the well-defined spaces in *absentia* and in *presentia* generates confusion. In fact, due to the infinite fractionary dimensions in between these former spaces, a single image – a fixed image – becomes an infinite narrative space (Ax. II) that can be infinitely linked to other spaces. Further, being a reflection of the Whole in its totality (Def. III; Ax. III), the single fractal image expresses the continuity of the Whole. Thus, the single fractal image expresses a temporal dimension – this last coming from the nature of the Whole – through the embedded links as well as the possibility to embed links.

Proposition XXVII

Fractal images impose a new idea of choice in the creation of narrative spaces.

Proof: As the fractal image is a reflecting entity in which the Whole is reflected in its totality (Ax. I, III), the choice is no longer determined by an action of placing images in a linear suite in order to produce a sequence, but by the displacement of the point of view through the whole database, which is infinite and in constant becoming (Def. IV, V). Certainly, the choice that derives from it is highly determined by the relationship that the fractal image imposes between humankind and machine.

Corollary: It follows that the new choice deals with infinite narrative spaces consisting of many links that express a center in function of the viewer, and from which many links can be followed or freely created. Further, being an infinite, multidimensional space (Def. III; Ax. II), the fractal image allows infinite possibilities to build narratives spaces. Consequently, one cannot theorize rules to guide the creation of fractal narrative spaces. These narrative spaces are open (Def. IX); thus they are free from any grammar. The construction of these spaces is essentially guided by both technological improvements, from which new relationships between the human component and the machine can emerges, and the free will of the viewer to create paths of lectures and to add new images into the infinite space.

List of Illustrations

Fig. 1.1 The measurement of the pyramid by observation of the length of its shadow.
From: http://fr.wikipedia.org/wiki/Thal%C3%A8s
Fig. 1.2 Graphic representation of Zeno's paradox of the dichotomy.
From: http://en.wikipedia.org/wiki/Zeno%27s_paradoxes
Fig. 1.3 Diagram illustrating Euclid's parallel postulate.
From: http://en.wikipedia.org/wiki/File:Parallel_postulate_en.svg.
Fig. 1.4 Peano curve.
From: http://upload.wikimedia.org/wikipedia/commons/5/58/Peano_curve.png
Fig. 1.5 The topologic phenomenon of Homeomorphism: a *Homeotasse.*
From: http://commons.wikimedia.org/wiki/File:Homeo_tasse.png
Fig. 1.6 Lorenz Attractor.
From: http://en.wikipedia.org/wiki/File:Lorenz.png
Fig. 1.7 Cantor Set in seven iterations.
From: http://en.wikipedia.org/wiki/File:Cantor_set_in_seven_iterations.svg
Fig. 1.8 Koch Snowflake.
From: http://es.wikipedia.org/wiki/Copo_de_nieve_de_Koch
Fig. 1.9 Sierpinski Triangle evolution.
From: http://en.wikipedia.org/wiki/File:Sierpinski_triangle_evolution.svg
Fig. 1.10 Sierpinski Carpet Process.
From: http://en.wikipedia.org/wiki/Sierpinski_carpet
Fig. 1.11 Irregular line.
From: Author's personal archive.
Fig. 1.12 Sierpinski carpet.
From: http://en.wikipedia.org/wiki/File:Sierpinski_carpet.png
Fig. 1.13 Menger Sponge.
From: http://en.wikipedia.org/wiki/Menger_sponge
Fig. 1.14 Graphic comparing the differences between Topological dimension, Fractal dimension and Euclidean dimension.
From: Fan L.T. – Neogi D. – Yashima M. 1991, p. 15.
Fig. 2.1 Graphic of the projection exerted by mathematical perspective.
From: http://en.wikipedia.org/wiki/Perspective_%28graphical%29
Fig. 2.2 The Ames chair demonstrations.
From: Grombrich E.H. 1960[11] fig. 213, p. 246.

Fig. 2.3 A. Dürer From *Underweysung der Messung.*
From: Grombrich E.H. 1960[11] fig. 214, p. 251.

Fig. 2.4 Rabbit or Duck?
From: http://www.spring.org.uk/2012/01/duckrabbit-illusion-provides-a-simple-test-of-creativity.php

Fig. 2.5 Müller-Lyer Illusion.
From: http://en.wikipedia.org/wiki/M%C3%BCller-Lyer_illusion

Fig. 2.6 A. Dürer's *Draughtsman Manking a Prespective Drawing of Woman* (1525).
From: http://www.naturalpigments.com/education/images/draughtsman.jpg

Fig. 2.7 Diagram of the eyes and related nerves (from Kitab al-Manazir, *Book of Optics*, by Ibn al-Haytham Istambul).
From: Steffends B. 2007, p. 198 (figure 12.1a)

Fig. 2.8 Diagram illustrating principles of the camera obscura (from a *Résumé of Optics* by Kamal al-Din al-Farisi).
From: Steffends B. 2007, p. 200 (figure 12.2)

Fig. 2.9 Roger Bacon's circular diagrams relating to the scientific study of optics, in *Perspectiva.*
From:http://upload.wikimedia.org/wikipedia/commons/archive/b/bd/20111230212953!Roger_Bacon_optics01.jpg

Fig. 2.10 Figure from Bacon's *Perspectiva,* demonstrating how the sphere can be the recipient of an infinity of perpendiculars, and thus, comparing it with human eyes.
From: Lindeberg D.G. 1996, p. 59.

Fig. 2.11 A 16th century pictorial representation of a camera obscura, Gemma Frisius's camera. First published illustration of a camera obscura: observing a solar eclipse in January 1544.
From: Gernsheim H. 1955, fig. I, p. 3.

Fig. 2.12 Athanasius Kircher's large portable camera obscura 1646.
From: Gernsheim H. 1965[3], p. 12.

Fig. 2.13 Engravings showing landscapes with both a camera obscura and its portable version.
From: http://www.precinemahistory.net/1750.htm.

Fig. 2.14 Reflex Camera obscura Johannes Zahn 1685.
From: Gernsheim H. 1955, Fig. 5, p. 15.

Fig. 2.15 An Artist using a 19th century camera obscura to trace an image.
From: Gernsheim H. 1955, fig. II, p. 18.

Fig. 2.16 Janssen's microscope of three draw tubes with lenses inserted into the flaking tubes.
From: Bradbury S. 1967, p. 23.

Fig. 2.17 Robert Hooke's microscope.
From: Robert Hooke's *Micrographia.*

Fig. 2.18 Robert Hooke's illustration of a Flea seen with the microscope.
From: Robert Hooke's *Micrographia.*

Fig. 2.39 Standard Coat of arms of the Crow of Aragon,
From: http://commons.wikimedia.org/wiki/File:Aragon_Arms.svg

Fig. 2.40 Emblems showing a Dimidiated Coat of arm.
From: Franklyn J.–Tanner J. 1970, fig. 54 p. 37.

Fig. 2.41 Emblems showing a Impaled Coat of arm case.
From: Franklyn J.–Tanner J. 1970, fig. 43 p. 33.

Fig. 2.42 Series of images showing the process of *party per cross* and, as an example, the coat of arms of the United Kingdom without the scutcheon of Hanover.
From: http://en.wikipedia.org/wiki/File:Royal_Coat_of_Arms_of_the_United_Kingdom.svg

Fig. 2.43 Quartered Arms - Temple Nugent Brydges Chandos Grenville.
From: www.familyarms.net.

Fig. 2.44 Coat of Arms of the United Kingdom (1816-1837). In this figure one can see the arms of England, Scotland and Ireland, and the escutcheon of Hanover in abyme.
From:http://en.wikipedia.org/wiki/File:Coat_of_Arms_of_the_United_Kingdom_%281816-1837%29.svg

Fig. 2.45 'Self-portrait' of the scribe who placed the book in *abyme*.
From:http://www.bodley.ox.ac.uk/dept/scwmss/wmss/medieval/jpegs/imagecat/500/imac0968.jpg

Fig. 2.46 Mosaic placed in the southwestern entrance of Hagia Sophia in Istanbul
From:http://upload.wikimedia.org/wikipedia/commons/e/e9/Hagia_Sophia_Southwestern_entrance_mosaics_2.jpg

Fig. 2.47 Droste effect.
From: http://en.wikipedia.org/wiki/File:Droste.jpg, author Johannes Musset.

Fig. 2.48 Horce-Bénédict de Saussure, *Prospect geometrique des montagnes neigées, dittes Gletlcher, telles qu'on les découvre en temps favorable, depuis le Chateau d' Arbourg, dans les territoires des Grisons du Canton d'vry, et de l'oberland du Canton Berne.*
From: Sammlung Ryhiner, http://www.zb.unibe.ch/maps/ryhiner/sammlung/?group=volume&dir=3209&pic=Ryh_3209_16.jpg

Fig. 2.49 Panorama of London, 50" X 60", based on daguerreotypes by Claudet, *Illustrated London News*, 1842.
From: Gernsheim H. 1955, Fig. 62.

Fig. 2.50 Caspar David Friedrich, *Frau am Fenster* (1822).
From:http://commons.wikimedia.org/wiki/File:Caspar_David_Friedrich_018.jpg

Fig. 2.51 Cross-section of the auditorium and picture emplacement of the Diorama, London.
From: Friedberg A. 1994, p. 27.

Fig. 2.52 Daguerre, *A midnight Mass at Saint-Etienne-du-Mont* (1834).
From: Mannoni L. – Pesenti Campagnoni D. – Robinson D. 1995, p. 135.

Fig. 2.68 Runner wearing shoes equipped with a device that records the rhythm and speed.
From: Marey E.J. 1873, p. 131. (Fig. 27).

Fig. 2.69 Horse with recording devices of the pressure of the feet on the ground. The rider wears a recording cylinder.
From: Marey E.J. 1873, p. 156. (Fig. 44).

Fig. 2.70 Bird transmitting an electromagnetic signal of the beats of its wings to a myograph.
From: Marey E.J. 1873, p. 240. (Fig. 94).

Fig. 2.71 Mechanism of the *fusil photographique*. Details of the photographic plates and the interior of the photographic gun.
From: Marey E.J. 1895, pp. 111-113 (Figs. 75-77).

Fig. 2.72 Scheme of the functioning of the *Chronographe à plaque fixe*, and front view of the same device.
From: http://www.mif-sciences.net/francais/mag/marey/marey-pompidou.htm

Fig. 2.73 Chronographie of a man wearing a half-white – half-black suit. 1883.
From:http://4.bp.blogspot.com/-ji4uUSbUC4E/TjyECHtHJUI/AAAAAAAAAm4/6M_vkSHiwzE/s1600/marey.jpeg

Fig. 2.74 Man dressed in black, with white lines and points for the chronographic study of the movement of the important parts of the body.
From: Marey E.J. 1895, p. 60. (fig. 41).

Fig. 2.75 Images of a runner reduced to a system of bright lines for representing the position of his limbs (geometrical chronophotography).
From: Marey E.J. 1895, p. 61. (fig. 42).

Fig. 2.76 Internal structure of the photographic chamber 1890.
From: Bulletin de la société Française de photographie.

Fig. 2.77 Conoid engendered by the movement of a white thread.
From: Marey E.J. 1895, p. 27. (fig. 17).

Fig. 2.78 Air movement meeting different shapes of bodies placed in a field of parallel threads of smoke (1900-1901).
From: Marey E.J. 1895, p. 96.

Fig. 2.79 Movement of a liquid meeting a flat obstacle (*chronographie*, 1893); below, *chronographie* of movements rippling through bright pellets suspended in a liquid.
From: Marey E.J. 1895, p. 94 (fig. 63 above – fig. 64 bellow).

Fig. 3.1 P. Picasso *Les Demoiselles d'avignon* (1907).
From: http://en.wikipedia.org/wiki/File:Les_Demoiselles_d%27Avignon.jpg

Fig. 3.2 Aerial view of the village of Labbezanga in Mali, a photo by Georg Gerster.
From: Eglash R. 2005, fig 2.5 a, p. 32.

Fig. 3.3 Fractal graphic.
From: Eglash R. 2005, fig. 2.5 b, p. 32.

Fig. 3.4 Stylized sculpture of a bat (Museum of African Art, N.Y).
From: Eglash R. 2005, fig. 4.2, p. 52.

Fig. 3.23 Graphic of Baker's Map.
From: http://en.wikipedia.org/wiki/File:Ising-tartan.png (created by Linas Vepstas).

Fig. 3.24 Series of images from Fritz Lang's *Metropolis* (1927).
From: Author's personal archive.

Fig. 3.25 Graphic representing the composition of a video line.
From: http://www.maximintegrated.com/app-notes/index.mvp/id/4186

Fig. 3.26 Series of images from S. Vasulka's *Orbital Obsession* (1977).
From: Author's personal archive.

Fig. 3.27 Images from S. Vasulka's *Study No. 25* (1975) and Vasulka W.'s *Artifacts* (1980).
From: Author's personal archive.

Fig. 3.28 Image from Vasulka W.'s *Artifacts* (1980).
From: Author's personal archive.

Fig. 3.29 Series of images from Rybczynski's *Orchestra* (1990).
From: Author's personal archive.

Fig. 3.30 Series of images from Rybczynski's *Orchestra* (1990).
From: Author's personal archive.

Fig. 3.31 B. Mandelbrot *Julia set.*
From: http://en.wikipedia.org/wiki/File:Mandel_zoom_00_mandelbrot_set.jpg

Fig. 3.32 Image from S. Vasulka's *Violin Power* (1978).
From: Author's personal archive.

Fig. 3.33 Silver Grain in photography (1904).
From: http://commons.wikimedia.org/wiki/File:Film_Grain.jpg

Fig. 3.34 Image showing the effect of image noise.
From: http://en.wikipedia.org/wiki/Noise_%28video%29

Fig. 3.35 Series of images from Rybczynski's *Kwadrat* (1972).
From: Author's personal archive.

Fig. 3.36 Series of images from Rybczynski's *Nowa Ksiazka* (1975).
From: Author's personal archive.

Fig. 3.37 Series of images from Rybczynski's *Oj! Nie Moge Sie Zatrymaci!* (1976).
From: Author's personal archive.

Fig. 3.38 Series of images from Rybczynski's *Oj! Nie Moge Sie Zatrymaci!* (1976).
From: Author's personal archive.

Fig. 3.39 Series of images from Rybczynski's *Oj! Nie Moge Sie Zatrymaci!* (1976).
From: Author's personal archive.

Fig. 3.40 Series of images from Rybczynski's *Oj! Nie Moge Sie Zatrymaci!* (1976).
From: Author's personal archive.

Fig. 3.41 Series of images from Fellini's *Roma* (1972).
From: Author's personal archive.

Fig 3.42 Series of images from Rybczynski's *Oj! Nie Moge Sie Zatrymaci!* (1976).
From: Author's personal archive.

Fig. 3.63 A Series of images from Wachowski Brothers' *The Matrix Reloaded* (2003).
From: Author's personal archive.

Fig. 4.1 A figure representing an information structure with center.
From: Author's personal archive.

Fig. 4.2 A figure representing a centerless space, a network of information.
From: Author's personal archive.

Fig. 4.3 A banner of a demonstration in Paris during the social movement of 1968.
From: http://archives.strasbourg.fr/mai_68.htm

Fig. 4.4 Fractal image by Paul W. Carlson.
From: Jackson W. J. 2004, Fractal image C4STKJ01.PNG.

Bibliography

Aarseth J.E. 1994, "Nonlinearity and Literary Theory", in: G.P. Landow (ed.), *Hyper / Text / Theory*, Baltimore, pp. 51- 86.

1997, *Cybertext. Perspectives on Ergodic Literature*, Baltimore.

Adams G. 1771, *Micrographia illustrata, or the Microscope Explained in Several New Inventions*, London.

Alberti L.B. 1950 (1435), *Della Pittura* (Edited by L. Mallè), Firenze.

Algarotti F. 1963 (1762), *Saggio sopra la pittura* (Edited by G. Da Pozzo), Bari.

Allouche J.P. – Shallit. J. 2003, *Automatic Sequences: Theory, Applications, Generalizations*, Cambridge.

Angelet C. 1980, "La mise en abyme selon le « Journal » et la « Tentative Amoureuse » de Gide", in: F. Hallyn (ed.), *Onze études sur la mise en abyme*, Paris, pp. 8-20.

Apollinaire G. 1965, *Les peintres cubistes*, Paris.

Argentieri M. 1979, *L'occhio del regime*, Firenze.

1998, *Il cinema in guerra. Arte, communicazione e propaganda in Italia 1940-1944*, Roma.

Aristarco G. 1977, "Pasolini: le cinéma comme 'langue'", *Études cinématographiques* 41, pp. 109-126.

Arnheim R. 1932, *Film als Kunst*, Berlin.

1974, *Art and Visual Perception. A Psychology of the Creative Eye* (Expanded and revised edition of the original publication of 1954), Berkeley – Los Angeles – London.

Ascott R. 2003, *Telematic Embrace. Visionary Theories of Art, Technology, and Consciousness* (Edited by E.A. Shanken), Los Angeles.

Aubin D. – Dalmedico A.D. 2002, "Writing the History of Dynamical Systems and Chaos : Long Durée and Revolution, Disciplines and Cultures", on: http://www.aos.princeton.edu/WWWPUBLIC/gkv/history/Aubin-Dahan-chaos02.pdf

Bachelar G. 1932, *L'intuition de l'instant*, Paris.

1964 (1958), *La poétique de l'espace*, Paris.

Bacon F. 1960 (1620), *The New Organon and Related Writings* (Edited by H.A. Fulton), New York.

Bacon R. 1928, *The Opus Majus of Roger Bacon* (Edited by R.B. Burke), Philadelphia – London.

1988 (c. 1292), *Compendium of the Study of Theology* (Edited by T.S. Maloy), Leiden.

1996, *Roger Bacon and the Origin of Perspectiva in the Middle Ages. A Critical Edition and English Translation of Bacon's* Perspectiva *with Introduction and Notes* (Edited by D.C. Lindberg), New York.

Baker H. 2009 (1743), *The Microscope Made Easy*, London.

Balázs B. 2001, *Der Geist des Films*, Frankfurt am Main.

Baltrušaitis J. 1969, *Anamorphoses ou magie artificielle des effets mervelleux*, Paris.

1984, *Anamorphoses, les perspectives dépravées*, Paris.

Bapst G. 1899, *Essai sur l'histoire du théâtre et de la mise en scène*, Paris.

1891, *Essai sur l'histoire des Panoramas et des dioramas: Extrait des rapports du jury international de l'exposition universelle de 1889*, Paris.

Barbier F. – Bertho Lavenir C. 1996, *Histoire des médias de Diderot à Internet*, Paris.

Barrow J.D. 2005, *The Infinite Book. A Short Guide to the Boundless, Timeless and Endless*, New York.

Barthes R. 1964, "Rhétorique de l'image", *Communications* (Numéro Spécial « Recherches sémiologiques »), pp. 40-51.

1970, *S/Z*, Paris.

1980, *La chambre claire. Notes sur la photographie*, Paris.

Bataille G. 1949, *La part maudite*, Paris.

Baudrillard J. 1976, *L'échange symbolique et la mort*, Paris.

1989, "Videowelt und fraktales Subjekt", in: Ars Electronica (Hrsg.), *Philosophien der neuen Technologie*, Berlin, pp. 113-131.

1991, *La guerre du Golfe n'a pas eu lieu*, Paris.

1995, *Le crime parfait*, Paris.

Baudry J.-L. 1975, "Le dispositif: approches métapsychologiques de l'impression de la réalité", *Communications* 23/1, pp. 56-72.

Bazin A. 2008 (1975), *Qu'est-ce que le cinéma ?*, Paris.

Benjamin W. 2002a (1935), "Daguerre oder die Panoramen", in: W. Benjamin, *Medienästhetische Schriften* (Auswahl und Nachwort von D. Schöttker), Frankfurt am Main, pp. 127-128.

2002b (1936), "Pariser Brief (2): Malerei und Photographie", in: W. Benjamin, *Medienästhetische Schriften* (Auswahl und Nachwort von D. Schöttker), Frankfurt am Main, pp. 329-340.

2002c (1936/1939), "Das Kunstwerk im Zeitalter seiner technischen Reproduzierbarkeit", in: W. Benjamin, *Medienästhetische Schriften* (Auswahl und Nachwort von D. Schöttker), Frankfurt am Main, pp. 351-383.

Berardi F. 1995, *Neuromagma. Lavoro cognitivo e infoproduzione*, Roma.

2006, *Skizomedia. Trent'anni di mediattivismo*, Roma.

Berardi F. – Guarneri E. (ed.) 2007, *Alice è il diavolo*, Milano.

Bergson H. 1889, *Essai sur les données immédiates de la conscience*, Paris.

1896, *Matière et mémoire*, Paris.

1907, *L'evolution créatrice*. Paris.

Berkeley G. 1964 (1709), *An Essay Towards a New Theory of Vision*, in: A.A. Luce – T.E. Jessop, *The Works of George Berkeley, Bishop of Cloyne*, vol. I, London.

Boehm G. 2007, *Wie Bilder Sinn erzeugen. Die Macht des Zeigens*, Frankfurt am Main.

Böhm D. – Hiley B. J. 1993, *The Undivided Universe: An Ontological Interpretation on Quantum Theory*, London.

Bolter J.D. 1991, *Writing Space: The Computer, Hypertext, and the History of Writing*, New Jersey.

Bolter J.D. – Grusin R. 2000, *Remediation. Understanding New Media*, Cambridge (Massachusetts).

Bonilla D. 2006, "La estructura como narrativa. El uso de algoritmos estadísticos para el control de una narrativa hypermedia no lineal", *Razón y palabra* 49 (Ejemplar dedicado a: V Bienal Iberoamericana de la Comunicación (2/2)), p. 104.

Bonitzer P. 1982, *Le champ aveugle*, Ligugé.

Bonola R. 1955, *Non-Euclidean Geometry. A Critical and Historical Study of its Development*, New York.

Bordini S. 1984, *Storia del Panorama. La visione totale nella pittura del XIX secolo*, Roma.

Bordwell D. 1985, *Narration in the Fiction Film*, Madison, Wisconsin.

Borges J.L. 1997 (1949), *El Aleph*, Madrid.

Börsch-Supan H. 1960, *Die Bildgestaltung bei Caspar David Friedrich*, München.

Börsch-Supan H. – Jähnig K.W. 1973, *Caspar David Friedrich. Gemälde, Druckgraphik und bildmäßige Zeichnungen*, München.

Borsò V. – Görling R. (ed.) 2004, *Kulturelle Topografien*, Stuttgart.

Burch N. 1969, *Praxis du cinéma*, Paris.

Bush V. 1945, "As We May Think", *The Atlantic Magazine* (July 1945), on: http://www.theatlantic.com/magazine/archive/1945/07/as-we-may-think/3881/#

Bowring J. (ed.) 1843, *The Works of Jeremy Bentham*, vol. iv, London.

Boyer C.B. 1959, *The History of Calculs and Its Conceptual Development*, New York.

Bradbury S. 1967, *The Evolution of the Microscope*, Edinburg.

Bresson R. 1975, *Notes sur le cinématographe*, Paris.

Breton A. 1985 (1924), *Manifestes du surréalisme*, Malesherbes.

Browand F.K. 1986, "The Structure of the Turbulent Mixing Layer", *Physica18D*, p. 135.

Brownlow K. 1980, "Silent Films. What was the Right Speed?", *Sight and Sound* 49/3 (Summer 1980), pp. 164-167.

Cantor G. 1883, "Über unendliche, Lineare Punktmannigfaltigkeiten V", *Mathematische Annalen* 21, pp. 545-591.

Caronia A. 2006, "L'incoscio della macchina. Ovvero: come catturare il significante fluttuante", in A. Caronia – E. Livraghi – E. Pezzano (ed.), *L'arte nell'era della producibilità digitale*, Milano, pp. 125-140.

Caronia A. – Livraghi E. – Pezzano E. (ed.) 2006, *L'arte nell'era della producibilità digitale*, Milano.

Castells M. 2001, *The Internet Galaxy. Reflections on the Internet, Business, and Society*, Oxford.

Chinn W.G. – Steenrod N.E. 1966, *First concepts of topology. The Geometry of Mappings of Segments, Curves, Circles, and Disks*, Washington, D.C.

Chomsky N. – Herman E.S. 1988, *Manufacturing Consent : The Political Economy of the Mass Media*, New York.

Clark D.M. (ed.) 2008, *Berkeley: Philosophical Writings*, Cambridge.

Coe B. 1976, *The Birth of Photography. The Story of the Formative Years 1800-1900*, London.

Cohen G.L. – Shannon A.G. 1981, "John Ward's Method for the Calculation of Pi", *Historia Mathematica* 8/2, pp. 133-144.

Comolli J.-L. 1971-1978, "Technique et idéologie", *Cahiers du cinéma* nos. 229-240.

Condé S. 1993, *Fractalis. La complexité fractale dans l'art*, Paris.

Conklin J. 1987, "Hypertext: An Introduction and Survey", *IEEE Computer* 20/9 (September 1987), pp. 17-41.

Cortazár J. 2008 (1963), *Rayuela*, Madrid.

Couchot E. 1988, "La mosaïque ordonnée ou l'écran saisi par le calcul", *Communications* 48, pp. 79-87.

1989, "La question du temps dans les techniques électroniques et numériques de l'image", in: *3 ^{e} semaine internationale de vidéo, Saint-Gervais Genève (novembre 1989)*.

1993, "Zwischen Reellem und Virtuellem: die Kunst der Hybridation", in: F. Rötzer – P. Weibel (Hrsg.), *Cyberspace. Zum medialen Gesamtkunstwerk*, München, pp. 340-349.

2007, *Des images, du temps et des machines dans les arts et la communication*, Paris.

Court de Gébelin A. 1782, *Monde Primitif, Analysé et Comparé avec le Monde Moderne*, vol. 1, Paris.

Court T.H. – Clay R.S. 1932, *The History of the Microscope*, London.

Crochiere R.E. – Rabiner L.R. 1983, *Multirate Digital Signal Processing*, New Jersey.

Croft W.J. 2006, *Under the Microscope : A brief History of Microscopy*, Singapore.

Crutchfield J.P. 1984, "Space-Time Dynamics in Video Feedback", *Physica*, pp. 191-207.

1988, "Spatio-Temporal Complexity in Nonlinear Image Processing", *IEEE Transaction on Circuits and Systems* 35/7 (July 1988), pp. 769-780.

Cubitt S. 1991, *Timeshift. On video Culture*, London.

2004, *The Cinema Effect*, Cambridge.

Curi U. 2009, *L'immagine-pensiero. Tra Fellini, Wilder e Wenders : Un viaggio filosofico*, Milano.

D'Arcy W.T. 1969³, *On Growth and Form*, Cambridge.

Dalí S. 1930, "L'âne pourri", *Le surréalisme au service de la révolution* 1 (juillet 1930), pp. 9-12.

1977, *La conquista de lo irracional*, Barcelona.

Dällembach L. 1977, *Le récit spéculaire. Essai sur la mise en abyme*, Paris.

Dantzig T. 1954⁴, *Number, The language of Science*, Toronto.

Davis P. 1992, "Is the Universe a Machine?", in: N. Hall (ed.), *The New Scientist, Guide to Chaos*, London, pp. 213-221.

Debord G. 1967, *La société du spectacle*, Paris.

Debray R. 1991, *Cours de médiologie générale*, Paris.

1992, *Vie et mort de l'image*, Paris.

De Kerckhove D. 1991, *Brainframes. Technology, Mind and Business*, Utrecht.

De Kerckhove D. - Tursi A. (ed.) 2006, *Dopo la democrazia ?*, Milano.

Deleuze G. 1966, *Le bergsonisme*, Paris.

1983, *Cinéma 1. L'immage-mouvement*, Paris.

1985, *Cinéma 2. L'image-temps*, Paris.

1988, *Le Pli, Leibniz et le baroque*, Paris.

Deleuze G. - Guattari F. 1980, *Capitalisme et schizophrénie 2. Mille plateaux*, Paris.

1991, *Qu'est-ce que la philosophie ?*, Paris.

Della Porta G.B. 2008 (1589), *La Magia Naturale*, Firenze.

Descartes R. 1925 (1637), *The Geometry of René Descartes* (Ed. by D.E. Smith - M.L. Lathem), New York.

Dickinson H.W. 2009, *Robert Fulton, Engineer and Artist. His Life and Works*, New York.

Dicks D.R. 1970, *Early Greek Astronomy to Aristotle*, Ithaca.

Didi-Huberman G. 1990, *Devant l'image*, Paris.

Dierkesmann M. - Lorentz G.G. - Bergmann G. - Bonnet H. 1967, "Felix Hausdorff zum gedächtnis", *Jahresbericht der Deutschen Mathematiker-Vereinigung* 69, pp. 51-76.

Dieudonné J. 1989, *A History of Algebraic and differential Topology 1900-1960*, Boston.

1994, "Une brève histoire de la topologie", in: J.-P. Pier (ed.), *Development of Mathematics 1900-1950*, Basel, pp. 35-155.

Duarte G.A. 2009, *La scomparsa dell'orologio universale. Peter Watkins e i mass media audiovisivi*, Milano.

2011, *Reificación mediática*, Bucaramanga.

Eco U. 1985, *Sugli specchi e altri saggi. Il segno, la rappresentazione, l'illusione, l'immagine*, Milano.

2003, *Dire quasi la stessa cosa. Esperienze di traduzione*, Milano.

2005⁸ (1964), *Apocalittici e integrati. Comunicazione di massa e teorie della cultura di massa*, Milano.

2006⁷ (1962), *Opera aperta. Forma e indeterminazione nelle poetiche contemporanee*, Milano.

Eglash R. 2005, *African Fractals. Modern Computing and Indigenous Design*, New Yersey.

Einsenstein S.M. 1943, *The Film Sense* (Edited and translated by J. Leyda), London.

1949, *Film Form: Essays on Film Theory* (Edited and translated by J. Leyda), London.

Ekeland I. 1995, *Le Chaos*, Paris.

Elsaesser T. 2009, "Tales of Epiphany and Entropy: Around the Worlds in Eighty Clicks", in: P. Snickars – P. Vonderau (eds.), *The YouTube Reader*, Lithuania, pp. 166-186.

Engell L. 1999, "Fernsehen mit Gilles Deleuze", in: O. Fahle – L. Engell (Hrsg.), *Der Film bei Deleuze / Le cinéma selon Deleuze*, Weimar, pp. 468-481.

2003, *Bilder des Wandels*, Weimar.

Epstein J. 1946, *L'intelligence d'une machine*, Paris.

1974, *Écrits sur le cinéma, Tome 1*. Paris.

Evans R. 1971, "Bentham's Panopticon. An Incident in the Social History of Architecture", *Architectural Association Quarterly* 3/2 (April-July 1971), Oxford – New York, pp. 21-37.

Fahle O. 1999, "Deleuze und die Geschichte des Films", in: O. Fahle – L. Engell (Hrsg.), *Der Film bei Deleuze / Le cinéma selon Deleuze*, Weimar, pp.114-126.

2005, *Bilder der Zweiten Moderne*, Weimar.

2007, "Die Transtemporalität des Fernsehens", in: K. Greiser – G. Schweppenhäuser (Hrsg.), *Zeit der Bilder Bilder der Zeit*, Weimar, pp. 123-136.

Fan L.T. – Neogi D. – Yashima M. 1991, *Elementary Introduction to Spatial and Temporal Fractals*, Berlin.

Fauvel J. – Gray J. 1987, *The history of Mathematics: A Reader*, London.

Ferrier J.L. 1977, *Holbein, les Ambassadeurs, Anatomie d'un tableau*, Paris.

Fihman G. 1999, "Bergson, Zénon d'Élée et le cinéma /Bergson, Deleuze und das Kino", in: O. Fahle – L. Engell (Hrsg.), *Der Film bei Deleuze / Le cinéma selon Deleuze*, Weimar, pp. 62-85.

Fleischer I. – Hinz B. – Schipper I. – Mattausch R. 1974, "Friedrich in seiner Zeit. Das Problem der Entzweiung", in: W. Hofmann – C. David (Hrsg.), *Friedrich und die deutsche Nachwelt*, Frankfurt am Main, pp. 17-27.

Flusser V. 2008, *Kommunikologie weiter denken. Die Bochumer Vorlesungen*, Frankfurt am Main.

1996, *Ins universum der Technischen Bilder*, Göttingen.

Foras (de) A. 1883, *Le Blason, dictionnaire et remarques*, Grenoble.

Foucault M. 1966, *Les mots et les choses*, Paris.

1969, *L'archéologie du savoir*, Paris.

1975, *Surveiller et punir. Naissance de la prison*, Saint-Amand.

1984, "Des espaces autres", *Architecture, Mouvement, Continuité* 5 (octobre 1984), pp. 46-49.

Fox-Davies A.C. 2006, *A Complete Guide to Heraldry*, London.

Fragier J.-P. 1989, "Z. Rybczynski et G. Hill: la ligne, le point, le pli", *Cahiers du cinéma* (janvier 1989).

Frahm L. 2010, *Jenseits des Raums. Zur filmischen Topologie des Urbanen*, Bielefeld.

Franklyn J. – Tanner J. 1970, *An Encyclopaedic Dictionary of Heraldry*, New York.

Freud S. 1904, *Zur Psychopathologie des Alltagslebens (Ubre Vergesse, Versprechen, Vergreifen, Aberglauben und Irrtum)*, Berlin (Kindle edition).

Friedberg A. 1994, *Windows Shoping: Cinema and the Postmodern*, Los Angeles.

Furlong L. 1983, "Notes Toward a History of Image-processed Video: Steina and Woody Vasulka", *Afterimage, Visual Studies Worshop* 11/5 (December 1983), p. 15.

Galbreath D.L. 1948, *Handbüchlein der Heraldik*, Lausanne.

Galimberti U. 2005[4] (1999), *Psiche e Techne. L'uomo nell'età tecnica*, Milano.

Gardies A. 1993, *L'espace au cinéma*, Paris.

Gaudreault A. 2002, "Dal Semplice al multiplo o il cinema come serie di serie…", in: A. Antonini (ed.), *Il film e i suoi multipli, Atti del IX Convegno internazionale di studi sul cinema, Udine, 20-23 marzo 2002 Gorizia*, Udine, pp. 29-35.

Gazzano M.M. 1995, "Sulle tracce del fuoco degli dei", in: M.M. Gazzano (ed.), *Steina e Woody Vasulka. Video, media e nuove immagini nell'arte contemporanea*, Roma, pp. 11-24.

Genette G. 1982, *Palimpsestes. La littérature au second degré*, Saint-Amand-Montrond (Cher).

Gernsheim H. 1955, *The History of Photography. From the Earliest Use of the Camera Obscura in the Eleventh Century up to 1914*, London – New York – Toronto. 1965[3], *A Concise History of Photography*, New York.

Gernsheim H. – Gernsheim A. 1956, *L.J.M. Daguerre (1787-1851). The World's First Photographer*, Cleveland.

Gide A. 1951, *Journal 1889-1939*, Paris.

Gleick J. 1987, *Chaos, Macking a New Science*, New York.

Gleizes A. 1969, *Puissances du cubisme*, Chambery.

Gleizes A. – Metzinger J. 1993, *Du Cubisme*, Frankfurt.

Godard J.-L. 1985, *Jean-Luc Godard par Jean-Luc Godard*, Paris.

Goldberg V. 1988, *Photography in print : Writings from 1816 to the Present*, New York.

Gombrich E.H. 1960[11] (1957), *Art and Illusion. A Study in the Psychology of Pictorial Representation*, Hong Kong.

Grassmann H. 1878, *Die Ausdehnungslehre von 1844 : oder Die Lineale Ausdehnungslehre, ein neur Zweig der Mathematik*, Leipzig.

Gray J. 1989[2], *Ideas of Space. Euclidean, Non-Euclidean, and Relativistic*, New York. 1994, "Curves", *Companion Encyclopedia of the History and Philosophy of the Mathematical Sciences*, volume 2, London, pp. 860-865.

Großklaus G. 2003, "Zeitbewusstsein und Medien", in: C. Funken – M. Löw (Hrsg.), *Raum – Zeit – Medialität. Interdisziplinäre Studien zu neuen Kommunikationstechnologie*, Hemsbach, pp. 23-38.

Grusin R. 2009, "YouTube at the End of New Media", in: P. Snickars – P. Vonderau (eds.), *The YouTube Reader*, Lithuania, pp. 60-67.

Günzel S. 2007, "Raum – Topographie – Topologie", in: S. Günzel (Hrsg.), *Topologie. Zur Raumbeschreibung in den Kultur- und Medienwissenschaften*, Bielefeld, pp. 13-29.

Hallin D. 1989, *The "Uncensored War": The Media and Vietnam*, Oxford.

Hallyn F. 1980a, "Holbein: La mort en abyme", in: F. Hallyn (ed.), *Onze études sur la mise en abyme*, Paris, pp. 165-181.

1980b, "Le microcosme", in: F. Hallyn (ed.), *Onze études sur la mise en abyme*, pp. 183-192. Paris.

Hartlaub G.F. – Weißenfeld F. 1958, *Gestalt und Gestaltung: Das Kunstwerk als Selbstdarstellung des Künstlers*, Krefeld.

Hatanaka M. – Koizumi K. – Sekiguchi M. (ed.) 1998, *Steina & Woody Vasulka Video Works*, Tokyo.

1951, *Zauber des Spiegles. Geschichte und Bedeutung des Spiegels in der Kunst*, München.

Heath T. 1981, *A History of Greek Mathematics. From Thales to Euclid*, Vol I, Toronto.

Heelan P.A. 1988, *Space-Perception and the Philosophy of Science*, Los Angeles.

Heidegger M. 1954 (1930), *Vom Wesen der Wahrheit*, Frankfurt am Main.

1977 (1950), *Holzwege*, Frankfurt am Main.

Heilbroner R.L. 1996[3], "Do Machines Make History?", in: M.R. Smith – L. Marx L. (eds.), *Does Technology Drive History? The Dilema of Technological Determinism*, London, pp. 53-65.

Helmholtz H. 1876, "The Origin and Meaning of Geometrical Axioms", *Mind* 1/3 (Jul. 1876), pp. 301-321.

Henderson L.D. 1983, *The Fourth Dimension and Non-Euclidean Geometry in Modern Art*, New Jersey.

Hennessy J.L. – Patterson D.A. 2003, *Computer Architecture: A Quantitative Approach*, Amsterdam.

Herbert S. 2000, *A History of Pre-Cinema*, Vol-1, London.

Heuser M.-L. 2007, "Die Anfänge der Topologie in Mathematik und Naturphilosophie", in: S. Günzel (Hrsg.), *Topologie. Zur Raumbeschreibung in den Kultur- und Medienwissenschaften*, Bielefeld, pp. 181-200.

Hick U. 1999, *Geschichte der optischen Medien*, München.

Hilbert D. 1891, "Über die stetige Abbildung einer Linie auf ein Flächenstück", *Mathematische Annalen* 38, pp. 459-460.

1962 (1899), *Grundlagen der Geometrie*, Stuttgart.

Himanen P. 2001, *The Hacker Ethic and the Spirit of the Information Age*, New York.

Hinz S. 1974, *Caspar David Friedrich in Briefen und Bekenntnissen*, Berlin.

Holmes O.W. 1861, "Sun-Painting and Sun-Sculpture; with a Stereoscopic Trip across the Atlantic", *Atlantic Monthly* 8/45 (June 1861), 13-29.

Hooke R. 1961 (1665), *Micrographia or Some Physiological Descriptions of Minute Bodies Made by Magnifying Glasses with Observations and Inquiries Thereupon*, New York.

Horkheimer M. – Adorno T.W. 1947, *Dialektik der Aufklärung. Philosophische Fragmente*, Amsterdam.

Hörl E. (Hrsg.) 2011, *Die technologische Bedingung. Beiträge zur Beschreibung der technischen Welt*, Berlin.

Hughes T.P. 1987, "The Evolution of Large Technological Systems", in: W. Bijker – T.P. Hughes – T. Pinch (eds.), *The Social Construction of Technological Systems*, Cambridge, Massachussets, pp. 45-76.

1998, *Rescuing Prometheus*, New York.

Hulten P. 1977, "Etienne-Jules Marey et la mise à nu de l'espace/temps", in: *E.J. Marey. 1830/1904 La photographie du mouvement* (Centre Nacional d'art et de culture George Pompidou), Paris, pp. 7-8.

Hunt R. 1839, "On the Applications of Science to the Fine and Useful Arts", *The Magazine of Science and School of Arts* no IV.

Jackson W.J. 2004, *Heaven's Fractals Net. Retrieving Lost Visions in the Humanities*, Bloomington.

James D.E. (ed.) 1992, *To Free the Cinema. Jonas Mekas & the New York Underground*, New York.

Jay P. 1976, *Niépce et Daguerre*, Chalán-sur-Saône.

1983, *Nicéphore Niépce*, Paris.

1988, *Niépce, Genèse d'une invention*, Chalon-sur-Saône.

Kappelhoff H. 2005, "Der Bildraum des Kinos. Modulationen einer ästhetischen Erfahrungsform", in: G. Koch (Hrsg.), *Umwidmungen. Architektonische und kinematographische Räume*, Berlin, pp. 138-149.

Kessler F. - Schäfer M.T. 2009, "Navigating YouTube: Constituting a Hybrid Information Management System", in: P. Snickars - P. Vonderau (eds.), *The YouTube Reader*, Lithuania, pp. 275-291.

Kermabon J. 1990, "Zbigniew Rybczynski, l'autre dimension", *Bref* (May -July).

Kittler F.A. 2001, "Computer Graphics: A Semi-Technical Introduction", *The Grey Room*, no. 2, (Winter 2001) pp. 30-45.

Kolb D. 2009, "Other Spaces for Spatial Hypertexts", *Journal of Digital Information* vol. 10/3, online version: http://journals.tdl.org/jodi/article/view/171/485

Kolmogorov A.N. - Yushkevich A.P. 1996, *Mathematics of the 19th Century. Geometry Analytic Function Theory*, Basel.

Konermann R. 1991, *Lebendige Spiegel. Die Metapher des Subjekts*, Frankfurt am Main.

Körner S. 1960, *Philosophy of Mathematics*, London.

Kracauer S. 1997, *Theory of Film. The Redemption of Physical Reality*, Princeton.

Kraemer H. 1985 (1900), *Die Ingenieurskunst auf der Pariser Weltausstellung 1900*, Düsseldorf.

Krämer S. 1998, "Was haben die Medien, der Computer und die Realität miteinander zu tun", in: S. Krämer (Hrsg.), *Medien, Computer, Realität. Wirklichkeitsvorstellungen und Neue Medien*. Frankfurt, pp. 9-26.

Kristeva J. 1969, *Sèméiotikè. Recherches pour une sémanalyse*, Paris.

Laffay A. 1964, *Logique du cinéma*, Paris.

Landow G.P. 2006, *Hypertext 3.0. Critical Theory and New Media in a Era of Globalization*, Baltimore.

Lange K. - Fuhse F. 1970 (1893), *Dürers Schriftlicher Nachlass* (New Edition 1970), Halle.

Lavin I. 1980, *Bernini and the Unity of the Visual Arts*, London.

Lawder S. 1975, *The Cubist Cinema*, New York.

Leadbeater C.W. 1910, *L'autre côté de la mort*, Paris.

Lefèbvre H. 2000[4], *La production de l'espace*, Paris.

Leibniz G.W. 1996a (1765), *Nouveaux essais sur l'entendement humain / Neue Abhandlungen über den menschlichen Verstand*, in: G.W. Leibniz, Philosophische Schriften Band 3.1 and 3.2 (Edited by W. von Engelhardt – H.H. Holz), Frankfurt am Main.

1996b (1695), *Systeme nouveau de la nature et de la communication des substances, aussi bien que de l'union qu'il y a entre l'ame et le corps / Neues System der nature und des verkehrs der Substanzen sowie der verbindung, die es zwischen seele und körper gibt*, in: G.W. Leibniz, Kleine Schriften zur Metaphysik. Philosophische Schriften Band 1 (Edited by W. von Engelhardt – H.H. Holz), Frankfurt am Main, pp. 191-320.

1996c (1714), *Monadologie / Monadologie*, in: G.W. Leibniz, Kleine Schriften zur Metaphysik. Philosophische Schriften Band 1 (Edited by W. von Engelhardt – H.H. Holz), Frankfurt am Main, pp. 438-483.

1996d (1768), *Eclaircissement des difficultés que monsieur Bayle a trouvées dans le Systeme Nouveau de l'union de l'ame et du corps. / Erläuterung zu den Schwierigkeiten, die Bayle in dem Neuen System der Vereunigung der Seele un des Körpers gefunden hat*, in: G.W. Leibniz, Kleine Schriften zur Metaphysik. Philosophische Schriften Band 1 (Edited by W. von Engelhardt – H.H. Holz), Frankfurt am Main, pp. 252-270.

1996e, *De Primae philosophiae emendatione, et de notione substantiae /Über die verbesserung der ersten philosophie und über den Begriff der Substanz*, in: G.W. Leibniz, Kleine Schriften zur Metaphysik. Philosophische Schriften Band 1 (Edited by W. von Engelhardt – H.H. Holz), Frankfurt am Main, pp. 194-199.

Leiris M. 1946, *L'âge d'homme*, Paris.

Leonesi S. – Toffalori C. 2007, *Matematica, Miracoli e Paradossi. Storie di Cardinali da Cantor a Gödel*, Parma.

Leroi-Gourhan A. 1964-1965, *Le geste et la parole*. Vol I: *Technique et langage*. Vol II: *La mémoire et le rhythmes*, Paris.

Lévy P. 1997, *L'intelligence collective. Pour une anthropologie du cyberspace*, Paris.

Lévi-Strauss C. 1987, *Race et histoire*, Saint-Ammand.

Lewis C.A. 1975, *A Historical Analysis of Grassmann's Ausdehnungslehre of 1844*, Michigan.

L'Herbier M. 1946, *Intelligence du cinématographe*, Paris.

Lillestrand R.L. 1972, "Techniques for Change Detection", *IEEE Transactions on Computers* C-21/7, pp. 654-659.

Lindeberg D.C. 1996, *Roger Bacon and the Origins of Perspectiva in the Middle Ages. A Critical Edition and English Translation of Bacon's* Perspectiva *with Introduction and Notes*, Oxford.

Listing J.B. 1848, *Vorstudien zur Topologie*, Göttingen.

Lyotard J.F. 1979, *La condition postmoderne*, Paris.

Lyssy A. 2009, "Monaden als lebendige Spiegel des Universums", in: H. Busche (Hrsg.), *Gottfried Wilhelm Leibniz Monadologie* (Klassiker Auslegen Band 34), Berlin, pp. 145-160.

Malraux A. 1940, "Esquisse d'une psycologie du cinéma", *Verve* 2/8, pp. 69-73.

1946, *Esquisse d'une psychologie du cinéma*, Paris.

Mandelbrot B. 1963a, "A New Model for the Clusterning of Errors on Telephone Circuits", *IBM Journal of Research and Development* 7, pp. 224-236.

1963b, "The Variation of Certain Speculative Prices", *The Journal of Business* 36, pp. 394-419.

1967, "How Long is the coast of Britain? Statistical self-similarity and fractional dimension", *Science* 156, pp. 636-638.

1983, *The Fractal Geometry of Nature*, New York.

1995, *Les objets Fractals. Forme, hasard et dimension*, Manchecourt.

1997, *Fractales, Hasard et Finance*, Manchecourt.

Mandelbrot B. – Lorenz E. – Peitgen H.O. 1990, *Fraktale in Filmen und Gespräche*, Heidelberg.

Mannoni L. – Pesenti Campagnoni D. – Robinson D. 1995, *Light and Movement. Incunabula of the Motion Picture*, Gemona.

Manovich L. 2001, *The language of New Media*, Cambridge.

2007, "Database as Symbolic Form", in: V. Vesna (ed.), *Database Aesthetics, Art in the Age of Information Overflow*, Minneapolis, pp. 39-60.

Maor E. 1987, *To Infinity and Beyond. A Cultural History of the Infinite*, Boston.

Marcuse H. 1964, *One Dimensional Man. Studies in the Ideology Of Advanced Industrial Society*, Boston.

Marey E.J. 1863, *Physiologie médicale de la circulation du sang, basée sur l'étude des mouvements du cœur et du pouls artériel, avec application aux maladies de l'appareil circulatoire*, Paris.

1868, *Du mouvement dans les fonctions de la vie*, Paris.

1873, *La machine animale, locomotion terrestre et aérienne*, Paris.

1885, *Développement de la méthode graphique par l'emploi de la photographie. Supplément à La Méthode Graphique*, Paris.

1890, *Le vol des oiseaux*, Paris.

1895, *Movement*, New York.

Marks L.U. 2010, *Enfoldment and Infinity. An Islamic Genealogy of New Media*, Cambridge.

Martens M. – Nowicki T.J. 2003, "Ergodic Theory of One-Dimensional Dynamics", *IBM Journal of Research and Development* 47/1, pp. 67-76.

Martin B. 1742, *The Micrographia Nova: Or a New Treatise on the Microscope, and Microscopic Objects*, London.

McLuhan M. 2003 (1964), *Understanding Media. The Extension of Man* (Critical Edition Edited by W.T. Gordon), Corte Madera, California.

Merleau-Ponty M. 1945, *Phénoménologie de la perception*, Paris.

1964, *L'œil et l'esprit*, Paris.

Meteyard E. 1970 (1865), *The Life of Josiah Wedgwood*, London.

Metz C. 1968, *Essais sur la signification au cinéma*, Paris.

1977, *Essais sémiotiques*, Paris.

Michaud J.Fr. – Michaud L.G. (éd.) 1968 (1811-1962), *Biographie universelle ancienne et moderne*, 79 vols., Paris.

Michotte Van Den Berk A. 1948, "Le caractère de la réalité des projections ciné-matographiques", *Revue internationale de filmologie* 1/3-4, pp. 249-261.

Mitry J. 1963a, *Dictionaire du cinéma*, Paris.

1963b, *Esthétique et psychologie du cinéma*, vol 1., Paris.

1987, *La sémiologie en question*, Paris.

Mondzain M.-J. 1998, *Image, icône, économie : Les sources byzantines de l'imaginaire contemporain*, Paris.

Morin E. 1956, *Le cinéma ou l'homme imaginaire*, Paris.

2005, *Introduction à la pensée complexe*, Paris.

Müller E. 2009, "Where Quality Matters: Discurses on the Art of Making a YouTube Video", in: P. Snickars – P. Vonderau (eds.), *The YouTube Reader*, Lithuania, pp. 126-139.

Mullin T. 1992, "Turbulent Times For Fluids", in: N. Hall (ed.), *The Newscientist Guide to Chaos*, London, pp. 59-68.

Murria J.H. 1997, "The Pedagogy of Cyberfiction: Teaching a Course on Reading and Writing Interactive Narrative", in: E. Barret – M. Redmond (eds.), *Contextual Media: Multimedia and Interpretation*, Cambridge, pp. 129-162.

Musha T. – Higuci H. 1976, "The 1/f Fluctuation of a Traffic Curren ton a Express-way", *Japanese Journal of Applied Physics* 15, pp. 1271-1275.

Muybridge E. 1955, *The Human Figure in Motion*, New York.

1979, *Complete Human and Animal Locomotion,* vol. I, New York.

Nagel E. 1939, "The Formation of Modern Conceptions of Formal Logic in the Devel-opment of Geometry", *Osiris* 7, 142-223.

Neubecker O. 1976, *Heraldry: Sources, Symbols and Meaning*, London.

Newhall B. 1982, *The history of Photography from 1839 to the Present*, (Revised and enlarged edition), London.

Niépce I. 1841, *Historique de la decouverte improprement nomée Daguerréotype*, Paris.

Noake R. 1988, *Animation Techniques. Planning & Producing Animation UIT Today's Technologies*, New York.

Oettermann S. 1980, *Das Panorma. Die Geschichte eines Massenmediums*, Frankfurt am Main.

O'Reilly T. 2005, *What is Web 2.0. Design Patterns and Business Models for the Next Generation of Software*, On: http://oreilly.com/web2/archive/what-is-web-20.html#mememap

Panofsky E. 1954, *Galileo as a Critic of the Arts*, La Haye.

1974, "Style and Medium in the Motion Pictures", in: G. Mast – M. Cohen (eds.), *Film Theory and Criticism: Introductory Readings*, London.

1969, *Renaissance and Renascences in Western Art*, Stockholm.

2009[5], *Perspective as Symbolic Form*, New York.

Pasolini P.P. 2000, *Empirismo eretico*, Milano.

Peano G. 1890, "Sur une courbe, qui remplit toute une aire plane", *Mathematische Annalen* 36, pp. 157-160.

Peitgen H.O. – H. Jürgens – D. Saupe. 1992, *Chaos and Fractals, New Frontiers of Science*, New York.

Pfeifer P.J. – Obert M. 1989, "Fractals: Basic Concepts and Terminology", in: Avnir D. (ed.) *The Fractal Approach to Heterogeneus Chemistry*, pp. 11-43, Chichester.

Pfau L. 1877, *Kunst und Gewerbe*, Part I, Stuttgart.

Poncelet J.V. 1822, *Traité des propriétés projectives des figures*, Paris.

Poincaré H. 1953a (1892), "Comptes rendus", in: *Oeuvres*, vol. VI, Paris, pp. 189-192.

1953b (1895), "Analysis Situs", in: *Oeuvres*, vol. VI, Paris, pp.193-288.

1902, *La Science et l'hypothèse*, Paris.

1908, *Science et Méthode*, Paris.

Poser H. 2009, "Innere Prinzipen und Hierarchie der Monaden (§§ 9-9, 82 f.)", in: H. Busche (Hrsg.), *Gottfried Wilhelm Leibniz Monadologie* (Klassiker Auslegen Band 34), Berlin, pp. 81-94.

Potonniée G. 1925, *Histoire de la découverte de la photographie*, Paris.

Pudovkin V.I. 1970, *Film Technique and Film Acting*, New York.

Quart A. 2005, "Networked: Don Roos and 'Happy Endings'" on: http://www.alissaquart.com/articles/2005/08/networked_don_roos_and_happy_e.html

Ramonet I. 2001, *La tyrannie de la communication*, Paris.

Reed D. 1995, *Figures of Tought. Mathematics and Mathematical Texts*, London.

Reis M. 2007, "Zur Topologie des Kinos – und darüber hinaus", in: S. Günzel (Hrsg.), *Topologie. Zur Raumbeschreibung in den Kultur- und Medienwissenschaften*, Bielefeld, pp. 297-308.

Riemann B. 1919, *Über die Hypothesen, welche der Geometrie zu Grande liegen*, Berlin.

Riley R. 1996a, "Steina and Woody Vasulka: Machine Media", in: R. Riley – M. Sturken (eds.), *Steina and Woody Vasulka: Machine Media*, San Francisco, pp. 9-11.

1996b, "Instalations", in: R. Riley – M. Sturken (ed.), *Steina and Woody Vasulka: Machine Media*, San Francisco, pp.12-25.

Risholm E. 2001, "Film, Raum, Figur: Raumpraktiken in F.W. Murnaus Film Nosferatu – Eine Symphonie des Grauens", in: S. Lange (Hrsg.), *Raumkonstruktionen in der Moderne. Kultur – Literatur – Film*, Bielefeld, pp. 265-288.

Rondinella L.F. 1929, *More About Muybridge's Work. The General History and Historical Chronicle*, Philadelphia.

Ropars-Wuilleumer M.-C. 1999, "Le tout contre la partie: une fêlure à réparer / Das Ganze gegen das Teil: ein Riß, der zu schließen ist", in: O. Fahle – L. Engell (Hrsg.), *Der Film bei Deleuze / Le cinéma selon Deleuze*, Weimar, pp. 242-267.

Ross A. 1991, "A Semiological Exploration of Dalí's Paranoiac-Critical Method", on: http://www.dr-yo.com/writing_semiotic.html

Rubin W. – Fluegel J. 1980, *Pablo Picasso. A Retrospective*, New York.

Rutherford D. 2009, "Simple Substances and Composite Bodies (§§ 1-5)", in: H. Bus-che (Hrsg.), *Gottfried Wilhelm Leibniz Monadologie* (Klassiker Auslegen Band 34), Berlin, pp. 35-48.

Rybczynski Z. 1997, "Looking to the Future – Imagining the Truth", in: F. Penz – M. Thomas (eds.), *Cinema & Architecture. Méliès, Mallet-Stevens, Multimedia*, London.

2007, "Kwadrat", in: L. Ronduda – F. Zeyfand (eds.), *1,2,3...Avant-Gardes. Film/Art Between Experiment and Archive*, Berlin, p. 139.

Sadoul G. 1949, *Histoire du cinéma mondial, des origines a nos jours*, Orléans.

Sartre J.-P. 1940, *L'imaginaire. Psychologie Phénoménologique de l'imagination*, Paris.

Scharf A. 1968, *Art and Photography*, London.

Scheele C.W. 1777, *Aeris atque ignis examen chemicum*, Leipzig (English translation: *Chemical Observations and Experiments on Air and Fire*, London 1780).

Schiavo L.B. 2003, "From Phantom Image To Perfect Vision: Physiological Optics, Commercial Photography, and the Popularization of the Stereoscope", in: L. Gitelman – G.B. Pingree (eds.), *New Media, 1740- 1915*, Cambridge, Massachusetts, pp. 113-137.

Schickore J. 2007, *The Microscope and the Eye*, Chicago.

Schier J. 1992, "Description of the George Brown Multi-Level Keyer (april 21, 1992)", in: Daniel Langlois Foundation, Steina and Woody Vasulka Founds, VAS B37-C2-3.

Schmeling M. 1977, *Das Spiel im Spiel. Ein Beitrag zur Vergleichenden Literaturkritik*, Saarbrücken.

Schuster M. 2000, "Das Ende der Bilder in endlosen Bildern? Beweguns-Bild und Interaktions-Bild", in: H. Beller (Hrsg.), *Onscreen/Offscreen. Grenzen, Übergänge und Wandel des filmischen Raumes*, Stuttgart, pp. 123-158.

Serres M. 1968, *Le système de Leibniz et ses modèles mathématiques*, Paris.

1993, *Les origines de la géométrie*, Paris.

Shapiro S. 1997, *Philosophy of Mathematics. Structure and Ontology*, New York.

Shipman III F.M. 1999, "Spatial Hypertext: An alternative to navigational and semantic Links", on: http://www.cs.brown.edu/memex/ACM_HypertextTestbed/papers/37.html

Shipman III F.M. – Furuta R. – Marshall C.C. 1997, "Generating Web-based Presentations in Spatial Hypertext", in: *IUI'97. Proceedings of the 2nd Internacional Conference on Intelligent User Interfaces*, New York, pp. 71-78.

Simmel G. 1908, *Soziologie. Untersuchungen über die Formen der Vergesellschaftung*, Leipzig.

Smith A. 1966 (1759), *The Theory of Moral Sentiments*, New York.

Smith D.E. - Latham M.L. 1925, *The Geometry of René Descartes*, New York.

Smith M.L. 1996 (1994), "Recourse of Empire: Landscapes of Progress in Technological America", in: M.R. Smith – L. Marx (eds.), *Does Technology Drive History? The Dilema of Technological Determinism*, London, pp. 37-52.

Smith M.R. 1996 (1994), "Technological Determinism in American Culture", in: M.R. Smith – L. Marx (eds.), *Does Technology Drive History? The Dilema of Technological Determinism*, London, pp. 1-35.

Smith M.R. – Marx L. (eds.) 1996 (1994), *Does Technology Drive History? The Dilema of Technological Determinism,* London.

Snelders H.A.M. 1982, "Antoni Van Leeuwenhoek's Mechanistic View of the World", in: L.C. Palm – H.A.M. Snelders (eds.), *Antoni van Leeuwenhoek 1632-1723*, Amsterdam, pp. 57-78.

Sobchack V. 1999, "Nostalgia for a Digital Object: Regrets on the Quickening of Quicktime", *Millennium Film Journal* 34, pp. 29-38.

Solar G. 1979, *Das Panorama und Seine Vorentwicklung bis zu Hans Conrad Escher von der Linth*, Zurich.

Sorval (de) G. 1981, *Le langage secret du blason*, Paris.

Spielmann Y. 2004, "Video and Computer", on: http://www.fondation-langlois.org/html/e/page.php?NumPage=461#intro.

2005, *Video. Das reflexive Medium*, Frankfurt am Main.

Stauff M. 2010, "The Governmentality of Media : Television as 'Problem' and 'Instrument'", in: L. Jäger – E. Linz – I. Schneider (eds.), *Media, Culture and Mediality. New Insights into the Current State of Research*, Bielefeld, pp. 263-281.

Steffends B. 2007, *Ibn al-Haytham First scientist*, North Carolina Greensboro.

Sternberger D. 1955, *Panorama, oder Ansichten vom 19. Jahrhundert*, Hamburg.

Stewart I. 1975, *Concept of Modern Mathematics*, New York.

1992, "Portraits of Chaos", in: N. Hall (ed.), *The Newscientist Guide to Chaos*, London, p. 44-58.

Stiegler B. 2009, "The Carnival of the New Screen : From Hegemony to Isonomy", in: P. Snickars – P. Vonderau (eds.), *The YouTube Reader*, Lithuania, pp 40-59.

Sturken M. 1995, "Exploring the Phenomenology of the Electronic Image", in: M.M. Gazzano (ed.), *Steina e Woody Vasulka. Video, media e nuove immagini nell'arte contemporanea*, Roma.

1996a, "Videotapes",in: R. Riley – M. Sturken (eds.), *Steina and Woody Vasulka: Machine Media*, San Francisco, 26-34.

1996b, "Steina and Woody Vasulka: in Dialogue With the Machine", in: R. Riley – M. Sturken (eds.), *Steina and Woody Vasulka: Machine Media*, San Francisco, pp. 35-48.

Talbot H. F. 1969, *The Pencil of Nature*, New York.

Toepell M. 1986, *Über die Entstehung von David Hilberts « Grundlagen der Geometrie »*, Göttingen.

Torretti R. 1978, *Philosophy of the Geometry. From Riemann to Poincaré*, London.

Toth I. 1991, "Le problème de la mesure dans la perspective de l'être et du non-être. Zénon et Platon, Eudoxe et Dedekind : une généalogie philosophico-mathématique", in: R. Rashed (éd.), *Mathématiques et philosophie. De l'antiquté à l'âge classique*, Paris, pp. 21-99.

Uttal W. 1978, *Psychobiology of Mind*, Hilsdale, New Jersey.

Van D'Elden S.C. 1976, *Peter Suchenwirt and Heraldic Poetry*, Wien.

Valenciennes P.H. 1820 (1800), *Éléments de perspective pratique a l'usage des artistes*, Paris.

van Leeuwenhoek A. 1939-, *Alle de brieven von Antoni van Leeuwenhoek: The Collected Letters of Antoni van Leeuwenhoek* (Edited and Annotated by a Committee of Dutch Scientists), 19 vols., Lisse.

Vandenbunder A. 1999, "La rencontre Deleuze-Pierce", in: O. Fahle – L. Engell (Hrsg.), *Der Film bei Deleuze / Le film selon Deleuze*, Weimar, pp. 86-113.

Vaughan W. 1979, *German Romanticism and English Art*, London.

Vertov D. 2011, *L'Occhio Della rivoluzione. Scritti dal 1922 al 1942* (Ed. by P. Montani), Milano.

Vesna V. 2007, "Seeing the World in a Grain of Sand: The Database Aesthetics of Everything", in: V. Vesna (ed.), *Database Aesthetics, Art in the Age of Information Overflow*, Minneapolis, pp. 3-38.

Virilio P. 1977, *Vitesse et politique*, Paris.

1989, "Le phénomène Rybczynski", *Cahiers du cinéma* (janvier 1989).

1994, *La machine de vision*, Paris.

Vries L. (de) 1975, *Tolle Erfindungen des 19. Jahrhunderts*, Hamburg.

Wade N.J. 2005, "Accentuating the Negative: Tom Wedgwood (1771 – 1805), Photography and Perception", *Perception* 34/5, pp. 513-520.

Wagner A.R. 1939, *Heralds and Heraldry in the Middle Ages*, London.

Wark M. 2004, *A Hacker Manifesto*, Cambridge, Massachussets.

Wartofsky M. 1980, "Art History and Perception", in: J. Fisher (ed.), *Perceiving Artworks*, Philadelphia, pp. 23-41.

Whatling S. 2009, "Putting Mise-en-abyme in its (Medieval) Place", on: www.courtauld.ac.uk.

Weber T. 2008, *Medialität als Grenzerfahrung. Futurische Medien im Kino der 80er und 90er Jahre*, Berlin.

Wedgwood T. – Davy H. 1802, "An Account of a Method of Copying Paintings Upon Glass, and of Making Profiles, by the Agency of Light Upon Nitrate of Silver", *Journal of the Royal Institution* 1, p. 170.

Wiesing L. 2005, *Artifizielle Präsenz. Studien zur Philosophie des Bildes*, Frankfurt am Main.

Winston B. 1998, *Media Technology and Society. A History: from the Telegraph to the Internet*, New York.

2009, *Technologies of Seeing. Photography, Cinematography and Television*, London.

Withe J. 1957, *The Birth and Rebirth of Pictorial Space*, London.

Wolfe H. E. 1945, *Introduction to Non-Euclidean Geometry*, New York.

Wolfram S. 2002, *A New Kind of Science*, Winnipeg.

Wolton D. 2000, *Internet et après? Une théorie critique des nouveaux médias*, Paris.

Wu Q. – Merchant F.A. – Castleman K.R. 2008, *Microscope Image Processing*, San Diego.

Youngblood G. 1970, *Expanded Cinema*, New York.

Zglinicki F. V. 1979, *Der Weg des Films*, Hildesheim.

Zielinski S. 1999, *Audiovisions, Cinema and Television as entr'actes in History*, Amsterdam.

2002, *Archäologie der Medien. Zur Tiefenzeit des technischen Hören und Sehens*, Hamburg.

Zinna A. 2004, *Le interfacce degli oggetti di scrittura. Teoria del linguaggio e ipertesti*, Roma.

Zuylen (van) J. 1982, "The Microscopes of Antoni Van Leeuwenhoek", in: L.C. Palm – H.A.M. Snelders, *Antoni van Leeuwenhoek 1632-1723*, Amsterdam, pp. 29-55.

Ancient Authors

Aeschylus

The Prometheus Bound (Edited by Th. George, New York 1979).

Aristotle

Metaphysics (Edited with commentaries and glossary by H.G. Apostle, Bloomington, Indiana 1966).

Posterior Analytics (Edited by T. Huch, Cambridge, Massachusetts 1960).

The Poetics (Edited by H.W. Fyfe, London 1965).

Cicero

De Natura Deorum (Edited by H.M.A. Rackham, London 1933).

Euclid

Elements: The Thirteen Books of Euclid's Elements, (Edited by L.H. Thomas 3 vols 2nd Ed., Cambridge 1926).

Plato

Phaedrus (Ed. by R. Hackforth, Cambridge 1952).

Theaetetus (Ed. by H.N. Fowler, London 1921).

Proclus

Elements of Theology (Ed. by E.R. Dodds, Oxford 2004).

A Commentary On the First Book of Euclid's Elements (Ed. by G.R. Morrow, Princeton 1970).